Contents

ANALYSING SOCIAL POLICY CONCEPTS AND LANGUAGE

Comparative and transnational perspectives

Edited by Daniel Béland and Klaus Petersen

First published in Great Britain in 2015 by

Policy Press
University of Bristol
1-9 Old Park Hill
Bristol BS2 8BB
UK
+44 (0)117 954 5940
pp-info@bristol.ac.uk
www.policypress.co.uk

North America office:
Policy Press
c/o The University of Chicago Press
1427 East 60th Street
Chicago, IL 60637, USA
t: +1 773 702 7700
f: +1 773 702 9756
sales@press.uchicago.edu
www.press.uchicago.edu

British Library Cataloguing in Publication Data
A catalogue record for this book is available from the British Library

Library of Congress Cataloging-in-Publication Data
A catalog record for this book has been requested

ISBN 978-1-4473-0643-6 paperback

Cover design by Qube Design Associates, Bristol
Printed and bound in Great Britain by CMP, Poole
Policy Press uses environmentally responsible print partners.

List of figures and tables

List of figures

List of tables

Acknowledgements

This project emerged in the context of the Nordic Centre of Excellence NordWel, which is funded by Nordforsk. Daniel Béland acknowledges support from the Canada Research Chairs Program. Klaus Petersen has received support from the Carlsberg Foundation, through his project on Danish welfare state history.

Some of the chapters in the volume were presented at the 2012 annual Social Science History conference in Vancouver, where Jenny Andersson (Science-Po, Paris) provided helpful comments. We also thank the anonymous reviewers from Policy Press for offering very constructive criticism. Many thanks to the Policy Press editorial team for their support, especially Rebecca Tomlinson, Laura Vickers, and Emily Watt. We also acknowledge the work of our copy editors: Tanya Andrusieczko, Steven Sampson, and Sarah Hoffmann Nielsen. Last but not least, we thank the contributors for their willingness to participate in this attempt to set a new research agenda in comparative welfare state research.

Notes on contributors

Zsófia Aczél is a doctoral student in the Department of Social Policy at Eötvös University of Sciences, Hungary. Her research focuses on gendered patterns of communication in social work and the history of social services in Hungary. Her publications include 'A jóléti állam és a nők: a 'maternalista' szociálpolitika' (with Dorottya Szikra), in Adamik, M. (ed.) *Bevezetés a szociálpolitika nem szerinti értelmezésébe* (Eötvös University of Sciences, 2012).

Jean-Claude Barbier is emeritus CNRS researcher at University Paris 1 (Panthéon Sorbonne), France. He conducts comparative research on social protection systems, especially in Europe. His research interests also include epistemological and methodological issues of the very practice of comparison. His recent publications include: *Le système français de protection sociale* (La Découverte, 2009); *Social Policies: Epistemological and Methodological Issues in Cross-National Comparison* (Peter Lang, 2005); and *La longue marche vers l'Europe sociale* (PUF 2008, adapted in 2013 for Routledge as *The Road to Social Europe: A contemporary approach to political cultures and diversity in Europe*).

Daniel Béland is Canada Research Chair in Public Policy (Tier 1) and professor at the Johnson-Shoyama Graduate School of Public Policy (University of Saskatchewan campus). A political sociologist studying public policy from an historical and comparative perspective, he has published 10 books and more than 80 articles in peer-reviewed journals. Recent books include *What is Social Policy?* (Polity, 2010); *The Politics of Policy Change* (Georgetown University Press, 2012, with Alex Waddan); and *Ideas and Politics in Social Science Research* (Oxford University Press, 2011, co-edited with Robert Henry Cox).

Nils Edling is university lecturer and researcher in the Department of History, Stockholm University, Sweden. His main research interest is the comparative history of unemployment in Scandinavia from the 1850s to the 1920s. He is currently working on the project 'The struggle over the welfare state: A conceptual history of welfare in Sweden 1850–2000'. Recent publications include 'Regulating unemployment the Continental way: the transfer of municipal labour exchanges to Scandinavia 1890–1914', *European Review of History - Revue Européenne d'Histoire*, 15(1), 2008: 23–40, and 'The primacy of welfare politics: notes on the language of the Swedish Social Democrats and their adversaries in 1930s', in Haggrén, H., Rainio-Niemi, J. and Vauhkonen, J. (eds) *Multi-layered Historicity of the Present: Approaches to Social Science History* (Helsinki University 2013).

Ana M. Guillén is professor of sociology and head of department at the University of Oviedo, Spain. She has written extensively on welfare state development, health policy, Europeanisation and comparative social policy, especially on South European welfare states. She has acted as a consultant to the European Commission and several European Union presidencies. Recent publications include *Work-Life Balance in Europe. The Role of Job Quality*, co-edited with Sonja Drobnic (Palgrave Macmillan, 2011); *The Spanish Welfare State in European Context*, co-edited with Margarita León (Ashgate, 2011); and *Health Care Systems in Europe under Austerity: Institutional Reforms and Performance*, co-edited with Emmanuele Pavolini (Palgrave Macmillan, 2013).

Kees van Kersbergen is professor of comparative politics in the Department of Political Science and Government at Aarhus University, Denmark. He has published widely on comparative welfare state issues in general, and the Dutch welfare state in particular. He is co-editor (with Philip Manow) of *Religion, Class Coalitions and Welfare States* (Cambridge University Press, 2009). His latest book (co-authored with Barbara Vis) is *Comparative Welfare State Politics: Development, Opportunities, and Reform* (Cambridge University Press, 2014).

Pauli Kettunen is professor of political history at the University of Helsinki, Finland. He has published widely on social movements and labour history, industrial relations and welfare state, globalisation and nationalism, and the conceptual history of politics. His recent publications include *Beyond Welfare State Models – Transnational Historical Perspectives on Social Policy*, co-edited with Klaus Petersen (Edward Elgar, 2011), and 'Reinterpreting the historicity of the Nordic model', *Nordic Journal of Working Life Studies*, 2(4), 2012: 21–43.

Jennifer Klein is professor of history at Yale University, USA. Her main research interest is 20th century US history, labour history, political economy, and social policy. She is the author of *For All These Rights: Business, Labor, and the Shaping of America's Public-Private Welfare State* (Princeton University Press, 2003), and *Caring for America: Home Health Workers in the Shadow of the Welfare State*, co-authored with Eileen Boris (Oxford University Press, 2012). Klein is senior editor of the journal *International Labor and Working-Class History*.

Huck-ju Kwon is professor at the Graduate School of Public Administration, Seoul National University, South Korea. His research interests are comparative social policy in East Asia, international development policy and global governance. His publications include *Transforming the Developmental Welfare State in East Asia* (Palgrave, 2005); *The East Asian Welfare Model: the State and Welfare Orientalism* (Routledge, 1998; co-authored); and *The Korean State and Social Policy* (Oxford University Press, 2011, co-authored).

Stephan Lessenich is professor of comparative sociology at the University of Jena, Germany, where, since 2010, he has also been the dean of the Faculty of Social and Behavioral Sciences. He is also president of the German Sociological Association (DGS) and has for several years been chair of the DGS's Research Committee on Social Policy. His publications include the edited volume *Wohlfahrtsstaatliche Grundbegriffe* (Campus Verlag, 2003) and an introduction to theories of the welfare state, *Theorien des Sozialstaats zur Einführung* (Junius Verlag, 2012).

Neil Lunt is a reader in social policy at the University of York, UK. Between 1997 and 2007, he taught policy studies in New Zealand. His main research interests are around the organisation, management and delivery of health and social services, the role of research within policy and practice, welfare policy, migration and welfare, and medical tourism. Lunt has published many articles and book chapters on social policy issues. Recent publications include 'From welfare state to social development: winning the war of words in New Zealand', *Social Policy and Society*, 7, 2008: 405–418.

David Luque is junior lecturer of sociology at the University of Oviedo, Spain. His research areas include industrial conflict and social policy. He is co-author of *Crisis and Social Fracture in Europe. Causes and Effects in Spain* (Colección Estudios Sociales, Fundación 'la Caixa', 2012) and author of *Las huelgas en España 1905–2010* (Germania, 2013).

Rianne Mahon holds the Centre for International Governance Innovation (CIGI) chair in comparative social policy at the Balsillie School of International Affairs and Wilfrid Laurier University in Canada. Her earlier work focused on the politics of industrial and labour market restructuring with particular attention to the role of trade unions. More recently, Mahon has produced numerous articles and book chapters on the politics of childcare, with a particular focus on Canada and Sweden. Her current research focuses on transnational social governance, including the policy discourses of international organisations like the Organisation for Economic Co-operation and Development (OECD) and the World Bank. With Stephen McBride she co-edited *The OECD: Transnational Governance* (UBC Press, 2008); and with Roger Keil, *Leviathan Undone: Toward a Political Economy of Scale* (UBC Press, 2009).

Jørn Henrik Petersen is professor in social policy at the Centre for Welfare State Research, at the University of Southern Denmark. He has for a significant time studied social policy, has been an advisor to several governments and is a well-known commentator in Danish public debates. His many publications include numerous books and articles in multiple languages on the history of, and contemporary challenges to, the Danish welfare state. He is currently one of the main editors and contributors to a six-volume *History of the Danish Welfare State*. The first volume was published in November 2010 and volume six will be published in August 2014. He has (with Klaus Petersen) recently published in *Journal of European Social Policy*, *Church History* and *Journal of Church and State*.

Klaus Petersen is professor of welfare state history and director of the Centre for Welfare State Research at the University of Southern Denmark. His main research interests include family policy, political history of the Nordic welfare state, pension policies, war and social policy, and the comparative history of the term 'welfare state.' His recent publications include *American Foundations and the European Welfare States* (University of Southern Denmark Press, 2013, co-editor); and 'Confusion and divergence: the term 'welfare state' in Britain and Germany ca. 1840–1960', *Journal of European Social Policy*, 23(1), 2013: 37–51 (with Jørn Henrik Petersen).

Toshimitsu Shinkawa is professor of political science at Kyoto University, Japan. His current research interests lie in the political economy of welfare regime transformation, social policy responses to population decrease, and the new politics of social integration in national welfare states. His recent publications include 'Substitutes for immigrants? Social policy responses to population decreases in Japan', *American Behavioral Science*, vol. 56 (August 2012); and 'Beyond Familialism? Welfare regime transformation in Japan' in Magara Hideko and Stefano Sacchi (eds.) *The Politics of Structural Reforms: Social and Industrial Policy Changes in Italy and Japan* (Edward Elgar, 2013).

Dorota Szelewa is an assistant professor at Institute of Social Policy, Warsaw University. Her research interests and publications focus on the questions of gender, family policy and childcare, especially in Central and Eastern Europe. Her publications include 'Gender and class: comparing the situation of single-parent households in seven European countries', forthcoming in the *European Journal of Social Security*; and 'Who cares? Changing patterns of childcare in Central and Eastern Europe', *Journal of European Social Policy,* 18(2), 2008: 115–131 (with Michał Polakowski).

Dorottya Szikra is an associate professor at Eötvös University, Hungary. Her research has centred on the history of social policy and social work. She has been investigating the evolution of social insurance and family policy systems in Central and Eastern Europe from a comparative perspective. Her recent publications include 'Tradition matters: child care and primary school education in modern Hungary.' in: Hagemann et al (eds) *Child Care and Primary Education in Post-War Europe* (Berghahn Books, 2011).

Yuki Tsuji is an associate professor of political science at Kyoto University, Japan. Her research interests focus on the gender politics of Japan, including the discursive politics of restructuring a 'familialist' welfare regime, the gendered relationship between the state and civil society, and the political representation of women. Her most recent publication in English is 'Re-imagined intimate relations: elder and child care in Japan since the 1990s' in: Rianne Mahon and Fiona Robinson (eds.) *Feminist Ethics and Social Policy: Towards a New Global Political Economy of Care* (UBC Press, 2011).

Antje Vetterlein is associate professor in the Department of Business and Politics, Copenhagen Business School, Denmark. Her research area is international political sociology, with particular interests in the role actors such as international organisations or multinational corporations play in the system of global governance. Publications based on one of her research projects investigating policy change in the World Bank and the International Monetary Fund (IMF) include 'Seeing like the World Bank on poverty', *New Political Economy*, 17(1), 2012: 35–58; and *Owning Development: Creating Global Policy Norms in the IMF and the World Bank* (with S. Park, Cambridge University Press, 2010).

Daniel Wincott is Blackwell Professor of Law and Society, and head of the Cardiff Law School, Cardiff University, UK. He has published widely on the welfare state, including 'Images of welfare in law and society: the British welfare state in comparative perspective', *Journal of Law and Society*, vol 38, 2011; and *The Political Economy of European Welfare Capitalism* (with Colin Hay, Palgrave MacMillan, 2012).

Jaap Woldendorp is assistant professor at the Department of Political Science, VU University, Amsterdam. He has published in Dutch and internationally on the Dutch welfare state, corporatism, party government, and institutions and macroeconomic performance. Recent publications include 'Enhancing and improving data on party government', in H. Keman and F. Müller-Rommel (eds), *Party Government in the New Europe* (Routledge, 2012); and 'Examining variation in economic performance using fuzzy-sets', *Quality and Quantity*, 47, 4, 2013: 1971–1989 (with Barbara Vis and Hans Keman).

Introduction: social policy concepts and language

Daniel Béland and Klaus Petersen

Exploring social policy language and concepts

Social scientists, historians, and linguists have noted that the terms, metaphors, and concepts we use are far from innocent and are closely tied to political struggles and international exchanges.[1] Therefore, from a comparative and international perspective, studying terminology and concept formation is an important part of both political and policy analysis (Williams, 1976; Sartori, 1984; Farr, 1989; Heywood, 2000; Daigneault, 2012). This is also the case when it comes to social policy. The words we use to make sense of social policy and the way we use them need to be properly studied to get the definitions right while grasping the political consequences of social policy language. But so far, relatively little has been done in that respect.

In recent years, researchers have rightly complained about the vagueness of core concepts used in contemporary social policy debates. For example, following well-known predecessors such as Asa Briggs (1973–74, 1985) and Richard Titmuss (1963), John Veit-Wilson (2000, 2003) and Daniel Wincott (2001, 2003) have criticised the tendency among social policy students and practitioners to use the concept of 'welfare state' without offering any coherent definition of it. As Wincott (2001: 409) puts it, 'While the expression of "the welfare state" has many interpretations and connotations – both academic and popular – there are surprisingly few clear discussions of the concept. . . . [The] field does need to be mapped'. Social policy concepts are subject to many interpretations, partly because they are dynamic historical constructions. Thus, one way to map this field and explore the boundaries of social policy is to take a comparative look at the history of concepts like 'welfare state' (Béland, 2011; Petersen and Petersen, 2013). Even though a number of key social policy concepts (such as '*Wohlfahrtsstat*,' '*Sozialstaat*,' or '*Sozialpolitik*') have a German origin, most of the English language discussions on social policy language (for example in Flora and Heidenheimer, 1981; Alber, 1988; Lowe, 1999; Powell and Hewitt,

---

[1] Some of the material in this chapter is adapted from Béland, 2011.

2002;Titmuss 1963) focus on Great Britain , as it was British Archbishop William Temple (1941) and others who popularised the term 'welfare state' during the Second World War, and paved the way for its political breakthrough in the late 1940s (Figure I.1).

Figure I.I: Number of hits searching 'welfare state' 1945–65

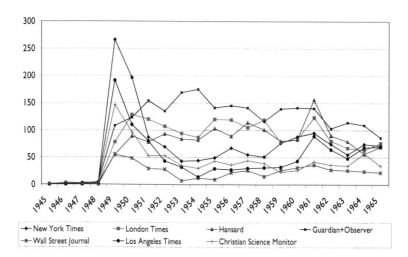

Source: Figure prepared by the authors using *The Times* online archive and ProQuest Historical Newspapers.

Since then, this English language term and its foreign language equivalents have been used around the world (Barbier, 2008), adding to the semantic confusion Wincott (2001) refers to. While there is a need for more comparative and historical research about the phrase 'welfare state,' isolating it from other key social policy concepts is potentially misleading, because concepts are typically defined in relationship to one another.

The objective of this volume is to draw attention to social policy concepts and language and to outline a new research agenda for social policy scholars. We have invited leading scholars in the field to share their empirical findings and discuss the development and importance of social policy language and concepts. Hence, this edited volume offers comparative, historical, and political surveys of the international development of social policy language and concepts, and the changing boundaries such development entails. In this volume, we offer comparative and transnational perspectives on social policy language and key social policy concepts in countries belonging to the

Organisation for Economic Co-operation and Development (OECD). What characterises social policy language in the individual countries and regions? How do social policy language and concepts travel between countries and what role have transnational institutions (such as the International Labour Office (ILO), the European Union (EU), the World Bank, and the OECD) played in that respect? Which are the dominant social policy concepts and how are they contested? How did they become dominant and how does this relate to the institutional legacies of different types of welfare regime? The individual chapters, written by a cross-disciplinary group of leading social policy researchers, explore these questions. The chapters address not only broad, widely diffused core concepts such as 'welfare state', but also what we may call secondary concepts, which have typically played an important role in specific national, institutional, and/or historical settings (for instance, the concept of Japanese-style welfare society in Japan). When it comes to the second type of social policy concepts, we can expect significant cross-national variation.

Exploring core concepts used to define the role of the state and other actors in the allocation of social benefits and services, this book presents international perspectives on the language of social policy through the analysis of the changing meaning of, and the political struggles over, broad concepts such as 'welfare', 'welfare state', and 'social security' (including the German variant *Sozialstaat* (Ritter, 1991) and the French concept of *État-providence* (Béland, 2011)), which are involved in drawing and redrawing the boundaries of state intervention in the social policy realm. These concepts change over time, as newer terms replace or supplement older ones, which is precisely why an historical perspective on social policy language is a necessity.

More generally, the analysis of social policy language and the boundaries it helps to define and redefine must draw on a variety of disciplines, such as history, sociology, and political science. This volume brings together social policy scholars from various disciplinary backgrounds in order to clarify the evolving meanings of some of the most crucial concepts in the field. As suggested by the chapters in this book, a reflexive, comparative, and historically informed discussion of key social policy concepts is a necessary starting point for research and teaching in the field.

Analytical considerations

This volume is not devoted to any single theoretical framework. Studying social policy language should not be reserved for one discipline or one theoretical approach. Our point of departure is that words matters, but also that the semantic field of social policy language is largely unknown territory for welfare state research. Hence, we need to approach it with an open mind. Still, this volume is related to the growing attention social policy scholars have been paying to ideas, discourse, and conceptual history. The resulting discussions fall into two major strands of literature: one stressing the role of ideas and the other focusing on concepts and terminology. A brief discussion of the related literature helps locate the volume within ongoing academic debates in policy research.

First, a growing number of scholars have stressed the role of ideas (and by extension discourse and concepts) in social policy development. This literature draws our attention to the structuring impact of ideas and discourse in social policy development (for example, Blyth, 2002; Campbell, 2004; Padamsee, 2009; Béland and Cox, 2011). Importantly, some of the literature on policy ideas and discourse is grounded in post-structuralist and constructivist approaches inspired by the work of Michel Foucault (2002) and his many followers, such as the proponents of critical discourse analysis (Fairclough, 1995), who all stress the close relationship between discourse, language, and asymmetrical power relations. The work of feminist scholars Nancy Fraser and Linda Gordon (1994) on the genealogy of the concept of 'dependency' in the United States illustrates this Foucault-related stream within the contemporary ideational scholarship. Other ideational scholars, for instance Peter Hall (1993) and Vivien Schmidt (2011) have moved away from Foucault to study ideas and discourse from an institutionalist, political science perspective.

A key insight of the contemporary literature on ideas and social policy that informs this volume is the recognition of the role of transnational actors and processes in the diffusion of policy ideas and concepts from one country to another (for example, Rodgers, 1998; Dolowitz and Marsh, 2000; Orenstein, 2008; Stone, 2008). For instance, ideational scholars have written about the importation of the American concept of 'workfare' to Great Britain in the mid to late 1990s and early 2000s (King and Wickham-Jones, 1999; Daguerre and Taylor-Gooby, 2004). Yet, despite the undeniable role of transnational actors and processes, the ideational literature also stresses that the weight of national cultures and intellectual traditions remains strong (Campbell, 2004) and the analysis of social policy language must place concepts in their national context, which is what the country chapters of this volume do. When we study countries that have different national languages, perhaps the most obvious issue at stake is translation, in the strict sense of the term (that is, the translation from one national language to another). For instance, a long time ago, Asa Briggs (1985: 185) raised this issue by pointing to the fact that the English term 'self-help' is extremely difficult to translate into French, at least if one is to preserve its original meaning. Yet, despite the challenges of linguistic translation, policy concepts are integrated into a country's existing cultural and institutional repertoires (Campbell, 2004). In the United States, for instance, the term 'welfare' took on a different meaning than in other countries because, by the 1960s, it became closely related to a controversial social programme targeting poor single mothers (Steensland, 2008).

Second, another stream of literature that is most helpful in framing this volume is conceptual history. The assumption of this approach is that key concepts are 'essentially contested' and part and parcel of the political struggle of modern societies. Conceptual history is basically a critique of anachronistic understandings of terms and concepts, striving to place terms and their meanings in their original historical context. German historian Reinhart Koselleck (1979) has stressed the importance of combining diachronic analysis (the quasi-archaeological unearthing of the historical layers of meanings attached to a single concept) and synchronic analysis (studying a concept in its social and political context) in taking into account the relationship between concepts within a particular semantic field. British historian Quentin Skinner (1989) turned his attention to the process of 'rhetorical redescriptions,' in which concepts, through the agency of actors, are used in a new context, in the form of 'rhetorical strategies' or 'innovating ideologists'.

However, within conceptual history, studies of social policy concepts are quite rare, with the exception of the pioneering book *Wohlfahrtsstaatsliche Grundbegriffe* (Lessenich, 2003), which explores the semantic field of the German welfare state. Yet, increasingly, language and concepts are becoming a research topic for contemporary political historians (Frevert and Haupt, 2005) and for students of welfare state development (for example, Rodgers, 1998; Kettunen and Petersen, 2011; Wincott, 2011; Petersen & Petersen, 2013). For instance, British historian Noel Whiteside (2005: 213) has, on the basis of a detailed study of the different meanings and understandings of unemployment in Great Britain and France, noted the importance of integrating conceptual analysis with comparative welfare state research, which is 'plagued by problems of similar policies disguised by different terminology and different policies, agencies and instruments that possess almost similar labels. Words get in our way'.

Traditionally, conceptual historians have focused on pre–1900 eras and on major political concepts such as democracy, state, or liberalism (see Leonhard, 2001; Nevers, 2011). Only more recently have they turned to the 20th century and broadened the analysis from the study of concepts to the study of 'semantic fields' (Steinmetz, 2007, 2012). We believe social policy language is a semantic field where concepts, language, ideas, discourses, and narratives are intertwined in the ongoing political struggles over social programmes.

Interestingly, conceptual history and contemporary ideational analysis have so far lived very separate lives. Conceptual history has overwhelmingly been the trade of historians, whereas the literature on the role of ideas has been dominated by social scientists. There have been attempts at bridge building, with historians studying the role of policy ideas, especially from a transnational perspective (Rodgers 1998; Conrad 2011). Yet even today, the two approaches differ in various ways. Conceptual history has a very strong emphasis on words and concepts, whereas the ideational literature focuses on the relationship between actors, ideas, and policy change. This means that conceptual history tends to become descriptive while the ideational literature seeks to analyse power relations and to explain policy outcomes. In addition, conceptual history addresses long-term historical processes by discussing the career of concepts over centuries, whereas ideational literature typically focuses on more recent trends, episodic policy changes, and well defined paradigm shifts.

Both of these perspectives are valid and necessary for developing a new research agenda on social policy language. These two perspectives have different analytical strengths and combining them allows us to take into account social policy concepts and the agents uttering them when studying the development of social policy language (see Koselleck, 1979: 21). This is precisely why this volume, which focuses on the historical development of ideas, concepts, and language as they are related to specific actors and policies, draws on insights from both the ideational and the conceptual history perspectives.

Case selection and chapter outline

The volume focuses on OECD countries located on four continents: Asia, Australasia, Europe, and North America. This international take on social policy language and concepts allows us to explore issues such as the transnational diffusion of social policy concepts and discourses across national boundaries. In combining in-depth, single country analyses with broader comparative chapters, this volume seeks to strike a balance between comparative, transnational, and international perspectives and detailed case studies. Due to the limited space available, most chapters focus on post-1900, and especially post-1945, developments.

Regarding the selection of our cases, we follow a well-established tradition in comparative welfare state research, of comparing developed countries belonging to the OECD. Historically, these countries have helped set the social policy agenda around the world, far beyond the OECD itself. One of the major challenges for comparative research concerns the issue of transnational diffusion (Obinger, Schmitt and Starke, 2013), which refers to the fact that ideas and social policy concepts travel across national borders (see, for example, Rodgers, 1998; Kettunen and Petersen, 2011). In this volume, we address the role of diffusion not only within the national contexts described in the country chapters, but also regionally and institutionally, with a spotlight in the first part of the book on Scandinavia and Eastern Europe, and on several key institutions involved in the development of an international social policy language: the EU, the World Bank and the International Monetary Fund (IMF), and the OECD. The decision to include Scandinavia in the comparative chapters stems from the prominent international position of the Scandinavian welfare state model in the comparative literature, while the inclusion of the Hungarian–Polish comparison enables us to explore how the major transformations in Eastern Europe (from market economy to socialism and back again) have influenced the development of social policy language over nearly a century.

The choice of the countries selected for our case study chapters comprising the rest of our volume is based on an attempt to represent all major welfare regimes (Esping-Andersen 1990; 1999) as well as the main regions of the advanced industrial world, which is culturally, economically, and institutionally diverse (Hall and Soskice, 2001). We have attempted to include smaller and larger countries. We have also limited the number of English speaking countries to three (the United Kingdom, the United States, and New Zealand) to make sure that as many different national languages as possible were featured among our eleven case studies. Finally, because no country is totally isolated from the others, authors of these case studies stress transnational influences, when relevant.

The structure of this book is straightforward. The first five substantive chapters offer historical and comparative perspectives on the evolution of social policy language over time and across countries. These five chapters are primarily devoted to the diffusion and the historical development of social policy ideas and concepts over time and space.

Four chapters cover the following four topics: 1) the comparative history of the concept of the welfare state in Scandinavia; 2) the evolution of social policy language in Eastern Europe, with a focus on Hungary and Poland, before and after state socialism; 3) the tension between social policy concepts and languages within the European Union; and 4) the role of the World Bank and the IMF, and the OECD, covered in chapters four and five, respectively, in the construction of a transnational social policy language. The next ten chapters are case studies focusing primarily on the politics of social policy language in Britain, France, Finland, Germany, Japan, South Korea, the Netherlands, New Zealand, Spain, and the United States. All these country specific chapters explore shifts in social policy language over time, and analyse the debates about key concepts. In both parts of the volume, the authors adopt the format (chronological or thematic) and time frame they consider most appropriate for their individual chapter and topic. The volume's conclusion stresses the commonalities and differences among these rich and diverse case studies, before sketching an agenda for future research on social policy language and concepts, within the OECD and beyond.

References

Alber, J. (1988) 'Continuities and changes in the idea of the welfare state,' *Politics & Society*, 16(4): 451–468

Barbier, J.-C. (2005) *Social Policies: Epistemological and methodological issues in Cross National Comparison*. Brussels: PIE Pieter Lang

Barbier, J.-C. (2008) *La longue marche de l'Europe sociale*. Paris: Presses Universitaires de France.

Béland, D. (2011) 'The politics of social policy language,' *Social Policy & Administration*, 45(1): 1–18.

Béland, D. and R.H. Cox (eds) (2011) *Ideas and Politics in Social Science Research*. New York: Oxford University Press.

Blyth, M. (2002) *Great Transformations: Economic Ideas and Institutional Change in the Twentieth Century*. Cambridge: Cambridge University Press.

Briggs, A. (1973-74) 'Welfare state', in P. P. Wiener (ed.), *The Dictionary of the History of Ideas*, vol 4. New York: Scribner.

Briggs, A. (1985 [1961]) 'The welfare state in historical perspective', in Asa Briggs, *Collected Essays of Asa Briggs. Volume II: Images, Problems, Standpoints, Forecasts*. Brighton: The Harvester Press, pp. 177–211.

Campbell, J. L. (2004) *Institutional Change and Globalization*. Princeton: Princeton University Press.

Castles, F.G. et al. (eds) (2010) *The Oxford Handbook of the Welfare State.* Oxford: Oxford University Press.

Conrad, C. (2011) 'Social policy history after the transnational turn', in P. Kettunen and K. Petersen (eds), *Beyond Welfare State Models. Transnational Historical Perspectives on Social Policy*, London: Edward Elgar: 218-240.

Daguerre, A. and Taylor-Gooby, P. (2004) 'Neglecting Europe: explaining the predominance of American ideas in New Labour's welfare policies since 1997,' *Journal of European Social Policy*, 14(1): 25-39.

Daigneault, P.-M. (2012) 'Introduction to the symposium "Conceptual Analysis in Political Science and Beyond"', *Social Science Information*, 51(2): 183-187.

Dolowitz, D. and Marsh, D. (2000) 'Learning from abroad: the role of policy transfer in contemporary policy-making,' *Governance*, 13(1): 5-24.

Esping-Andersen, G. (1990) *The Three Worlds of Welfare Capitalism.* Princeton University Press.

Esping-Andersen, G. (1999) *Social Foundations of Postindustrial Economies.* Oxford: Oxford University Press.

Fairclough, Norman. (1995) *Critical Discourse Analysis: The Critical Study of Language.* Harlow, Essex: Longman.

Farr, J. (1989) 'Understanding conceptual change politically', in T. Ball et al (eds), *Political Innovation and conceptual change.* Cambridge: Cambridge University Press.

Flora, P. and Heidenheimer, A. J. (1981) 'The historical core and changing boundaries of the welfare state', in P. Flora and A. J. Heidenheimer (eds), *The Development of Welfare States in Europe and America.* New Brunswick: Transaction Books, pp. 17-34.

Foucault, Michel, (2002 [1969]) *The Archaeology of Knowledge.* London: Routledge.

Fraser, N. and Gordon, L. (1994) '"Dependency" demystified: inscriptions of power in a keyword of the welfare state,' *Social Politics*, 1(1): 4-31.

Frevert U. and Haupt, H.G. (eds) (2005) *Neue Politikgeschichte. Perspektiven eine historischen Politikforschung.* Frankfurt: Campus Verlag.

Glennerster, H. (2000) *British Social Policy Since 1945* (second edition). London: Blackwell.

Hall, P. A. (1993) 'Policy paradigms, social learning and the state: the case of economic policymaking in Britain,' *Comparative Politics*, 25(3): 275-296.

Hall, P. and Soskice, D. (eds) (2001) *Varieties of Capitalism: the Institutional Foundations of Comparative Advantage.* Oxford: Oxford University Press.

Heywood, A. (2000) *Key Concepts in Politics.* Basingstoke: Palgrave.

Kettunen, P. and Petersen, K. (eds) (2011) *Beyond Welfare State Models: Transnational Historical Perspectives on Social Policy*. London: Edward Elgar.

King, D. and Wickham-Jones, M. (1999) 'From Clinton to Blair: the democratic (party). Origins of welfare to work,' *Political Quarterly*, 70(1): 62-74.

Koselleck, R. (1979) 'Begriffsgeschichte und Sozialgeschichte', in K. Koselleck, *Vergangene Zukunft. Zur Semantik geschichtlicher Zeiten*. Frankfurt: Suhrkampf: 107-129.

Leonhard, J. (2001) *Liberalismus. Zur historischen Semantik eines europäischen Deutungsmusters*. München: Oldenbourg Wissenshaftsverlag.

Lessenich, S. (ed.) (2003) *Wohlfahrtsstaatsliche Grundbegriffe. Historische und Aktuelle Diskurse*. Frankfurt: Campus Verlag.

Lowe, R. (1999) 'Introduction: the road from 1945', in H. Fawcett and R. Lowe (eds), *Welfare Policy in Britain: The Road to 1945*. Basingstoke: Macmillan Press, pp. 1-18.

Nevers, J. (2011) *Fra skældsord til slagord. Demokratibegrebet i dansk politisk historie*, Odense: University of Southern Denmark Press.

Obinger, H., Schmitt, C and Starke, P, (2013) 'Policy Diffusion and policy transfer in comparative welfare state research', *Social Policy & Administration*, 47 (1): 111-129.

Orenstein, M.A. (2008) *Privatizing Pensions: The Transnational Campaign for Social Security Reform*. Princeton: Princeton University Press.

Padamsee, T. (2009) 'Culture in connection: re-contextualizing ideational processes in the analysis of policy development,' *Social Politics*, 16(4): 413-445.

Petersen, J. H. and Petersen, K. (2013) 'Confusion and divergence: origins and meanings of the term 'welfare state' in Germany and Britain, 1840-1940,' *Journal of European Social Policy*, 23(1); 37-51

Powell, M. and Hewitt, M. (2002) *Welfare State and Welfare Change*. Buckingham: Open University Press.

Ritter, G.A. (1991) *Der Sozialstaat. Entstehung und Entwicklung im Internationalen Vergleich*. München: Oldenbourg.

Rodgers, D.T. (1998) *Atlantic Crossings: Social Politics in a Progressive Age*. New York: Belknap Press.

Sartori, G. (1984) *Social Science Concepts: A Systematic Analysis*, Beverly Hills: SAGE.

Schmidt, Vivien. (2011) 'Reconciling ideas and institutions through discursive institutionalism' in Daniel Béland and Robert Henry Cox (eds) *Ideas and Politics in Social Science Research*. New York: Oxford University Press.

Skinner, Q. (1989) 'Language and political change', in T. Ball, J. Farr and R.L. Hansen (eds), *Political Innovation and Conceptual Change*, Cambridge: Cambridge University Press: 6-23.

Steensland, B. (2008) *The Failed Welfare Revolution: America's Struggle over Guaranteed Income Policy*. Princeton: Princeton University Press.

Steinmetz, W. (2007) '40 Jahre Begriffsgeschichte – the state of the art', in H. Kämper and L.M. Eichinger (eds), *Sprache–Kognition–Kultur*. Berlin: Walter de Gruyter: 174-197.

Steinmetz, W. (2012) *Political Languages in the Age of Extremes*. Oxford: Oxford University Press 2012.

Stone, D. (2008) 'Global public policy, transnational policy communities, and their networks,' *Policy Studies Journal*, 36(1): 19-38.

Temple, W. (1941) *Citizen and Churchman*. London: Eyre and Spottiswoode.

Titmuss, R. M. (1963) 'The Welfare state: images and realities,' *Social Service Review*, 37(1): 1-11.

Veit-Wilson, J. (2000) 'States of welfare: a conceptual challenge,' *Social Policy & Administration*, 34(1): 1-25.

Veit-Wilson, J. (2003) 'States of welfare: a response to Charles Atherton,' *Social Policy & Administration*, 36(3): 312-317.

Whiteside, N. (2005) 'Conventions, institutions and frameworks for welfare state comparisons: an analysis of pension development in France and Britain since the Second World War', in J.C. Barbier and M.T. Letablier (eds), *Politiques sociales: enjeux epistemologiques des comparaisons internationales*. Brussels: Peter Lang: 211-229.

Williams, R. (1976) *Keywords*. London: Fontana.

Wincott, D. (2001) 'Reassessing the Social foundations of welfare (state) regimes', *New Political Economy*, 6(3): 409-425.

Wincott, D. (2003) 'Slippery concepts, shifting context: (national) states and welfare in the Veit-Wilson/Atherton debate,' *Social Policy & Administration*, 37(3): 305-315.

Wincott, D. (2011) 'Images of welfare in law and society: the British welfare state in a comparative perspective', *Journal of Law and Society*, 38 (3): 343-375.

ONE

Social policy language in Denmark and Sweden

Nils Edling, Jørn Henrik Petersen and Klaus Petersen[2]

The term 'welfare' is of Nordic origin. The Old English *wel faran*, meaning getting along and/or doing well, comes from Old Norse *velferð*, which in modern English means welfare (Hoad, 1996). This linguistic connection should certainly not be exaggerated, but the Nordic welfare states definitely enjoy a special position in international political and scholarly discourses. The Nordic or Scandinavian welfare state is a well-established model, and there would seem to be widespread agreement that the Nordic welfare state is something special. The question we pose here is: does this Nordic welfare state also come with a distinct social policy language?

In this chapter, we address this question by studying aspects of social policy language in Denmark and Sweden. The two countries have their separate histories, distinct national contexts and political cultures – and these national features naturally influence the terminology. Even so, there are shared characteristics. As North Germanic languages, Danish and Swedish are closely related. The Nordic setting is also characterised by a high level of transnational economic, political and cultural exchange, which also influences the development of social policy and social policy language (Petersen, 2011). Intra-Nordic diffusion and emulation, however, are not a self-contained system. On the contrary, the social policy languages of the open economies of Northern Europe have been influenced continuously by outside debates and reforms. In the following analysis, we use 'Nordic' and 'Scandinavian' interchangeably, but strictly speaking Denmark, Norway and Sweden are the Scandinavian countries, whereas 'Nordic countries' also include Finland and Iceland.

---

[2]   A previous version of this paper was presented at 5th NordWel Key Concept Seminar in Rome, September 2012 and at the Social Science & History Associations Meeting in Vancouver, November 2012. We thank the participants for valuable comments.

Answers to the workers' question

The 'social question', or the 'workers' question' (Danish: *Arbejdersporgsmaalet*, Swedish: *arbetarfrågan*) as it was also labelled, concerned 'the conditions of the labouring classes in primarily economic, social and political respects', as articulated in 1896 by the Swedish Liberal politician and writer Ernst Beckman in a major new dictionary (Beckman, 1896: 317).This question, formulated in various ways with growing anxiety from the 1870s onwards, concerned the social and economic position of a growing class of wage earners. Beckman argued that the complexity of the social question called for a variety of responses. He pointed out three pathways: 'individual self-help, help-to-self-help from society and help from the state'.The concrete remedies would be various forms of moral reform, help-to-self-help and social legislation.There was little uniquely Nordic about the construction of 'the workers' question', that is to say, the concrete issues and policies were of course framed in specific contexts, but in general, the issue was a transnational one, in which the transfer of concepts, categories and policies played an important part (Rodgers, 1998).

Prompted by moral and political concerns created by industrial and urban growth and the demands from nascent working-class movements, the social question created the demand for new social science information. Social scientists benefited from this demand for detailed surveys and inquiries into wages, working and living conditions which, simultaneously, defined the social and economic problems of the day while suggesting answers to them (Andersen, 2010; Edling, 2010). Although the social policy language of the time included numerous innovations, it was basically reactive. It was the social policy language of the established social and political elite.

According to Swedish and Danish encyclopaedias published around 1900, social policy (*socialpolitik*), a new concept imported from Germany in the 1870s and 1880s, concerned various measures introduced by the state 'in the interest of the common good in order to regulate or direct the relations between different classes in society or to improve the conditions of one particular class' (Nordisk Familjebok, 1890: 1553; Salmonsen, 1905:318).This was a new conception of the state and its right and obligation to intervene in and regulate markets and society in the interest of the common good and to assist the economically weaker class. The target group for social policy was primarily the 'labouring classes' or the 'working class', but it was statistically difficult to define the 'worker'. In Scandinavian societies, one could hardly exclude the majority of the working population who were agricultural labourers or small-scale farmers but who could not be considered 'wage earners' in the proper sense of the term. Consequently, the vaguer notion of 'people without means' (*de ubemidlede*, Danish) or 'people of limited or lesser means' (*obemedlade och mindre bemedlade*, Swedish) signals broader reforms and universal coverage (J.H. Petersen, 2010: 359; Edling 1996: 42–44).

The practices of poor relief, philanthropy and new social policies had their distinctive concepts and discourses, with language legacies from earlier poor laws and their practices as well as the influence of religion on philanthropy (Lützen, 1998; Green, 2011). In the period from the mid-19th century well into the interwar decades, the language of the old poor law permeated social policy discourses. It was especially the distinction between the 'worthy' (*værdige*, in Danish) and the 'unworthy' (*uværdige*) that formed a dividing line in both the older practices, directly related to poor relief systems, and the new policies, introduced to provide rudimentary social protection outside the poor law.

Social policy was about prevention, insurance and new risk categories, yet it retained criteria of worthiness or deservingness as the core of eligibility. We see this in the preparation of the 1891 Danish Pension Law and Poor Law, where principles such as compulsion versus voluntariness, and premium-financed insurance versus tax-funded provision for older people, were up for discussion (Petersen, 1985). These reforms were modern, yet in various ways they made use of the old poor law dichotomies. A guiding idea was to include the deserving poor in the new schemes and to refer the 'unworthy' (loafers, vagrants and other 'undeserving' people) to the older, unpopular poor relief system. Furthermore, economists and high ranking civil servants were not the only ones interested in social problems and potential solutions to them. The civil society or non-state sphere, with its many associations, and above all Christian philanthropic organisations, were key providers of welfare. This sector provided services and set up institutions to rescue, feed and reform orphans, 'juvenile delinquents' and prostitutes, as well as to provide care for older and disabled people. Philanthropy had its own language. 'Insurance' had no place in this discourse. Instead, the actions were articulated as 'acts of charity and compassion' (Danish: *Kærlighedsgerninger*, Swedish: *kärlekshandlingar*), moral reform and responsibility, and as expressing 'compassion', supporting 'family' and 'home', a reflection of both bourgeois patriarchal relations and family ideals (Jordansson, 1998; Lützen, 1998). Philanthropic initiatives, often with an openly anti-state language, contributed to creating what we would call today the 'welfare service sector', and this sector has since retained an emotional terminology based on 'care' (*omsorg*) – a language very different from that found in income related social insurance systems. These initiatives established the concept of the 'home' (*hjemmet, hemmet*) in Danish and Swedish social policy language (K. Petersen, 2010; Södling 2010, chs. 4–5). Even today, popular discourse uses 'home for older people' (*alderdomshjem, ålderdomshem*) and 'children's home' (*børnehjem, barnhem*), colloquial expressions included in the official terminology. Consequently, the languages of social reform in the late 19th century were not particularly state-centred, although social policy conceptually had strong links to state activity. Insurance, help-to-self-help, philanthropy and service provision constitute the main concepts of social policy, as was repeatedly stated at the turn of the 20th century.

The sociopolitical language of the nation-state 1920–45

The development of social policy has always been linked to nation building – this remark applies to both Denmark and Sweden. The First World War and the profound economic crisis of the 1930s paved the way for the state to play a more central role in social policy. In the words of the leading Danish economist Frederik Zeuthen (1919), social politics was:

> an organ in the body of society which has a number of important roles in ensuring the health and wellbeing of the whole ... As with every organ, social legislation has to be of a suitable size for the entire body and to be positioned where it can cooperate with the other parts.

Put simply, two major and interconnected prime movers brought about this widened role for the state: the social engineers and the Social Democratic labour movements. The 'social engineers' – political economists, architects, town planners, doctors and other professionals with a recognised claim to exclusive expert knowledge – pushed for a 'rational' and state-centred social policy. Sweden's famous couple Alva and Gunnar Myrdal provide the best known example of such experts. In a lecture from the early 1930s, Gunnar Myrdal criticised the old 'sentimental' approach to social policy with his new 'intellectualistic and coldly rationalistic' approach, which was to be a 'matter of fact. Its romanticism is that of the engineer' (Myrdal, 1932). In Denmark Jørgen S. Dich, at the time adviser to the Ministry of Social Affairs, voiced similar views (Dich, 1938).

The new experts advocated planned social reforms, using a technical, more scientific language; they did not always have a decisive influence on the outcome of reforms, but they changed the language of social policy. Myrdal stressed the prophylactic character of the social policies to come and their pronatalist bestseller, *Crisis in the Population Question* (*Kris i befolkningsfrågan* 1934, in Danish, 1935) turned the problem of the declining birth rate on its head. An issue previously conceived in conservative and nationalist terms was reshaped as a problem of social reform, of rational policies supporting the family (Hirdman, 2008: 174–188). This made population policy (*befolkningspolitik*, in Swedish and Danish) an important keyword in the 1930s and 1940s, and the new family policies introduced in Sweden from the 1930s and after 1945 in Denmark included measures to protect pregnant women, mothers and children and to encourage couples to have children (Lundqvist, 2011; Petersen, 2011). The qualitative aspects of the population were at the forefront of these reform initiatives, where the public authorities intervened into new areas of societal life. After the war, 'population policies' were replaced by the less radical, statist concepts of 'family policy', but the basic ideas and policies remained very much the same.

The other political driving force behind the growing role of the state was the Social Democratic parties, which assumed dominant roles in the Scandinavian countries in the 1920s and 1930s. From having originally been classic working-class parties anchored in a socialist concept of society and politics, these parties developed in a more pragmatic direction as national coalition parties and as guarantors of democracy and order. This also meant that the parties adopted a new sociopolitical position. It was to a great extent based on the existing system and on the existing use of language, but in particular, it contained two innovations linked to the concepts of 'folk' and 'rights'.

In the years 1928–33, the Swedish Social Democrats completed the change from a reformist party for the working class to a reformist party representing the entire population, the 'folk'. The 'folk' were understood here as the entire nation in its civic and ethnic sense (Trägårdh, 2002). In a now famous speech in 1928, party leader Per Albin Hansson touched on the building of a national home (people's home/*folkhem*) characterised by inclusive and comprehensive social reforms, a home for all citizens, all the people, as the political objective.[3] This new national orientation constituted a change in socialist reformist ideology and political practice, and became a vital element in the Social Democrats' subsequent electoral triumphs. The 'folkish' turn undermined the ongoing criticism from the Conservative camp that the Socialists defended class interest whereas the Conservatives represented the national interest and the people as a whole. The crisis agreement of May 1933, followed by Sweden's swift recovery from the Depression, created the new buzzword 'welfare politics' or 'welfare policies' (*välfärdspolitik*) – the key concept launched by the Social Democrats.[4] For the Social Democrats, 'welfare politics' encapsulated the socially inclusive and economically productive reforms. Since the 1930s, 'welfare' has been the contested key concept in Swedish politics.

The concept of the folk, the people, had a parallel in Denmark with the Social Democratic Party programme of 1934, *Denmark for the People (Danmark for Folket)*, which was popularised both as a song and as a feature film with popular actors. Also Denmark, the use of the concept included a strategic element. When minister of social affairs K.K. Steincke, in 1935, set up a commission to formulate a population policy, part of his agenda was to recapture such key concepts as 'people' and 'family' from the Conservatives (Banke, 2003).

The interwar years were also the period when the concept of rights made its entry into the social policy language. The Social Democrats had a history of insisting that obligations and rights should go hand in hand. 'Do your duty, claim your rights' was the traditional banner. It was in particular the Danish Social Democrat K.K. Steincke who, in both word and deed, placed social rights on the political agenda. The basic flaw in existing social policy, argued Steincke, lay in the principle of charity or compassion, that is to say that help was offered according to a (state or philanthropic) organisation's independent assessment of the degree of need in each individual case. If help were to be given only at the expense of the recipient first having to swallow their self-esteem, it would diminish the feeling of being someone

---

[3]   'Folk' was certainly a key concept, but, contrary to widespread belief, *folkhem* has never been the central organising concept in Swedish politics. From the mid-1930s, *folkhem* has lacked strong political connotations and it has been used mainly as a non-contested metaphor for Swedish society in general. (See Edling, 2013).

[4]   Like many other languages, the Scandinavian languages have a single term, *politik*, for both politics and policy (see Heidenheimer, 1986). On the importance of the concept welfare politics/policies in the 1930s, see Edling (2013).

who was independent and autonomous. For Steincke, there was also an administrative point connected to the concept of rights. The task of the state was not to offer charity but to determine citizens' rights (Steincke, 1912). The state as loving benefactor doling out gifts out of kindness was a fundamental misconception. The state was in power, and legislation was the implementation of the ruling conception of 'rights'. This 'principle of rights' (*retsprincippet*), as Steincke typically referred to it, would gradually gain ground in sociopolitical legislation over the following decades.

Building on this, in Sweden, the longstanding Social Democratic Minister of Social Affairs, Gustav Möller, launched a similar reform of sociopolitical thinking and language. In 1913, the *Riksdag* had passed the first pension law, creating what was officially called general insurance (*den allmänna försäkringen*) but early on known as 'the people's pension' (*folkpension*). The pension provided very limited benefits, and the call for revision comprised an important part of the Social Democrats' platform in the 1920s. 'Liberate the elderly from poor relief' and 'make the pensions large enough to ensure the elderly a degree of independence from their next of kin', demanded Möller, who drew inspiration from the Danes (Möller, 1936: 10). A fair pension was described as a right accorded all hard working and decent citizens. The reforms of 1935 and 1937 introduced a short period of redistribution, where those earning and paying more received less than actuarially-sound benefits and increased the supplements. Coverage became universal, as this was said to serve the 'common good' (*det allmänna bästa*), but the supplements remained income related, that is to say they targeted lower income groups (Berge, 1999). Making the supplements universal was never the objective of the reform, and Social Democrats of the 1920s and 1930s adhered to the old division between the deserving and non-deserving poor.

This change to a more statist sociopolitical language did not take place unopposed, despite the international stereotype of the pragmatic, state-friendly Nordic consensus model having existed as far back as the interwar period (Musial, 2002). The increasing role of the state, however, was in fact highly controversial. The Conservative camp was strongly critical of the increasing taxes, emphasising that individual responsibility and the family comprised a zone where the state should not intervene. 'Welfare' and related concepts were contested.

In the mid-1930s, the Swedish Conservatives criticised the irresponsible and expensive reforms as 'welfare policies that undermine welfare' (Bagge, 1937: 78). Professor Gustav Cassel, a leading Swedish economist of the older generation, hit out at 'the degeneration of public relief policies' while claiming that social reforms created a welfare mentality (*understödstagaranda*) (Carlson, 1994, chs 8, 12). His arguments were repeated by the Conservatives and the Taxpayers' Association (*Skattebetalarnas Förening/Skatteborgerforeningen*) in both Sweden and Denmark. For Cassel, the new welfare reforms of the 1930s would pave the way for a nanny state (*försörjningsstat*), where high taxes and state regulations thwarted individual freedom and responsibility.

The 'welfare state' 1940s–1970s

In the late 1930s and during World War II, the social policy agenda was mainly about making the existing system work but, especially during the last year of the war, planning for the post-war era started. Even though, compared to the rest of Europe, Denmark and Sweden were only moderately affected by the war, it created a consensus that proved a good breeding ground for future social reforms. In the decades after 1945, a whole series of reforms placed new welfare amenities on the agenda, improved the quality of services and facilitated access to the existing amenities. During this period, the Nordic welfare states really began to assume the characteristics typically associated with the Nordic model. It was during this period that the term 'welfare state' came into use. However, this was not an unequivocal welfare revolution. It was based on ideas launched in the interwar period and on institutions whose roots went back to the end of the 19th century. The mantra of 'building on what already exists' was clearly stronger in Denmark, but it was reflected in the sociopolitical language of both countries, where existing semantic strata lived on and coexisted with linguistic innovations such as, for example, the new concept of 'welfare state'.

As in the rest of Western Europe, planning for post-war society gained momentum in Denmark and Sweden during the mid-1940s. All political parties drew up new programmes and devoted more attention to social reforms. Conservatives, Liberals and Social Liberals – in Sweden the latter two were united into a single party – spoke about restoring the existing system and laid out plans for future reforms using formulas such as 'productive social policies' (Swedish Conservatives), 'help-to-self-help' (Danish Conservatives), 'social liberalism' (Swedish Liberals), and 'neither state socialism, nor laissez-faire', according to the Danish Social Liberals (Ljunggren, 1992, ch 2; Larsson, 1998: 141–201; Petersen, Christiansen and Petersen 2011: 110–116). Sweden's Social Democrats formulated the most ambitious post-war programme, with over 200 pages and listing 27 topics centred on three main themes: full employment, fair distribution of economic resources and improved standard of living and, finally, improved efficiency and increased democracy in the private sector (conceptualised as 'economic democracy') (Sainsbury, 1980). This caused immediate political controversy and heated debates about 'state regulation' and 'socialisation'. Anti-planning resistance (*planhushållningsmotståndet*) became the catch phrase as Swedish Conservatives and Liberals mobilised between 1944 and 1948 (Lewin, 1967). The Danish debate echoed the Swedish one in many ways, even though it lacked its intensity. In both countries, Social Democrats had to back away ideologically from the ideas of increased planning and state regulation, and it was as part of this ideological retreat that the two parties turned their attention to 'welfare' and the 'welfare state'.

Both Danish and Swedish Social Democrats in the 1940s and 1950s talked about welfare politics and policies (*velfærdspolitik, välfärdspolitik*), and the latter used 'Social Sweden' (*Social-Sverige*) as the general label for the new society. It was only in the mid-1950s that the term 'welfare state' was frequently employed, when it was imported from Britain and the US. At the 1953 Social Democratic Party convention in Denmark, the 'welfare state' was linked to the social reforms with a discussion of the 'social welfare state'. In 1956, Danish Prime Minister Jens Otto Krag could affirm that 'The welfare state is the sum of our social policy legislation' (Krag, 1956). In the 1950s and early 1960s, however, the term 'welfare state' was still used critically in Scandinavia (as elsewhere in the world). In Denmark especially, we find a heated debate about the meaning and connotations of the 'welfare state' related to the discussion about pension policy in the 1950s. The objections to the 'welfare state' were of three types: the economic critique (high taxes and low incentives); a critique of the welfare state as authoritarian (*formynderstat*) and a threat to personal integrity and freedom; and a Marxist-inspired critique of the welfare state as being part of the state capitalist system. In Sweden, we had calls for a *Revolt against the Welfare State*, a Swedish book from 1958 (Thuresson). Two years later, the leading Danish Social Democrat and Minister of Finance, Viggo Kampmann, asked: 'Is the welfare state just a scapegoat in line with the finance ministers and other unpopular concepts?' (Kampmann, 1960:16) Consequently, we rarely find the concept of 'welfare state' used in the Social Democratic Party's propaganda – the party instead prefers to talk about less overtly ideological concepts such as 'security' (Danish: *tryghed*, Swedish: *trygghet*).

In Sweden, the debates over economic planning and socialism and the international climate of the Cold War, with its anti-communism, pushed the Social Democrats to use other concepts in order to defuse any potential conflicts between freedom and welfare. As a replacement for 'welfare state', the Social Democrats launched the 'strong society' (*det starka samhället*), a concept introduced by Prime Minister Tage Erlander but also adopted and developed by his successor Olof Palme. In its first formulation from 1954, Erlander avoided all other welfare terms except 'welfare politics/policies', and this became the standard procedure. The Social Democrats' party programmes, platforms, posters and pamphlets from the 1950s and 1960s did not mention the 'welfare state' at all; instead, 'society', 'security', 'change', 'growth', 'welfare' and 'freedom' were the catchwords. The guiding principle of the 'strong society' was the assertion that increased economic prosperity in a society with full employment increased the demand for further social reforms, and that there was absolutely no conflict between comprehensive social policies and individual freedom (Erlander, 1954, 1962; Andersson, 2006, ch 2). The concept of 'welfare state' was somewhat de-politicised in the latter half of 1950s in academic circles. Gunnar Myrdal, in *Beyond the Welfare State* (1960), expanding on his book *The International Economy* from 1956, argued that a new state characterised by coordination, planning and rationalisation had gradually emerged: 'all rich countries in the Western world, had become a democratic "welfare state"' (Myrdal, 1960) For Myrdal and other likeminded social science scholars, the 'welfare state' was a sociological (and rational) concept and not a matter of political opinion.

After the Social Democratic victory in the 1959 referendum on a new income related pension scheme (ATP), which split the non-socialist opposition, the Swedish Social Democrats were full of self confidence. Party leader Erlander, speaking at the 1960 party congress, declared that 'The pension reform represents a *new* kind of policy' that was not about securing 'decent living conditions for the elderly' but about 'securing the standard of living for families, the elderly and invalids' (SAP, 1960: 247).

Apart from this discussion about a sociopolitical master concept, extremely rapid development also took place on the more technical side of social policy language. Constant sociopolitical change brought with it new terminology, new types of institutions and new occupational groups. In the field of pensions, we find in Sweden new 'terms' or abbreviations for complicated measures such as 'ATP' (Labour Market Supplementary Pension, 1959) and in Denmark 'ITP' (Income related Supplementary Pension, which was never achieved). Within the family sphere in both countries, people began talking about 'family counsellors', 'aftercare' and 'adventure playgrounds'. Within social policy circles, from the 1960s onwards, people talked about 'rehabilitation', 'residual groups','relative poverty' and 'residual poverty'. Many of these new concepts were generated by experts and bureaucrats, and they often did not have a broad popular impact. They were more part of the way the welfare state spoke about itself than the way people spoke about the welfare state. They were closely linked to the professionalisation and bureaucratisation of the Scandinavian welfare states, which accelerated in the post-war era as the public sector expanded. This new expansion was noticed by people at the time, and in the 1960s and 1970s in particular, one notices increasing criticism of bureaucracy and the rule of experts which, among other things, targeted the special (power) language of this new technocratic class (see Dich, 1973).

In the early 1960s, there was a general acceptance that the welfare state had been realised. 'The myth of the welfare state won the election', lamented the Swedish Conservative leader Hjalmarson in 1960 after yet another defeat – a loss that soon dethroned him (Bohman, 1983: 55). A few years later, the conservative journal *Svensk Tidskrift* argued that the average citizen needed and wanted freedom of choice in the field of social policy. The journal complained that an ever expanding welfare system was now seen as inevitable and continued: 'To question the welfare state in its normal Western form is widely regarded as being "politically impossible"' (Svensk Tidskrift, 1963: 244). Swedish Social Democrats, labelling themselves on election posters as 'the guarantee for progress' (*framstegsgarantin*), had managed to solve the tension between economic growth and social security. Left on the to do list were reforms that within the given system reduced 'residual wants' (*restnöd*) (Andersson, 2006, ch 2). Similarly, in Denmark, the Social Democrats in 1960 used the slogan of 'Making good times better' (Petersen, 1998). In both countries, Social Democrat governments continued the expansion of tax-financed public services, the centre-right parties had to change to accommodate, and in the 1960s, their language became distinctly more welfare state-friendly. However, soon a new form of critique emerged which focused on the many inadequacies and problems in society; the Swedish book *The Incomplete Welfare* (*Den ofärdiga välfärden*), from 1967, pointed out the 'hidden poverty and deprivation' and attracted a lot of attention (Inghe and Inghe, 1967). In Denmark the book *Prosperity without Welfare* (*Velstand uden velfærd*) was published in several editions in 1969 (Hansen). Other books and reports followed, and the issue of social inequalities persisting despite economic growth and the problem of low wages for many unionised workers gained importance with the radicalisation of the political climate, also finding support within the Social Democratic labour movement.

The leftist critique, with its stronghold in the academic world, did not influence the language of social policy directly. Numerous publications appeared, describing social policies using Marxist concepts and theories, and we also find political pamphlets catering mainly for the already convinced. However, the criticism contributed to a change in the political rhetoric of Social Democrats and unions from a defence for the existing social policies towards a more leftist critique of the shortcomings of the realised reforms. It is noteworthy that the critical accounts mentioned above use the word 'welfare' without adding the state, turning attention to the outcomes of social policy rather than its ideals and the way it is provided.[5] This partly explains why the concept of 'equality' became so important in social policy language in the 1970s. Apart from equality, other new terms such as 'exclusion', 'redistribution', 'low income groups' and 'negative social background' left their mark upon the social policy discourse and helped to widen the ways in which welfare was perceived. The concept of 'welfare' gained a life of its own, referring to new groups and covering almost all aspects of social life. It was high time, declared Social Democratic Prime Minister Olof Palme at the 1972 party congress, to include working life and industrial relations in Social Democratic welfare policies. 'This means', he continued, 'an expansion of the old and familiar concept of welfare which will be of significance for the development of society' (Greider, 2011: 213). In both countries, a focus on equality became the answer to these new challenges to the dominant party, accused by the left of being a mere custodian of capitalist society. Most significant in the long run, however, was the impact of the feminists, who, supported by the Social Liberals and Social Democrats, made gender equality (Danish: *ligestilling,* Swedish: *jämställdhet*) a central concept; important reforms were introduced, and we see linguistic changes from mother oriented to parent oriented policies (Florin and Nilsson, 1999; Lundqvist, 2011; Petersen, 2012). This new language of gender equality is a trademark of Scandinavian welfare, with Sweden standing out as the special case, from the 1970s onwards, whereas the concept and language of gender equality gained less of a foothold in Denmark.

---

[5]   However, in everyday language, in the two countries, the concept of 'welfare' is not very clearly defined. It can refer to the outcome (the welfare of the individual citizen) as well as the system providing it, or even the general welfare of the nation (often in purely economic terms).

Towards a new welfare state language

Since the 1970s, the social policy languages of Denmark and Sweden have undergone significant changes. The two countries have followed the Western trend, where the Marxist-inspired critique from both the Old and the New Left was followed by more influential waves of criticism from Conservatives and neoliberals who argued that the welfare state was causing economic and social problems rather than solving them, that there was too much 'state' in the 'welfare state'. The economic crisis and its effects provided an impetus for the strong political and ideological comeback of New Right and Liberal ideas. In Denmark, the economic downturn hit hard as far back as the early 1970s, whereas Sweden was able to postpone the crisis until the early 1990s. Consequently, we find differences as to when and exactly how social policy language changed, and due to the hegemonic position of the Swedish Social Democrats – they were in government 1932–76 and 1982–91 – the ideological temperature ran higher in Sweden. In general, however, the Danish and Swedish discourses on social policy showed many similarities. The same concepts and semantic innovations appeared in both countries; the notion that the expansive era of social reform had come to end became an underlying common theme in Denmark as well as in Sweden.

In Denmark, the 1973 parliamentary election was a shock to the Danish political establishment. Five more parties entered parliament, all based on some kind of resistance to the establishment (anti-abortion, anti-capitalism and anti-tax). The outright winner of the election was the populist Progress Party (*Fremskridtspartiet*). Under the absolute leadership of the charismatic tax lawyer Mogens Glistrup, it became the second largest party overnight. Glistrup combined a radical neoliberal anti-tax ideology with a populist and innovative rhetoric arguing for limiting social benefits (except old age pension) and doing away with most of the public sector (Kuur Sørensen, 2013). Even though Glistrup was marginalised by the political establishment, he pioneered neoliberal anti-welfare state politics in Denmark and paved the way for a more critical framing of the social policy debate that also influenced more important political actors on the right in Denmark. This was demonstrated in a stream of books throughout the 1970s and early 1980s that complained about the inefficiency of the public sector and were anti-tax and anti-state (Petersen, 1998; Petersen, Christiansen and Petersen, forthcoming).

A few years later, the neoliberal wave came to Sweden, with orchestrated campaigns to counter the impact of the left on public opinion (Boréus, 1994). The political parties soon followed. In 1981, the chairman of the Swedish Moderates – the Conservatives changed their name in 1969 to *Moderata Samlingspartiet* – Gösta Bohman called for a 'liberal revolt against the dictatorship of the public sector, against increasing bureaucracy, against the on-going politicisation of social life and against the tendency to limit the freedom of the individual' (Bohman, 1981: 76; Smolander, 2004). The new Moderate Party's programme, from 1984, called for a state limited by the rule of law (*demokratisk rättsstat*), instead of a welfare state.

The Swedish political developments led to a marked changed in Swedish sociopolitical language. Non-state concepts such as 'market-based solution', 'competition', 'freedom of choice' and 'privatisation' entered the language of social policy. We find them in the programmatic statements of the new centre-right governments in Denmark between 1982 and 1993. In Sweden, the joint election manifesto from the Swedish Liberals and the Moderates in 1991, entitled 'New start for Sweden', argued for a freedom of choice revolution (*valfrihetsrevolution*) in the welfare sector in order to ensure economic efficiency and empower the citizens (Moderaterna & Folkpartiet Liberalerna, 1991). 'Privatisation', a word so confrontational in its attack on the welfare state as the leading provider of services, was replaced in Denmark (but not in Sweden) by the less controversial – and muddier – concept of 'contracting out' (*udlicitering*), by which tax-financed services were to be provided by private contractors. This general shift towards non-state solutions also paved the way for a comeback of the philanthropic tradition, repackaged as the 'third sector' and 'voluntary sector' (often funded from public money) as well as a concern for 'the 'civil society' (especially in Sweden. See Trägårdh, 2007). In both countries, the immediate reaction of the Social Democratic parties and fellow travellers was to vigorously defend the welfare state. The solution to the new social and economic problems was therefore presented as more sociopolitical reforms. The concept of 'welfare state' became more popular among those on the centre-left than ever before. The criticisms against the welfare state, however, also gradually gained ground within the sociopolitical language of the Social Democrats, initially as a kind of 'state scepticism'. Among Danish Social Democrats, for example, one can trace how the concept 'welfare society' (*velfærdssamfund*) in the 1980s gradually started to replace the 'welfare state' (Petersen, Petersen and Christiansen, forthcoming). The welfare society had been launched as a liberal alternative to the welfare state, as could be seen, for example, from the 1984 Swedish Conservative party programme (Moderata Samlingspartiet, 1984: 6–10, 45–46), but because the concepts of 'state' and 'society' are, to a certain extent, synonymous in the Scandinavian context, the Social Democrats were also able to use the word 'society', as the inclusive 'us', to defend the existing welfare model. In Sweden, this defence included reviving the old metaphor of the 'people's home' (*folkhem*) from the interwar period and making it synonymous with the universalistic welfare state (see footnote 3; Edling, 2013).

During the 1980s, Danish and Swedish Social Democrats started to rethink the welfare state model. Neoliberal attacks, the influence of New Public Management, as well as a general feeling that the welfare model, because of globalisation and demographic pressure, was not financially viable in the long run, led leading Scandinavian Social Democrats to formulate a new strategic position, presented in a joint report in the late 1980s (Lundberg, 2006; Petersen, 2011). To oversimplify slightly, one can say that the Social Democratic response to the challenge aimed at the welfare state was to use neoliberal tools to undertake a thorough modernisation of the welfare state. This led to a comprehensive change in sociopolitical language in the two countries (Petersen, 2011) – as well as a number of welfare reforms under the Social Democratic governments in both countries. In general, one could speak of a new sociopolitical language that was embedded in a new phraseology (the 'old' welfare state gave way to a 'new' welfare society) at both the national and the local levels, in both politics and the public debate generally. Clients and citizens now became 'users' or 'consumers' of public services. The public sector went from being a political mechanism to being perceived as a provider of services, the focus being on 'demand', 'budget control' and 'performance'. In sociopolitical debates, discussions of social services and measures invariably included reference to more 'incentives', citizen 'activation' and enhanced 'effectiveness'.

One can interpret this trend as the victory of neoliberalism. Yet the triumph of neoliberalism did not mean the end of the welfare state as such. Both Denmark and Sweden continue to have a very large tax-financed public sector and – despite widespread privatisation and contracting out – strong social welfare institutions. The new neoliberal strategy was politically successful for the two Social Democratic parties, which carried out a wide range of reforms that commanded international attention. The Swedish Prime Minister Göran Persson proudly spoke about the bumblebee that, despite gloomy prognoses, proved capable of flying. It was during this period that Denmark became famous for its 'flexicurity' model of labour market policy.

In both countries the right-wing parties were forced to acknowledge that a clear neoliberal course was not a sure path for them to gain political power. This awareness began around the turn of the millennium, what could be called a 'race to the centre'. The populations of the two countries were relatively satisfied with the existing social programmes and public services, and they were sufficiently dissatisfied with the existing tax burden to support more radical neoliberal change. This led to a completely new rhetorical style, with the right-wing parties relaunching themselves as defenders of the Scandinavian welfare model (Lundberg and Petersen, 2005) protesting against cuts in care of older people and claiming higher benefits for poor older people This was not so much a question of changing sociopolitical language use as such – it has remained relatively unaltered – but of changing the narrative about the welfare state (or 'welfare society', as the right-wing parties prefer to call it). Historically, the Social Democratic Party was until the 1980s mobilised around a powerful narrative, with the party adopting the role of a 'hero' championing social security, while the Social Democrats assigned the right-wing parties a much less prominent role in the history of the welfare state. That narrative has been successfully contested and even overturned in recent years, first in Denmark and, slightly later, in Sweden.

In Denmark, the Liberal politician Anders Fogh Rasmussen (Prime Minister 2001–10) from the late 1990s headed the introduction of a new welfare narrative that involved the creation of such new slogans as 'Welfare and Freedom of Choice', a retention of the neoliberal concepts discussed earlier, and a launching of the Liberal Party as Denmark's answer to Tony Blair's New Labour. Inspired by the Danish success, the Conservatives or Moderates, the dominant non-socialist party in Sweden, reinvented themselves using concepts formerly solely associated with the Social Democrats. This makeover into 'the New Labour Party' (a slogan actually used) brought them electoral success in 2006 and 2010. In both countries, control over concepts, sociopolitical language and narratives was an important part of this transformation (Lundberg and Petersen, 2005; Andersson, 2009).

The most recent example of the Swedish struggle for conceptual control is about the concept of the 'Nordic model'. The current Swedish centre-right government has claimed its birthright to the model with this reinvented history in a brochure entitled 'The Nordic Way', presented at the meeting of the World Economic Forum in Davos in 2012. The reaction of the Swedish Social Democrats was to officially register the 'Nordic model' as a Social Democratic trademark, an application which was approved by the Swedish Patent and Registration

Office in early 2012.[6] Even though it was presented as a political gimmick it attracted strong reactions and has been contested, but so far it means that formally the Social Democratic Party have reclaimed what they consider their birthright.

Conclusion

In this chapter we have tried to outline the path of social policy language in Denmark and Sweden from the emergence of modern social policy in the late 19th century to today. We have demarcated four historical phases: in the first phase, around 1900, the two countries imported and domesticated the general European (mainly German) social policy debate. In the second phase, 1920–40, the Social Democratic parties gained power and, together with the 'social engineers', formulated a more inclusive, comprehensive and rational social policy language based on concepts such as 'people', 'rights' and 'prophylaxis'. However, this development towards a more statist social policy language also made it more politically contested. This is also the case in the third phase, 1945–70, where the term 'welfare state' becomes a key concept. This fierce criticism of the 'welfare state' led the Social Democrats to avoid using it in the 1950s and partly also in the 1960s. Only after the economic crisis and the emerging neoliberal critique entered the scene (in the 1970s in Denmark and a decade later in Sweden) do we find a strong grasping of the concept 'welfare state'. However, this was not very successful. In the final phase, neoliberal criticism and neoliberal concepts (like 'competition', 'customers', 'performance measurement', and so on) gain a foothold and eventually become established when the Social Democratic parties in the two countries pick them up. In more recent years, we have witnessed a 'race to the centre', where the successful Social Democratic internalisation of neoliberal social policy language in the 1990s was paralleled – if not imitated – by a Liberal (in Denmark) and Conservative (in Sweden) strategy of rebranding themselves as defenders of the 'welfare society'. As a result, the contesting of welfare concepts has increased as all political parties claim ownership and struggle over the right to define national values, issues and policies.

---

[6]　See 'Socialdemokraterna har fått den nordiska modellen varumärkesskyddad', www.aip.nu/default.aspx?page=3&nyhet=41506; www.globalutmaning. se/wp-content/uploads/2011/01/Davos-The-nordic-way-final.pdf

The language of social policy is both complex and multifaceted, growing more specialised and technical over time and covering innumerable sectors of modern society. It should also be emphasised that the four analytical phases described above should be treated as historical underpinnings of the present day social policy language. In each phase, we find innovations and reformulations, but we also find that old concepts and narratives continue to play a role. The dictionary of present day social policy language in the two countries is the result of more than 100 years of state practices, discussions and adaptations. The Nordic welfare state, like all historic state formations, also comes with its distinct social policy language. As we have shown, this language does not comprise just one layer that slowly gives way to another. It is, rather, a more fractal process, where the different historical layers interact, fissure, or crash like tectonic plates. Welfare language, like welfare states, is dynamic.

References

Andersen, L. (2010) 'Between social radicalism and Christian socialism: Intellectuals, social knowledge and the building of the early Danish welfare state', in Å. Lundqvist and K. Petersen (eds), *In Experts We Trust. Knowledge, Politics and Bureaucracy in Nordic Welfare States*, University Press of Southern Denmark, Odense, 89-118.

Andersson, J. (2006) *Between Growth and Security: Swedish Social Democracy from a Strong Society to a Third Way*, Manchester University Press, Manchester.

Andersson, J. (2009) *The Library and the Workshop: Social Democracy and Capitalism in the Knowledge Age*, Palo Alto: Stanford University Press.

Bagge, G. (1937) *Politiska tal år 1937*, Stockholm.

Banke, C. (2003) 'Manden som kom cyklende med velfærdsstaten', Klaus Petersen (ed.), *13 historier om den danske velfærdsstat*, Syddansk Universitetsforlag, Odense: 113-124.

Beckman, E. (1896) 'Arbetarefrågan', in *Nordisk Familjebok: Konversationslexikon och Realencyklopedi*, Stockholm: C. & E. Gernandts förlagsaktiebolag, vol. 19: 317–334.

Berge, A. (1999) The 'People's Pensioner' in Sweden 1914–1954: On the Changing Moral Content of a Social Category', *Scandinavian Journal of History*, (vol. 24:3-4), Stockholm; Oslo; Copenhagen: Scandinavian University Press, 267–280.

Bohman; G. (1981) *Kurs mot framtiden: Ett friare och öppnare Sverige*, Norstedt, Stockholm.

Bohman, G. (1983) *Så var det: Gösta Bohman berättar*, Bonnier, Stockholm.

Boreus, K. (1994) *Högervåg: Nyliberalismen och kampen om språket i svensk debatt 1969-1989*, Tiden, Stockholm.

Carlson, B. (1994) *The State as a Monster: Gustav Cassel and Eli Heckscher on the Role and Growth of the State*, University Press of America, Lanham, Md.

Dich, J.S. (1938) 'Socialpolitikkens Udviklingstendenser', *Nationaløkonomisk Tidsskrift*, vol 3. No. 46: 4-33.

Dich, J.S. (1973) *Den herskende klasse*. Borgen, Copenhagen.

Edling, N. (1996) *Det fosterländska hemmet: Egnahemspolitik, småbruk och hemideologi kring sekelskiftet 1900*. Diss. Stockholm: Carlsson.

Edling, N. (2010) 'The Making of Nordic Unemployment Policies. Experts and Public Policy in Denmark and Sweden, 1890–1910', in Å. Lundqvist and K. Petersen (eds), *In Experts We Trust. Knowledge, Politics and Bureaucracy in Nordic Welfare States*, University Press of Southern Denmark, Odense, 119–148.

Edling, N. (2013), 'The Primacy of Welfare Politics: Notes on the language of the Swedish Social Democrats and their adversaries in 1930s', in H. Haggrén e.a. (eds). *Multi-layered Historicity of the Present. Approaches to social science history*, Helsinki University, Helsinki, 125–150.

Erlander, T. (1954) *Människor i samverkan*, Tiden, Stockholm.

Erlander, T. (1962) *Valfrihetens samhälle*, Tiden, Stockholm.

Florin, C. and Nilsson, B. (1999) ''Something in the Nature of a Bloodless Revolution...': How New Gender Relations became Gender Equality Policy in Sweden in the Nineteen-sixties and seventies', in R. Torstendahl (ed.), *State Policy and Gender System in the Two German States and Sweden 1945–1989*, Department of History, Uppsala University.

Green, T.H. (2011) *Responding to Secularization. The Deaconess Movement in Nineteenth-century Sweden*, Brill, Leiden.

Greider, G. (2011) *Ingen kommer undan Olof Palme*, Ordfront, Stockholm.

Hansen, B. (1969) *Velstand uden velfærd: en kritik af det danske klassesamfund*, København: Fremad.

Heidenheimer. A.J. (1986) '*Politics, Policy* and *Policey* as Concepts in English and Continental Languages: An Attempt to Explain Divergences', *The Review of Politics* (vol. 48:1), 3–30.

Hirdman, Y. (2008) *Alva Myrdal: The Passionate Mind*, Indiana University Press, Bloomington.

Hoad, T. F. (ed.) (1996) *The Concise Oxford Dictionary of English Etymology*, Clarendon, Oxford.

Inghe, G. and Inghe, M.-B. (1967) *Den ofärdiga välfärden*, Stockholm: Tiden.

Jordansson, B. (1998) *Den goda människan från Göteborg: Genus och fattigvårdspolitik i det borgerliga samhällets framväxt*, Arkiv, Lund.

Kampmann, V. (1960) 'På vej mod velfærdsstaten', in Fr. Nielsen and O.H. Petersen (eds), *Hug og Parade. Tolv indlæg om Velfærdsstaten og Kulturen*, Fremad, København, 16-24.

Krag, J.O. (1956) 'Velfærdsstaten', *Politiken*, 9 August 1956.

Kuur Sørensen, M. (2013) *Dansk Velfærdskritik* (unpublished manuscript)

Larsson, S-E. (1998) *Bertil Ohlin: Ekonom och politiker*, Atlantis, Stockholm.

Lewin, L. (1967) *Planhushållningsdebatten*, Almqvist and Wiksell, Uppsala and Stockholm.

Ljunggren, S-B. (1992) *Folkhemskapitalismen: Högerns programutveckling under efterkrigstiden*, Tiden, Stockholm.

Lundberg, U. (2006). 'A Leap in the Dark: From a Large Actor to a Large Area Approach: The Joint Committee of the Nordic Social Democratic Labour Movement and the Crisis of the Nordic model'. N. F. Christiansen e.a. (eds). *The Nordic Model of Welfare: A Historical Reappraisal.* Museum Tusculanum, Copenhagen, 269–297.

Lundberg, U. and Petersen, K. (2005) 'Socialdemokratiet, borgerlige partier og velfærdsstat – et essay om moderne velfærdspolitik', *Arbejderhistorie*, No. 4: 6-26.

Lundqvist, Å. (2011) *Family Policy Paradoxes: Gender Equality and Labour Market Regulation in Sweden, 1930-2010*, Policy, Bristol.

Lützen, K. (1998) *Byen tæmmes.* Hans Reitzels forlag, København.

Moderata Samlingspartiet (1984) *Partiprogram*, Stockholm.

Moderaterna and Folkpartiet Liberalerna (1991) *Ny start för Sverige*, Stockholm.

Möller, G. (1936) *Bättre folkpensioner*, Tiden, Stockholm.

Musial, K. (2002) *Roots of the Scandinavian Model. Images of Progress in the Era of Modernisation.* Baden Baden: Nomos Verlagsgesellschaft.

Myrdal, G. (1932) 'Socialpolitikens dilemma' I-II. *Spektrum*, vol. 2: 3-4, 1–13, 13–31.

Myrdal, G. (1956) *An international economy: Problems and prospects*, New York: Harper & Brothers.

Myrdal, A . and G. (1934) *Kris i befolkningsfrågan*, Bonnier, Stockholm.

Myrdal, G. (1960) *Beyond the Welfare State. Economic Planning and its International Implications. The Storr lectures, Yale University 1958.* Duckworth, London.

Nordisk Familjebok (1890) 'Socialpolitik', *Nordisk Familjebok: Konversationslexikon och Realencyklopedi*, Nordisk familjebok, Stockholm, vol. 14, 1533–1534.

Petersen J.H. (1985) *Den danske alderdomsforsørgelseslovgivnings udvikling I, Oprindelsen*. Odense: Odense Universitetsforlag.

Petersen, J.H. (2010) 'Kapitel 5. Debatten om alderdomsforsørgelse frem mod alderdomsforsørgelsesloven af 1891', in J.H. Petersen, K. Petersen and N.F. Christiansen (eds), *Dansk Velfærdshistorie bind I, Perioden 1536-1898*, Syddansk Universitetsforlag, Odense, 311-390.

Petersen, J.H. (2011) 'Marketization and free choice in the provision of social services. Normative shifts 1982-2008', in P. Kettunen and K. Petersen (eds), *Beyond Welfare State Models*, Edward Elgar, London, 170-198.

Petersen and N.F. Christiansen (eds), *Dansk Velfærdshistorie bind II, Perioden 1898-1933*, Syddansk Universitetsforlag, Odense, 643-758.

Petersen, J.H., N.F. Christiansen and K. Petersen (2011) 'Kapitel 2. Det socialpolitiske idélandskab', J.H. Petersen, K. Petersen and N.F. Christiansen (eds), *Dansk Velfærdshistorie bind III, Perioden 1933-1956*, Syddansk Universitetsforlag, Odense.

Petersen, J.H., Petersen K. and Christiansen, N.F. (eds) (forthcoming) *Dansk Velfærdshistorie Bind VI, Perioden 1993-2013*, Odense: Syddansk Universitetsforlag.

Petersen, K. (1998) *Legitimität und Krise. Die politische Geschichte des dänischen Wohlfahrtsstaates 1945-1973*, Berlin Verlag Arno Spitz, Berlin.

Petersen, K. (2010) 'Kapitel 9. Børnesagen. Dansk Familiepolitik', in J.H. Petersen, K.

Petersen, K. (2011) 'National, Nordic and trans-Nordic: transnational perspectives on the history of the Nordic welfare states', in P. Kettunen and K. Petersen (eds), *Beyond Welfare State Models*, Edward Elgar, London, 41-64.

Petersen, K. (2012) 'Kapitel 9. Familiepolitikkens storhedstid', J.H. Petersen, K. Petersen and N.F. Christiansen (eds), *Dansk Velfærdshistorie bind III, Perioden 1933-1956*, Syddansk Universitet, Odense, 579-588.

Rodgers, D.T. (1998) *Atlantic Crossings. Social Politics in a Progressive Age*, Belknap Press of Harvard University PressCambridge.

Sainsbury, D. (1980). *Swedish social democratic ideology and electoral politics 1944-1948: A study of the functions of party ideology*. Stockholm : Univ.. Stockholm.

Salmonsen (1905) 'Socialpolitik', *Salmonsens store illustrerede Konervsationsleksikon: En nordisk Encyklopaedi*, A/S J. H. Schultz Forlagsboghandel, Copenhagen, vol. 16, 318–319.

SAP (1960) *Sveriges Socialdemokratiska arbetarepartis 21:a kongress, Folkets hus, Stockholm den 6–10 juni 1960: Protokoll*, Stockholm.

Smolander, J. (2004) 'Neoliberalism or Economic Nationalism? Changes in the Welfare Policy of Finnish and Swedish Conservatives during the 1970s and 1980s', in A. Lahtinen and K.Vainio-Korhonen (eds), *History and Change,* Finnish Literature Society, Helsnki, 239–252.

Södling, M. (2010) *Oreda i skapelsen: Kvinnligt och manligt i Svenska kyrkan under 1920- och 1930-talen,* Uppsala.

Steincke, K.K. (1912) *Almisser eller Rettigheder,* Copenhagen: Gyldendalske Boghandel.

Svensk Tidskrift (1963) 'Dagens frågor: Välfärd och valfrihet', *Svensk Tidskrift* (vol. 50) 244–246.

Thuresson, L (1958) *Revolt mot välfärdsstaten,* Stockholm: Natur & Kultur.

Trägårdh, L. (2002) 'Crisis and the Politics of National Community Germany and Sweden, 1933/1994', in L. Trägårdh and N. Witoszek (eds), *Culture and crisis: The Case of Germany and Sweden,* Berghahn, Oxford/New York, 75–109.

Trägårdh, L. (2007) 'The 'civil Society' Debate in Sweden: The Welfare state Challenged', in L. Trägårdh (ed.), *State and Civil Society in Northern Europe: The Swedish Model Reconsidered,* Berghahn Books, Oxford/New York, 9–36.

Zeuthen, F. (1919) 'Den sociale Lovgivnings Formaal', *Samfundets Krav.* Copenhagen.

TWO

The changing language of social policy in Hungary and Poland

Zsófia Aczél, Dorota Szelewa and Dorottya Szikra

The modern history of Hungary and Poland, both belonging to Central and Eastern Europe (CEE), is characterised by turbulent political and economic changes and 'emergency' decisions in the field of social policy (Inglot, 2008). Forty years of an autocratic communist regime provides the strongest common legacy of social policy in the two countries. The subsequent liberal democracies, built up since 1990, have, however, brought to the surface long-forgotten patterns of mid-war social policy in both countries which now shape the language of social policy, together with that from their communist legacies. The neoliberal agenda of 'retrenchment' has penetrated Eastern European countries just when they were about to adjust their welfare institutions to capitalist democracy, making a strong impression on their social policy agendas and languages. During the process of accession to the European Union (EU), Poland and Hungary also adopted some of the social policy discourse of the EU, though not without controversies. The historical volatility of social policy programming in this region (Szikra and Tomka, 2009) is partly due to the sharp ideological division on this matter between Conservative and Socialist elites. This is why the issue of social policy, as we argue in this chapter, has been politicised ever since the introduction of the first state-run programmes. This is reflected in the translation of 'social policy' into both Polish and Hungarian, in relation to which we need to make a key remark right at beginning of our chapter: there is only one word for 'policy' and 'politics' in Hungarian and Polish, as both are called *'politika'* (in Hungarian) or *'polityka'* (in Polish). Thus the term 'social policy' has most often been translated as *'szociálpolitika'* in Hungarian and *'polityka społeczna'* in Polish.

In this chapter we demonstrate how historical legacies since the late 19th century – together with current internal, external and supranational influences – have formed the distinct social policy languages in these post-communist countries. Key terms and definitions used to describe the field and aims of social policy are investigated in the most important periods during which distinct developments in social policy language have been witnessed: first, from the late 19th century to the Second World War; second, from the state socialist period (late 1940s) to 1989; and third, from the eve of the political and economic transformation in 1989/1990 up until today.

From the late 19th century to the end of the Second World War

Hungary had partial autonomy within the Austro-Hungarian Empire from 1867 to 1920, when the Monarchy fell to pieces. Poland, at the same time, was carved up between Russia, Prussia and Austria, with a few enclaves of self-government, of which most were within the Austrian part (Galicia). In both countries, the emerging official social policy language was linked to a Bismarckian type of social insurance with strong German influence on the language of social policy.

The Hungarian state was eager to establish social insurance schemes compatible with the Austrian and German legislation of the time (Szikra, 2004). The language of the first social insurance legislation (Act XIV of 1891 on Sickness Insurance) mimicked that of the Austrian and German model as it was almost a word-for-word translation of relevant German language legislation. Similarly, in the Austrian part of Poland (Galicia) – which had more autonomy within the Habsburg Empire – several laws were taken from Austria (including the system of social insurances introduced in 1888), with the principles of subsidiarity and merit governing the distribution of welfare (Jakubiec, 2007). The process of transposing social policy legislation was facilitated by the widespread use of German in the multi-ethnic Austro-Hungarian Monarchy, where this language was used not only by the state apparatus but quite frequently by ordinary people. The independent Ministries of the Hungarian Kingdom only gradually changed their working language to Hungarian during the late 1880s and early 1890s, and used both languages for a short while.

Such German language domination was not the case in the Russian part of Poland, where, importantly, the basis for welfare entitlements was not predominantly insurance, but where welfare institutions targeted the poorest. Here the overall public administration was much less willing to build social security systems (Zalewski, 2006). In contrast, in the Prussian part's policies were typically centralised, based on the laws binding all the inhabitants of German lands. They were also highly bureaucratised and involved direct citizen control.

Already at this time, the development of a social policy vocabulary was taking place in these two countries with different understandings and connotations. In Hungary, the term 'social policy' (*szociálpolitika*) was used first and foremost as a synonym for 'workers' insurance' (*munkásbiztosítás*). The word 'worker' clearly referred to 'industrial worker', and not to 'agricultural worker'. The first social insurance legislation was called 'workers' assistance' (*munkássegélyezés*). This labelling shows the uncertainty of social policy language: there was no clear distinction yet between 'social insurance' and 'social assistance'. The second meaning of 'social policy' was 'workers' protection', or 'work protection' (*munkavédelem*), mainly from injuries, the enactment of which dates back to 1893, when a list of 'dangerous' industries was defined and related regulation of production was formulated (Bódy, 2011). The most important actors who influenced decision making on social policy – state bureaucrats as well as employers' and labour organisations – agreed that the state should not interfere with industrial affairs more than it did through the compulsory social insurance legislation. The relationship between the state and the economy was clear: the limits of social policy were set at a few percentage points of compulsory social insurance contributions, and very limited social assistance benefits were provided at the municipal level. This liberal approach was gradually replaced by the idea of a more interventionist state during and after the First World War (WWI), broadening the meaning of social policy and changing its language respectively.

The dividing line between two basic understandings of social policy in Poland was the scope of social policy. Polish intellectuals who eventually became the architects of the Polish welfare state after 1918 developed different social policy meanings and emphasised different priorities. A narrower, Bismarckian approach to social policy emphasised entitlements based on 'social insurances' (*ubezpieczenia społeczne*) as the basic response to the 'social question' (*Soziale Frage*) (Orłowski, 1912; Rysz-Kowalczyk, 2002). Others understood 'social policy' in a broader sense: as the overall policy approach for shaping social relations. An influential intellectual and feminist activist, Zofia Daszyńska-Golińska, wrote a brochure in which she defined 'modern' social policy in contrast to the term 'economic policy', thus criticising 'classical', market-oriented economic thought. Here 'social policy' (*polityka społeczna*) is understood very broadly, in the context of human rights. She also defined the group of intellectuals working on social policy concepts as 'the new school of social politicians' (*politycy społeczni*) and historical economists, also called 'socialists ex cathedra' (Daszyńska-Golińska, 1906: 6). However, while Hungarian social policy language had already developed as a part of official public policy vocabulary, these developments in the Polish land took place within the independence movement, and often beyond formal policy making.

Following the loss of the war in 1918, the Austro-Hungarian Monarchy fell apart and two thirds of the previous territories of the Hungarian Kingdom were taken away as a punishment. After the social democratic revolution in 1918 and a short communist dictatorship in 1919, a long period of Conservative rule started where the 'left' was pushed to the margins. Linked to the fear of the potential 'disappearance' of the Hungarian nation and the wish to regain lost territories, a nationalist discourse on social policy emerged. At the same time, with the end of the Great War, Poland regained independence. As early as 1918 Parliament adopted several important laws on labour relations and social security provisions. This made the Polish social security system one of the most developed in Europe (Czubiński, 1978; Albert, 1989). As Poland signed the Washington Treaty and joined the International Labour Organization (ILO) in 1919, the Constitution that was finally adopted in 1921 needed to include many important social rights. In contrast to the Hungarian case, where the right-wing parties were in a ruling position during the mid-war period, the Polish social policy agenda was dominated by the Socialists, especially in the first, critical phase of welfare state development following the years when independence was achieved.

Importantly, independence meant establishing a central administration that would bring Polish social policy research which had been carried out 'underground' to the documents and language of official public policy. The first central administration unit that was engaged in social policy issues was named the Ministry of Labour and Social Welfare (*Ministerstwo Pracy i Opieki Społecznej*). In fact, the term '*opieka społeczna*', used in the Ministry's name, could also be translated as 'social care' and understood in a broader sense: as the overall state effort (administered by this powerful Ministry) to 'protect' society against different social risks and to 'take care' of the inhabitants of the fledgling Polish state. This was also in line with the holistic philosophy of encompassing social policy as a state project and illustrated the paternalist role of the state. As noted by Inglot (2008), social policy (social 'care') was more directly part of a statist philosophy in Poland than in other countries of the region. The role of social policy was also to support the state-building project and was interrelated with the issue of (national) economic growth (Zawadzki, 1927). Overall, though, the language of official documents, especially in the Ministry of Welfare, included the use of terms such as 'struggle of the working class', 'exploitation', 'social justice', 'equality', and 'social progress'.

While the first years after WWI were important for the development of Polish social policies, in Hungary the important change came with the Great Depression of 1929, when the crisis boosted the idea that the state had to intervene in the free market for the purpose of the 'collective good' – even if it would be against the interests of individuals. This was closely linked to the nationalistic and Conservative politics of the interwar era, which abandoned the ideal of 'liberal' capitalist democracy. As the Minister of the Interior put it on the occasion of the opening ceremony of a 'social course' (*szociális tanfolyam*) for civil servants at the end of the decade: 'Instead of the unlimited ambition of the individual, the interest of the community has to come to the fore' thus 'the individual has to subsume his selfishness to the public' (Esztergár and Somogyi, 1940: 13). Experts and bureaucrats now argued that previous social policies were 'fragmented' and thus a new, 'organic' social policy was needed, especially in the field of social assistance, which by this time became explicitly separated from social insurance (Esztergár, 1941).

The emblematic programme of this period in Hungary was the so-called 'Productive Social Policy' (*produktív szociálpolitika, PSP*), which aimed at the 'uplifting' of the agricultural poor through providing loans and organising 'welfare co-operatives' (Szikra, 2012). Social assistance was no longer a mere 'waste of money', according to PSP, but 'contributed to the inclusion of lower classes in the circle of production and consumption' from which the economy as a whole benefited (Esztergár, 1941). The word 'productive' had gender connotations in this context: 'meaningful employment' for men, and 'reproductive' roles for women. According to the nationalist ideology, it was not just coping with the poverty of agricultural workers, but the 'protection' of the ethnically defined 'Hungarian family and nation' (Indoklás, 1940) that was at stake with the success of the new programme, which was closely interlinked with anti-Semitic legislation (Szikra, 2009).

This ideological underpinning gave PSP a larger role in discourse than in practice. While the programme had a rather limited scope, affecting only a small number of impoverished agricultural families, it was celebrated as a manifestation of the newly designed Hungarian 'active' or 'social state' (*szociális állam*). The German '*Sozialstaat*', as well as the Italian corporate state, served as models for the 'social state', an important feature of which was a new design of state bureaucracy. The state would be 'brought closer to the people' according to Zoltán Magyary, an influential expert on state bureaucracies (Magyary, 1939).

Compulsory 'social courses' were organised for local bureaucrats to make them sensitive to the needs of poor people and, not least, to propagate the merits of productive social policy (Esztergár and Somogyi, 1940).

Finally, Poland also suffered from the economic crisis of 1929. But while in Hungary the government (as in other countries) developed more comprehensive social policies, the post-crisis era in Poland can be characterised by retrenchment affecting the generous policies that had been created after 1918. However, other changes came as well: the domination of the Socialists in governments was over after the *coup d'état* of May 1926, which was led by the powerful political leader Józef Piłsudski. Though Piłsudski originally belonged to the Socialist camp, he left the Socialists and became the leader of the right-wing political forces called the '*Sanacja*' movement. *Sanacja* gained influence from the 1930s, as nationalist rhetoric increasingly gained ground in public policy. The political domination of *Sanacja* was also possible thanks to the quasi-authoritarian style of their rules: among *Sanacja*'s methods of removing political competitors was sentencing and imprisonment of political opponents. However, in relation to social policy language, these processes did not bring about significant change. Although the word 'labour' disappeared from the name of the Ministry for Social Welfare in 1932 (thus signalling the strengthening of the 'protectionist' and 'paternalistic' role of the state together with a diminishing emphasis on 'class struggle'), the infamous *Sanacja* rules in fact managed to centralise social insurance funds in 1933.

These developments left Hungary and Poland with two sets of discursive legacies with regard to social policy language. While in Hungary the term 'social state', as well as its propagators, was pushed aside for several decades following the Second World War (WWII), the ideas of central planning, the scientific organisation of state bureaucracy, and state intervention in the economic system in the name of the 'collective good' were given a new lease of life under Communist rule. However, in Poland the legacy of the first, post-independence social policies – inspired by socialist and leftist thought – continued to influence social policy language for decades to come.

State socialism

After the Communist takeover, the two countries received perhaps the most 'unifying' impulse in their history, though with different outcomes in the early Communist times and in the later state socialist regime.

The new 'soviet' model of social policy was implemented in different ways as it was confronted with different local conditions and legacies.

The period between the Communist turn (in 1949 in Hungary and 1944 in Poland) and the 1956 revolution in Hungary was that of a genuine Stalinist dictatorship in both countries (called 'Rákosi-regime' in Hungary). The second period after the revolution (called 'Kádár-regime') was marked by a 'compromise' between the state and the citizens in Hungary, with substantial welfare efforts being made from the 1970s onwards. For Poland the period after 1956 could be further divided according to the party leadership of Władysław Gomułka (1956–70) and Edward Gierek (1970–80), while the early 1980s were dominated by the Solidarity protests followed by a decade of economic decline.

In Hungary, the totalitarian dictatorship was based on the personality cult of Stalin and his Hungarian follower Mátyás Rákosi. A command economy was introduced with the first three year plan in 1947, and the one party system, coupled with the almost total nationalisation of the industry, in the following years. The inclusion of women and agricultural workers in the production of heavy industry were the prime aims of the communist regime, not least due to the preparations for a possible Third World War (Romsics, 1999: 312). Compulsory employment had major effects on social policy, not only because social rights became closely entwined with employment in the 'state sector', but also because it was supposed that the command economy and full employment would together solve all previously existing social problems, including poverty. Roma people (being the largest minority in the country, with about 5% of the total population), the majority of whom were excluded from mainstream society before WWII, were to be integrated into society by taking up the lowest skilled jobs in heavy industry. The essence of the so-called 'economic turn' is best summarised by Welfare Minister Anna Ratkó, just before her Ministry was dissolved in 1950 (only to be re-established in 1991): 'All the acts of the state are social policy' (Ferge, 1986: 158).

Social policy and social work as independent disciplines were thus deliberately excluded from the vocabulary of the party elites, and from scientific research and education because they would have highlighted the existence of poverty and social problems which, in theory, did not exist after the 'economic turn'. 'Social care' (*szociális gondozás*), however, was still carried out by district nurses under the supervision of doctors and the Ministry of Health. 'Social policy departments' (*szociálpolitikai ügyosztály*) continued to exist in local councils: their task was to provide small amounts of social assistance to those unable to work, such as people with disabilities or who were marginalised. Social assistance was given a low profile and people with disabilities or mental health issues were hidden from the view of the general population so as not to destroy the image of communist rule.

At the same time in Poland – subsequent to policy decisions already made in the 1940s – the communist leaders focused on restoring social insurances (especially health services) that had already existed before the war (Jackowiak, 1991). Although the basic principles of the prewar social insurance system were sustained, they gradually came to cover new occupational groups. Social policy was subjugated to the goals of economic policy, and economic plans involved the prioritisation of developing the industrial sector. In the 1940s, a new system of the public health was created, which was coordinated by the newly established Ministry of Health and Social Welfare ('social care') and which shared responsibilities with the Ministry of Labour and Social Affairs (*spraw socjalnych*).

The introduction of such central planning was accompanied by a change in the social policy discourse. As early as 1947, the 'productivist' approach had become apparent: the very first assumption of social policy in the context of the command economy was to bring every person to work (women, people with disabilities and others). The role of 'social care' (*opieka społeczna*) in a traditional sense was to become marginal; instead, the postulate was to 'make the social care institutions productive' (*uproduktywnienie instytucji opiekuńczych*). This was justified on moral grounds: for example, the practice of pushing people with disabilities and dependent individuals into an economically passive role was 'hard to think of in a system ruled by the people' (*ludowładztwo*) (Orlewicz, 1947). The communist party regarded social insurances as a tool for increasing the physical fitness and readiness of employees to work in heavy and dangerous conditions, all according to the requirements set out in the central plan. Social care was, therefore, regarded as unnecessary and having an 'incapacitating' (*ubezwłasnowolnienie*) effect on people (Radlińska, 1947).

Importantly, the term '*socjalizm*' in Polish and '*szocializmus*' in Hungarian (labelling the state political and economic system) is closer to the narrower translation of social policy, (*polityka socjalna; szociálpolitika*) (*Sozialpolitik* in German). This narrower translation is also reflected in how the social programmes were functioning, to a large extent being transferred to the factories and workplaces. The expression '*socjalna*' (narrow) instead of '*społeczna*' (broad, used in the first Polish social policy legislation) was also reflected in the name of the central ministry responsible for the coordination of these different social programmes.

In both countries, social policy language developed as a part of the official propaganda, with the predominant role of the state (and party) as the decisive benefit provider. The state provided 'societal benefits', as translated from the Russian (*társadalmi juttatások- социальные льготы*), in a paternalistic manner, where the state, as father, 'made sacrifices for the building of Hungarian workers' democracy'. In the language of communist leaders, expressions like 'our state' (*államunk*) and 'our people' (*népünk*) were frequently used with the connotation of the leaders themselves 'owning' the state and the people. This language was neither professional nor personal: it resembled the language of armed forces mixed with bureaucratic clichés.[7] In this way, the official language of policies, including social policy, became gradually distanced from the vocabulary of everyday people. Frequently used expressions served to delineate those who were 'building socialism' – and who belonged to the 'working class' (*munkásosztály*) – and those who were the so-called 'class aliens' (*osztályidegen*). The meaning of 'people' (*nép*) now marked the new society of 'socialist persons' (*szocialista ember*) whose place in the division of labour – rather than their social situation (their needs) – defined their social rights. The minority group of 'class aliens' was punished, not least through the means of social policy. For instance, privileges gained by civil servants in the prewar social insurance system were taken away; and agricultural workers not willing to enter state cooperatives did not receive free health care and sick pay and were excluded from receiving family allowance for years (Pető and Szakács, 1985; Ferge, 1986). As 'work' was put at the centre of 'building socialism' and was made the only basis of social rights, the legal category of 'publicly dangerous work-avoidance' (*közveszélyes munkakerülés, KMK*), which had already been established before WWII, gained special importance.

In a very similar manner, social policy programmes in Poland (*programy polityki socjalnej*) (so in a *narrow* sense) were put in place in favour of manual workers and the new category of intelligentsia: when describing the role of white-collar workers, the official propaganda made the distinction between the 'working intelligentsia' (*inteligencja pracująca*) and those who were not state employees, and therefore not considered as working (or 'producing'). While the former were mostly white-collar employees of the state (secondary to the 'working class') and in this sense a 'good' and 'deserving' intelligentsia, the latter were regarded 'undeserving', were therefore excluded from any right to use

---

[7]   The prototype of George Orwell's 'Newspeak' in *Nineteen Eighty-Four* (1984) is exactly this totalitarian language.

the privileges offered by the socialist state. As in Hungary, the notion of 'class enemy' (*wróg klasowy*) was used in relation to any actions undermining the legitimacy of the communist system (Chumiński, 2010). Importantly, Poland was the only country in the Soviet bloc where private farming was not eradicated through collectivisation. The existence of private land ownership was seen as 'alien' to the socialist economic order and had profound consequences for such farmers. The derogatory term 'kułak' (*кулак*) was used in propaganda with regard to the owners of larger farms in both countries and became the basis for inferior treatment, including reduced social policy entitlements.

Despite the compulsion to work, living standards in Hungary decreased relative to the 1930s (Ferge, 1986); thus the 1956 revolution in Hungary was partly a product of the social deprivation that the vast majority of the Hungarian population experienced. Following the suppression of the revolution, János Kádár's main invention was a 'welfare compromise' between party elites and the 'people', which led to an eventual increase in living standards and a decrease in inequalities as well as in poverty from the mid-1960s. The legitimacy of the system rested on increased wellbeing, which was based on the growth of centrally planned wages and low prices of basic goods, coupled with extending social insurance benefits. 'Strategic plans on social policy' were created from the early 1960s, thus the term 'social policy' re-entered the political (but not yet the public and scientific) discourse. This is also indicated by the fact that such documents remained 'top secret', to be read only by ministerial and high-ranking political officials. The widest possible definition of social policy was present in such plans, including those relating to social insurance, housing policy, health care, wages, family policy (under the name of the 'population question') and even the issue of holiday resorts for workers (Munkaügyi Minisztérium, 1960).

By the late 1970s the central terms of Hungarian social policy discourse became 'societal welfare' (*társadalmi jólét*) and 'quality of life' (*életszínvonal*), while 'work' in the 'socialist sector' remained the basis of eligibility to social benefits. The word 'protection' also reappeared in relation to needy and deserving social groups such as children, older people and those with disabilities. However, 'protection' meant not only social protection of the vulnerable but also the protection of the socialist ideal from the reality of social problems. Institutions for children, older people and those with disabilities continued to exist in remote mansions in the countryside, hidden away from the eyes of the majority of society.

In Poland the Stalinist phase was also over in 1956, and the country entered a period of 'small stabilisation' with the new leadership of Władysław Gomułka. The term 'social security' (*zabezpieczenie społeczne*) became more popular from late 1950s and early 1960s. The use of this notion was inspired by The Social Security Act of the New Deal legislation (1935), as well as by The Social Security Act of the Working People, issued by the Council of People's Commissars in revolutionary Russia in 1918 (Święcicki, 1971). 'Social security' was contrasted with 'social insurance', the former being wider in scope and not only departing from the actuarial principles but also with a classical catalogue of social risks (Święcicki, 1971). This broader approach to social policy became even more profound during the 1970s, when in the declaration of the party leaders, social policy was proclaimed as equally important as economic policy, and aimed at meeting 'citizens' needs' (Balicka-Kozłowska, 1975). Therefore, 'social planning' was to gain equal status with regard to economic planning (an aim that was present in Hungary) and received its own recognition and importance from the beginning of the 1970s, with Edward Gierek's term in office as the party leader (Piotrowski, 1979).

The language of 'needs' was accompanied, for the first time, by calls for the 'rationalisation' of social policy as a requisite for an increase in the 'efficiency of work' (PiZS, 1972). For example, the argument about the 'rationalisation of female employment' justified the introduction of longer maternity leaves (Jakubowicz, 1971). In a similar manner, 'efficiency' (that is, the withdrawal of mothers with small children from the workforce) justified the introduction of paid, three year long maternity leave in 1969 in Hungary (Szikra, 2011). In contrast to the Stalinist period, female employment started to be treated as 'complementary to that of men' (Jakubowicz, 1971). At the same time, faced by the looming economic crisis (especially the food crisis), the socialist state shifted its attitude with regard to private farmers. Even though still treated worse than industrial workers or those employed in collectivised agriculture, private farmers gained new social rights, including a separate pension system. In this way private farmers became (similarly to female workers) treated as 'complementary' to the socialist mode of economic production (Polakowski, 2010). Finally, important changes took place with regard to the name of central administration bodies: in 1960 the Ministry of Labour and Social Affairs was closed down and, instead, the Committee for Wages and Labour was established. The Ministry of Wages, Labour and Social Policy (*polityka socjalna*) was established in 1972 (Rybicki, 1978), with the word 'wages' disappearing from its title in 1987.

Alongside the extension of social rights, research into inequalities emerged in Hungary during the mid-1960s (Ferge et al, 1966). However, the words 'poverty' or 'poor' were carefully avoided: when the first representative research on the Roma minority was carried out in 1971, the leading sociologist István Kemény had to leave the country for raising the issue of the poverty of the Roma (Kemény, 1976). Other researchers used expressions like 'low income' or 'disadvantaged' (*hátrányos helyzetű*). One important study in the mid-1980s defined the term 'social inclusion disorder' (*[társadalmi beilleszkedési zavar – TBZ]*), a label resembling a psychiatric classification and referring to marginalised families where certain 'deviancies' caused the 'dysfunctional working of the family' (Dús, 1986). When the underground organisation 'Fund to Help the Poor' (*Szegényeket Támogató Alap - SZETA*) was created in the early 1980s, its members were persecuted by the police for the open usage of the word 'poor', which was seen as a critique of the state socialist system in itself (Pik, 2001). The official discourse still insisted that poverty could only exist in capitalist societies.

Polish experts also noted a growing discrepancy between, on the one hand, the official rhetoric of the equality of socialist society and, on the other, increasing inequalities and deprivation among benefit recipients and certain groups of workers. Several studies on poverty existed, but were never published, and, when talking about poverty, official documents only used euphemisms such as 'shortage of goods' (*niedostatek*) (Rakowski, 2009). The need to define minimum living standards as a benchmark for the assessment of living conditions was voiced by social policy experts as early as the 1970s. However, the demand to make them publicly available was only put forward by the independent trade union Solidarność in 1980 during its famous negotiations. The monetary value of the so-called 'social minimum' (*minimum socjalne*) was subsequently published (Tymowski, 2001). Together with the call for an official recognition of poverty, this revealed a failure of the Polish state to satisfy the needs of population (as articulated in the 1970s) and represented the protest against the primacy of economic policy over social goals (Zieliński, 1982).

At the same time, the 'rationalisation' approach was revived to limit the development of social policy for the purposes of 'not spending more than we produce' (Zieliński, 1982). Legislation was adopted in 1982 to deal with 'social parasitism' (*pasożytnictwo społeczne*), which mostly referred to those who avoided taking up employment (Szarfenberg, 2010). This was followed by the parliamentary resolution on 'fighting the phenomena of social pathology (*patologia społeczna*) and 'enhancing the moral health of society' in 1986. In this way, the productivist approach and the moral exclusion of those who did not work reappeared in official public policy during the period of the decline of state socialism.

It should be noted that research exchange with the Western world was severely limited. Only a select group of Hungarian state bureaucrats and experts could attend international meetings (for example the ILO assembly) and conferences (such as meetings of demographers) from the late 1960s. Consequently, the language of social policy was not much affected by the 'Western' concepts of the welfare state and social security. Interestingly enough, there was almost no connection with other countries of the 'Eastern bloc' until this period either; however, the Soviet hegemony caused important semantic changes in the language of social policy. Expressions like 'council' (*tanács - совет*) and 'societal benefits' (*társadalmi juttatások - социальные льготы*) were translations borrowed from their Russian counterparts.

Capitalist democracy after 1989

Although the political and economic transition from the communist system to a capitalist democracy brought about major changes in social policy, certain important continuations can also be observed in these institutions (Inglot, 2008; Szikra and Tomka, 2009). Social insurance remained the dominant social policy area in both countries. A radical change in that system only occurred in 1997 in Hungary, with partial privatisation of the pension system (Müller, 1999; Orenstein, 2008), a move which was only recently reversed. Experts and stakeholders in social insurance and local social policy (for example heads of nurseries, social administrators of municipalities and others) remained in place. Thus, although decentralisation of social services and the increased role of social assistance may be considered paradigmatic changes, certain continuities in the way social problems have been dealt with and the language that has been used by administrators and experts can also be observed.

Transition in Central and Eastern Europe (also called 'transformation' or 'velvet revolution'), took different forms in Hungary and in Poland. The 'big bang' package ('Balcerowicz Plan') led to a 'shock economic therapy' in the early 1990s in Poland, leaving many people below the minimum income level. Unlike that in Hungary, the social policy strategy had been to compensate for the loss of income, not to prevent this situation. Therefore, after massive outlays, many costly programmes of income compensation were introduced, together with a generous unemployment benefit scheme. However, when faced with so many unemployed people after the big bang, the government decided to cut the previous generous unemployment scheme and put more emphasis on establishing effective programmes of social assistance. Most of the programmes were, therefore, aimed at the poorest and involved the principle of income testing. The first comprehensive legislation in Hungary, called the 1993 'Social Act', aimed at defining the boundaries of 'deservingness' for adults, as separate from the issue of children, who, by definition, became eligible for various forms of assistance through the 1997 Child Protection Act. Decentralisation of responsibility for social policy was most visible in the sphere of care services.

Issues previously considered as taboos could now be openly expressed in both countries. Poverty, unemployment and homelessness could be discussed in the media and scholarly journals. Social policy as a scientific discipline was reborn, and a Department of Social Policy and Social Work was created at Eötvös University of Sciences, Budapest, followed by several other departments in major universities all over the country. While foreign – especially UK – influence was important, the founders of the new discipline also looked back in time to the prewar examples of social work and social policy courses and took inspiration from them.[8]

Most importantly, together with the fall of state socialism and the introduction of a democratic regime, an opportunity appeared for the various meanings and understandings of social policy to develop. In Poland, though, the narrow understanding of social policy as '*polityka socjalna*' continued. The new capitalist economy was contrasted with the communist (or socialist) policies. Social policy was required for alleviating poverty caused by the 'necessary costs of transformation'. The adjective 'social' in the narrow translation as '*socjalna*' became synonymous with 'fiscal burden'. The road towards the 'Western', 'modern', 'capitalist' economy was somehow 'disturbed' by the need to provide welfare for the 'losers of transformation'. The term 'welfare state' was already in use during the period of state socialism, mostly when describing developments in the West and linked to social democracy and 'socially oriented' economies (Rysz-Kowalczyk, 2002). The new rhetoric, often used by market oriented economists such as Leszek Balcerowicz, presented the 'welfare state' as the result of Western 'prosperity' (*dobrobyt*) and so the term 'welfare state' was typically

---

[8]   The development of courses, the interlinked nature of social work and social policy, and the importance of fieldwork to both social workers and social policy students were elements of social work and social policy training that were already present in the very first social policy course of the University of Economics in 1942.

translated as 'prosperity state' (*państwo dobrobytu*). According to such a line of argument, countries like Poland first 'need to get to the level of Western prosperity' and only then 'could we afford' to have a welfare state (Balcerowicz, 1997).

The newly (re)discovered term of 'social policy' has had two alternative meanings in Hungarian, which were used by the 'left' and the 'right' of the political spectrum, respectively. During the 1990s and mid-2000s the 'left' (the leading force of which was the post-communist Hungarian Socialist Party - MSZP) preferred an all-encompassing meaning of social policy that included social insurance, social assistance, family policies and social services. FIDESZ – Young Democrats' Alliance-Hungarian Civic Union (a Liberal party that turned to the right in the mid-1990s and has become the leading Conservative force since then) and the smaller Christian Democratic Party (KDNP) aimed at narrowing the meaning of social policy to social assistance provided to the poor. The shift to the more limited meaning was striking when FIDESZ was in power between 1998 and 2002, and recently, since 2010. Family policy is explicitly differentiated from social policy according to the Conservatives, where the former is aimed at increased fertility of the middle class and the latter at the marginal assistance of the poor. Social insurance is also separated from social policy and has been administered by the Ministry of National Economy since 2010. The Ministry of Welfare was closed and a giant Ministry of Human Resources was created, where family policy is handled separately from 'social inclusion', this latter including the issue of the Roma and people with disabilities.

The term 'welfare state' or 'social state' has its own post-1990 history as well. In the early 1990s the Conservative government of the Hungarian Democratic Forum (MDF) defined its own role as promoting the building up of the Hungarian '*Soziale Marktwirtschaft*' (*szociális piacgazdaság*), following the example of the newly unified Germany. Yet this ideal was soon forgotten, and has not been replaced by the Hungarian concept of 'welfare state' (*jóléti állam*). This term only exists as something that Hungary might reach in the (far) future, or as something that exists in wealthier parts of Europe. Only the short-lived Socialist Medgyessy government (2002–04) used the term to point out a relatively rapid change in the living standards of Hungarians when it called for a 'welfare change' in 2002. A similar attempt for paradigmatic shift was the Child Poverty Programme between 2006 and 2008; here the rhetoric of 'social investment' gained some ground for a short while.

Apart from these failed attempts, 'welfare systems' (*jóléti rendszer*) and – as they have frequently been called by economists – 'big systems of distribution' (*nagy elosztó rendszerek*) were contextualized as 'burdens' on the free market and obstacles for the Hungarian economy. Governments argued for a 'small state' (*kis állam*) and for retrenchment most of the time (apart from during election campaigns). The term 'social policy' became a difficult one: it could not easily (if at all) be integrated into everyday language because of its connotations of something that has to do with 'socialism' and 'politics'. The term 'social work' also fared ill, as it is connected to the word 'labour', which reminds people of the compulsion to labour under state socialism.

The dominance of a neoliberal discourse in the public approach to social policies was hard to break in Poland also. After 1989, consecutive governments tried to change this social policy language, but such discursive changes had no effect on actual policies. Jacek Kuroń, the first Minister of Labour and Social Policy after 1989, tried to 'explain' the reforms to the public by regular television appearances, where he famously wore a casual blue denim shirt (not a suit, like most of the other politicians and experts). Afterwards, the 'social democratic' (post-communist) governments of the mid-1990s declared a departure from austerity policies and hardship that 'people could no longer bear' (Inglot, 2008).

When justifying cuts in social policy spending, phrases such as 'laziness' and 'learned helplessness' remained reference points. Polish intellectual circles invented and/or popularised terms like '*homo sovieticus*', 'learned helplessness', or 'civilisational incompetence' (Ferge, 2008). For example, '*homo sovieticus*' was a representation of the type of person who was raised in the socialist ('communist', or 'Soviet') system, where the 'paternalistic' state was 'doing everything for him/her' and in this way made him/her passive and 'infantile' (Sztompka, 2000). The '*homo sovieticus*' was, according to the argument, completely 'unprepared' for the conditions of competition, where first and foremost the will to work and to perform were required in the new, capitalist and 'civilised' order (Hnatiuk and Kołodziejska, 2012). Thus, social policy instruments are constantly 'abused' by the groups displaying a 'demanding stance', because they are unable to 'adjust' to the new conditions.

Preparing for accession to the European Union (EU) further complicated the picture.[9] Hungary started to participate in EU financed programmes and adjust its legal system at the end of the 1990s, when it also had to learn EU jargon. The term 'equal opportunities' (*esélyegyenlőség*), for example, was disseminated during this process. But as 'gender equality' or 'equal opportunities for people with disabilities

---

[9]   Hungary and Poland entered the EU in 2004.

and people from minority ethnic communities' remained mainly on paper, the expressions describing such phenomena did not become part and parcel of mainstream social policy language. It is telling that no single word for 'gender' has emerged in Hungarian or Polish: in both languages, the notion of 'gender' is only understood when translated by a longer chain of words describing its meaning, which makes it hard to use expressions like 'gender roles', 'gender order', and 'gendered institutions'.

Concepts like 'social inclusion' *(társadalmi befogadás)* and 'exclusion' *(társadalmi kirekesztés)* could not easily be translated into Hungarian: prominent social policy experts lamented this situation on the eve of EU accession (Ferge, 2002; Szalai 2002). The EU tried to influence national social policy through the new terminology with limited success. Documents like the 'National Action Plan for Social Inclusion' were prepared by bureaucrats but actual discrimination against women, the Roma, people with disabilities and migrants continued over time.

In Poland, neoliberal discourse was partially strengthened by the workfare orientation of EU policies aimed at improving 'employability'. The somewhat bureaucratic language of EU social policy has also been introduced primarily via the use of the European Social Fund. Interestingly, the right-wing, Eurosceptic and Conservative Party 'Law and Justice' *(Prawo i Sprawiedliwość 'PiS')* was in fact one of the few political organisations that openly criticised the market orientation of the post-1989 Polish transformation and postulated stronger state engagement in economic and social policy. It was in 2005 that the first Prime Minister of the Conservative Coalition changed the name of the Ministry of Labour and Social Policy to one which included the broader translation of the term 'social policy' *(polityka społeczna)*, removing the 'old' adjective *'socjalna'* that had a bad connotation and was mostly used when talking about social programmes for poor people.

Although civil control over social policy increased during the first half of the 1990s in Hungary, and even if 'self-governance' of the social insurance system was created to include the participation of employers and workers, we now see a gradual reversal of the process. Nationalisation recently carried out by the Conservative government of Viktor Orbán is also reflected in the change of social policy language. 'Protection', reflecting the language of both the 1930s and the 1980s, became a key concept in this context. For example, when private pension savings were confiscated by the state in 2011, the person responsible for the process was named 'Commissioner of the Protection of Pensions' *(nyugdíjvédelmi biztos)*. The recent suggestion by the Prime Minister to build a 'society based on work' instead of a 'welfare state' suggests that 'work' and 'welfare' are opposing notions, where 'work' is a positive force, strengthening society, whereas 'welfare' is defined as 'social assistance' for those who are unable to work, and thus only impose a burden on the 'working' society.[10]

Conclusion

The goal of this chapter was to trace the shifting meaning of social policy vocabulary in Hungary and Poland, two countries that experienced state socialism. We began our analysis with developments in the 19th century and continued to the interwar period, when the formation of the nation-states of both Poland and Hungary started and in which social policy played a central role. In the 1920s and 1930s, the term 'social policy' was used in Poland in a broader sense as *polityka społeczna,* where *społeczny* means 'social', and where social policy was driven by intellectuals from socialist circles linked to international initiatives and networks. The term 'social policy' developed during the Dual Monarchy in Hungary, and by the 1930s 'social state' or even 'active state' became central. These notions referred to the state's increased intervention in the social affairs and the behaviour of its citizens. During state socialism, these terms lost their importance as social policy and social work became 'inexistent': central economic planning was supposed to eradicate poverty and all other social problems. However, a central pillar of social policy – that is, social insurance – continued to exist. The language of social policy discourse was ideologically loaded from the outset of the transformation to a market economy in both countries. After the fall of communism in Poland the term 'social policy' was understood as 'socialist' policy and hence had negative connotations. The dominating discourse was to depart from the period of state socialism. Simultaneously, there was the discourse of '*homo sovieticus*' – 'civilisational incompetence' – that justified social policy cuts. However, social policy and social work have been re-established as academic disciplines in both countries and thus created their new language, with intended references to the interwar period.

The term 'welfare state' has been understood as a state of prosperity with generous social provisions and thus it has been referred to in connection with 'Western' or 'Northern' countries 'that can afford it'. The prevalence of the rule of the market over social policy is

---

[10] Viktor Orbán: Nem jóléti állam, hanem munka alapú társadalom épül. (We do not build a welfare state; we build a society based on work.) 18 October, 2012. www.fidesz.hu/index.php?Cikk=185467

rarely contested in Hungary and Poland and the term 'social policy' is frequently equated with 'poor policies' or 'social assistance'. Social policy vocabulary thus often describes benefit recipients as 'immature' and 'passive,' delegitimising the very existence of such programmes. EU related social policy language seems to be going more in the direction of actually supporting the idea of individual responsibility, though with the European Social Fund absorption process, at least gender equality and equal opportunity slogans are gaining some ground in both countries.

References

Albert, A. (1989) *Najnowsza Historia Polski*. London: Polonia Book Fund.

A Magyar Szocialista Munkáspárt központi Bizottságának beszámolója (1993). In: *A Magyar Szocialista Munkáspárt VIII. kongresszusa*. Budapest: Kossuth Könyvkiadó.

Általános Munkás- Betegsegélyző Pénztár. Jelentés a Pénztár forgalmáról és működéséről. 1870-1898. Táblázatos kimutatásokkal és statisztikai adatokkal. Budapest, 1899.

Arató, A. (1993) *Forradalom, restauráció és legitimáció. Az államszocializmusból való átmenet ideológiai problémái* Politikatudományi Szemle, 3, 5-44.

Augusztinovics, M. (ed.) (2000) *Körkép reform után. Tanulmányok a nyugdíjrendszerről*. Budapest: Közgazdasági Szemle alapítvány.

Balcerowicz, L. (1997) *Socializm, kapitalizm. Szkice z przełomu epok*. Wydawnictwo Naukowe PWN.

Balicka-Kozłowska, H. (1975) Niektóre problemy opiekii pomocy społecznej. *Praca i zabezpieczenie społeczne* xvii(12).

Bicskei, É. (2006) 'Our greatest treasure, the child': the politics of child care in Hungary, 1945-1956'. *Social Politics*, vol 13, Nr.2.

Bódy, Z. (2001) 'A 'szociális kérdés' kezelésének alternatívái a XIX. század végén. Az 1891-es kötelező betegbiztosítási törvény keletkezése', *Korall*, September.

Bódy, Z. (2011) *Az ipari munka társadalma - Szociális kihívások, liberális és korporatív válaszok Magyarországon a 19. század végétől a második világháborúig*. Budapest: Argumentum.

Chumiński, J. (2010) Mentalne bariery rozwoju gospodarczego PRL. *Modernizacja czy pozorna modernizacja? Społeczno-ekonomiczny bilans PRL 1944-1948*. Gajt, Wrocław: 92-232.

Czubiński, A. (1978) 'Polska w okresie dwudziestolecia miedzywojennego'. *Dzieje Polski*. J. Topolski (ed.), Warsawa: Polskie Wydawnictwo Naukowe, 612-778.

Daszyńska-Golińska, Z. (1906) *Teoretyczne podstawy polityki społecznej w XIX stuleciu*. Warszawa: Nakładem Księgarni Naukowej.

Dús, Á. (ed.) (1986) *Társadalmi beilleszkedési zavarok.* Budapest: Kossuth Kiadó.

Ecseri, L. (1884) *A munkássegélyezés ügye Magyarországon.* Pesti Könyvnyomda Rt., Bp.

Esztergár, L. (1941) 'Társadalomépítés.' *Sorsunk,* 1–2. Pécs, Dunántúl Pécsi Egyetemi Könyvkiadó és Nyomda Rt.

Esztergár, L. and Somogyi, F. (1940) *A magyar szociálpolitika feladatai: A vármegyei szociális tanácsadók és közjóléti előadók pécsi országos szociálpolitikai értekezletén elhangzott előadások.* Pécs, Kultúra.

Ferge, S. e.a. (1966) *Társadalmi rétegződés Magyarországon: 15 000 háztartás 1963. évi adatai.* Budapest: KSH.

Ferge, Z. (1986) *Fejezetek a szegénypolitika történetéből.* Budapest: Magvető Kiadó.

Ferge, Z. (2002) 'Az EU és a kirekesztés.' In. *Esély* 2002. 6. 3-13.

Ferge, Z. (2008) Is there a specific East–Central European welfare culture? W. van Oorschot e.a. (eds) *Culture And Welfare State. Values and Social Policy in Comparative Perspective,* London: Edward Elgar, 141-161.

Heller, F. (1947) *Közgazdaságtan. II. kötet. Alkalmazott közgazdaságtan.* Budapest: Mérnöki Továbbképző Intézet kiadása.

Hnatiuk, M. and M. Kołodziejska (2012) Pożegnanie z homo sovieticus: próba empirycznej weryfikacji kategorii oraz analiza jej obecności w socjologicznym dyskursie o transformacji. Maciej G. and P. Sadura (eds) *Style życia i porządek klasowy w Polsce,* Warszawa: Scholar.

Horváth, S. (2012) *Két emelet boldogság. Mindennapi szociálpolitika Budapesten a Kádár-korban.* Budapest: Napvilág kiadó.

Indoklás. (1940) XXIII. törvénycikk az Országos Nép- és Családvédelmi Alapról. Magyar törvénytár, 1941, Franklin, Budapest.

Inglot, T. (2008) *Welfare States in East Central Europe, 1919-2004,* Cambridge: Cambridge University Press.

Jackowiak, C. (1991) Po drugiej wojnie swiatowej: kierunki rozwoju ubezpieczen spolecznych. *Rozwoj ubezpieczen spolecznych na ziemiach polskich,* edited by C. Jackowiak. Ossolineum, Wroclaw.

Jakubiec, D. (2007) *Pierwsze polskie instytucje ubezpieczen spolecznych. Zarys historii i ustroju.* Warszawa: Zaklad Ubezpieczen Spolecznych.

Jakubowicz, M. (1971) Racjonalne zatrudnienie a praca kobiet. *Praca i zabezpieczenie spoleczne* xiii(4)

Kemény, I. (1976) *Beszámoló a magyarországi cigányok helyzetével foglalkozó, 1971-ben végzett kutatásról.* Budapest: MTA Szociológiai Intézet.

Kornai, J. (1980) *Economics of Shortage.* Amsterdam: North-Holland, 1980.

Lackó, M. (1961) *Ipari munkásságunk összetételének alakulása 1867-1949.* Budapest: Táncsics.

Magyary, Z. (1936) *A nemzeti szocialista községi közigazgatás.* Különlenyomat a Városi Szemle 22. évfolyamából, Budapest.

Magyary, Z. (1939) 'A közigazgatás és az emberek. Eredmények és tanulságok.' In. Magyary, Zoltán and Kiss, István. 1939. *A közigazgatás és az emberek.* Dunántúl, Budapest. 353-373.

Magyary, Z. (1939) 'Közigazgatás – szociális közigazgatás.' In. *Közigazgatási továbbképző tanfolyam.* Budapest, Állami Nyomda, 1939. 103-110.

Magyary, Z. (1941) (ed.) *A szociális vármegye. A Komárom vármegyei Közjóléti és Gazdasági Szövetkezet működése.* Magyar Közigazgatástudományi Intézet, Budapest. 24-41.

Müller, K. (1999) *The Political Economy of Pension Reform in Central-Eastern Europe.* Cheltenham, Northampton.

Munkaügyi Minisztérium, Szociálpolitikai Főosztály (1960) *A szociálpolitikai intézkedések 20 éves távlati terve.* 'Szigorúan Titkos.' Hungarian National Archives, XIX-C-5, 147. doboz.

Orenstein, M.A. (2008) *Privatizing Pensions: The Transnational Campaign for Social Security Reform.* Princeton University Press.

Orlewicz, T. (1947) Polityka społeczna Polski w obliczu Planu Gospodarczego. *Praca i opieka spoleczna* 1 (XXI):27-35.

Orłowski, A. (1912) *Ubezpieczenia robotnicze w dumie państwowej.* Warszawa: Skład Główny w Księgarni G. CenterSzwera i S-ki.

Orwell, George (1949) *Nineteen Eighty-Four (1984).* Secker and Warburg, London.

Pető, I. and Szakács, S. (1985) *A hazai gazdaság négy évtizedének története 1945-1985.* I.kötet. Budapest: Közgazdasági és Jogi Könyvkiadó.

Pik, K. (2001) *A szociális munka története Magyarországon, 1817-1990.* Budapest: Hilscher Rezső Szociálpolitikai Egysület.

Piotrowski, J. (1979) 35 lat społecznego rozwoju. *Praca i zabezpieczenie spoleczne* xxi(7).

PiZS. (1972) Ministerstwo obietnic i nadziei. *Praca i zabezpieczenie spoleczne* xiv(7).

Polakowski, M. (2010) *The Institutional Transformation of Social Policy in East Central Europe. Poland and Hungary in Comparative and Historical Perspective.* Maastricht: Boekenplan.

Radlińska, Helena. (1947) Zagadnienia opieki społecznej (Ze skrzyżowań teorii i praktyki). *Praca i opieka spoleczna* 4 (xxi):277-285.

Rakowski, T. (2009) *Łowcy, zbieracze, praktycy niemocy.* Warszawa: Słowo/ obraz terytoria.

Romsics, I. (1999) *Hungary in the 20th Century.* Budapest: Corvina Kiadó.

Rybicki, Z. (1978) *Administracje gospodarcza w PRL.* Warszawa: Polskie Wydawnictwo Naukowe

Rysz-Kowalczyk (ed.). (2002) *Leksykon polityki społecznej,* Warszawa: Oficyna Wydawnicza Aspra-jr,.

Saád, J. (2000) *Magyary Zoltán.* Budapest: Új Mandátum.

Szabó, M. (2003) *A diszkurzív politikatudomány alapjai. Elméletek és elemzések.* Budapest, L'Harmattan Kiadó.

Szalai, J. (1985) 'A szociálpolitika nyelve- amit kifejez és amit eltakar.' In. Medvetánc 1984-1985. 4-1. 105-119.

Szalai, J. (1992) 'A társadalombiztosítás érdekviszonyairól.' In: *Szociológiai Szemle 2. szám.* 27 - 43.

Szalai, J. (2002) A társadalmi kirekesztődés egyes kérdései az ezredforduló Magyarországán.' [Some questions about social exclusion in Hungary at the turn of the Millenium.] In. *Szociológiai Szemle* 2002. 4. 34–50.

Szalai, J. (2007) *Nincs két ország…?* Budapest, Osiris Kiadó.

Szarfenberg, R. (2010) Marginalizacja i wykluczenie społeczne - panorama językowo teoretyczna. R. Szarfenberg e.a. (eds) *Ubóstwo i wykluczenie społeczne perspektywa poznawcza.* Warszawa: Elipsa.

Szikra, D. (2004) 'The thorny path to implementation: Bismarckian social insurance in Hungary in the late 19th century.' *European Journal of Social Security,* vol. 6, no 3, September, 255-272.

Szikra, D. (2009) 'Social policy and anti-semitic exclusion before and during World War II in Hungary. The case of the productive social policy', in Hauss, G. and Schulte, D.: *Amid Social Contradictions. Towards a History of Social Work in Europe.* Opladen and Farmington Hills: Barbara Budrich Publishers, 111-131.

Szikra, D. (2011) 'Tradition matters: child care and primary school education in modern Hungary', in Hagemann, K. et. al. (eds) *Child Care and Primary Education in Post-War Europe.* New York and Oxford, Berghahn Books. 2011.

Szikra, D. (2012) "Welfare Co-operatives"and social policy between the two World Wars in Hungary', in Hilson, M. et. al. (eds) *Co-operatives and the Social Question: The Co-operative Movement in Northern and Eastern Europe, 1880-1950.* Cardiff :Welsh Academic Press, 153-167.

Szikra, D. and B. Tomka. (2009). 'Social policy in East Central Europe. major trends in the 20th century', in Cerami, A. and P. Vanhuysse (eds) *Post-Communist Welfare Pathways: Theorizing Social Policy Transformations in Central and Eastern Europe.* Basingstoke: Palgrave Macmillan.

Święcicki, M. (1971) Ubezpieczenia społeczne a prawo pracy. *Praca i zabezpieczenie społeczne* xiii (8-9).

Sztompka, P. (2000) *Trauma wielkiej zmiany : społeczne koszty transformacji.* Instytut Studiów Politycznych Polskiej Akademii Nauk, Warszawa.

Tomka, B. (2003) *Szociálpolitika a 20. századi Magyarországon európai perspektívában*. Budapest, Századvég Kiadó.

Tymowski, A. (2001) Z perspektywy czasu: początki 'minimum socjalnego'. *Polityka społeczna* vol. 11-12/2001.

Zalewski, D. (2006) *Opieka i pomoc społeczna. Dynamika instytucji.* Wydawnictwa Universytetu Warszawskiego, Warszawa

Zawadzki, W. (1927) *Polska polityka socjalna a gospodarstwo społeczne.* Towarzystwo Ekonomiczne, Kraków.

Zieliński, T. (1982) Podstawowe problmy reformy ubezpieczeń społecznych w PRL. *Praca i zabezpieczenie spoleczne* xxiv(4).

THREE

Languages of 'social policy' at 'the EU level'

Jean-Claude Barbier

What one could cursorily call the 'language' question in European Union (EU) social policy is generally overlooked by social scientists. Under the apparently benign use of one of the varieties of 'international English', the EU perhaps provides the clearest illustration of the tendency to blur the frontiers between politics, social science and political communication. This *mélange des genres* affects the participants in the production of the languages of social policy[11], the spaces where they craft them, and the ensuing discourses that travel across Europe and beyond. After a short section devoted to the definition of 'social policy' at the EU level, we outline a theory of the production and circulation of social policy languages within the borders of the EU.[12] In a third section, we provide examples of this production and circulation of social policy languages.

The empirical base for the chapter is twofold: the first is a reflection originating from the author's continual participation – as a non-native speaker of English – in various academic forums over the last 20 years. The second is the writing over the same period of a series of monographs about social policy concepts. Most of the time, the sociological unease experienced in 'international research situations' (Barbier, 2005) triggered the writing of these monographs, none of which, incidentally, was commissioned. To give an illustration at the start: one of the first experiences of uneasiness occurred with the concept of 'welfare state' at a time when the notion was extremely hegemonic

---

[11] There are languages and not one language, because, as we shall see, the forums where they circulate are numerous and partly fragmented according to policy areas, sectors or countries.

[12] The focus of this chapter is the European Union, and for the sake of brevity, we shall not deal directly with the circulation and production of social policy languages beyond its frontiers, although the mechanisms involved are entirely similar.

(Barbier and Théret, 2001). Concurring with Merrien (1997), we argued that the notion of '*État-providence*' in French was inadequate for many reasons, notably for its focus on the state as the only actor: social protection (*la protection sociale, soziale Sicherung, la protezione sociale,* and so on) was a more encompassing notion, involving structural social relationships (a 'nexus') between politics, economics and the family. In France and the United States, it found its place gradually as a notion complementary to, but also competing with, social security or *sécurité sociale* (Barbier, 2008, ch1; see also chapter seven, this volume, by Daniel Béland). Social protection was also a more useful and adequate notion than the British-centric 'welfare state', with its specific origin and history. The concept of 'social protection' can also encompass societal forms that existed before the British welfare state, but in addition forms that now exist across a wide variety of countries and continents. More than 15 years after the author, and François-Xavier Merrien (1997), both raised the argument, the mainstream currency of that phrase has received strong support in the comparative literature by virtue of its use by international organisations dealing with poor people and with social programmes in the developing countries. While it is true that this particular usage has often remained focused on the basic components of 'social protection', it can also easily be observed that the political–administrative expression 'social protection' has become so common at the EU level[13] that it would be useless and cumbersome to examine it in detail in the huge output of the 'Brussels' administration.

'Social policy' at 'the EU level': linking two problematic notions with one another

There is no doubt about the existence of a broad aggregation of 'social matters' that are of interest to politicians and officials belonging to the formal institutions of the EU, as well as their counterparts in the nation-states. Whether this hotchpotch of programmes and social topics extending across 28 nation-states stands as a sociologically objectifiable 'policy' is another matter. If the EU has never been a significant player for redistribution (Majone, 1993), it is indeed difficult to accept that it

---

[13] Here are two typical instances of this use: on 10 October 2012, American economist Joseph Stiglitz, discussing inequality on *France Culture* radio, talked of 'social protection' and not of 'welfare'; in one of its editorials dealing with China and Asia, *The Economist* stated that 'pressure is growing for public pensions, national health insurance, unemployment benefits and other hallmarks of social protection' (8 September 2012, p 9).

has ever had classic 'social policies'. Hence, it is only *by extension* that one can accept that there is such a thing as a genuine 'EU social policy'. Instead, rather than a fully fledged policy, the substance of 'EU social policy' lies in the organisation of ideas, concepts, rules and norms that EU elites promote: the eventual outcome of their continuous struggles between 'social models' (as the expression goes) lies in the legitimisation of a certain discourse about the state of the world among elite actors. They are all intensely engaged in the use of these categories in the transnational debate in their own national polities (Barbier, 2013).

Despite its very common use, the expression 'at the EU level' is no less problematic. While we now have a significant and convincing body of literature on the multilevel governance of the EU (Scharpf, 1999), the image of 'levels' it conveys is ambiguous when it comes to identifying the *spaces* where social policy languages originate and have currency. If one may identify EU institutions (for example the Parliament, the Council) as clearly different from national institutions (for example governments, national legal systems), the spaces where discourses are crafted and disseminated are populated with actors such as individuals and interest groups, lobby groups and representatives of various constituencies, members of epistemic communities, and participants in advocacy coalitions. Empirically, these participants can never be identified as only belonging to a 'European' level, or for that matter to a national one; as administrators, journalists, researchers, politicians, lobbyists, experts, consultants, spin doctors, and others, all have crucial links with one or more national interests and entities (for example universities, firms, parties, institutions), while at the same time they all belong to the EU and to national places, forums and arenas. This is why it is impossible to clearly separate the so-called 'EU level' from the 'national level'. This situation is all the more relevant for the object of the present reflection, that is, the trans-, inter-, and cross-national language of social policy. In the absence of alternative concepts, however, we will use the expression EU level without inverted commas in the rest of this chapter.

The production and circulation of social policy languages in EU public forums

Since Max Weber, the social science literature has generated many concepts to discuss the role of 'ideas'; one of these concepts is the French notion of *référentiel*, which offers advantages vis-à-vis other concepts. It clearly features among social science concepts that are not strictly translatable. When he wrote in English, its creator with

Pierre Muller, Bruno Jobert, used the expression 'cognitive framework' (Jobert and Muller, 2003), while when he wrote in French (Jobert, 1998), he stressed that the cognitive aspect was only one element of *référentiel*, together with its expressive (images) and normative (values and norms) components. The existence of this expressive aspect points to a substantial difference between *référentiel* and Hall's (1993) concept of 'policy paradigm', which only features 'ideas' (as discussed later). Second, it is essential to identify the spaces where these cognitive *and normative* frameworks – here seen mainly as 'languages' – are produced: these 'forums' are described and it is shown how they are differentiated. However differentiated though, the rule of the games played in transnational forums has often been one of confusion between political and social science languages. In addition, it should be noted that the languages of social policy at the EU level are produced in international English*es* (Ostler, 2011[14]), and this has crucial consequences.

Ideas and cognitive and normative frameworks

Any sociological analysis of discourses should start from the basic Weberian assertion about world-views and ideas which function as 'shunters' (*Weichensteller*) for the channelling of interests. After this initial proposition, social science literature has proposed various concepts for analysing the role of world-views and ideas that it is not possible to review here systematically: Hall used the concept of paradigm, which was explicitly discussed by Jobert (1998). Although less often cited in the English language literature, Jobert's (1998) notion of *référentiels* is very useful for the analysis of social policy languages in the EU. *Référentiels* comprise the set of values, norms, algorithms (theories of action) and images that underpin a particular policy. In contrast to policy paradigms, they also have an *explicit* normative dimension. The fact that they comprise images points to the expressive aspect of language. Moreover, *référentiels* have a cultural link to the polities, the political cultures and the national languages where they find their origin (Barbier, 2008). In the EU context, this latter aspect is obviously more complex to objectify methodologically, because policy making is carried out in a 'multicultural', multilingual context, but this does not prevent the use of the concept. Understanding the production and dissemination

---

[14] Contrary to the mainstream belief that English is unified, empirical demonstration of its variety abounds. N. Ostler has shown that this variety has increased, and that there exist many varieties of international English, hence international English*es*.

of social policy languages at this 'level' also means including the cultural and linguistic aspects that are generally ignored. Written by English speaking researchers and politicians, many social policy texts are conceived as if the whole world was uniformly Anglophone and dealing with universal forms of policies and concepts. Social policy languages at the EU level thus provide various discursive arrangements of *référentiels*. In this sense, as may be seen in the third section, there exist *référentiels* for 'employment', 'labour market', 'activation policies', 'flexicurity strategies', 'social investment policies' and the like. These languages are produced in certain spaces and staged in certain scenes by various groups of actors.

Forums and arenas

As already hinted at, it is impossible to strictly delineate the spaces where the production of social policy languages occurs between national and 'European'. This is true because today, within the EU, whatever the 'level' or 'scale', no forum can strictly be 'national'.[15] These are public spaces, in the sense that there are groups of actors deemed to act in the realm of the public interest: the extent to which they really are public, however, remains to be assessed empirically each time we deal with one of them. The basic typology (Jobert, 1998: 133–37; 2003) distinguishes between arenas and forums, and among forums, between three types: 'forums of political communication', 'forums of policy communities', and 'scientific forums'. Such forums are active for each policy area or domain; although they often overlap, the 'employment' forums are not the same as the 'pension' forums. For any policy domain at the EU level, there are three main forums where actors debate and fight about the language. Sectoral forums together form the 'social policy forum,' which is discussed here for the sake of simplicity.

The concept of 'field', inspired by Bourdieu, has sometimes been used for the same purpose, but it is at the same time too vague and too constraining (Favel and Giraudon, 2011: 21). It is thus preferable not to use this concept for fear of implicitly buying into the entire corpus of Bourdieusian conceptual paraphernalia ('habitus', 'struggle', 'forms of capital', 'symbolic violence', and so on). *Arenas* are different

---

[15] In a very bold statement made before the French Parliament on 15 October 2012, V. Reding, Vice President of the EU Commission, stated that there was no such thing anymore as *'politique intérieure'*: any policy and politics, she meant, was now European (see www.assemblee-nationale. fr/).

from forums, not only because they are much more selective: they group together a small number of actors who make decisions, notably about legislation. The Employment Committee, mandated to help the Council in the field of employment and social affairs is such an arena, and the EU Commission is another. In arenas, debates and compromises take place, but they are not the locus par excellence for the crafting of social policy languages, and this is why we concentrate here on *forums*. Obviously, those active in the arena also take part in one or more of the forums, where they may also participate in the production of social policy languages.

The first type of forum is the 'forum of political communication'. Within national public spaces, this forum brings together citizens, the media, politicians and their spin doctors. This is the forum where politicians argue about their solutions and where various coalitions compete for elections on a national basis. The transnational forum of political communication dedicated to social policy is so large that no existing media can cover the entire European situation. Debates are segmented according to national languages and polities, and there exists no homogenous EU electoral process (Barbier, 2013). Yet for social policy language, the role of this forum is extremely important: its key actors are the Commissioners, the President of the Commission and the Council, the members of the European Parliament, and Brussels based journalists and think-tanks.[16] However, this forum is very seldom the place where social policy languages originate: more generally, this forum uses languages crafted elsewhere.

European international English is the language of this elite forum, which is essentially populated by English speakers who read *The Economist* and the *Financial Times*. However, the fact that this forum brings together members of a very exclusive elite does not mean that political communication about social policy is reserved for internal consumption. The EU Commission has never abandoned the project of convincing (and sometimes manipulating) European citizens. As the political communication (propaganda) tool that it increasingly is, Eurobarometer[17] plays a key role, as demonstrated by an example about 'flexicurity'. From 2005, as the Barroso presided Commission had limited its social projects to a minimum (Barbier, 2008), the

---

[16]   Again, note that the individuals concerned are at the same time members of the 'EU level' and one or more 'national level' forums.

[17]   Eurobarometer is the standard opinion survey funded and managed by the European Commission. It is one of the very few really cross-national sources of data in the EU.

Commission was looking for a cross-cutting discursive theme in order to appear to be pursuing social goals of its own. Social Affairs Commissioner Špidla thus used 'flexicurity' as a catchword that could possess both vague and flexible meanings. The problem was that no one really knew what 'flexicurity' meant. Nevertheless, the Commission commissioned a special Eurobarometer survey and asked samples of European citizens to approve or disapprove a set of five assertions.[18] Notwithstanding the fact that interviewees and interviewers did not know the meaning of 'flexicurity', the authors of the resulting report eventually concluded that European citizens 'indirectly' applauded 'flexicurity' in huge numbers because a large majority of respondents approved each of the five assertions. This example is typical of the way the forum of political communication contributes to the formulation and diffusion of social policy language at the EU level.

The second forum is the forum for the 'social policy community' (for a parallel notion, see Falkner, 1998). Within this forum, some members form an 'epistemic community' and interact with people who are especially involved in the conception and implementation of a specific type of social policies, as envisaged at the EU level. The forum welcomes all sorts of administrators, experts, journalists, lobbyists (and various advocacy coalitions and non-governmental organisations (NGOs)), as well as social scientists specialising in social policy. Even more than in the case of the 'political communication forum', national 'social policy community forums' cannot remain insulated from their EU level counterparts. In the third section, its functioning is illustrated with empirical cases.

Finally, there is the scientific forum for social policy. By definition, because of the universal claim of social science analysis, scientific forums in general are transnational. However, the 'universal' characteristic is controversial. Note that Bourdieu (2002) has rightly alluded to this, stressing that the conditions for production of ideas, their contexts, and the 'dominant national traditions' should be taken into consideration. The features of the social policy scientific forum at the EU level still differ greatly today from their national level counterparts. The social policy scientific forum is characterised by its multidisciplinary profile

---

[18] Hence: 'regular training improves one's job opportunities'; 'lifetime jobs with the same employer are a thing of the past'; 'being able to change easily from one job to the other is a useful asset to help people to find jobs nowadays'; 'work contracts should become more flexible to encourage job creation' and, finally, 'many people retire too early' (Eurobarometer, October 2006, no 65.3, question 18).

and the dominant role played by EU funding. The latter explains the fact that, compared with national social science forums, the EU level forum is much more 'policy oriented'. 'Policy lessons' have become, together with 'dissemination', a crucial criterion for selecting research projects for funding. This has important consequences for the production of social policy languages at the EU level: the research topics in the forum are formulated directly in political terms, and the political language used by politicians, experts and administrators is used directly in the scientific forum. The amount of time and research the forum devotes to conceptual issues is therefore very limited (Barbier, 2005). This key aspect of the *mélange des genres* is illustrated in the third section of this chapter but, at this point, it is important to stress that the language used for formulating both political problems and EU social policy categories and theories, is one form of international English, if not entirely Commission-speak or Eurospeak. Researchers are involved in evaluation studies, consultancy, and various scientific and dissemination activities, and are aware that participation in these scientific forums overlaps to a large extent with the policy community forum. Traditional research ethics, on the other hand, would normally prevent social scientists from participating as such in the 'political communication' forums.[19]

The mélange des genres

At the EU level, it is thus very difficult to establish clear separations between the policy community and the scientific forums as concerns their role in the production and dissemination of social policy languages. One of the main challenges in this respect is the blurred nature of the documents, reports and analyses produced at this level, and the uncertain contexts of their production (commissioning, evaluation of their quality, and so on). Sometimes, as the example of the annual report *Employment in Europe* shows, documents feature a mix of political statements and scientific studies (Barbier, 2005). Normally, one of the features of the scientific forum is that its products are assessed among peers – that is to say, social scientists of the same discipline. Social scientists are at pains to establish clear-cut distinctions between the work they produce as consultants and their genuine scientific output, generally published in peer-reviewed journals and books. Some social

---

[19]   Nevertheless, we observe an increasing number of cases where social scientists directly and explicitly participate in the political communication debate, as promoters of specific policy (see Vanderbroucke et al, 2011).

scientists, however, question the very legitimacy of this distinction. Economists, especially welfare economists, argue that their discipline inevitably entails the production of normative conclusions, whereas many sociologists argue in favour of the opposite contention (Barbier, 2008). All in all, the special characteristics of the scientific forum at the EU level tend to downplay conceptual and theoretical discussion, they bring together different disciplinary approaches without controlling for their conditions of cooperation, and tend to minimise, if not ignore altogether, the dangers of mixing politics and research. This is the fate of 'international research situations' that often lead to the reality that – except for orthodox economics – *publishable* academic work is seldom written in the strict context of research contracts funded by the EU (within the scholarly community, a report for the European Commission hardly passes for material acceptable in refereed journals): social scientists have thus to rework their material in order to produce texts that live up to academic criteria (Barbier, 2005).

English as the lingua franca of social science

The role of English as the *lingua franca* of both EU research and politics is a major one. Within the limits of the present chapter, it is impossible to formulate a detailed discussion about the unfairness that the domination of English has produced in Europe since the 1970s. We limit ourselves here to the consequences of this domination in the production of social policy language at the EU level. To go directly to the main point: for social scientists (economists are a special case here), 'Eurospeak' and the European English language constitute the first obstacle to overcome, if they want to remain faithful to the values of their discipline. Translation at the EU level inevitably leads to erasing diversity, accuracy and, in the end, 'scientific truth'. And yet, in sociology and political science, while it is generally recognised that language (and hence languages) are essential in political activity, these disciplines implicitly postulate that language is a secondary aspect of research and that the problems it raises will eventually be solved through translation – *into English*. Few comparative researchers assign explicit importance to languages, even though linguistic questions constantly arise in ethnographic observation, statistical categories, and the history of political action. The central importance of this issue has to do with the fact that language cannot be reduced to a code, because of its signifying or expressive dimension (Hagège, 1985). Nevertheless, the importance of language for research, beginning with concepts, is seldom genuinely stressed. Moreover, as has been shown, concepts that are essential for social policy are often not directly translatable into English, or the other way round, from English into other languages (note the examples of 'welfare state', *'rapport salarial'*, *'politiques d'insertion'*, to take just a few – for a wider exploration of this see Barbier, 2013). These problems are, de facto, ignored most of the time in the social policy scientific forum at the EU level. What is lost in translation in the forum is more often than not 'scientific truth' as a discourse contestable among peers.

The antidote to the instrumental impoverishment of social science analysis lies in in-depth studies, but these are unfortunately often impossible to implement in 'international research situations'. The problem and obstacle that European English constitutes for research in social policy is further illustrated later, but the present section is concluded with a typical Danish social policy example. In Denmark there used to be two social 'programmes' that enabled people to retire early: one was called *førtidspension*, the other *efterløn*. The botched instrumental English translation used by international organisations designates both programmes as 'early retirement'. Yet any researcher working in Denmark realises that these programmes operated quite differently and derived their legitimacy from different sources. The language that differentiates them makes this clear: the first is early retirement due to disability or inability to continue work, literally a 'pension' given 'beforehand' (*førtid*); the second, early retirement in the period prior to a formal pension, consists of wages (*løn*) received afterwards (*efter*). An in-depth study shows that the latter programme is supported by an optional contribution by employees, who thereby earn their early departure from the labour force; the *førtidspension,* however, is the result of a social partner's decision that grants those unable to continue working to leave 'beforehand'. Anyone who fails to make this distinction and simply refers to both as 'early retirement' cannot have understood why the two programmes were reformed in very different ways over the last ten years.

Social policy forums and language at the EU level: three illustrations

In one national language and within the boundaries of a certain country, it is possible to analyse historically the genesis of elements (notions, concepts, images, and so on) of social policy language and assess their evolution and currency over the years. When it comes to the EU level (or the transnational level more generally), the task of exhaustively exploring the production and diffusion of social policy languages appears impossible because of the sheer number of forums and national and transnational interactions: each social policy language at the EU level has various national–historical roots.[20] The concepts used in the European social policy languages could each provide ample material for writing as many books as there are social policy concepts, if one took into account the various national–historical roots in all the European idioms.[21] In this section, this is obviously not achieved. Instead, three concepts are discussed as illustrations. The three concepts are flexicurity, workfare/activation and social investment.

Flexicurity

The term 'flexicurity' was never a concept in the German and French sense of a concept (*Begriff* and *concept*). Contrary to English, where the concept–notion distinction is blurred, in both German and French, a clear separation exists between *concept/Begriff* (abstract and scientific construct), on the one hand, and the vaguer *notion/Idee-Vorstellung*, on the other (see Barbier, 2005: 59). Far from a proper scientific concept, 'flexicurity' instead acquired wide currency and a central position in social policy language at the EU level in the years 2005–08, as a political notion used in all the three forums explored in this chapter. Its manipulative use in the 'political communication forum' has already been mentioned. The 2008 financial crisis marked an end to this spin doctoring success, but the notion of flexicurity is still (moderately) used today in the 'policy community' and the 'scientific' forums. The fate of this term is also an illustration of the fact that social policy language at the EU level is constantly subjected to fads.

Although it is derived from two English words (flexibility and security), the term has identified roots in Dutch forums (scientific and policy community ones). It was first coined for political communication by the Dutch sociologist Hans Adriaansens, acting as an advisor to the socialist politician Ad Melkert in 1995 (Wilthagen, 1998: 13). This was the time when the *Wet Zekerheid en Flexibilitet* (Act) was being debated in the Netherlands. It made sense in the context of the Dutch political project of the late 1990s (Wilthagen, 2002; Madsen, 2006; Barbier, 2007). Essentially, this project was to negotiate with unions a reform of social protection and labour market legislation in order to have more flexible employment contracts and to enhance access to social security benefits for part-time workers.

---

[20] Examples are the French *insertion*; the Swedish *arbeidjslinjen*; the British welfare state; the German *Zumutbarkeit* (see Barbier, 2013).

[21] For an excellent illustration in German, see Lessenich (2003).

Outside the Netherlands and its forums, the dissemination of the notion is clearly attributable to the EU forums[22], and can historically be ascribed to the pioneering work of two academics, acting as consultants and advisors to political actors and labour unions: the move is typical of the functioning of the scientific and policy community forums at the EU level. The first, Ton Wilthagen (Sociology Professor at Tilburg University) was involved in the Dutch debate. The second, Per Kongshøj Madsen (Economics and Political Science Professor at the Universities of Copenhagen and, then, Aalborg) was involved in the Danish debate. In Denmark, consensual policy had been pursued with social partners (strictly speaking 'labour market parties' in Danish) for a long time and the 'importation' of 'flexicurity' was easy. As late as in 1999, however, a Danish policy report ignored the term 'flexicurity' altogether. Instead, it discussed the so-called *gyldne trekant* (golden triangle) of the Danish labour market. Due to Per K. Madsen's borrowing of the word 'flexicurity' in the early 2000s especially, the notion quickly became a catchword for Danes in the promotion of their model abroad, and most especially within the three EU forums. Hence, Madsen started from the 'golden triangle' of the labour market, describing it as a virtuous nexus existing between low employment protection, high unemployment benefits, and efficient active labour market policies able to foster the training and requalification of workers. He then moved to 'flexicurity'. We do not discuss here the fact that flexicurity had different social meanings in the two sets of forums, the Dutch and the Danish; what is of interest for the present analysis is that the initiation of the debate at the EU level provided the motive for the use and dissemination of the word 'flexicurity' in the policy community, but also in the scientific forums at the EU level. Because such national forums are so much increasingly interconnected, these debates had effects and counterparts in many countries.

In the initial stages of the diffusion of the term 'flexicurity' in EU social policy language, Wilthagen aimed to formulate a sociological theory of flexicurity in the scientific forum; he presented flexicurity as a 'strategy' of certain actors (Wilthagen, 1998) that could favour the advent of 'transitional markets', a concept borrowed from Günther

---

[22] Take a typical forum event: ministers are invited by the European Commission in Brussels for a 'stakeholder conference' about flexicurity (20 April 2007). On the same panel sit Ton Wilthagen, a sociologist and Franz Müntefering, former German Social affairs minister. Incidentally, the minister declares that flexicurity is a dishonest term (*"es ist ein unechtes Wort"*).

Schmid (1993). He subsequently theorised flexicurity as a *nexus* – a social nexus he compared to the regulationist concept of wage earner nexus (Wilthagen, 2002: 3). As the policy community forum at the EU level became increasingly interested in the concept, in 2004, Wilthagen presented it in a more pragmatic mode, as a 'matrix' linking various 'forms' of flexicurity and security and combining them (Wilthagen and Tros, 2004). By 2007, he was an official expert and rapporteur of a working group composed primarily of economists.

What characterises social policy language at the EU level is that it originates in national forums and diffuses across the EU forums towards other national forums, but also cross-national ones. Starting in 2004, flexicurity became an object for benchmarking countries in the Organisation for Economic Co-operation and Development's (OECD) *Employment Outlook* (Barbier, 2007). Finally, the incorporation of flexicurity into EU social policy language also illustrates the fact that the multidisciplinary nature of the EU scientific forums relegates to the background any theoretical–definitional effort. Because mainstream economic thought was not concerned with precise definitions of what was seen merely as a 'mechanism' without precise actors, sociologists were at pains to air their claim that insufficient conceptual research would make the alleged 'reconciliation' of flexibility and security largely illusory: the wage earner nexus was certainly not significantly altered by random and hotchpotch reforms introduced in various countries under the magic label of flexicurity (Barbier, 2007). Instead, we observe the temporary – faddish – triumph of a buzzword in the policy community forum. Emerging cross-disciplinary controversies were not welcome in the EU scientific, English speaking forum.

Workfare and 'activation'

Under the *apparently uniform* political banner of 'workfare', 'welfare to work' and 'activation,' in the late 1980s, reforms were implemented in countries such as France and the United States. These reforms then spread to a larger group of countries and caught the attention of experts and policy makers, with the term 'activation' becoming one of the most typical words in EU social policy language. One can trace the pathways of 'activation' and 'workfare' at the EU level and in some of the forums identified previously.

In the scientific forums – at both national and EU levels – despite 20 years of the dissemination of policies that were called 'active' or 'activating' by politicians, 'activation' per se has never become a rigorous sociological concept (Barbier, 2002, 2008). Nevertheless, it has enjoyed constant currency within the EU's policy community forums. In these forums, 'activation' has been used within the economics and political science literature, as well as in political communication – especially in the discourse promoted by international organisations such as the OECD, as a code word for decreasing social benefits (on this issue, see Rianne Mahon's chapter on the OECD in this volume). The term 'activation' expresses a normative objective set by politicians, who contend that 'activation' is a good thing for European citizens in general. Politicians have received much backing in this respect from the academic community, most notably mainstream economists, sometimes directly intervening in national political communication forums.[23] While this intervention took place before the 2008 financial crisis, the concept has remained. In the political use of the term, 'activation' has remained logically ill-defined and fuzzy. 'Active policies' may be seen as only one part of 'activation' in general. Other components of 'activation' include 'active labour market policies'; 'welfare to work' schemes in the UK (for people with disabilities, young people, single parents, and others); *'aktivering'* in Denmark; and *'insertion'* programmes in France. All these programmes apparently belong to the same type and are seen as such in the EU policy community forum, but the use of the term never spilled over significantly into the EU level political communication forum.[24]

Again, as in the case of flexicurity, the EU scientific forum was not really interested in precise definitions and here, too, the quick fix characterisations of mainstream economics were seen as sufficient. More seriously, 'activation of social protection' (Barbier, 2002, 2008) can be understood in the context of the welfare state restructuring approach (Pierson, 2001), where it constitutes one of the many dimensions of the restructuring tendencies affecting (to varying degrees) all social policy systems in developed countries. Before the recent crisis, the tendency to 'activate social protection' had been linked to the economic rationale of the reforms in an era of austerity and the domination of the neoliberal paradigm. This was never really explicitly accepted in the policy community forums at the EU level, where the tradition is to treat economic and social policies separately. Logically, the mainstream debate

---

[23] One typical instance is Lord Richard Layard's intervention in the French election campaign, 'Unemployment, France should follow European ways', Telos, 7 February 2007, www.telos-eu.com/en/article/unemployement_france_should_follow_european_ways

[24] This is very different in Denmark, where one of the original words was created: *aktivering*.

in these forums, and also – marginally – in the political communication forum, has focused on the question of 'activating' poor and unemployed people. In EU social policy language, the main message was to stress the introduction (or the reactivation or reinforcement) of an explicit linkage between gaining or retaining access to social protection and labour market participation.

It is important to stress a second aspect with regard to the close interconnection of the EU level and the national forums. While the 'activation of social protection' displayed characteristics of change, it was never entirely new. This is no surprise, because the EU social policy language cannot exist without clear historical roots in nations. For instance, 'active labour market policies' first emerged in Sweden and in Swedish (*aktiv arbetsmarknadspolitik* – see also *aktiva arbetsmarknadsåtgärder* (labour market measures). Gösta Rehn brought these to the OECD, and to international English, when he was Head of the OECD Directorate for Manpower and Social Affairs, in Paris, from 1962 to 1974 (Barbier, 2008). Systems of social protection in Europe – even the most 'de-commodified' ones – had always been based upon some variety of full employment, and they had always been 'activated' de facto: there was a strong link between employment and access to benefits across countries. Since the 19th century, social protection schemes have included job search obligations and employment history. However, the notion of 'activation' was not (or seldom) used in national forums: the EU (and international) forums (both scientific and policy community) helped create the opportunity for existing policies to be *discursively* reinterpreted. For instance, workfare in the United States and the *Revenu Minimum d'Insertion* in France (both adopted on a significant scale in 1988) became known as 'activation policies' after this new discursive fad was disseminated from Denmark (1993) and by New Labour (1997) in the UK. Hence the 'new activation' is typical of the functioning of the EU level forums. Actually, it has only been new to the extent that the existing linkage was reinforced or introduced for some programmes where it had not been present *directly*. In the EU forums, however, the 'newness' of the reforms was promoted, even in an overblown manner. At the system level, the change appeared explicitly when governments talked about transforming the architecture of existing social policy systems into 'active welfare states', enhancing the systemic role of what is known as 'paid work' in international English.[25]

---

[25] In German (die *Beschäftigung*) and in French (*l'emploi*) the counterpart concepts have very different connotations.

It is worth noting that before the vocabulary of 'activation' firmly took hold in the EU languages of social policy, a differently framed debate, focused on 'workfare', was going on within the transnational scientific forum. 'Workfare' was an American invention coined in 1969 by journalist William Safire on behalf of his patron Richard Nixon, describing a programme imposing work obligations on assistance recipients (mainly black lone mothers). In the late 1990s, European and especially Scandinavian researchers picked up the American word and used it. However, when analyses of the ongoing reforms kept piling up (Morel, 2000; Lødemel, 2004), it became clear that there existed very different ways to 'activate the poor', and the EU forum turned to 'activation' instead of sticking to workfare. In the political communication forum, this turn of events also offered important advantages because, despite its 'cross–party' political backing in the US, linking the Nixon and the Clinton eras, the American connotation of workfare nevertheless carried with it the bad reputation of forced labour (Barbier, 2002). Shedding the term 'workfare' was also convenient within the British political communication forum, where actors such as the British Trades Union Congress (TUC) had been showing support for the main Labour reforms introduced in the UK after 1997, that is to say, the New Deal programmes and extension of tax credits. The TUC certainly did not want to be associated with US-style programmes, and they would later signal that the 2008 reforms were to be opposed as the 'introduction of workfare' in the UK. Workfare was definitely too blunt and too 'foreign' (US-born) a concept for use in the euphemistic political language of the EU forums.

Social investment

Sociology tends to be uneasy with macroconcepts that originate from political struggles. There is an increasing list of such concepts flying around in the EU forums: 'activation', 'flexicurity', and 'workfare' are among them, as well as many others, like 'modernisation of social protection'. We end this short illustration with the concept of 'social investment'. The use of the term is illustrative of the *mélange des genres* existing between scientific and policy community forums. With this, social scientists and politicians seem to use the one and only language of seemingly reasonable, depoliticised reform at the EU level.

On the scientific side, though, the proponents of the notion of 'social investment' have never been entirely clear as to what the concept did and did not encompass. Its invention has been attributed to Anthony Giddens in 1998, then Tony Blair's policy guru, even if the phrase 'social investment' had been used before. What is certain is that, strictly speaking, social investment has never been a social science concept in the sense of a French '*concept*' or a German '*Begriff*' (Jenson, 2009: 41, proposed to label it a 'quasi-concept'). Nowadays, it is clearly a political notion expressed in international English in the EU policy community forum, but rarely used in the political communication forums, despite its success in Britain. The difference certainly has to do with the widely different functioning of political communication at the national and EU levels. 'Social investment' was included by Blairites, as was earlier the term 'social inclusion', after the rejection of 'social exclusion' in the late 1990s. 'Social investment' makes immediate sense in English and is used by British politicians addressing British people in the media. This is a benefit and a significance such a phrase could never achieve for a cross-national public in the EU. In French, or in German for that matter, the special connotation is lost on ordinary people, whereas it can still be shared in English, among elites. Hence, in contrast with 'flexicurity' and even 'activation', 'social investment' can function only as a technical, specialised term for elites.

At a certain level of abstraction, the notion of an 'enabling state', initially coined by Neil and Barbara Gilbert (1989)[26] was very similar, although applied only to the US (and not to Europe, although Gilbert later extended the 'enabling state' to Europe). Morel et al (2012: 1, 8) acknowledge the similarity of both approaches, a similarity that should be explored in greater detail. These authors nevertheless reached the conclusion that there were actually at least two polar approaches to social investment, one 'social democratic', the other 'third way,' which coexisted under the same 'umbrella' (Morel et al, 2011: 19), a very large umbrella indeed. For his part, contributing to the EU policy community forum, Hemerijck (2012) did not address the definitional aspect of the question. In a symposium, he *implicitly* defined 'social investment' by distinguishing what he called 'social investment spending' from 'non-social investment spending' (Hemerijck, 2012 : 21-24), admitting that there was no 'agreed definition of social investment spending'. The author did not provide a precise justification as to why state outlays for 'old-age, survivors, disability pensions, excluding the rehabilitation expenses, and unemployment spending thus excluding expenses on active labour market programmes' (p. 21) should be seen as 'non-social investment'. From a normative and political standpoint, the potential implications of this list of programmes excluded from

---

[26]   The Gilberts' basic motto was 'public support for private responsibility', as Gilbert (1995: 153) later wrote.

'social investment' are extremely problematic. But this discussion is a good illustration of the *mélange des genres* that prevails in the EU forums. Because of the lack of rigorous social policy concepts and languages, because of the impoverishment brought by the exclusive usage of European English, genuine scientific discussions are discouraged. These discussions nevertheless survive in academic publications, hopefully, as the alternative interpretations of 'social investment' have shown (Cantillon, 2011; De la Porte and Jacobsson, 2012; Morel et al, 2012).

Conclusion

Formulated in European English, social policy languages at the EU level express the state of compromises and battles fought for by narrow elites intervening in three distinct types of forums (political communication, policy community and scientific). Each of these forums has special features, yet they are all linked together. Irrespective of their original status (scientists, politicians, administrators, journalists, and activists), actors may belong to several of them, a situation that leads to much blurring of the frontiers between types of forums.

The conditions of production of these languages profoundly influence their nature, and they are never cut off from their deep cultural–historical roots or national origins. The close study of 'EU level' forums shows that they are not at all separated from national ones. A clear feature, nevertheless, distinguishes the British forum from all others: however specific, European English still remains one among many English*es*. This is why British politicians, unlike Italian, or for that matter, German ones, are often directly able to influence the languages of social policy at the EU level. Tony Blair, and his former advisor Anthony Giddens, were once typical examples of such political personnel. Nevertheless, as the earlier discussion about 'workfare' alluded to, British English and European English point to different types of policies, in terms of their imaginary and political meanings. The distinction between national policies and 'EU level' policies is inevitably greater in this respect, because they are formulated essentially in national languages, and not in English. This complex interplay of languages explains why, when studying the 'EU level', social scientists are first confronted with social policies in English and in English speaking forums. This fact highlights the important methodological obligation for social scientists to cast a critical look at the continual production of new concepts and terms linked to the specific type of politics taking place at the EU level. This will help social scientists discard the highly misleading illusion according to which they feel they can fathom the complexity of 'social policy languages' in Europe just by listening to interviewees in Brussels, and by downloading the proliferating literature posted on the Commission's website by its politicians and officials.

References

Barbier J.-C. (2002) 'Peut-on parler d' 'activation' de la protection sociale en Europe?', *Revue française de sociologie*, n° 43-2, avril-juin : 307-332.

Barbier J.-C. (2005) 'Dealing anew with cross-national comparison: when words matter' in J.-C. Barbier and M.-T. Letablier (eds) *Politiques sociales/Social Policies: Enjeux méthodologiques et épistémologiques des comparaisons internationales/Epistemological and methodological issues in Cross National Comparison,* Brussels: PIE Pieter Lang, 45-68.

Barbier J.-C. (2007) 'From political strategy to analytical research and back to politics, a sociological approach of "flexicurity"', in H. Jørgensen and P.K. Madsen (eds), *Flexicurity and Beyond, Finding a New Agenda for the European Social Model,* Copenhagen: DJØF Publishing, 155-188.

Barbier J.-C. (2008) *La longue marche vers l'Europe sociale,* Paris : PUF, Le lien Social.

Barbier J.-C., (2013) *The Road to Social Europe: A Contemporary Approach to Political Cultures and Diversity in Europe,* Abingdon: Routledge.

Barbier J.-C. and Théret B. (2001) 'Welfare to work or work to welfare: the French case' in N. Gilbert and R. Van Voorhis, *Activating the Unemployed: A Comparative Appraisal of Work-Oriented Policies,* Rutgers, New Jersey: Transaction Publishers, 135-183.

Bourdieu P. (2002), 'Les conditions sociales de la circulation internationale des idées', *Actes de la Recherche en sciences sociales*, 145 (1): 3-8.

Cantillon B. (2011) 'The paradox of the social investment state: growth, employment and poverty in the Lisbon era', *Journal of European Social Policy*, 21 (5): 432-449.

De la Porte C. and Jacobsson K. (2012) 'Social investment or recommodification: assessing the employment policies of the EU states', in S. Morel., B. Palier and J. Palme (eds), *Towards a Social Investment State: Ideas, Policies and Challenges*, Bristol: Policy Press, 117-152.

Falkner G. (1998), *EU Social Policy in the 1990s*, London: Routledge.

Favell A. and Guiraudon V. (eds) (2011), *Sociology of the European Union*, Basingstoke: Palgrave MacMillan.

Gilbert N. (1995) *Welfare Justice: Restoring Social Equity*, New Haven and London: Yale University Press.

Gilbert N. and B. (1989), *The Enabling State: Modern Welfare Capitalism in America*. New York: Oxford University Press.

Hagège C. (1985) *L'homme de paroles, contribution linguistique aux sciences humaines,* Paris: Fayard (Folio).

Jobert B. (1998) 'La régulation politique: le point de vue d'un politiste', in J. Commaille et B. Jobert, *Les métamorphoses de la régulation politique,* Paris : LGDJ, 119-144.

Jobert, B. (2003) 'Europe and the recomposition of national forums: the French case', *Journal of European Public Policy,* 10(3): 463-477.

Jobert B. and Muller P. (1987) *L'État en action, politiques publiques et corporatismes,* Paris, PUF.

Hall P. A. (1993) 'Policy paradigms, social learning, and the state: the case of economic policymaking in Britain', *Comparative Politics,* 25 (3): 274-296.

Hemerijck A. (2012) 'When changing welfare states and the Eurocrisis meet', *Sociologica,* 2012/1, www.sociologica.mulino.it/doi/10.2383/36887

Jenson J. (2009) 'Redesigning citizenship regimes after neoliberalism: moving towards social investment' in N. Morel, B. Palier and J. Palme, (eds), *What Future for Social Investment,* Stockholm, Institute for Future Studies Research Report, pp. 27-44.

Lessenich S. (ed.) (2003) *Wohlfahrtsstaatliche Grundbegriffe,* Frankfurt-New York, Campus Verlag.

Lødemel I. (2004) 'The development of workfare within social activation policies', in D. Gallie (ed), *Resisting marginalization, Unemployment Experience and Social Policy in the European Union,* Oxford: Oxford University Press, 197-222.

Madsen P.K. (2006) 'How can it possibly fly? The paradox of a dynamic labour market', in J. L. Campbell, J. A. Hall and O.K. Pedersen O.K. (eds) *National Identities and the Varieties of Capitalism: The Danish Experience,* Montreal and Kingston: McGill-Queen's University Press, 321-355.

Majone G. (1993) 'The European Community between social policy and social regulation', *Journal of Common Market Studies,* 31(2): 153-170.

Merrien F.-X. (1997) *L'État-Providence,* Paris, PUF, 'Que sais-je ?'

Morel S. (2000) *Les logiques de la réciprocité, les transformations de la relation d'assistance aux États Unis et en France,* Paris: PUF.

Morel S., Palier B. and Palme J. (eds) (2012) *Towards a Social Investment State: Ideas, Policies and Challenges,* Bristol: Policy Press.

Ostler N. (2011) *The Last Lingua Franca, English Until the Return of Babel*, London: Penguin Allen Lane.

Pierson, P. (ed.) (2001). *The New Politics of the Welfare State*, Oxford: Oxford University Press.

Scharpf F. *(1999), Governing Europe: Effective and Democratic*, Oxford: Oxford University Press.

Schmid, G. (1993), *Übergänge in der Vollbeschäftigung, Formen und Finanzierung einerzukunftsgerechten Arbeitsmarktpolitik* FS 93-208, Berlin:WZB.

Vanderbroucke F., Hemmerijck A., Palier B. (2011) 'The EU needs a social investment pact', OSE Paper, Brussels, no 5, May.

Wilthagen,T. (1998) 'Flexicurity – a new paradigm for labour market policy reform?', Berlin:WZB Discussion Paper, FSI, 98-202.

Wilthagen T. (2002) 'The flexibility-security nexus: new approaches to regulating employment and labour markets', OSA working papers 2002-18,Tilburg University.

Wilthagen,T. and F.Tros (2004) 'The concept of "flexicurity": a new approach to regulating employment and labour markets', *Transfer*, 10 (2): 166-187.

FOUR

The OECD's search for a new social policy language: from welfare state to active society

Rianne Mahon[27]

The International Labour Organisation (ILO) was the first international organisation with an explicit social mandate, but by the 1960s it had been joined by a plethora of UN related and other international organisations, including the Organisation for Economic Co-operation and Development (OECD). Although the OECD's primary mission was to promote economic cooperation among advanced capitalist economies, it has also become an important node in transnational social policy networks, working alongside other key international organisations and in close cooperation with the European Commission.[28] Some see the OECD as an important contributor to the neoliberal assault on the welfare state (Armingeon and Beyeler, 2004). Yet it – or, more precisely, its Directorate for Employment, Labour and Social Affairs (DELSA)[29] – has also been seen as one of the early (1990s) promoters of the idea of 'social investment' as an alternative to the neoliberal conception of the welfare state as a barrier to the efficient operation of labour markets (Jenson, 2010).

[27] Research for this paper was made possible by a grant from the Social Science and Humanities Research Council of Canada. I would also like to thank Karen Atkinson and the staff at the OECD archives, who could not have been more helpful during my two week visit, in March 2012.

[28] For an excellent overview of the OECD history and mode of operation, see Woodward (2009). See also Mahon and McBride (2008) and Martens and Jakobi (2010).

[29] The Directorate, initially called Social Affairs, Manpower and Education, became the Directorate for Education, Employment, Labour and Social Affairs in the 1990s. A decade later, a separate Education Directorate was established, giving it its current title.

These two views need not be at odds with one another: just as there were varied conceptions of the welfare state in the Keynesian era, so too is social investment understood in different ways (Mahon, 2010a). What this paper shows is that already in the twilight of the Keynesian era, the OECD had begun to talk about the need for a shift towards a more 'positive' and 'preventive' conception, while the two oil shocks and stagflation helped to open the way for the break with Keynesian ideas. By the end of the 1970s, the OECD was set to host the conference often seen as promoting the adoption of the 'welfare state as burden' language. It is argued here, however, that while the conference did stress the need to curb social expenditure, it also accelerated the search for a new conception of social policy, but it was not until the first meeting of social policy ministers (1988) that the new understanding got its name – 'active society.' Although the active society was initially translated into terms that fit with the organisation's neoliberal Jobs Strategy,[30] resistance to the Strategy within the Social Policy Directorate and among certain member states opened the way for a more equity oriented interpretation.

From 'quality of life' to 'welfare state in crisis'

The OECD was formed in 1961, built on the foundations laid by the Organisation for European Economic Co-operation (OEEC).[31] Initially it understood the world through Keynesian ideas and in the 1960s it became an important source for the transmission of 'Keynes plus' conceptions such as 'active labour market policy'(Hansen, 1986). One of the first of the OECD's famous peer reviews in fact focused on labour market and social policies, beginning with Sweden, which was a pioneer in the field of active labour market policies, and the United States, where there was a very active debate on the need for 'manpower' policies to improve the employment prospects of 'disadvantaged' groups (Gordon, 1964). In the early 1970s, the OECD's growing interest in human capital formation led to the creation of the new Directorate of

---

[30] The OECD's Jobs Strategy, adopted in 1994, was a major, cross-cutting programme. Although developed by an interdepartmental team, the Economics Department was given the major role in defining performance criteria and monitoring country compliance, but the Directorate for Employment, Labour and Social Affairs also retained a role. For more detail on the Jobs Strategy see McBride and Williams (2001); Jacobsson and Noaksson (2010); and Mahon (2011).

[31] The OEEC was set up in 1948 to manage post-war reconstruction of Western Europe (Wolfe, 2008).

Social Affairs, Manpower and Education (SAME). At this juncture, its conception of social policy was influenced by the social mobilisations of the1960s – from the student revolts and the emergence of second wave feminism to the wave of strikes that had swept across Western Europe. The concern thus sparked in 'quality of life' issues and de-bureaucratisation that marked SAME's initial projects, however, came to share space with pessimistic assessments of prospects for stable growth and increasingly vociferous claims that the welfare state was inhibiting economic adjustment.

The social unrest of the 1960s inspired then Secretary General, Thorkil Kristensen, and others within the organisation to address 'quality of life' issues. The importance attached to quality of life issues was reflected in SAME's social indicators project. Social indicators were needed because 'growth is not an end in itself but rather an instrument for creating better conditions of life. Increasing attention must be given to the quality aspects of growth, and to the formulation of policies with respect to broad economic and social choices in the allocation of growing resources'.[32] The list of common concerns compiled testifies to the breadth of the organisation's conception of the quality of life and social policy's role in enhancing this: a healthy life through all stages of the life cycle; individual development through learning, from childhood through to self-development in adulthood; attention to the quality of working life, with its promise of greater industrial democracy, as well as to the quantity of jobs; the quality, range of choice and accessibility of public and private goods and services; and 'the extent of opportunities for participation in community life, institutions and decision-making.'[33]

At the same time the organisation was beginning to grapple with inflation and unemployment. A new internal study – *Expenditure Trends in OECD Countries 1960-1980* (1972) – had revealed a 'surprising leap' in government transfer payments, which were seen to fuel inflation as workers sought wage increases to compensate for

---

[32] OECD Press Release, PRESS/A(70)28 22 May 1970 cited in MAS (78) 26 Manpower and Social Affairs International Conference on Social Policy in the 1980s?

[33] MS/M/107/47 25 June 1973 Future Orientation of Activity in Manpower, Social Affairs Fields: National Positions. A Note by the Secretariat.

the tax hikes introduced to pay for the new social programmes.[34] In addition, there was growing acceptance of the view that social policies were contributing to unemployment. Thus Working Party 4 (Social Aspects of Income Transfer Policies) was tasked with assessing the effect of social transfers on work incentives. At this time, however, the country representatives on the working party had still to be convinced that unemployment compensation contributed significantly to unemployment.[35]

As unemployment and stagflation assumed greater importance, the Secretariat began to suggest that social policy planning needed to go beyond improved cost effectiveness to a more profound rethinking of the goals of social policy. Here we see the beginnings of what would later be named the 'active society'. Thus the Secretariat noted that

> the present dilemma in fact reinforces the need for more *active social policies* by changing their emphasis from mainly remedial measures to repair the damage to individuals ... in favour of *positive and preventive measures* to improve the access of all citizens to work, income and satisfactory working and living conditions. [36]

This emphasis on a 'positive and preventive' approach also featured in the rationale for its integrated social policies study, where it was argued that, given the centrality of employment to a 'positive approach' to social policy, it was important to examine the interaction of social policies with labour market and industrial relations policies. Related to the rethinking of social policy goals and language was a reassessment of the means to achieving these – away from the 'bureaucratic welfare state' towards a 'welfare society'. As the Working Party preparing the ministerial meeting noted, 'The burden on the economy of income

---

[34] The author of the report noted that during the 1960s OECD economists had ignored transfers when calculating government expenditure. When *Expenditure Trends* introduced the concept of 'pure private consumption' it became clear that in some countries, the latter had declined 'because of the rapid growth of transfers and income redistribution of all forms' (Marris, 1983: 17).

[35] MAS/WP4/M (78) 1 Working Party on the Social Aspects of Income Transfer Policy Record of the 7th meeting held at the Chateau de la Muette, Paris, 2–3 February 1978.

[36] MO (74) 6 1st Revision Committee of Manpower and Social Affairs Programme of Work for 1975. A Note by the Secretariat, p 3. Emphasis added

---

redistribution [sic] and welfare services, *involving heavy bureaucratic machinery*, calls for a re-examination of the positive role of employment as a main instrument of wellbeing'.[37] At this point, the antibureaucratic theme reflected the Secretariat's response to criticisms of the Keynesian welfare state from the left as well as the right. This would later change.

These ideas would be elaborated in the documents prepared for the conference on social policy in the 1980s, 'The welfare state in crisis.' The Secretariat's position was that circumstances had changed and this required a rethinking of the aims and means of social policy, not its abandonment: 'Lower growth means that we cannot avoid the need to remodel our social policies, whilst still ensuring the necessary minimum levels of protection which a modern industrialised democracy is bound to provide for its citizens. *It is not the axe which is needed, but some skilful social surgery*' (OECD, 1981: 6).

While some OECD conferences are organised largely to enable the Secretariat to incorporate new ideas, others have as their primary goal the exposure of member state representatives to new language. The 1980 conference was of the latter sort: it was designed to promote new ways of thinking about social policy. This is hinted at in Angus Maddison's[38] letter seeking funding for the conference. Lamenting the dearth of analytical social policy work, Maddison hoped that participation in the conference 'would encourage Member governments to give greater funding for research and would tend to broaden the range of policy options open to consideration in individual countries, because it would gradually develop a view less constrained by national institutional experience'.[39] In preparing the key background document (OECD, 1981: 73–93) and constructing the questions to guide the discussion, the Secretariat played an active role in framing the debates.

The Secretariat clearly continued to be concerned with 'quality of life' issues such as work time and the role of the 'third or fourth' sector. Thus in the session on work, leisure and employment, Gass posed the following questions:

---

[37] MO (75) 24 Special Working Party on Preparation for the Ministerial Meeting, Possible Item #2: Manpower and Social Implications of Future Period of Steady and Sustained Growth, p 4. Emphasis added.

[38] Maddison was head of the Central Analysis Division, associated with the Directorate of Social Affairs, Manpower and Education 1971–78.

[39] Draft letter to David Bell, Vice President of the Ford Foundation, from Angus Maddison, 24 October 1977.

> Should not discussions on the various ways of redistributing
> and sharing work – hitherto mainly focused on a generalised
> reduction of working hours – deal not only with a broader
> concept of the distribution of working time, with varied
> effects on weekly, yearly and lifetime work patterns, but
> also with the redistribution of income and leisure time?
>
> Should not greater attention be given to workers' aspirations
> to a higher 'quality of working life', particularly with more
> decentralised processes of collective bargaining?
>
> Would it not be desirable for the definition of work in
> society and the choice of job opportunities available to the
> community, to be broadened ... by legitimising certain new
> forms of paid or unpaid work (typified by such concepts as
> the 'self-service economy', the 'third or fourth sector', the
> 'underground economy' and various forms of 'community'
> or 'co-operative' enterprises)? (OECD, 1981: 57)

Moreover, the continued concern with the original social indicators
was reflected in the framing document's reference to the desirability
of a coordinated approach to social and economic policies, based on
'a definition of well-being which also includes income distribution,
leisure, the quality of working life and questions of environment,
rather than simply continue with one confined solely to real output'
(OECD, 1981: 76).

At the same time, the paper emphasised SAME's emerging
conception of how to modernise social policy and administration. Here
again the need for a shift from a remedial to a preventive approach,
via the integration of human resources and social policies surfaces.
This time, however, it is clear that such an approach should target 'the
disadvantaged': 'If the main result of the recent recession is that the
burden of unemployment is falling disproportionately on disadvantaged
groups, should not the accent shift to more targeted, integrated, multiple
programmes for such groups – with a major link to employability?'
(OECD, 1981: 77).

More broadly, the Secretariat's emerging conception of social policy
involved a rejection of the 'welfare state' in favour of a 'welfare society.'
In fact, the poster prepared for the conference did not mention the
'crisis of the welfare state', but rather heralded the emergence of the
'welfare society.' This represents an important shift in OECDs social
policy strategy and language:

> The competing strategies [for social policy reform] appear in large part to boil down to the relative weights assigned to the traditional centralist ('Welfare State') option, as compared to a much more decentralised, disaggregated and selective ('Welfare Society') approach. The traditional centralised approach depends on tax/transfer mechanisms, uniformity in the delivery of social services, universality, and the protection of individuals through impersonal transactions with non-discriminatory eligibility conditions. The disaggregated approach, which has emerged in the seventies, is based on more selectivity (to target groups) in income transfers and the delivery of services; greater decentralisation and the localisation of services; greater responsibilities by local authorities, community groups, employers and trade unions, and more monitoring of effectiveness. (OECD, 1981: 82)

The idea of a welfare society fit well with the neoliberal emphasis on greater targeting, as resources could be shifted to programmes for the 'disadvantaged' and away from universal programmes, as the latter included an increasingly affluent middle class, now considered able to shoulder at least part of the costs itself. It, would, moreover, be willing to do so if offered greater 'choice' by subjecting public sector ('bureaucratic') providers to private (non- and for-profit) competition.

At this time, the concept of 'welfare society' was still inspired more by the antibureaucratic thinking of the 'autogestion' New Left than New Public Management theory, which would later become so influential. The push to engage private actors – employers, voluntary organisations, and even individuals and households – would subsequently come to fit well with neoliberal calls for privatisation. At this point, however, the Secretariat remained concerned about the implications for 'equity' of breaking completely with the welfare state. It thus argued that 'the extension of coverage and benefit by private institutions would need to take place within a framework of public policy if blatant inequalities are to be avoided' (OECD, 1981: 81). In other words, to combine equity and efficiency, the welfare society needed to rest on the foundations provided by the welfare state.

From welfare society to active society

If, when the 1980 conference was being planned, there was a delicate balance between the conception of 'quality of life' stimulated by the

1960s social movements and nascent neoliberalism, Ronald Reagan's election in 1980, following the electoral victory of Margaret Thatcher in 1979, announced the shift towards neoliberalism at the global scale. This is not to suggest the veracity of Thatcher's claim that 'there is no alternative'. In France, where the OECD is located, the Mitterrand government (1981–86) had come to office proclaiming a 'third way' (between Keynes and monetarism) and, although the unions were increasingly coming under attack, corporatist bargaining continued in a number of OECD countries. Of particular importance for social policy, the neoliberal solution to unemployment – an attack on 'labour market rigidities' associated with employment protection legislation and certain social policies – was contested by those arguing instead for flexible working time and the functional flexibility made possible by a highly qualified workforce.

The debate over the most appropriate response to the economic crisis influenced the OECD. The McCracken report (1977) is credited with marking the organisation's (or, at least, its influential Economics Department's) neoliberal turn. In 1984, moreover, van Lennep was replaced as Secretary General by Jean-Claude Payé.[40] Under Payé's direction, the organisation launched its own 'structural adjustment' project, which was to engage all units, including SAME. In addressing the Working Party on Social Policy, Secretary General Payé made clear that his conception of structural adjustment involved

> the need to remove obstacles to the creativity, adaptability and mobility of the labour force, the need for a reassessment of the tax/benefit system, the need for measures to strengthen the capacity of the young and the long term unemployed to enter or re-enter activity and the necessity of strengthening the capacity of OECD countries for investment, enterprise and innovation.[41]

The Secretary General's special task force on structural adjustment also clearly identified social expenditures on health, pensions and unemployment compensation as a 'potential bottleneck to adjustment.'[42]

---

[40] Payé, a senior French civil servant, would subsequently serve in the centre-right government of Raymond Barre.

[41] MAS/WP1/M (85) 1 Summary of the Second Meeting of the Working Party on Social Policy 1–12 June 1985, p 2.

[42] MAS WP1 M (87) 1 Summary of the 4th Meeting of the Working Party 23–25 March 1987.

On the whole, however, the Manpower and Social Affairs Committee (MASC), favouring a more 'positive' approach, called for exploration of ways that social policy could make such a contribution. This request would later spur SAME to develop its new conception of social policy, but for most of the decade SAME's research focused on containing – and restructuring – social expenditures, which were seen as contributing to unemployment and poverty or, in the language of American Conservatives, the emergence of an 'underclass' dependent on social assistance benefits.[43] The change from 'welfare society' to 'active society' would thus emphasise measures to promote the latter's labour market (re-)integration.

The new social policy conception SAME had begun to enunciate in the 1970s finally got its name – active society – at the first meeting of OECD social policy ministers. Although the term 'active society' did not actually appear in *The Future of Social Protection* (1988), the background document prepared by the Secretariat clearly reflected this line of thinking.[44] Thus *The Future* began by arguing that while those in charge of social policies cannot afford to ignore 'any' negative impact on economic performance, nevertheless, social policies can make a positive contribution to structural adjustment *if* they go beyond passive supports for unemployed people to help the latter develop the 'skills and characteristics' that could improve their position in the labour market (OECD, 1988: 7). More broadly, employing the language of social, rather than neo-, liberalism, it argued that 'the role of public policy in the 1990s must be to design interventions so as to maximise both the number of people who have *opportunities* for active social roles, and the durations of their lives over which they can experience such activity' (OECD, 1988: 30).

The term 'active society' however appeared in a 'room document' provided by the Secretariat and MASC agreed that it was the introduction of this term that was 'one of the important outcomes' of the Ministerial that warranted further development. For the SAME, an active society policy orientation was defined as:

> one that welcomes – rather than resists – the entry of new groups into the labour market. It recognises the demand

---

[43] The Secretariat was well aware of the differences in the languages adopted in Europe (for instance, 'the excluded'/'*les exclus*') and the US ('underclass').

[44] MAS WP1/M (88) 02 Working Party on Social Policy Summary Record of the 6th Meeting 8 July 1988.

> for participation in economic and social life which now characterises most groups in the population, and seeks to enhance the effective productivity of the population as a whole by drawing on previously unused talents and harnessing them in a more efficient and comprehensive division of labour. The role of public policy through social provision becomes one of removing obstacles to individual activity (such as unduly restrictive age retirement rules) and of ensuring that individuals have the skills to make such activities personally and/or economically rewarding. An Active Society becomes possible when individuals are enabled to have such choices.[45]

In other words, the role of social policy was not to *force* social assistance recipients into the labour force (although 'disincentives' needed to be removed) but rather to *enable* those currently at the margins to 'participate' by helping them to develop their talents and skills. The 'active society' strategy and language was also connected with the idea of enhancing 'choice': it not only enhanced possibilities for greater 'personal independence,' but also the freedom to choose (schools, health and elder care, pension plans), by fostering competition between the public sector and private providers.

As noted, the idea of a change from remedial to preventive policy had already surfaced within SAME in the 1970s. The 'naming' of the approach and the choice of a name that had positive, yet ambiguous, connotations, however, constituted an important step towards the consolidation of a new conception of social policy. In addition to public support for individual development, long central to social liberalism but given new meaning by the social movements of the 1960s, the emerging social policy language fit the dominant economic language, which stressed investment over consumption. Thus the active society was cast as an 'investment' that would pay dividends in the future: 'a fundamental change is taking place: while formerly emphasis was placed on the social costs of structural transformation, there is an increasing awareness that appropriate social policies represent an investment in the future. They create the essential preconditions in terms of consensus for effective and equitable change.'[46] At the same time, as *The Future*

---

[45] MAS (89) 1 Draft Programme of Work for 1990. Note by the Secretariat. Emphasis added.

[46] MAS (90) Proposed Ministerial Level Meeting on Social Policies. A Note by the Secretariat

---

recognised, 'The extent to which a consensus for adaptive change can be achieved may be a function of the degree to which changes are trusted to be part of the continued support of generally agreed broad social objectives, as distinct from being an attack on them' (OECD, 1988: 30). In other words, the argument gained momentum by using language that resonated with the earlier principles of social liberalism, while managing to 'modernise' this to fit the ideas stressed by neoliberals. The concept of 'active society' thus reflected a public commitment to help all who need and want it, to develop the capacities required to survive in the increasingly competitive environment unleashed by neoliberal economic reforms.

The very elements of interpretive ambiguity in SAME's strategy for creating an active society were also in its favour. As Jenson (2010) has argued, the polysemic character of certain concepts facilitates their diffusion. The addition of the term 'investment' thus increased the acceptability of the active society, enabling it to be heard in a universe of policy discourse dominated by neoliberal ideas. At the same time as an active society represented a break with the Keynesian emphasis on the importance of maintaining mass consumption, however, it broke with the neoliberal conception of social policies as a burden: animated by the 'active society', the state had a role to play, one of investing in people's capabilities.

The language adopted in the first social policy ministerial was developed in the core documents prepared for the second, *New Orientations for Social Policy* (1992). *New Orientations* began with an acknowledgement of its roots in the 1988 meeting: 'When they last met at the OECD in 1988, the Ministers for Social Policy accepted that, particularly in a climate of budgetary restraint, an *active society* in which all members have a constructive role, was a primary goal for social policy' (OECD, 1994: 9). Such an approach was deemed to contribute to the macroeconomic policy agenda of stable, noninflationary growth (OECD, 1994: 12). In order to do so, social programme costs would have to be reconciled with fiscal restraint, through the promotion of greater effectiveness and efficiency. More broadly, however, 'the emphasis should be on the encouragement of human potential as an end in itself, as well as a contribution to market efficiency. Consistent with this objective, income transfer programmes should be structured to foster self-sufficiency through earnings, without sacrificing the goals and systems of social protection' (OECD, 1994: 16). Like the 'welfare society' of the early 1980s, *New Orientations* called for a different kind of state, one that would maximise 'choice' by creating an enlarged role for private sector provision and for individual financial responsibility.

Thus the assumptions behind the active society were consistent with the change 'from welfare to workfare', although, as will be seen, the Directorate (now DEELSA: Directorate for Education, Employment, Labour and Social Affairs) initially saw a continued role for social protection. This changed when the Directorate sought to spell out the policy implications through two studies, The Battle Against Exclusion and Making Work Pay and it did so largely as a result of the Directorate's involvement in the wider OECD Jobs Strategy,[47] which grew out of a major interdepartmental initiative to tackle unemployment. Although DEELSA had been involved in its development, the major role was assigned to the Economics Department (Mahon, 2010c). As an organisation-wide initiative, however, DEELSA was expected to play its part.

A number of the Jobs Study's recommendations focused on social assistance recipients and a group within DEELSA had come to be increasingly concerned about the growth of social exclusion, 'new poverty' and benefit dependency.[48] In fact, the plans for conducting the social assistance review had begun a year before the adoption of the Jobs Strategy. Consistent with the 'active society' and in contrast to the Economics Department's single-minded focus on 'efficiency', DEELSA aimed to strike a balance between efficiency and equity. Thus the studies aimed to explore 'how best to minimise the problem of poverty traps while maintaining a decent level of income supplements for poor households'.[49] Therefore, while the Battle Against Exclusion supported the 'activation' of social assistance recipients, it also concluded that 'good' programmes, targeted at social assistance recipients, necessarily rested on all three pillars – cash assistance (set at a level to ensure adequate living standards ... but consistent with incentives to re-enter the labour market), supportive social services for those (with disabilities, lone parents, homeless people, people with addictions) who need them and labour market programmes capable of combining work socialisation

---

[47]   In fact, the original Jobs Study had reflected an uneasy amalgam between the neoliberal ideas championed by the Economics Department, and DEELSA's more equity oriented position, although the recommendations reflected the stronger hand of the former (Mahon, 2010b).

[48]   SAME documents from the 1980s refer to the difference between European discourses on the 'new poverty' and the American and British Conservatives' conception of the 'new underclass' dependent on social benefits. SAME itself came increasingly to use the term 'social exclusion', a term that had appeared in French debates during the 1970s, and been picked up by both the right and the left. See Silver (1994).

[49]   DEELSA/ELSA (94) 1 Project Report Fact Sheets 11.

---

with training.[50] Nevertheless, the Directorate's analysis failed to make the important distinction between progressive and neoliberal 'work first' workfare programmes.[51]

Making Work Pay carved out a tougher position, one more in line with neoliberal workfare. It made the following recommendations:

1. Out-of-work benefits should ensure a reward for work, which may involve cutting level of remuneration and duration 'to encourage reappraisal of acceptable wages by those who do not rapidly find work'.
2. Low wage work should not be overtaxed.
3. Employment conditional benefits should normally be used to increase in-work incomes of families with children.
4. The cost of hiring low wage workers should be reduced.
5. Job search efforts should be more strictly policed.
6. Non-employment benefits such as sick pay or early retirement, should not be used as alternatives to unemployment benefits.
7. Part time employment of certain categories – lone parents, the long term unemployed – should be encouraged.
8. Spouses of the unemployed should have an incentive to work (which does not happen when benefits are means-tested on a family basis).[52]

The neoliberal language of these recommendations, however, contrasts with the conclusions of a later OECD seminar on making work pay, which made it clear that such schemes work best in countries with low tax-benefit environments, relative low wage floors and wide earnings distribution, such as the US, although *Make Work Pay* arguably tacitly acknowledged this in the caveats ('adjustment for national circumstances') introduced for recommendations 3–5. In the seminar, it was also noted that make work pay schemes are no substitute for the longer-term path of upgrading educational attainment and skills.[53] This conclusion was in line with those drawn by DEELSA's Employment

---

50 DEELSA/ELSA/WP1 (97) 4 Social Assistance: Battle Against Exclusion: Outline of a Report to the Ministers prepared by the Secretariat. The report also noted that good policies required complex coordination as between national and local levels of government and as between governmental and nongovernmental agencies.

51 See Peck and Theodore (2000) for a nicely developed distinction between the two.

52 DEELSA/ELSA/WP1 (96)1/Final page 3.

53 DEELSA/ELSA (99) 14 Make Work Pay Report on the joint ELSA/ ECO Workshop 10–11 September 1999.

Division, that 'obtaining a job is just part of the battle. Remaining in employment with a good prospect for climbing up the earnings ladder proves quite difficult for many low paid workers, not the least women, mature adults and the less skilled'.[54]

What this suggests is that even while *Making Work Pay* was being conducted as part of the broader Jobs Strategy, a more critical language was being developed within DEELSA. The latter was first reflected in the Directorate's premier publication, the *Employment Outlook* in 1996, which laid out the following challenges to the neoliberal assumptions underpinning the Economics Department's interpretation of the Jobs Strategy: 1) the incidence of low pay was highest where earning inequality was the most pronounced, most notably in the Jobs Strategy 'stars', the United States and the United Kingdom; 2) in countries with higher rates of unionisation and collective bargaining coverage and higher minimum wages and welfare benefits, a wage floor existed, limiting the incidence of low wages without necessarily threatening employment creation; and 3) 'countries with higher cross-sectional earnings inequality do not appear to have correspondingly higher relative earnings mobility' (OECD, 1996: 60). In other words, the Economics Department's claims that its neoliberal recommendations support 'dynamic equity,' appeared ill-founded.

The contradictory interpretations of the active society articulated by different parts of the Directorate occurred against the backdrop of broader resistance to neoliberal globalisation that was reaching a crescendo on the eve of the new millennium. In addition, the adverse consequences of the brute neoliberal adjustment strategies imposed on Eastern Europe were beginning to become apparent. The OECD was directly affected by both developments. Its attempt to negotiate a multilateral agreement on investment (MAI) sparked the mobilisation of protests that saw more than 600 groups disrupt the OECD's 'normally tranquil Paris citadel' and contributed to the termination of the agreement (Woodward, 2008: 83). In addition, through its involvement in the Eastern European reforms, the OECD became aware of the limits to simple 'one size fits all' neoliberal solutions (Pal, 2008: 73). The then newly appointed Secretary General, Donald Johnston, was also well aware of the need to temper neoliberal ideas with positive social policies. As he noted:

---

[54] DEELSA/ELSA (97) Meeting of the Labour Ministers Theme 1 Draft Analytical Report: Policies for Low Paid Workers and Unskilled Job Seekers. Page 24.

I am concerned that we risk a backlash against this strategy because of the impression that it places too little emphasis on social objectives. Indeed we have already been witnessing in some OECD countries signs of social unrest and protest movements as well as low popularity ratings for many governments and a 'feel bad' factor which may reflect a lack of confidence in these policies (OECD, 1997: 9).

Within DEELSA, the message was being driven home via resistance to the Jobs Strategy by the Employment, Labour and Social Affairs Committee (ELSAC) (Mahon, 2010b). Thus as early as 1994, representatives reacted negatively to a presentation on the Strategy by the head of the Economics Department, arguing

> that it failed to give due weight to the positive side of unemployment and related social benefits, nor did it emphasise sufficiently the role of education and training. It was also considered too negative on active labour market policies ... and failed to pay attention to the potential and benefits of fostering social consensus and cooperation between the social partners.[55]

Again in 1997 the Economics Department's report to ELSAC was greeted sceptically. The minutes note that 'many delegates' felt that the paragraphs dealing with equity–efficiency trade-offs were unbalanced. In particular the Norwegian and Belgian representatives challenged the report's claim that narrow wage dispersion provides a poor signal for investing in human capital, while the Canadian felt there should be more stress on policies reinforcing security.[56]

The combination of committee member resistance and in-house research resulted in the 2002 recommendation of the labour ministers, that the Jobs Strategy be reviewed, which in turn led to the negotiation of the 'revised' Jobs Strategy (Mahon, 2010b). This had an impact on the work of Working Party 1 (WP1). Thus material provided for WP1 in preparation for the 2005 social policy ministerial suggested that *Battle Against Exclusion* was now outdated. The question now was 'how best to reconcile goals for ensuring an adequate standard of living

---

[55] DEELSA/ELSA M (94) Summary Record of the 84th Session of the Employment, Labour and Social Affairs Committee, page 10.

[56] DEELSA/ELSA M (97) 2 Summary Record of the 90th Session of the Employment, Labour and Social Affairs Committee, page 9.

for, and for encouraging self-reliance among, social assistance clients, *in a context where many of the jobs available to them may not pay enough to escape poverty?*'[57] While reaffirming the principles of the active society, the ministers' final communiqué, prepared by the committee, referred to the *reassessed* Jobs Strategy, with its 'flexicurity' option, as combining activation and equity. Moreover, 'making work pay' was now understood to include 'measures to provide adequate wages'.[58]

In other words, as the title for the 2005 meeting of the social policy ministers – 'How Active Social Policy Can Benefit Us All' – suggests, the Directorate and the Committee remained committed to the active society. Yet an important shift in how this was articulated had taken place: the problem posed by the proliferation of 'atypical' forms of employment, which offer low wages and/or unstable employment, was now understood as a barrier to successful labour market reinsertion.

While the incorporation of the concept of 'atypical' work brought a more critical edge to the active society, its extension from a preoccupation with disadvantaged people to an 'active society for all' reflected the increased emphasis placed on the modern 'adult earner' family, and its needs for supportive policies such as childcare and flexible working time. Of particular importance here was the high level conference, 'Family, Market and Community.' The latter featured important contributions by Gøsta Esping-Andersen and Chiara Saraceno, both of whom underlined the centrality of the changing family 'as a source of social problems and as a resource for addressing these same problems' (Saraceno, 1997: 81). Reflecting its adoption of this conception, the Secretariat outlined three important challenges facing member countries: to provide adequate resources to families with children; to foster optimal allocation of labour market resources while facilitating the reconciliation of work and family life and to work towards an 'efficient and sustainable balance of responsibility between governments, employers and families with children'.[59] The final communiqué of the 2005 social policy ministerial accordingly stressed that 'providing *all* parents with better choices about how to balance work and family life extends opportunities, especially for women, and

---

[57] DELSA/ELSA (2003) 7 Proposed Meeting of the Social Policy Ministers, page 5. Emphasis added.

[58] DELSA/ELSA/Min (2005) 2 Communiqué of Ministers Responsible for Social Policy, page 3.

[59] DEELSA/ELSA (99) 13 Family-Friendly Social Policy: A Project Proposal on the Reconciliation of Work and Family Life.

---

creates economic gains'.[60] Thus the active society had been expanded to re-embrace universality, if only for the modern adult earner family.

Conclusion

The OECD thus became involved in inventing a new language for thinking about the role and nature of social policy as early as the 1970s, when the egalitarian 'quality of life' ideas championed by the social movements of the 1960s began to be confronted by an ascendant neoliberalism, in a context of rising unemployment, inflation and slow growth. While the Secretariat's initial attempt to rethink social policy strongly bore the marks of the first, by the end of the decade both influences were reflected in SAME's conception of the 'welfare society'. The language used to describe the latter – the centrality of employment to economic security; an emphasis on a 'preventive' approach to social policy, involving its coordination with labour market policy; and a shift from a state-centric to a mixed model of provision and financing – was subsequently elaborated and given a name, 'the active society'.

The Secretariat's discovery of this new language for thinking about social policy, with its emphasis on promoting labour force participation, may well have been facilitated by the fact that, from the outset, those dealing with 'social affairs' formed part of a larger unit whose main remit was labour market policy, broadly defined. Nevertheless, it took some time, and the continuing pressure of political and economic events in the wider world, for the seeds to germinate. In other words, changes in the wider political–economic environment created political space for the introduction of new ideas and new social policy language. In addition, it was not just the development of new ideas about social policy but also the ability to give them a name that resonated with dominant ideological currents. This involved the shift first from the 'welfare state' through the 'welfare society' and then from the latter to the 'active society'. The latter moreover was a polysemic term could be heard by neoliberals and their critics alike. For the former, it provided a justification for the turn from welfare to workfare. For the latter, it promised a way for including the marginalised, by helping them to develop their capabilities.

The core elements of this new language continue to mark DELSA's social policy advice more than two decades later. This does not mean that there have not been important shifts in the way the active society

---

[60] DELSA/ELSA/Min (2004) 2 Communique of Ministers responsible for social policy, page 2.

has been interpreted. Initially the Secretariat's conception involved an articulation of neoliberal concerns to 'end benefit dependency' with elements of social liberalism that envisaged a role for the state in helping people to develop their capabilities. In the 1990s, the key attempts to spell out the policy implications – The Battle Against Exclusion and Make Work Pay – were influenced by the adoption of the OECD's Jobs Strategy. Resistance to that strategy, as articulated by the powerful Economics Department, within DEELSA, and by member country representatives, however, helped to open space for a more progressive conception, one which recognised the problems posed by spread of low wage, unstable jobs. Similarly, as WP1 and the Social Policy Division began to reflect on the social policy implications of changing gender relations, a combination of learning from outside experts (Esping-Andersen, Saraceno), exposure to national debates via country visits (Mahon, 2010c), and the input of member country representatives opened the way to the reintroduction of the principle of universality and a greater concern with class (and gender) inequality.

References

Armingeon, K. and M. Beyeler (eds) (2004) *The OECD and the European Welfare States,* Cheltenham: Edward Elgar

Esping-Andersen, G. (1997) 'Welfare states at the end of the century: the impact of labour market, family and demographic change' in *Family, Market and Community: Equity and Efficiency in Social Policy,* Paris: OECD, 63–80

Gordon, M.S. (1964) 'US manpower and employment policy: a review essay' *Monthly Labor Review* 87 1314-1321

Hansen, G.B. (1986) 'US employment and training policy: a twenty-five year review 1960-1975' *Economica & Lavoro* vol XX, no 3 141-147.

Jacobsson, K. and Noaksson, N. (2010) 'From deregulation to flexicurity: the makeover of the OECD's jobs strategy' in K. Martens and A. Jakobi (eds), *Mechanisms of OECD Governance – International Incentives for National Policy Making,* Oxford: Oxford University Press p. 119-138.

Jenson, J. (2010) 'Diffusing ideas after neo-liberalism: the social investment perspective in Europe and Latin America,' *Global Social Policy* 10(1) 59-84

Mahon, R. (2010a) 'After neoliberalism? The OECD, the World Bank and the child', *Global Social Policy,* 10:2, 172-192

Mahon, R. (2010b) 'The jobs strategy: from neo- to inclusive liberalism' *Review of International Political Economy,* December, 18:5, 570-591

Mahon, R. (2010c) 'Learning, forgetting, rediscovering: producing the OECD's 'new' family policy' in *Mechanisms of OECD Governance: International Incentives for National Policy-Making?* K. Martens and A.P. Jakobi (eds), Oxford: Oxford University Press

Mahon, R. (2011) 'The jobs strategy: from neo- to inclusive liberalism?' *Review of International Political Economy*, 18:5 570-591.

Mahon, R. and S. McBride eds. (2008) *The OECD and Transnational Governance*, Vancouver and Toronto: University of British Columbia Press

Marris, S. (1983) *My History of My Time at the OECD: Record of Two Seminars given by Steven Marris to the OECD Secretariat 24th and 30th June 1983*

Martens, K. and A.P. Jakobi eds. (2010) *Mechanisms of OECD Governance: International Incentives for National Policy-Making?* Oxford: Oxford University Press

McBride, S. and R. Williams (2001) 'Globalization, the restructuring of labour markets and policy convergence: The OECD 'jobs strategy' *Global Social Policy*, 1(3), 281-309

McCracken, P. (1977) *Toward Full Employment and Price Stability: A Report to the OECD by a Reference Group of Independent Experts*, Paris: OECD

OECD (1972) *Expenditure Trends in OECD Countries 1960-1980*, Paris: OECD

OECD (1981) *The Welfare State in Crisis*, Paris: OECD

OECD (1985) *Social Expenditure 1960-1990: Problems of Growth and Control*, Paris: OECD

OECD (1988) *The Future of Social Protection*, Paris: OECD

OECD (1994) *New Orientations for Social Policy*, Paris: OECD

OECD (1996) *Employment Outlook 1996*, Paris: OECD

OECD (1997) *Family, Market and Community: Equity and Efficiency in Social Policy*, Paris: OECD

Pal, L.A. (2008) 'Inversions without end: the OECD and global public management reform', in *The OECD and Transnational Governance*, R. Mahon and S. McBride (eds), Vancouver: UBC Press, 60-76

Peck, J. and N. Theodore (2000) 'Beyond employability', *Cambridge Journal of Economics* 24(6), 729-749

Saraceno, C. (1997) 'Family change, family policies and the restructuring of welfare' in *Family, Market and Community: Equity and Efficiency in Social Policy*, Paris: OECD, 81-100

Silver, H. (1994) 'Social exclusion and social solidarity' *International Labour Review*, 133 (5-6), 531-78

Theodore, N. and J. Peck (2012) 'Framing neoliberal urbanism: translating 'common sense' urban policy across the OECD zone' *European Urban and Regional Studies,* 19(1), 20-44

Wolfe, R. (2008) 'From reconstructing Europe to constructing globalization: the OECD in historical perspective' in R. Mahon and S. McBride (eds), *The OECD and Transnational Governance,* Vancouver and Toronto: University of British Columbia Press 25-42.

Woodward, R. (2008) 'Towards complex multilateralism: civil society and the OECD' *The OECD and Transnational Governance* R. Mahon and S. McBride (eds), Vancouver: UBC Press, 77-95.

Woodward, R. (2009) *The Organisation for Economic Co-operation and Development (OECD)* London and New York: Routledge

The discursive power of international organisations: social policy language and concepts in the World Bank and the International Monetary Fund

Antje Vetterlein

In a system of global governance, international organisations (IOs) are increasingly shaping domestic policies. This is particularly the case for policy fields such as social policy, where the nation–state seems to lose power and control in times of globalisation. The World Bank and the International Monetary Fund (IMF) are two powerful IOs. They not only set policy agendas but also, at least in developing countries, have sanctioning power through their financial interventions. In addition, insofar as they define the meaning of development using particular social policy language and concepts, they also impact global discourses of social policy in developed countries.

The objective of this chapter is to trace the social policy language and concepts in both organisations over a period of more than three decades, from the 1970s onwards, when both organisations began to deal with issues of poverty and social policy in developing countries. Using documents and interviews, three distinct periods are identified for both organisations. How the language of development has changed, and thus, the role social policies play therein[61], are examined, from a dynamic

---

[61] The relationship between social policies, poverty and development is seen as follows, throughout this chapter. If one follows development theories and practice, development seems to have two main objectives, economic growth and poverty reduction. In order to achieve them, different policy instruments can be utilised, including economic and social policies. Depending on which objective is emphasised within a development strategy and how their relationship is perceived, one type of policies is privileged over the other. For instance, if poverty reduction is perceived as a precondition of economic growth, then social policies will be prioritised over economic policies.

understanding of social policy as a shift from social welfare (1970s) to social protection (1980s–90s), and finally, to social development (2000s). Based on this descriptive analysis it is argued that despite many attempts to change the development language, the econocentric orientation of both organisations leads to only half-hearted outcomes that might not be sustainable in the long run. In other words, while there has been a change in the language of development over time, the underlying meaning has remained rather stable.

In conclusion, the chapter offers a critical assessment of the impact of different social policy concepts in the broader development discourse. Language or discourse can be considered as a medium through which meaning is constituted intersubjectively. Words, ideas or thoughts come into existence only by employing language. Thus, language is constitutive of thought, and thought in turn is constitutive of reality. In this way, language is central to the constitution of reality. Consequently, definitions of social policy in the three periods not only have policy consequences but also shape people's lives through the underlying meanings they convey. This chapter shows the impact of the framing of development in these three periods. While the development language and social policy concepts used in the 1970s turned people in developing countries into a development category and thus depicted them as victims needing assistance, today's language of ownership and participatory development tends to shift responsibility to the respective actors themselves. In other words, language always carries a deeper meaning that can help us understand the impact of discourses on the ground.

Discursive power of international organisations

The increasing influence of international organisations in the setting of global standards and public policies is one of the most significant characteristics of the changing nature of global politics. This chapter is concerned with the discursive power of IOs, and operates on the assumption that this discourse affects the policy recommendations they provide to member states, and ultimately, has implications for people on the ground. Conventional theoretical positions in the field of International Relations (IR) saw IOs mainly as a playing field for nation-states. These theories were concerned principally with the question of who has the power to dictate what IOs do (for example Krasner, 1985). Recent studies have focused on the social life inside these organisations and have explored principal–agent relations (Hawkins et al, 2006), organisational culture (Weaver, 2008), or specifically, the professional background of staff (Chwieroth, 2010) as crucial elements that explain the factors behind the policies that form the backdrop to IOs. A critical assessment of their discursive power, or indeed the language and concepts they adopt, is often missing in these IR studies. In contrast, work in the field of development studies often casts a more critical eye on these IOs, deconstructing the discourses they produce (Manzo, 1991; Escobar, 1995; Shestra, 1995), critically assessing their policy practices (Bøås and McNeill 2003; McNeill and St. Clair, 2009), and offering solutions in the form of development ethics (St. Clair, 2005). This chapter builds on these latter works, analysing the social policy language of the World Bank and the IMF in the broader context of development discourse. At the same time, it assumes the position of many recent IR studies, which see IOs as autonomous actors forming global discourses shaped by, but also independent of, the interests of member states. In that sense, the language studied here is that of the World Bank and the IMF.

The World Bank and the IMF were set up in 1944 at the Bretton Woods Conference, with the aim of preventing world economic crises such as the 1930s one, which was perceived as one factor leading to World War II. The headquarters of these two organisations are in Washington, DC, and by now almost all the countries in the world are members of these organisations (188 in 2012). The Bank's main purpose is to provide low interest loans, free credits and grants to developing countries. Such loans are usually used for specific development projects, such as building schools or hospitals, or investing in infrastructure. Mainly during the 1980s, with its engagement in concessional lending in the form of structural adjustment lending, the Bank moved itself closer to the Fund's area of intervention, that is, programme lending. Programme lending refers to loans given to a government. The Fund's main objective is macroeconomic stability and securing balance of payments. Its main tools to do so are the provision of short-term loans to countries, as well as technical advice and surveillance activities. In that sense, both organisations differ in the way they (can) practice social policy. Whereas the Bank, as an aid organisation, deals explicitly with social policies and projects, the IMF is only indirectly engaged with social policy instruments via its broad policy recommendations. In the early 1990s, for instance, the IMF began to focus on social safety nets, which meant that loan conditionalities paid attention to the social policies of the borrowing country. It has also embraced goals such as environmental sustainability or poverty reduction, which becomes apparent in its language and discourse.

Escobar (1995) proposes to study development as a discourse. The advantage of such an approach is that it highlights development as a social construction of reality as well as maintaining a focus on power. It was only after World War II, in the context of decolonisation, that 'development' became a dominant representation of social reality (Escobar, 1995; McMichael, 1996). Foucault (1972) offers an approach to analysing the dynamics of discourse and power in the representation of social reality. Specifically, he shows how a certain order of discourse produces and promotes specific modes of being and thinking while diminishing others. For instance, regarding development, the discourse represented developing countries as being 'underdeveloped' or 'backward' (Shestra, 1995), and people in those countries as 'powerless' and 'in need', leaving no room for alternative perspectives. IOs such as the World Bank and the IMF significantly contributed to such definitions with their specific way of framing development as an economic issue. Such a perspective implicitly assumes Northern standards of progress and modernisation as the benchmark against which to evaluate the situation in the global South, which is debatable. Yet, even within the framework of development, the language of development itself has changed over time, with economic arguments giving way to 'human development' and to today's 'sustainable development'. This chapter traces such changes, deconstructing their underlying meanings with a special focus on the role of social policies.

Following such an understanding of discourse, the analysis focuses on three dimensions to capture the Bank's and the Fund's discourse on development (as a summary, see Table 5.1). It traces the changing *definition* of development as articulated by the two organisations, highlighting the underlying forms of economic knowledge and theories used to justify different positions. Second, it identifies the social policy *language and concepts* corresponding to these changes in the framing of development strategies. In this respect, it is important to note the close link between concepts and policies. For instance, 'social safety net' can be perceived as a crucial social policy concept coined by the World Bank and then used by the IMF throughout the 1990s. Yet, simultaneously, 'social safety net' is also a policy tool. It will be shown that for the three periods discussed, the meaning of social policies varied from social welfare to social protection and, finally, social development. Finally, the *consequences* of this changing social policy language is examined and critically assessed. The main argument here is that while the development discourse and social policy language have changed over time, the underlying assumptions guiding policy development have remained stable. The explanation for this relative stability is that instead

Table 5.1: Changes in the social policy language of the World Bank and the International Monetary Fund

Period	Definition of development/ underlying theoretical knowledge	Social policy language/concepts and justification	Consequences
1950/60s: development as underdevelopment	Progress Modernisation theory	Food/nutrition, population planning, rural development	Infantilisation
1970s: development as technology and modernisation	Economic and human development Modernisation theory and Keynesianism	Investment Þ EG Þ trickle down to PR Social welfare: basic human needs such as food/ nutrition, health	Technologisation
1980/90s: development as a political issue	Economic development Orthodox economic theory	Structural adjustment Þ EG Þ PR Income distribution or social costs of adjustment From belief in trickle down mechanisms of EG to the insight that EG is necessary but not sufficient Social protection: opportunity for and empowerment of the poor, social safety nets (SSN)	Politicisation/ planning
2000s: development as a holistic approach	Economic and socially sustainable development 'New' development approaches, e.g. by Sen (1999) or Stiglitz (1998)	Poverty reduction and social conditions might be a precondition for economic growth Social development: participation, partnership, ownership, the country in the driver's seat, CDF	Self-responsibility/ de-politicisation

of embracing a truly alternative counter-discourse to a development perspective that highlights economic aspects, the changes to the social policy language towards a more holistic development approach have remained within the overall framework of development being an economic process. With such underlying assumptions, policies cannot change significantly. In addition, the new focus on 'partnership' and 'ownership' pushes responsibility for policy failure to the countries themselves, thus serving as a legitimising strategy for both organisations.

Development as a technological and modernisation issue

The first period of the development discourse in the 1970s is characterised by a solid belief in science and *technology*. Based on modernisation theory and given the positive example of the US and the success of the Marshall Plan in Europe after World War II, the belief was that such progress was both possible and desirable for the so-called Third World. Linked to this faith in science and technology was the uncontested belief in economic growth. Hence, this period laid the groundwork for the argument used in the decades to come: that economic growth was the main objective of development, as it would trigger wealth in developing countries and thus lead to poverty reduction. Yet, there was one major difference between this post-war period and the 1980s and 1990s: public spending legitimised by Keynesianism was not seen as problematic for levels of inflation, which required that supply-side policies, including social policies, were not seen as detrimental for enhancing economic growth. What did this understanding of development mean for the social policy language and concepts used by both organisations?

The IMF did not have a proper social policy language at that time. Set up as a financial institution, few examples may be found of engaging with the topic of social policy in the 1970s, that were framed in the context of welfare state language and with reference to the social security arrangements in developed countries (see IMF 1976, 1979a, 1979b). These papers dealt with the role and impact of social security on household savings and the link between inflation and welfare. What becomes clear from these documents is that, while at the time the Fund had already assumed the position of orthodox economic theory, it had also to defend claims for less inflation and less involvement of the public sector rather than – as would be the case a few years later – just referring to them as commonly known 'truths'. The Fund argued that the link between inflation and growth through public investment could not be supported:

> Since inflation rates are higher in many [Least Developed Countries] (LDCs) than can be justified under any of the welfare approaches examined in this paper, *'the less inflation the better'* is the motto appropriate for most of them. From this point of view, the concern in much of the academic literature about raising government expenditures and involuntary private saving through more inflation appears misdirected. How to control the growth of the public sector and how to raise explicit taxes so as to lower budget deficits and inflationary pressures appear to be more salutary concerns. (IMF, 1979a: 30, emphasis added)

While it seemed to be common sense that public investment financed through inflationary policies was an option for developing countries, the Fund now argued, on the basis of economic research, that private investment might be more efficient to stimulate economic growth. Consequently, low inflation and a decrease in public expenditure should be the goal. This argumentation signals the beginning of a strategy of development based upon classical economic theory.

As more and more developing countries turned to the Bank for assistance, it was forced to deal with poverty as a substantive issue. While the IMF dealt with social security at the theoretical level in some research papers, but not as one of its policy matters, during the 1970s, the Bank started to become actively involved in social policies in two different ways. First and foremost, public investment, focused especially on large infrastructural projects and the enhancement of a country's production capacity, were seen as stimulating economic development, which would in turn help a country's social development, including fighting poverty. The Bank was thus active in project lending in order to provide for the industrialisation of developing countries. Second, under the presidency of Robert McNamara (1968–81), the Bank turned into an aid agency. McNamara oriented the organisation's main objective towards poverty alleviation and social policy, a new priority declared publicly in 1973 at the Annual Meeting in Nairobi. He criticised the 'trickle down' theory of economic growth and development, arguing against the assumption that pursuing social policies does harm growth. This position is reflected in the 1980 World Development Report (WDR) on poverty:

> While there is now increasing recognition that growth does not obviate the need for human development and other steps to reduce poverty, it must be stressed that the converse is true as well – direct steps to reduce poverty do not obviate the need for growth. (World Bank, 1980: 35)

And further:

> human development is not only, or even primarily, an economic [problem]. Less hunger, fewer child deaths and a better chance of primary education are *almost* universally accepted as important *ends* in themselves. (World Bank, 1980: 32, emphasis added)

In summary, the 1970s were characterised by an understanding of development as both economic and human (see WDR: World Bank, 1980). Hence, both objectives, economic growth and poverty reduction, were – not only in rhetoric – pursued equally, and thus, economic and social policies were simultaneously adopted.[62] At the time, the meaning of social policy and the language surrounding it was starkly influenced by the experiences of modernisation in developed (welfare) states, as adjusted to developing countries. Under McNamara's leadership, the understanding of social policies (in the context of development) as basic human needs and some social protection for vulnerable groups (for example population health and nutrition) was supported by social policies such as education, food, and health care, thus adding a component of social welfare (Table 5.1; see also Kapur et al, 1997; Vetterlein, 2012, 2007).

Development as a political priority

The 1980s and 1990s were marked by a focus on achieving development using the 'correct' *policy mix*. In the late 1970s and early 1980s, in a bleak economic context, the world's leading economies, such as the US, Germany, Great Britain and Japan, saw conservative parties come to power. This had consequences for the kind of development policies advocated by the World Bank and the IMF. At the end of the 1970s, the management of both organisations had contemplated adopting the

---

[62] This becomes obvious in the Bank's discourse and policy practice. The Fund, as pointed out earlier, did not have a language for social policy at that time.

'basic needs approach' (BNA), which would have shifted development programmes away from economic policies towards social policies. The core of the BNA is to measure absolute poverty and define the resources necessary for physical wellbeing and then make the measurements and resources part of economic development models. For Bank and Fund programmes, it would have meant developing a framework that incorporates financial constraints into an economic model in which development depends on the economic ability to provide for the *basic needs* of the poor (Borpujari, 1980). This concept, promoted by the International Labour Office (ILO) in 1976, proved rather controversial within the Bank and the Fund. With the rise of political conservatism, BNA was abandoned and a new era began, often referred to as neoliberalism. Not only did economic growth become the main objective of development, with poverty to be reduced automatically once certain growth levels were reached, but promoting social policies was seen as detrimental for economic growth. In the 1980s, each organisation adopted a slightly distinct social policy language. The IMF framed its engagement with poverty in terms of income distribution, a concept that emerged together with the BNA and was then given priority over the more social approach. In contrast, the Bank used the language of social policy explicitly by addressing the social impacts caused by the structural adjustment lending programmes. Due to the experience of policy failure, in particular in Africa during the 1980s, and the criticism consequently voiced against the World Bank and the IMF, both organisations adjusted their discourse and policies during the 1990s. As a consequence, the single-minded focus on economic growth was replaced by a more nuanced perspective, whereby economic growth had to be supplemented by social policies in order to achieve poverty reduction. In both organisations, then, a new policy concept was born in the 1990s, that of 'social safety net'.

The IMF's main position with regard to social policies and poverty throughout the 1980s and most of the 1990s was to acknowledge that, in developing countries,[63] its adjustment programmes had had detrimental effects on poor people but that the Fund was unable to do anything. Due to the rise of conservatism in the main economic powers in the late 1970s and early 1980s, the Fund opted against a BNA approach, which had been seriously discussed as an option for

---

[63]   The IMF provided concessional lending to Low Income Countries (LICs) from the mid-1970s through the Trust Fund, which was replaced in 1986 by the Structural Adjustment Facility (SAF), followed in 1987 by the Enhanced Structural Adjustment Facility (ESAF).

its lending strategy (see Gerster, 1982; Vetterlein, 2010; Vetterlein and Moschella, 2013). Instead, the Fund's engagement with social issues was characterised by an economic approach, centred on achieving income distributional effects of its programmes. Fund-supported programmes inevitably affect poor people 'because they influence not only aggregate demand, supply, and the overall price level but also the composition of demand and supply and, therefore, relative prices (Heller et al, 1988: 8).

The language used in the policy documents in order to justify this policy choice was that such costs were seen as necessary, short-term sacrifices for achieving the long-term benefits of economic growth. The focus on short-term sacrifice and resulting social inequality is exemplified in the following quotation:

> Moreover, the associated reallocation of factors of production across sectors entails changes in the set of prices and sector payments that from a short-run egalitarian perspective may be undesirable and yet are necessary for the attainment of the economy's balance of payments and growth objectives. Thus, real wage rates may have to fall and real profit rates increase so as to encourage increased foreign capital inflow and private domestic capital formation. (Johnson and Salop, 1980: 23)

The Fund, therefore, saw no need to address these issues by reforming its policies. It was only at the beginning of the 1990s, after prompting of the World Bank through the Development Committee,[64] that it considered the design of social safety nets in order to deal with the economic programmes' adverse social impacts on poor people. These safety nets were defined as

> ad hoc or permanent arrangements that mitigate possible adverse effects of economic reform measures on the poor. Different countries have different social policy instruments which provide a basis for designing social safety nets and face varying financial constraints. In many countries, a core of social safety nets would include a mix of limited subsidies on basic necessities (particularly basic foodstuffs), social

---

[64] The Development Committee, established in 1974, is a ministerial level forum of the World Bank and the IMF. Its mandate is to advise the Boards of Governors of both IOs on development issues. Its 25 members, representing the membership of both organisations, meet twice a year.

security arrangements (such as pensions and unemployment benefits), and possibly public works programs adapted for this purpose. (IMF, 1993: 23)

Such social policy measures are justified, however, in mainly economic terms, that is, they should not jeopardise the IMF's economic adjustment programmes: 'Social safety nets are an important means of addressing *concerns for the poor*, particularly during a period of reform, and of providing a basis for enhancing the *political viability* of reform programs, including those supported by the Fund' (IMF, 1993: 1, emphasis in original). It is further argued that 'well-designed safety nets can encourage investment and growth by reducing risk' (IMF, 1993: 2). Thus, social safety nets can even be considered a condition for stimulating economic growth.

For the World Bank, the 1980s were characterised by a preoccupation with structural adjustment loans. Yet, compared to the IMF, the Bank, being an aid organisation[65] was better equipped to consider poor people and consequently engaged in the social costs of such adjustment programmes rather quickly. From the start, the World Bank put into place specific compensatory measures to address this problem (Development Committee, 1989: 8). It provided funds, such as social sector adjustment loans, in order to maintain social expenditure, or certain action programmes and social funds in order to mitigate the immediate social impacts of adjustment.[66] Yet, what was necessary was a more refined definition of poverty in order to identify the group of affected people and operationalise the compensatory measures designed to address such a group. That was the beginning of the idea of measuring poverty in relative terms as a threshold of one dollar per day (see World Development Report: World Bank, 1990) instead of as an absolute category.[67] The World Bank's main position during the 1980s was characterised by the perception of structural adjustment as being the ultimate objective in order to achieve economic growth, which in turn was supposed to lead to poverty reduction. The assumption was that not only investment projects but also policy reforms are

---

[65] Contrary to the IMF, development is stated as an objective in the Bank's Articles of Agreement.

[66] Examples are the Program of Action to Mitigate the Social Costs of Adjustment in Ghana or the Emergency Social Fund in Bolivia as well as financing of work schemes, food subsidies and more (see for example : African Development Bank, UNDP and World Bank 1990; Hicks 1993).

[67] In 2008, the World Bank adjusted this number from 1.08 USD to 1.25 USD per day.

necessary in order to create an environment that stimulates economic development. Hence, policy based lending was the main focus of the Bank during that time.

By the end of that decade, it had become obvious that neither objective, increasing growth rates or reducing the number of those in poverty, had been achieved. On the contrary, poverty had increased: in Latin America for instance, the poverty rate rose from 27 to 32% during the period from 1980 to 1989 (Hicks, 1993).[68] In addition, income inequality increased. The 1980s are thus also called the 'lost decade' (see for example Kapur et al, 1997; Hicks, 1993). It was now not only acknowledged that structural adjustment loans might have some adverse effects on poor people that need to be mitigated but also that economic policy reform might not be sufficient to integrate poor people in a sustainable way. The Bank therefore designed two new policy tools: 'social funds' and 'social safety nets', based on a new understanding of poverty outlined in the 1990 World Development Report. The language of social funds and safety nets implies an understanding of social policies as social protection rather than social welfare. Safety nets are about targeting specific groups of poor people instead of providing general welfare services. This understanding is in line with a perception of development as mainly economic and the notion that ensuring economic growth will automatically lead to poverty reduction.

This focus on the economy also expresses itself in the language used to justify this approach. The 1990 World Development Report put forward a 'two-pronged strategy' to combat poverty: opportunity and empowerment. The opportunity pillar was aimed at the expansion of employment and income earning opportunities for poor people, and is thus concerned with the nature and rate of economic growth. The second pillar aimed at enhancing the capacity of poor people to take advantage of these opportunities due to the direct improvement in their welfare, such as access to health care, education and other social infrastructure, thus empowering them to take part in economic processes. This strategy was supposed to be complemented by transfers or social safety nets in order to protect the poorest and most vulnerable, who, despite new opportunities, were not able to escape from poverty on their own. It was designed 'to ensure that the poor both gain from and contribute to growth' (World Bank, 1991: 12). In other words, the main function of social policy was seen primarily in its economic

---

[68] Poverty is defined as income of less than $60 a month per person (in 1985 purchasing power parity).

value for societies. The title of a working paper published by the World Bank makes this approach quite obvious: *Social Development is Economic Development* (Birdsall, 1993). This working paper further argues that social development is 'an excellent investment – in terms of its contribution to economic growth' (Birdsall, 1993: 1). Social development is 'good economics' and 'social programs are superb investments in future economic growth' (Birdsall, 1993: 1). Social programmes have an economic return. Social policies were understood as policies for education and health care, which does not come as a surprise, because not only are these policies the most obvious in terms of enhancing poor people's capability to respond to economic opportunities, but they are easy to operationalise into the organisation's technocratic understanding of development, and thus easier to implement.

Development as a holistic approach

The late 1990s witnessed a change in development discourse away from an exclusive focus on economic growth as the main development objective towards poverty reduction. Most remarkable was that the relationship between both objectives was suddenly reversed: poverty reduction, formerly a consequence of economic growth, was now seen as a precondition for economic growth. This in turn meant that social policies would be prioritised over economic policies. The theories underlying this new perspective were not necessarily new as such but were now voiced by well-known economists such as Amartya Sen (1999) or Joseph E. Stiglitz (1998). Furthermore, the overall development discourse outside the Bank and the Fund had started to turn in this direction at the beginning of the 21st century, as reflected in several strategies and policy agendas, such as the United Nations Development Programme (UNDP) *Human Development Report* in 1999, the UN *Millennium Declaration*[69] where the Millennium Development Goals (MDGs) were adopted, the 2000 Social Summit in Geneva, as well as the *Monterrey Consensus* in 2002 (United Nations, 2003). Development economists such as Dani Rodrik (2000) argued that the relationship between economic growth and poverty reduction is not precisely known but that it definitely goes in both directions. Thus, prompted by a mounting criticism against the Bank and the Fund following the 1997 East Asian financial crisis, a holistic approach to development was called for and then put into practice in 1999, with the

---

[69] www.un.org/millennium/declaration/ares552e.htm

World Bank setting up the Poverty Reduction Strategy Paper (PRSP) initiative, based on the concept of a Comprehensive Development Framework, that the Fund eventually followed.

In 1999, the IMF joined the Bank's PRSP initiative by setting up a new facility for Low Income Countries (LICs) that replaced the Enhanced Structural Adjustment Facility (ESAF). This new initiative, Poverty Reduction and Growth Facility (PRGF) thus made poverty reduction one of its priority objectives. Yet, as earlier, the Fund was a laggard in this regard and acted mainly due to the prompting of the World Bank. Throughout the 1990s, the Fund's internal rhetoric cites a 'moral imperative' and the strengthening of a 'broad social acceptability necessary for economic reform to succeed' (Gupta and Nashashibi, 1990: 14) in order to justify its engagement with social policies such as social safety nets (SSNs). What had been realised in the Bank much earlier was only officially argued at the end of the 1990s, that is, that economic growth was a necessary but not sufficient condition to achieve poverty reduction. As Michel Camdessus, Managing Director from 1987 until 2000, put it:

> we must maintain this emphasis on macroeconomic stabilization, and the trade liberalization, price reform, privatization, and other reforms that allow stabilization to take hold. But we have learned that this 'first generation' of reform is not, by itself, enough – either to accelerate social progress sufficiently, or to allow countries to compete more successfully in global markets. (Camdessus, 1997: 2)

The simple causal link between development objectives was questioned, and it was recognised that other factors, such as redistribution and investment in human capital, might stimulate economic growth. This new argument opened up space, discursively as well as politically, which then led to a redefining of the Fund's original aim in 1999 to include poverty reduction. When political pressures increased due to the East Asian financial crisis at the end of the 1990s, a policy shift towards more social policies was quickly executed. There are remarkable statements with regard to the Fund's language on social issues that go beyond its prior understanding of the relationship between poverty reduction and macroeconomic policies (IMF and World Bank, 2001). Not only did the Fund rename its lending facility to Low Income Countries (LICs) from Enhanced Structural Adjustment Facility (ESAF) to Poverty Reduction and Growth Facility (PRGF), but 'poverty' was now defined as 'a multidimensional problem that goes beyond economics to include, among other things, social, political and cultural issues' such that 'solutions to poverty cannot be based exclusively on economic policies' (IMF and World Bank, 2001: 1).

The same paper goes on to illuminate the relationship between growth and poverty while pointing out that this is not to be seen as a causal relationship but as an association, while further noting that 'the causality could well go the other way. In such cases, poverty reduction could in fact be necessary to implement stable macroeconomic policies or to achieve higher growth.' (IMF and World Bank, 2001: 5) The language of 'poverty' in relation to social policy had now entered the Fund, and this had implications at the operational level. For the first time in its history, the Fund hired social scientists, established a Poverty and Social Impact Analysis Unit and included social benchmarks in its conditionality (for more detail, see Vetterlein, 2010).

The World Bank was more of a forerunner with regard to this shift towards a holistic development approach. In 1995–96, James D. Wolfensohn, as newly appointed Bank President, launched several policy initiatives and internal reforms (the Strategic Compact). He also had a vision for Bank policy on poverty, which could well be regarded as a new concept for a holistic development approach, that is, the Comprehensive Development Framework (CDF). In this context, the PRSP can be seen as the operational vehicle that put this new policy concept into practice. What becomes obvious in this initiative, but also appears in other Bank policies (such as the bank-wide social development strategy in 2005, see Vetterlein, 2007), is a change in the language regarding poverty and social issues. Poverty is no longer perceived as mainly an economic issue, but as a multidimensional problem.[70] As a consequence, the understanding of 'development' broadened from purely economic to a more comprehensive, equitable, inclusive, and sustainable development (World Bank, 2003a: 5). In turn, policy responses have changed and brought social policies much more to the fore. And what is more, social policies now do not only refer to social protection or social welfare, but to cross-cutting issues such as partnership, ownership and participation, which are summarised under the broader concept of 'social development'.

---

[70] This notion of poverty as a multidimensional problem is based on *Voices of the Poor*, a background study conducted in preparation for the 2000 World Development Report. This study is based on interviews with about 60,000 poor people, who were asked how they would define what exactly poverty means to them. The major result was that poverty comprises much more than just an income dimension. Most particularly, it is about security.

A few quotations from Bank documents make that shift in language obvious: 'The end of the 20th century saw a major rediscovery of the role of the social in processes of national and international development' (World Bank, 2003a: 1). The failure of enhancing economic growth and decreasing poverty had raised 'troubling questions: Does the emphasis on structural adjustment ignore the poor?' (World Bank, 2003b: xvii). It was then realised that 'it is impossible to think about economic development, even in very restricted terms, without invoking assumptions about the *rest* of society and its social structures' (Smelser, 1997: 2, emphasis in original). The significance of 'the rest of society and its social structures' or more generally, the social foundation of development, seems open for discussion and interpretation. Within this discussion, the selection of themes regarding what development means and how it can be practised is broad and ranges from (good) governance, to institutions, as well as rules and norms of a society. There is also an increased emphasis on transparency, participation, and ownership within development practice that puts the developing countries and their peoples at the centre of attention. The PRSP process, for instance, not only requires the countries to write their strategies themselves (country ownership) but also mandates the adoption of a participatory approach, which means that not only policy makers and IO staff meet and discuss the new strategy but that non-governmental organisations (NGOs) and other local stakeholders are also invited and even obliged to contribute to the strategy.[71]

The gist of the development language at the turn of the century departs from the prior period's understanding that social policies and investment in human capital were sufficient: 'social development is not simply a matter of social service provision. It also depends on a range of political, economic, institutional, and cultural factors, that together play a critical role in poverty reduction and social inclusion' (World Bank, 2000: 1). And further:

> It is also clear that even well-intentioned social policies and programs too often do not reach poor people, especially women – and can, under certain circumstances, even undermine their well-being. The development community now recognizes that it needs greater understanding of community institutions, networks, norms, and values to enable

---

[71] Indeed, a PRSP has to include a chapter on the participatory process conducted while designing the strategy. Civil society participation is also assumed to increase country ownership.

people to capture the benefits of development and build their capacity to help themselves. (World Bank, 2001: 2)

It indeed looks like a 'new paradigm of development, premised on the argument that without attention to the social underpinnings of development, it is difficult for economic growth and development to succeed – and virtually impossible for it to be sustained' (World Bank, 1998: 2).

In summary, the analysis of the Bank's and the Fund's social policy language and concepts from the 1970s to the 2000s has shown significant changes in their understanding of, and approach to, the problem of development: from human and economic, to purely economic and, eventually, sustainable development. In turn, this last framing of development refers back to differences in the underlying theoretical assumptions about the importance of economic growth and the relationship between economic growth and poverty reduction. Consequently, the meaning of poverty also changed over time. From the empirical analysis, three periods were identified, where the definition of poverty begins with a needs based approach in the 1970s, to a problem of income distribution in the 1980s and, finally, in the 2000s, to poverty as a multidimensional issue that goes beyond economics. That, in turn, has consequences for social policy, the meaning of which changed from social welfare to social protection and, finally, social development, a concept that goes well beyond traditional social programmes and spans cross-cutting themes such as participation, ownership, and transparency. For each period, different social policy concepts also emerged and were closely linked to specific policy initiatives. While the 1970s were characterised by the idea of a BNA, the main concept in the 1980s–90s was the 'social safety net', which was later replaced by a comprehensive approach to development.

So far, this chapter has outlined these three periods for the Bank and the Fund, the different forms of knowledge and theories underlying these concepts, and the way this knowledge was deployed as justification to legitimise policy practices. We observed that the IMF used the language of social policy, but only when pushed to do so by the World Bank. Despite these changes, however, criticism of both organisations for their development policies can still be observed. Beyond the criticism that they are but instruments of their most powerful member states and thus follow geopolitical interests (Escobar 1995; McMichael, 1996), the Bank and the IMF have also been criticised for worsening the situation in developing countries through the policies adopted (Cornia et al, 1987) or for addressing poverty merely as window-dressing (Jayasuriya 1999; Fine 2001). In other words, the impact of the new social policy language and concepts on the ground is part of the answer to the question of whether the changes in discourse signify a new development strategy and are thus sustainable. The last section of this chapter offers such a critical assessment.

A critical assessment: social policy in word and deed

The changes in Bank and Fund social policy language cannot be denied. They can be referred back to a changing understanding of the meaning of development. Yet how sustainable are these changes? Engaging with a critical assessment of these developments raises two specific questions. First, what are the consequences of Bank and Fund discourse on the ground? Second, how much does the new language depart from the old development paradigm to be able to change practices significantly? Specifically, did the changes in language have implications for development practice?

As outlined earlier, the language used to describe things has an impact on people's practices, since it demarcates what it is possible to do and say, and thus shapes people's identities. The different framing of the development problem over the past decades has had different consequences for the way we talk about development and the way in which people in developing countries have come to perceive themselves as 'underdeveloped'. Poverty and the idea of development as such have existed only since the post–World War II era. Before that, the possibility of development in what were still colonies was not imaginable, as their capacity for economic development was perceived as non-existent (Adas, 1989). With the process of decolonisation, the developing world was depicted as 'a child in need of adult guidance' (Escobar, 1995: 30). This infantilisation in the 1950s and 1960s, as Escobar (1995) argues, fits nicely with an image of 'salvation' for those who give charity to poor people.

The making of poor people as a group and their image as being 'backward' or 'not modern' started with the change in development discourse to mean a lack of modernisation and the practice of development aid (Shestra, 1995). Suddenly, development became an issue of technology and industrialisation in the 1970s, which also meant that poor people were primarily in need of the right kind of knowledge and skills (and even mind-set) in order to partake in processes of modernisation. Given the situation in developing countries at the time, social policy was understood as a basic need, especially for the most vulnerable groups. The language was directed towards the concept of social welfare, as borrowed from developed countries. In addition to the basics such as nutrition or shelter, other provisions, particularly health policies but also education, were deemed necessary.

While this meaning of development as modernisation did not disappear, another conceptual layer was added during the 1980s and 1990s when development also became a matter of policy adjustment. After realising that huge investments did not lead to an increase in growth, as expected according to Rostow's theory (1960), the lack of success was attributed to political conditions. Development became a matter of economic modelling and planning, yet also more politicised since now governments of developing countries could be blamed for the lack of growth by not following the Bank's and the Fund's recommendations.[72] Poor people themselves still needed assistance in developing the capabilities to take up the opportunities offered by a modern economy. Therefore, the 1990s in particular saw a surge in SSNs and education and health policies. The language used to justify such policies invoked terms such as 'opportunity' and 'empowerment'. Poor people were to get the chance (via education and better health) to take part in economic activities, which in turn would empower them to gain further rights in the future.

Finally, the new language of holistic development shifted responsibilities again. After two decades of structural adjustment lending and little success, arguments became stronger that the economic models might be wrong or that the recommended policies would not work because they had been imposed on countries that did not 'own' them and thus did not fully engage in them. The new language of ownership and participation promoted by the concept of social development addresses this issue. They go hand in hand. The participation of civil society groups and other stakeholders, such as the actual beneficiaries of these programmes, is supposed to feed into the development process, which in turn should enhance ownership of programmes and projects. Taking part in designing such strategies themselves, and thus 'owning' them, rather than being told what is best to do, is based on a premise which is supposed to lead to a higher success rate. The often used metaphor of the 'country sitting in the driver's seat', however, can also have a different connotation. It is sometimes the person in the back seat that tells the driver where to go. But even if the new participatory

---

[72] To illustrate this perspective held by both organisations, I quote one of my interviewees: "The state remains sovereign. What they do in the end … is hard to monitor for the Fund. These are sovereign states"(translation by the author, interview with IMF staff 19 March 2004).

approach of PRSPs might lead to more ownership, this new discourse has managed to do something else: it has shifted responsibility for development back to the developing countries themselves. If a country writes its own strategy and then fails to achieve it, the Bank and the Fund can no longer be blamed. Opponents of the Bank and the Fund (for example McGee et al, 2002) consider the emphasis on participation as a strategic move to co-opt NGOs and other critical voices, and thus to use 'participation' as a means of depoliticising development, to keep critical voices quiet while enhancing their own institutional reputation as democratic and inclusive.

Given these criticisms, and leading on to the second question, of how different is this new holistic development approach from the 'neoliberal' perspective that had preceded it, besides the rhetorical use of ownership, participation and transparency discourses, the main difference lies in the focus on poverty and social development, and how it is linked to economic growth as a development objective (for more detail see Vetterlein, 2013). While this was truly the main spirit at the turn of the century and after the East Asian financial crisis, evidence can be found in the discourse that the strong focus on economic growth has not completely disappeared. Documents show a potential swing back to a priority on economic growth (for example World Bank Institute 2000; Dollar and Kray 2001; also interview with IMF staff on March 19, 2004). One quote puts it like this:

> However, the MDG initiative also presents some risks. Perhaps most importantly, the emphasis on non-income targets could distract attention from the absolutely critical role that economic growth plays in reducing income and non-income poverty, particularly in many low-income countries where sustained growth has been difficult to achieve. (World Bank, 2003c: 3)

The same is true for the IMF, which in April 2012 changed the name of its Poverty Reduction and Growth Facility (PRGF) that explicitly indicates a poverty focus to 'Extended Credit Facility'. In other words, the changes in 1999 do not seem to be sustainable.

International Relations studies would explain these observations by referring to organisational imperatives. Hypocritical behaviour of IOs (Weaver, 2008) or pathologies (Barnett and Finnemore, 2004) can be explained by the disconnect of external pressure and internal culture and by constraints of policy making which favour efficiency, simplicity and quantification, all of which contrast with a holistic approach to development yet fit particularly well with economic knowledge (St. Clair, 2005; see also Crouch, 2007). One could also argue, however, that the established counter-discourse of holistic development has not been successful in fully changing development practice because it remains within the same framework of modernisation, instead of offering a real alternative to theorising development. If the underlying ideas of development still refer to progress and becoming modern, then even the most critical counter-discourse is still trapped inside what Manzo calls 'logocentrism' (Manzo, 1991, borrowing from Derrida, 1978), that is, a disposition to impose a hierarchy between certain dichotomies such as North/South, male/female, modern/traditional. In other words, even though the dichotomy is turned around at least in the social policy language in favour of poverty reduction, as long as the problem is presented as a lack of economic progress, the logic remains intact and one cannot completely step out of the present dominant discourse. As Manzo argues further (1991: 8), the pervasiveness of logocentric thinking in development studies might explain why truly alternative counter-discourses are not taken seriously. Thinking outside the economic growth–poverty reduction nexus seems somehow impossible, at least for policy makers.

References

Adas, M. (1989) *Machines as the Measure of Man*, Ithaca: Cornell University Press.

African Development Bank, UNDP and World Bank (1990) *The Social Dimension of Adjustment in Africa. A Policy Agenda,* Washington, DC: World Bank.

Barnett, M. and Finnemore, M. (2004) *Rules for the World: International Organizations in Global Politics,* Ithaca, London: Cornell University Press.

Birdsall, N. (1993) *Social Development is Economic Development,* WPS 1123, Washington, DC: World Bank, Policy Research Department.

Borpujari, J.G. (1980) *Toward a Basic Needs Approach to Economic Development with Financial Stability,* IMF Departmental Memorandum DM/80/16, Washington, DC: IMF.

Bøås, M. and D. McNeill (2003) *Global Institutions and Development: Framing the World?*, London: Routledge.

Camdessus 1997 (1997) 'Fostering an enabling environment for development', address presented at the high-level meeting of the UN Economic and Social Council, Geneva, July 2, www.imf.org/external/np/speeches/1997/mds9710.htm.

Chwieroth, J.M. (2010) *Capital Ideas: The IMF and the Rise of Financial Liberalization*, Princeton, N.J.: Princeton University Press.

Cornia, G.A. e.a. (1987) *Adjustment with a Human Face,* 2 volumes, Oxford: Oxford University Press.

Crouch, C. (2007) 'Neoinstitutionalism: still no intellectual hegemony?' *Regulation and Governance* 1(3): 261-70.

Derrida, J. (1978) *Writing and Difference,* London: Routledge and Kegan Paul.

Development Committee (1989) *Strengthening Efforts to Reduce Poverty,* Development Committee Pamphlet No. 19, prepared by the staffs of the World Bank and the IMF for the Development Committee, Washington, DC: World Bank.

Development Committee (1990) *Development Issues, Presentations to the 39th Meeting of the Development Committee,* Development Committee Pamphlet No. 26, Washington, DC: IMF.

Dollar, D. and Kray, A. (2001) *Growth Is Good For the Poor,* Policy Research Working Paper 2587. Washington, DC: World Bank.

Escobar, A. (1995, [1952]) *Encountering Development. The Making and Unmaking of the Third World,* Princeton, N.J.: Princeton University Press.

Fine, B. (2001) 'Neither the Washington nor the post-Washington consensus: an introduction', in B. Fine, C. Lapavitsas, and J. Pincus (eds) *Development Policy in the Twenty-First Century,* London, New York: Routledge, 1-27.

Foucault, M. (1972) *The Archaeology of Knowledge,* Part II: Discursive Regularities, Tavistock Publication Limited.

Gerster, R. (1982) 'The IMF and basic needs conditionality', *Journal of World Trade Law* 16, Nov./Dec., 497-517.

Gupta, S. and Nashashibi, K. (1990) 'Poverty concerns in fund-supported programs', *Finance & Development* 27, 12-14.

Hawkins, D. e.a. (eds) (2006) *Delegation and Agency in International Organizations.* Cambridge: Cambridge University Press.

Heller, P.S. e.a. (1988) *The Implications of Fund-Supported Adjustment Programs for Poverty: Experiences in Selected Countries,* Occasional Paper No. 58, Washington, DC: IMF.

Hicks, N.L. (1993) *Poverty, Social Sector Development and the Role of the World Bank,* HROWP, Washington, DC: World Bank.

IMF (1976) *Intragenerational Equity Under Social Security,* Internal Document DM/76/23, Washington, DC: IMF, Fiscal Affairs Department.

IMF (1979a) *Inflation, Taxes and Welfare in LDCs,* Internal Document DM/79/42, Washington, DC: IMF, Research Department.

IMF (1979b) *The Influence of Social Security on Household Savings: A Cross-Country Investigation,* Internal Document DM/79/64, Washington, DC: IMF, Fiscal Affairs Department.

IMF (1993) *Social Safety Net in Economic Reform,* Internal Document EBS/93/34. Washington, DC: IMF, The Secretary.

IMF and World Bank (2001) *Macroeconomic Policy and Poverty Reduction, Washington,* DC: World Bank.

Jayasuriya, K. (1999) The new touchy-feely Washington. *AQ: Journal of Contemporary Analysis* 71(6): 5-7.

Johnson, O. and Salop, J. (1980) 'Distributional aspects of stabilization programs in developing countries', *Staff Papers* 27 (March): 1-23.

Kapur, D. e.a. (1997) *The World Bank. Its First Half Century,* Washington DC: Brookings Institution.

Krasner, S.D. (1985) *Structural Conflict: The Third World Against Global Liberalism,* Berkeley, London: University of California Press.

Manzo (1991) 'Modernist discourse and the crisis of development theory', *Studies in Comparative International Development* 26(2):3-36.

McGee, R. et al (2002) 'Assessing participation in poverty reduction strategy papers: a desk-based synthesis of experience in Sub-Saharan Africa', Research Report 52, Brighton, Sussex: Institute of Development Studies.

McMichael, P. (1996) *Development and Social Change: A Global Perspective* London: Pine Forge Press.

McNeill, D. and St. Clair, A.L. (2009) *Global Poverty, Ethics and Human Rights: The Role of Multilateral Organisations,* London: Routledge.

Rodrik, D. (2000) 'Growth and poverty reduction: what are the real questions?', in: http://ksghome.harvard.edu/-drodrik/poverty.PDF.

Rostow, W.W. (1960) *The Stages of Economic Growth: A Non-Communist Manifesto,* Cambridge University Press.

Sen, A. (1999) *Development As Freedom,* Oxford: Oxford University Press.

Shestra, N. (1995) 'Becoming a development category' in Crush, J., (ed.) *Power of Development,* London: Routledge.

Smelser, N.J. (1997) *Social Dimensions of Economic Development,* Social Assessment Series No. 48, Washington, DC: World Bank.

St. Clair, A.L. (2005) 'Third Stage development ethics: global institutions, scientific uncertainty and the politicization of moral worth', paper prepared for The International Conference and Workshop on Ethics and Development, Michigan State University, April 2005.

Stiglitz, J.E. (1998) 'Towards a new paradigm for development: strategies, policies, and processes', 1998 Prebisch Lecture at UNCTAD in Geneva, Switzerland, www.worldbank.org/html/extdr/extme/jssp101998.htm.

United Nations (2003) *Monterrey Consensus of the International Conference on Financing for Development*, UN: New York.

United Nations Development Programme, UNDP (1999) *Human Development Report 1999: Globalization with a Human Face*, Technical Report. UNDP, New York.

Vetterlein, A. (2007) 'Economic growth, poverty reduction and the role of social policies. the evolution of the World Bank's social development approach', *Global Governance* 13: 513-533.

Vetterlein, A. (2010) 'Lacking ownership: the IMF and its engagement with social development as a global policy norm', in: S. Park and Antje Vetterlein (eds): *Owning Development: Creating Global Policy Norms in the IMF and the World Bank*, Cambridge University Press: 93-112.

Vetterlein, A. (2012) 'Seeing like the World Bank on poverty', *New Political Economy*, 17, 1, 35-58.

Vetterlein, A. (2013) 'The role of the World Bank and the International Monetary Fund in poverty reduction: limits of policy change', in R. Surender, R. Walker, R. Van Niekerk (eds) *Social Policy in a Developing World: Comparative Developments and Debates*, Edward Elgar: 37-57.

Vetterlein, A. and M. Moschella (2013) 'International organizations and organizational fields: explaining policy change in the IMF', *European Political Science Review*, available on FirstView CJO2013. doi:10.1017/S175577391200029X: 1-23.

Weaver, C. (2008) *Hypocrisy Trap: The World Bank and the Poverty of Reform.*, Princeton, NJ: Princeton University Press.

World Bank (1980) *World Development Report 1980*, New York, Oxford University Press.

World Bank (1990) *World Development Report: Poverty*, New York: Oxford University Press.

World Bank (1991) *Assistance Strategies to Reduce Poverty*, A World Bank Policy Paper, Washington, DC: World Bank.

World Bank (1998) *Social Development Update: Making Development More Inclusive and Effective*, SDD Paper Series No. 27, Washington, DC: World Bank.

World Bank (2000) *New Paths to Social Development: Community and Global Networks in Action*, Washington, DC: World Bank.

World Bank (2001) *Dynamic Risk Management and the Poor. Developing a Social Protection Strategy for Africa*, African Region Human Development Series, Washington, DC: World Bank.

World Bank (2003a) *A Social Development Agenda for the 21st Century. The World Bank's Strategy for Social Development in the Latin American and the Caribbean Region*, Washington, DC: World Bank.

World Bank (2003b) *Toward Country-Led Development. A Multi-Partner Evaluation of the Comprehensive Development Framework,* Washington, DC: World Bank.

World Bank (2003c) *Poverty Reduction and the World Bank: Progress in 2002,* Washington, DC: World Bank.

World Bank Institute (2000) *The Quality of Growth,* Washington, DC: World Bank.

SIX

Original and imitated or elusive and limited? Towards a genealogy of the welfare state idea in Britain

Daniel Wincott

Britain occupies a pivotal and peculiar position in the historiography of the welfare state, looming large in the dominant – largely taken for granted – periodisation of welfare state history. Structured around a (roughly) thirty-year 'golden age' after 1945 (Wincott, 2013), the iconography of this metanarrative begins and ends with Britain. So 'British reforms introduced between 1945 and 1948' 'designed the first *coherent* and *systematic architecture* of a *universalistic* welfare state' (Ferrera, 2005: 64, emphasis added). While its precise endpoint is harder to date, Margaret Thatcher's assumption of the British premiership often appears as a decisive moment in the welfare state's demise. Claims about the origins of social policy language and concepts reflect or embody these assumptions: writing in the early 1960s (during the supposed heyday of welfare statism), distinguished social historian Asa Briggs asserted that the 'phrase "welfare state" ... was first used to describe labour Britain after 1945. From Britain the phrase made its way round the world' (1961: 221).

Today, claims of historic British patrimony over the concept of the welfare state have a peculiar quality. They do not seem to ring true. Specialists may quibble over the precise dates, but we have now lived through a period of post ('golden age') welfare statism longer than the putative 'golden age' itself. After this long denouement, the British welfare state now looks as if it was always comparatively limited, niggardly and 'ungrounded' (Dunleavy, 1989), making it hard to believe that Britain was ever (perceived) to have been the world leader. This sense that the chain of history is broken – that the past does not link to the present – may reflect a tendency towards anachronism in welfare state analysis. Elsewhere, the present author has analysed the fallacious assumption that the cluster of concepts adhering to the welfare state today can be projected back into history and had the same resonance, meaning and significance to contemporaries as they have today (Wincott, 2011, 2013). There are strong tendencies towards the fallacy of anachronism in most comparative welfare analysis. Even so, there is something especially peculiar about the British case.

In addressing 'British peculiarity' the focus here is on the putative moment of genesis for the modern idea of the welfare state and it is shown that *both* widespread assumptions of British patrimony in the welfare state concept *and* that of 1945 as a decisive moment its development are at best half correct: in fact, each might be regarded as seriously misleading. The same argument can be made generally for the historical development of welfare state institutions (see Wincott, 2013), but the concern here focuses specifically on the historical sociology of welfare concepts and language (see Somers, 2008 on the historical sociological of concepts). With respect to the issue of timing, the choice of 1945 as a decisive date is both too early and too late. Although the literature is very recent, scholars have made considerable progress towards debunking key misconceptions in the historiography of social policy language and concepts. Petersen and Petersen (2013) have decisively demonstrated that the 'welfare state' phrase was used in print with reference to Britain as early as the 1920s. Equally, the evidence suggests that this phrase was *not* used between 1945 and 1948 to describe post-war Labour social reforms. Instead, it only began to come into widespread use after 1949 and its value as a conceptualisation of these reforms remained fiercely contested – particularly by supporters of these social policies – for at least a decade.

The question of British 'ownership' of the welfare state concept is linked to the issue of timing. It is clear that the term *Wohlfahrtsstaat* was coined and widely used in Germany before its British equivalent was in general use (Petersen and Petersen, 2013). Equally, key proponents of interwar social reform in Britain and the authors of early English language texts in which the 'welfare state' was mentioned (among whom there was close contact) had a good knowledge of developments in Germany. That the relationship between German and British concepts and developments was complex is clear, but its precise character has yet to be described – and requires further research. Although more work is also needed on the post-war career of the welfare state concept, some of its characteristics are already reasonably clear. In particular, rather than being an indigenous development, the post-war (re-?) emergence of welfare state language to describe British social policy may have emanated from across the Atlantic. The US Right deployed the welfare state concept to counterattack the perceived spread of socialism before the phrase was widely used in post-war Britain.

The emergence of the welfare state concept in Britain before 1945

William Temple – who became Archbishop of Canterbury during the Second World War – is central to the conventional historiography of the welfare state concept, being widely regarded – celebrated – as its intellectual source. *The* senior figure in the Established Church of England, Temple was remarkably radical and politically engaged. Substantively, his association with 1940s social reform is justified. Temple led the Churches to support the 1944 Education Act and was an eloquent advocate of the Beveridge Report (1942), *Social Insurance and Allied Services*, in public meetings and the House of Lords (earning irate criticism from conservative Anglicans). Temple famously described the Report as "the first time anyone had set out to embody the whole spirit of the Christian ethic in an Act of Parliament" and, in a House of Lords debate on 25 February 1943, emphasised the positive impact on the "morale of the Army" of a clear government statement of intent to implement it. The Archbishop knew Beveridge well – and officiated at the religious ceremony to mark Beveridge's 1942 marriage. Temple was arguably politically the more radical man – unlike Beveridge, he had been a member of the Labour Party (between 1918 and 1925). His reputation as a social reformer probably rests most heavily on *Christianity and Social Order* (1976 [1942]), which set out a general case for Church involvement in public affairs and a detailed social reform programme.

Christianity and Social Order might be read as a companion volume to *Social Insurance and Allied Services* (Beveridge, 1942): together they helped to generate wartime support for social reform. For a historian of concepts they share another striking feature: neither used the term 'the welfare state'. It is well established that Beveridge disliked the phrase (see Harris, 1977: 459–64); to him it evoked a Santa Claus-like gift-giving state, not the contribution based social insurance scheme he proposed. By contrast, Temple did deploy the 'welfare state' phrase – doing so in *Citizen and Churchman* (1941), a more scholarly and abstract text published immediately before *Christianity and Social Order*. Temple affirmed the welfare state as based on 'Christian presuppositions' (1941: 35). But there is something elusive about Temple's 'welfare state': he used the term only once in *Citizen and Churchman*. Its meaning is established as much through negation as the elements it denoted directly. The

'Welfare-State' is not a 'Power-State'; its 'essence' is not power, but 'its function as the fountain and upholder of Law' ... which possesses ... 'force [only] ... because Law must be enforced' (1941: 35). Temple's use of the 'welfare state' term only once in *Citizen and Churchman* poses something of a puzzle, particularly because it has been treated as the original statement of the concept (Petersen and Petersen, 2013 identify Bruce, 1961; Titmuss, 1963; Heidenheimer, 1983; and Gregg, 1967; Woodroffe, 1968 and Lowe, 2005 with, respectively, the first use, first written use or popularising of the term). Might we expect a new idea to have been produced with more of a flourish? This lonely reference does suggest that Temple did not see the welfare state as a key term or overarching framework for social reform. Despite his major contribution to social reform in 1940s Britain, it is tempting to conclude that Temple's place in the pantheon of founding figures for (the idea of) the 'welfare state' is based on a post hoc conflation of his two (important) texts. Together they could be (mis)taken as a social plan based on a coherent welfare state concept.

By the mid-1980s, the historiographic problem posed by Temple seemed to have been dissolved. Historians (Pelling, 1985; Ashford, 1986) identified an earlier 'welfare state' reference in Alfred Zimmern's 1934 lecture *Quo Vadimus?* (Zimmern, 1934a; Bruce, 1961; Woodroffe, 1968 had mentioned Zimmern, but without a written source.) Zimmern was a colleague and friend of Temple – both were classicists and had been young academics together at Oxford in the early years of the 20th century. Zimmern went on to become the founding figure for the discipline of International Relations in British academia, being the inaugural holder of both the Woodrow Wilson Chair of International Politics at Aberwystwyth (the first position of its kind anywhere in the world) and of the Montague Burton Chair of International Relations at Oxford. In *Never Again* (1992) Peter Hennessy had powerfully underscored the priority of Zimmern over Temple in deploying the welfare state concept. But the story does not stop here. Although neglected in mainstream British and welfare state historiography (until Petersen and Petersen, 2013 – earlier references in Nicholls, 1989: 31–60, Grimley, 2004), Temple had used the welfare state even earlier, in his *Christianity and the State* lectures, published in 1928. Here, Temple addressed the Church–State issue, covering both the internal and external relations of the state. Once more the 'Welfare-state' was defined in contrast to the 'power-state' and, again, Temple used the term once in 200 pages.

In themselves, these earlier uses of the welfare state term do little to resolve the problem of its origin: they were only marginally less gnomic than that in *Citizen and Churchmen*. As mentioned earlier, Temple and Zimmern were close friends as young dons at Oxford. Despite their friendship, however, there is no evidence of cross-referencing in the key published works. Nevertheless the two men shared a strikingly consistent usage of the 'welfare state' phrase between 1928 and 1941. They shared the contrast between 'power' and 'welfare' state (Temple hyphenated both expressions) which connected the internal principles and values of a state to its expected behaviour in international – or more precisely interstate – relations. The temptation to speculate that Temple and Zimmern may have discussed or collaborated on these concepts – or owe them to some common, unknown source or wider circle – is strong. It would also be a mistake to assume that the power/welfare state distinction remained an obscure obsession of a few (admittedly influential) Oxford intellectuals: it was a key target of E.H. Carr's coruscation of 'utopian' international relations theory in his hugely influential and widely discussed *Twenty Years Crisis* (1939).

Two further points need to be made about the Temple/Zimmern welfare state concept. First, Petersen and Petersen rightly emphasise that neither 'Zimmern nor Temple understood the term "welfare state" in the modern sense as a social security system' (2013: 10), although perhaps they go too far in asserting that Temple's use of the 'contrast to the power state' meant that 'hence … it had *nothing to do with the welfare state as we understand it today* (as a social security system).' (2013: 9, emphasis added). Although the interwar English notion of the welfare state was not the same as the concept that was later applied to social insurance and social services, it denoted a state which served the community (in contrast, all other priorities were subservient to state power for the power state). Both men tended to focus on the characteristic external strategies of welfare or power states (collaborative peaceful liberalism and aggressive warmongering respectively). Equally, however, each sketched (closely similar) images of the internal character of the welfare state. While these images did not touch on social security or social insurance systems (about which, of course, Temple and Zimmern would have been aware), they were not inconsistent with wider normative characterisations of the welfare state that developed in the decades after the Second World War. Thus, for example, Temple wrote of 'inauguration of a new epoch' in which the 'State' operating 'under a specifically moral pressure, found itself impelled in the direction of regulating the welfare of its citizens in general' (1941: 32). Moreover, some 13 years earlier, he had argued 'it is plain that the State, which gives sanctions to such [property] rights, is fully entitled to determine what rights it will sanction, and is *as completely at liberty to redistribute property* as to protect its present owners in possession of it' (1928: 97, emphasis added). All in all, then, important family resemblances exist between themes in Temple and Zimmern and the broad conception of the welfare state that developed during the second half of the twentieth century.

Second, the Temple/Zimmern contrast between 'Power' and 'Welfare' has implications for the historiography of German influences on English ideas of the welfare state. Recent historiographical research has established that the term *Wohlfahrtsstaat* was used in Germany as early as the 1840s, and was deployed by prominent intellectuals through the 1870s and into the early decades of the twentieth century, albeit without much conceptual consistency (Petersen and Petersen, 2013: 3). That is, there is clear evidence of the concept having German, rather than British origins. Moreover, those who first deployed the welfare state phrase in Britain were familiar with German (academic) debates. There is, however, no direct evidence from the key texts that either Temple or Zimmern drew or borrowed from German usage.

Petersen and Petersen (2013: 6) 'found no examples of the term "Wohlfahrtsstaat" in political discussion of Bismarck's social reforms' and suggest 'the term did not truly enter the German political vocabulary before the interwar period' – indeed the authors argue that 'welfare state' was rarely used' during the 1920s, only coming into use 'in the very last years of the' Weimar 'Republic' (in other words, from about 1932). So the 1928 publication of *Christianity and the State* means Temple used the term *before* it came into political prominence in Germany. While in principle, the later usage by Temple and Zimmern could have been influenced by public debates in Germany, if Petersen and Petersen are correct, it is impossible that these debates influenced Temple's first published use of the 'welfare state' term.

More fundamentally, whatever its source, the content of the Temple/Zimmern power state/welfare state analysis suggests that it was *neither* rooted in, *nor* deeply influenced by, the German *Wohlfarhtsstaat* concept. Whether or not they saw the *Wohlfarhtsstaat* in a positive normative light, German analysts generally saw it in at least one of two ways: as quintessentially German (sometimes explicitly in contrast to Britain) and/or in opposition to the *rechtsstaat* or 'rule of law' (see Petersen and Petersen, 2013: 3–7). By contrast, in the original published statement of the English position, Temple identified Austria and Prussia as power states, while suggesting that England (and France) were welfare states (1928: 170). Relatedly, he attributed the 1914–18 War to a 'struggle between *Kultur* and the ideas of 1789 (1928: 169). Temple hoped that the 'establishment of the League of Nations' meant that 'the power state' had been 'swept into the limbo of forgotten idolatries' (1928: 171). Although Zimmern devoted much attention to the League, by 1934 he was understandably much more pessimistic about its prospects. Noting 'a recrudescence among the German people of the spirit and philosophy of militarism, accompanied by methods on the part of the government in power which run counter to the Rule of Law, and indeed to "civilisation itself"', Zimmern contrasted

> the political types represented on the one hand by the British Commonwealth and on the other by sovereign states of the conventional European kind … [the] one is a Realm of Law: the other is a portion of Power. … [In] the one … the state is simply an instrument needed to establish the good life for human beings, whilst in the other it becomes an object in itself to which human beings are subservient. We may call the one the Welfare State and the other the Power State. (Zimmern, 1934a: 31–2)

The contrast with Germany is, perhaps unexpectedly, effectively absent from Temple's wartime publications. He expressed some concern about the 'totalitarian state' (1941: 33; 1976 [1942]: 63), but his primary concern was with the church–state relationship. This absence of anti-German sentiment weakens any notion that Temple used the 'welfare state' idea as a motivating slogan for wartime anti-Nazi effort. Although the English theorists might have seen the Weimar Republic as an episode of welfare statism (as they understood the term) we have no evidence to support this interpretation. In short, for all that the *Wohlfahrtsstaat* term was better established from before the 1920s and more widely used in public debate during the 1930s, their use of the welfare state term does not appear to owe much to the prior German usage.

Finally, Temple and Zimmern generally seem to understand the welfare state and the rule of law as mutually supporting concepts. In contrast, some (not all) earlier German theorists contrasted the rule of law and welfare statism (see Petersen and Petersen, 2013: 4–5 – later US debates show a similar theme). While Temple 'readily admit[ted] that the State, as organ of the community, may … be concerned with all that takes place in the life of its community' and noted the 'moral pressure' impelling the state towards 'regulating the welfare of its citizens in general', he was also concerned that in 'such developments we see at work the principle which, if allowed free play unchecked and unbalanced, produces the Totalitarian State' (1941: 33). This was, nevertheless, a risk that existed at one extreme of what he understood as basically a sound social and political system, within which the state essentially served the community. He did note the 'equal concern' of non-state agencies with questions of welfare and the life of the community and their potential role as 'instruments for fulfilling' state 'Welfare' purposes (1928: 33). While offering a similar basic analysis of its relationship to the rule of law, Zimmern seemed less concerned that the welfare state might give way to a totalitarian form. This optimism was rooted in Zimmern's rosy view of the British Empire and Commonwealth, indeed ultimately of the government on the island of Britain itself, itself partly based on what he saw as the '*de-politicized nationality*' of the English (1934b [1926]: 186). By detaching English identity from British and Commonwealth political structures, Zimmern believed that the British State and Empire or Commonwealth had in them 'a principle of vitality ... the spirit of liberty'. 'The British Empire', he continued 'lives today because its institutions are free institutions' (1934b [1926]: 1–2). Making sense of this rich and pungent conceptual stew would require a separate analysis.

British State social reform from the mid-1940s

The British State embarked on a famous programme of social legislation from the mid-1940s. It began under the wartime coalition with the Education Act (1944) and Family Allowances Act (1945), but is most closely associated with Clement Attlee's post-war Labour government, which passed Acts for National Insurance (1946), National Health (1946) and National Assistance (1948). Given that the standard 'golden age' periodisation treats 1945 as *the* moment of 'welfare state' emergence, it is noteworthy that these legislative innovations were neither developed nor discussed under the welfare state rubric at the time. In fact, after Temple's brief allusion to the concept in 1941, there is little or no evidence of British social reforms being advanced or described in the language of the welfare state until the very end of the 1940s. Of course, Temple was an assiduous and eloquent advocate of the Beveridge report and allied social reforms more or less until he died in 1944. Yet he does not seem to have deployed the phrase 'the welfare state' in any of this advocacy – or no such record has yet been reported. So, although he did present social reform as a positive motivation for the British war effort, contrary to the standard historiography he did not do so in the language of the welfare state (compare Pierson, 1998: 99).

The phrase may not have been entirely unknown in Britain during the immediate post-war period. In fact, the first published post-war use of the term the present author has found dates from a 1946 article in *The Times*. Intriguingly, however, this is an article from *The Times*'Washington Correspondent concerned with November US mid-term elections. The analysis focuses on the likely Republican House of Representatives majority, which would 'return to the people' those 'extra-governmental functions' which the Democratic Administration has 'wrested' from states, counties and citizens. These 'extra-governmental functions' were associated with the ongoing creation of 'a "welfare" state, a process to which the first two years of Woodrow Wilson and the pre-war years of Franklin Roosevelt powerfully contributed'. Two other points are worth making here. First, in an echo of some themes from the early German debate, the 'welfare' state was explicitly depicted as superseding the 'legal' state. Second, the Washington Correspondent identified Britain as undergoing the same transformation from 'legal' state to 'welfare' state – a change described as occurring 'more fitfully' in the US than Britain (*The Times* 2 November 1946: 5). This suggests that the term welfare state was not entirely alien in Britain (at least to the extent that editors at *The Times* felt their readers would be able to make sense of it as a description of Britain) and that Britain served as a negative model of welfare state development in US political debate.

If Britain was used as a (negative) model welfare state in US political debate from 1946, this usage does not seem either to reflect or to have influenced the terms of British debate over ongoing Labour-led social reforms. While the 'golden age' epochalism which dominates commentary suggests 1945 as the welfare state's 'start date', sensitivity to the particular pattern of legislative and policy reform in Britain might point to a somewhat later date, say 1948, when (on 5 July) the new 'system' of social security came into operation, as the moment of emergence for the British welfare state. Even so, whether we look to political cartoons (Wincott, 2011: 359–60), the record of British Parliamentary debate (Hay and Wincott, 2012: 17), or textual evidence from newspapers (as the editors of this volume indicate in the introduction), 1949 stands out as the year in which the 'welfare state' phrase broke through into political debate. In other words, the application of this term to Britain occurred, it seems, only after the completion of the Attlee-led social reform legislation. On the eve of the operationalisation of the new system, Attlee broadcast a speech on 'The New Social Services and the Citizen' (1949). While he emphasised the systematic nature of the new policies, the conceptual framework within which he understood them was primarily that of social *security*, allied to social *insurance* and social *services*, but not the welfare state – a phrase he did not use in this speech.

The initial use of the welfare state phrase in parliamentary debate about Britain occurred in April 1949, as a derogatory term used by Conservative critics of Labour's social reforms (see Hay and Wincott, 2012: 17). The content of newspaper usage of welfare state language from 1949 is instructive. It is not clear that its initial major focus was social reform legislation or the institutions and policies it created – nor indeed that the discussion identified Britain as the leading example of a welfare state. So, for example, the first sustained discussion of the welfare states in *The Times* during 1949 seems to have been published in May and opened with the following statement:

> A movement towards the development of the welfare State, or the social democratic State, or whatever it may be called, has been common to most western European nations since the war. This was already true in the preceding quarter of a century, but the atmosphere of the period since the war has given fresh stimulus. The chief features are the increasing concern, some would say interference, of the Government with the day-to-day lives of the people, the growing influence of workers' representatives on the conduct of affairs, and provision for social security. (*The Times* 27 May 1949: 5)

This statement hardly accords with the suggestion that the post-war conception of the welfare state had distinctively British origins (as implied, for example, by Briggs, 1961), or with the notion that it was a specifically post-war phenomenon, or even with the suggestion that social security was central to the idea of the welfare state – never mind the National Health Service (NHS) or education. Indeed, the main theme of the article was the reluctance of the British government to use legislative compulsion to impose wage restraint or joint consultation between employers and workers. British voluntarism was contrasted with legislative action in both fields by the Benelux countries. This difference between the 'British' and 'the Continental preference' is one that has echoed through analyses of European political economy ever since. By offering a characterisation that seems to encompass wide swathes of industrial relations and economic organisation, it is also an analysis that offers an unusually broad characterisation of the British welfare state (one that may be more typical of conceptualisations of Continental welfare states).

It did not take long for an image of the welfare state that would, at least in some respects, be more familiar to contemporary British observers to emerge. By October 1949, *The Times* was reporting on a major speech by Attlee: the first reason for the familiarity of this speech was its discussion of abuse of the NHS – and the introduction of charges for medication prescriptions to curb one such abuse, the second its central theme of cuts in public spending (of £250 million) due to poor economic performance. In contrast to his speech welcoming the introduction of the New Social Services in July 1948, by October 1949 Attlee had begun to use the language of the welfare state as a positive label for these policies. It should be noted, however, that he did so *prospectively*, stating that 'creating the Welfare State, the state which seeks security and happiness for all' was a task 'we have set ourselves … in this country'. And while 'Great progress has been made. [T]he Welfare State can only endure if it is built on a sound economic foundation'. Attlee 'sought to make' the necessary 'heavy cuts in expenditure' 'in such a way as not to impair seriously the great structure of social services which has been built up and which we intend to preserve' (*The Times*, 25 October 1949: 2). Nevertheless the 'welfare state' term was introduced into British public debate not primarily as a celebration of the social reform successes of the Attlee government, but rather in the context of anxieties about economic performance and retrenchment. And these concerns were neither isolated nor passing: anxieties that would be familiar to observers from the late 1970s onwards were articulated in the press throughout the 1950s. For example, as early as February 1952, *The Times* carried an extended report over two consecutive days by a special correspondent on the very modern theme of 'Crisis in the Welfare State' (*The Times* 25 February 1952: 7, 26 February 1952: 5).

Even if 1949 marks the emergence of the welfare state as a term of widespread currency, it would be wrong to assume that any welfare state *concept* came to be widely accepted from that date across expert, policy and public debate as providing the appropriate language in which to discuss social insurance and services. The concept was certainly not an essential taken for granted part of the conceptual landscape of social analysis. For example, although subsequently widely understood and deployed as the key conceptual statement of its theory, T.H. Marshall did not use the term 'the welfare state' in his landmark 1949 lecture on *Citizenship and Social Class* (1992 [1950]). Instead, contemporary analysts tended to discuss 'the social services' and perhaps also 'social security' or 'social insurance' rather than the welfare state.

The 'welfare state' gained ground in public debate during the 1950s and into the 1960s as a term with positive connotations, as in the discussion of Poverty and the Welfare State by Rowntree and Lavers (1951). However, many key experts in social administration and social policy – who were generally also advocates of expanded social provision – displayed a striking ambivalence about or hostility towards its use. So, for example, in the early 1950s Titmuss was already discussing the 'so-called Welfare State' (1951: 412) and describing 'a nation' clinging 'sentimentally to the label of 'welfare state'' (1952: 260). By the late 1950s he was concerned to expose the 'welfare state myth', while worrying that state welfare might become cut off from other means of providing welfare (1963 [1958] , see the discussion in Wincott, 2011: 358–9). As early as 1951, Marshall lamented 'misconceptions about Britain … partly in consequence of the use of that imprecise term, the 'welfare State'' (*The Times* 14 September 1951: 5). Even Rowntree and Lavers whose analysis of poverty in York used the term in its title, referred to the welfare state no more than a couple of times in the body of the text (1951: 53, 58).

Use of the language of the welfare state as a positive term, signalling approval of the new social policies and practices did begin to emerge in the early 1950s, but it came largely from outside the mainstream of British social administration. Exemplary here is Wolfgang Friedmann's 1951 monograph *Law and Social Change in Contemporary Britain*. Although this early, sustained analysis of the British welfare state by a German émigré, London School of Economics (LSE) based academic lawyer might suggest a range of possible intellectual lineages and links, the evidence suggests that Friedmann was influential in US rather than UK welfare debates (Wincott, 2011: 364–66).

Instead, the development of the welfare state as a key concept for British social analysts probably occurred in left-wing circles – and through publications associated with the new left (such as *The New Reasoner* and *The Socialist Register*), rather than in more conventional academic journals. Once again, it began with a critique: John Saville analysed the problems posed to the Labour movement by the emergence of the welfare state (1957–58). Saville explicitly downplayed the significance of the post-war Labour government and traced the origins of the welfare state back through Edwardian and into Victorian Britain. Saville's analysis provoked an immediate response from critics, who seem to have been more sympathetic to Attlee's administration (Hatch, 1958: 125; Thompson, 1958: 127). Friedmann aside, Saville's critics may be among the first intellectuals to use the welfare state as a positive term broadly indicating approbation of these policies. Asa Briggs used the welfare state phrase more clearly as a term of approval at the start of the 1960s (Briggs, 1961). The earlier use of the 'welfare state' term by leading figures (Marshall, Titmuss) in the study of social administration had been critical (in the scholarly sense) – apparently seeking to delegitimise the phrase, even to squeeze it out of the debate. So, perhaps it is only once this attempt to marginalise it had failed that we can speak of the concept having become established as central to the conceptual framework for the analysis of state social provision in Britain. Arguably, that moment may only have come with the publication of Dorothy Wedderburn's (1965) review of the 'Facts and Theories about the Welfare State' – in a debate within British socialism, published in *The Socialist Register* – much later, that is, than the conventional wisdom would hold.

Conclusion

Only recently has the conceptual history of the welfare state begun to claim the attention it deserves. A major theme of the new conceptual historical sociology of welfare is the debunking of the myth of the welfare state's 'golden age'. And the British case occupies a pivotal position within that fantastic narrative: serving as the template for mythical origins of the welfare state as a post-1945 phenomenon. Here, we have begun to see that closer attention to the historical record suggests that welfare state concepts emerged both *too soon* and *too late* to accord with the standard account of the post-war welfare state. This combination is particularly damaging for the received theory – as it shows that the welfare state terminology *was* available to Labour's post-war social reformers, but *was not* taken up by them. Others have shown conclusively that the concept had a German history that significantly predates its use in the British case – although so far analysis of the emergence of the phrase in English does not suggest that it owes much to the earlier German literature. By contrast, there are some initial indications that the adoption of the term in post-war Britain may owe something to the way it was taken up in US political debate. More research is required on both topics. Finally, if the new conceptual historical sociology has quickly discovered that its foundations are shaky, we need to ask how our received image of a thirty year post-war 'golden age' of the British welfare state was constructed and why it has remained so strong. It seems likely that our understanding of the past was decisively shaped by (mis)conceptions thrown up in later struggles over welfare state development and, especially, retrenchment. In the long term, if later welfare provision is compared with an idealised image of a golden past that never actually existed, the terms of debate will be set against pro-welfare state propositions.

References

Ashford, D. (1986) *The Emergence of the Welfare State,* London: Basil Blackwell.

Attlee, C. (1949) *'The New Social Services and the Citizen'*, www.bbc.co.uk/archive/nhs/5147.shtml

Beveridge, W. (1942) *Social Insurance and Allied Services* (the 'Beveridge Report'), Cmnd 6404, London: HMSO.

Briggs, A. (1961) 'The welfare state in historical perspective', *Archives Européennes de Sociologie,* II: 221–258.

Bruce, M. (1961) *The Coming of the Welfare State,* London: Batsford.

Carr E.H. (1939) *The Twenty Years Crisis,* London: Macmillan.

Dunleavy, P. (1989) 'The United Kingdom: Paradoxes of Ungrounded Statism', in F. Castles (ed.) *The Comparative History of Public Policy,* Cambridge: Polity.

Ferrera, M. (2005) *The Boundaries of Welfare,* Oxford: Oxford University Press.

Friedmann, W. (1951) *Law and Social Change in Contemporary Britain* London: Steven and Sons

Gregg, P. (1967) *The Welfare State,* London: George G. Harrap & Co.

Grimley, M. (2004) *Citizenship, Community and the Church of England: Liberal Anglican Theories of the State between the Wars,* Oxford: Clarendon Press.

Harris, J. (1977) *William Beveridge: A Biography,* Oxford: Clarendon Press.

Hatch, S. (1958) 'The welfare state', *The New Reasoner,* Spring, 4: 125.

Hay, C. and D. Wincott. (2012) *The Political Economy of European Welfare Capitalism,* London: Palgrave.

Heidenheimer, A.J. (1983) 'Secularization patterns and the westward spread of the welfare state: two dialogues about how and why Britain, the Netherlands, and the United States have differed', *Comparative Social Research,* 6: 3–38.

Hennessy, P. (1992) *Never Again: Britain 1945–1951.* London: Vintage.

Lowe, R. (2005) *The Welfare State in Britain since 1945.* London: Palgrave.

Marshall T.H. (1992) [1950], 'Citizenship and social class' in T.H. Marshall and T. Bottomore *Citizenship and Social Class,* London: Pluto.

Nicholls, D. (1989) *Deity and Domination,* London: Routledge.

Pelling, H. (1985) *The Labour Governments 1945–1951,* London: Macmillan.

Petersen, K. and J.H. Petersen (2013) 'Confusion and divergence: origins and meanings of the term "welfare state" in Germany and Britain, 1840–1940', *Journal of European Social Policy,* vol 23, no.1: 1–15.

Pierson, C. (1998) *Beyond the Welfare State* (2nd edn), Cambridge: Polity.

Rowntree, B.S. and G.R. Lavers (1951) *Poverty and the Welfare State*, London: Longman.

Saville, J.(1957/58) 'The welfare state: an historical approach', *New Reasoner,* Winter, 3: 5-25.

Somers, M. (2008) *The Genealogy of Citizenship*, Cambridge: Cambridge University Press.

Temple, W. (1928) *Christianity and the State*, London: Macmillan.

Temple, W. (1941) *Citizen and Churchman*, London: Eyre & Spottiswoode.

Temple, W. (1976) [1942] *Christianity and Social Order*, London: Shepheard-Walwyn.

The Times (1946, 2 November: 5) 'US mid-term elections. Republican prospects in the lower house. Party alignments in a "welfare" state'.

The Times (27 May 1949: 5) The welfare state. Leading article.

The Times (25 October 1949: 2). Home news. Mr. Attlee's broadcast. the task of the welfare State.

The Times (14 September 1951: 5) The welfare state. Leading article.

The Times (25 February 1952: 7) Crisis in the welfare state. The "Beveridge Principles". By our special correspondent.

The Times (26 February 1952: 5) Crisis in the welfare state. Ends and means. By our special correspondent.

Thompson, D. (1958) The welfare state, *New Reasoner,* Spring, 4: 125-130.

Titmuss, R. (1951) 'Family problems in the welfare state', *The Listener,* 15 March: 411-412.

Titmuss, R. (1952) 'Crisis in the social services', *The Listener,* 14 February: 259-260.

Titmuss, R. (1963) 'The welfare state: images and realities', *Social Service Review,* 37, 1: 1–11.

Wedderburn, D. (1965) `Facts and theories about the welfare state', *Socialist Register,* 2: 127-146.

Wincott, D. (2011) 'Images of welfare in law and society: the British welfare state in comparative perspective' *Journal of Law and Society,* 38, 3: 343-375

Wincott, D. (2013) The (golden) age of the welfare state: interrogating a conventional wisdom, *Public Administration,* 91(4): 806-822.

Woodroffe, K. (1968) The Making of the Welfare State in England: a summary of its origin and development', *Journal of Social History* 1, 4: 303–324.

Zimmern, A. (1934a) *Quo Vadimus?* London: Oxford University Press.

Zimmern, A. (1934b) [1926] *The Third British Empire* London: Oxford University Press.

SEVEN

Social policy concepts and language in France

Daniel Béland[73]

This volume explores the politics and history of social policy language and concepts. A country associated with both universalism and a unique Republican political culture, France is an interesting case for the analysis of social policy language because of the contested nature of the very concepts that help define what social policy is about. Another reason to turn attention to France is the influence of this country on international policy debates, within the European Union and beyond. For instance, the concept of social exclusion, which has now entered the international policy vocabulary, first emerged as a 'keyword' in France, before it was diffused through international policy networks (Béland, 2007). Thus, the French case is fascinating in part because it allows us to understand the specific nature of national policy debates while acknowledging their international dimension.

This chapter is comprised of four main sections. The first two sections respectively explore the development of the concepts of *sécurité sociale* and *État-providence* in France. These sections each trace the history of one of these concepts, before explaining why is has become politically contentious. The last two main sections delve into the French Republican political culture and discourse to explore the ideas of solidarity and social exclusion, respectively. The chapter's Conclusion stresses some basic lessons drawn from the French case for the broad analysis of social policy language and concepts.

Social security

Popularised in the United States during and after the New Deal, the term 'social security' (*Sécurité sociale*) became an enduring 'keyword'

[73] The author thanks Jenny Andersson, Jean-Claude Barbier, and Klaus Petersen for their comments on previous drafts of this chapter. He also acknowledges support from the Canada Research Chairs Program.

(Williams, 1976; see also Fraser and Gordon, 1994) in France's social policy language in the aftermath of the 1944 Liberation.[74] At the time, the 1942 Beveridge report (*Social Insurance and Allied Services*) motivated what became a failed attempt to unify the fragmented social insurance system that had emerged in France during the first decades of the 20th century (for example Hatzfeld, 1971; Rosanvallon, 1981; Baldwin, 1990; Palier and Bonoli, 1995). In France, the term 'social security' typically refers to the social insurance schemes central to the French social policy system. In a textbook on 'social security', for instance, Georges Dorion and André Guionnet (1995: 14) enumerate the key components of that fragmented system: health insurance, parental leave, disability insurance, death insurance, workers' compensation, old-age insurance and family benefits. What is striking about this list is the absence of unemployment insurance. This absence stems from the fact that France did not create a modern unemployment insurance scheme until 1958.[75] Because this scheme was enacted long after the consolidation of 'social security' in 1945, and because unemployment insurance is not under state control but under the exclusive responsibility of the 'social partners' (that is to say, business and labour organisations), this major type of social insurance does not formally belong to French 'social security' (Barbier and Théret, 2004: 4). The same remark applies to social assistance programmes, which are formally distinct from 'social security', in part because they emerged before it (Bec, 1998). From this perspective, the exclusion of unemployment insurance and social assistance from what is commonly referred to in France as 'social security' reflects particular national – and historical – trends in social policy development.

Despite the relative consensus about the meaning of this term in France, when the 'social partners' and their relationship to the state are concerned, the boundaries of 'social security' have long been contested. From the start, labour unions became administrative players in the governance of the post-war 'social security' system. At a broad level, French unions saw 'social security' as a 'labour conquest' that became part of an effort to democratise France after the dark years of the Vichy regime (Galant, 1955; Palier, 2002: 86). As for business organisations, it is only after a long political struggle that they became full 'partners' within French 'social security', where they hold half of the

---

[74] This section and the next are adapted from Béland, 2011.

[75] Before the creation of this unemployment insurance system (ASSEDIC), social assistance was the only form of unemployment relief in France (Rosanvallon, 1981). On the history of social assistance in France see Bec (1998).

appointments on the various social insurance boards. Called *paritarisme*, this type of institutional arrangement means that labour and business organisations share half of the board appointments (Guillemard, 2000). At first, labour representatives boldly opposed business participation in social insurance boards, which they saw as an exclusive labour domain (Friot, 1998: 177–8). To this day, in France, the respective role of labour and business organisations in 'social security' remains controversial (Béland and Marier, 2006). This is also true of the state's involvement in the 'social security' system, which has increased in recent decades, in a context characterised by attempts to control costs and lower payroll contributions in the name of 'economic competitiveness'. Although the state has always played a key role in 'social security' by providing a legal framework for the system, since the 1980s, France has witnessed what has been understood as a gradual takeover of the state in policy areas like health care (Palier, 2002). On the left of the political spectrum, this growing financial and regulatory role of the state is sometimes depicted as an attack against the labour movement's prerogatives (Friot, 1998).

État-providence

This discussion about the role of the state in 'social security' leads to an analysis of the phrase *État-providence*, which is the French equivalent of the English language term 'welfare state'. More controversial than the concept of 'social security', *État-providence* is not a core element of French political discourse, and some academics and bureaucrats avoid the term altogether. For example, in a 1998 'bilingual glossary' on social policy, there is no entry for *État-providence* (Portonnier, 1998). In the same glossary, the discussion about the English language term 'welfare state' claims that *État-providence* is not an accurate translation of this term, partly because *État-providence* 'tends to have a negative implication' (Révauger and Spicker, 1998: 251). To understand this remark and why many French social policy experts perceive the concept of *État-providence* as problematic, at least two main factors must be taken into account: the historical origin of this French language expression, and its explicit emphasis on the state (*État*) as a 'providential' source of welfare benefits (which could imply it faces a passive citizenry and labour movement).

For Jean-Claude Barbier and Bruno Théret (2004: 3), one should avoid the term *État-providence* for the following reasons:

> Generally considered as the equivalent to what the British call the *welfare state*, the notion of *État-providence* seems

> unsatisfactory. Pierre Rosanvallon, in his short 1981 book *La Crise de l'État-providence*, re-popularized this old-fashioned expression, used pejoratively by liberal thinkers opposed to any social legislation, at the very moment when the legitimacy of social protection was contested on the political scene.[76]

The influence of Rosanvallon's 1981 book cannot be overstated, as this bestseller has been widely read and criticised in France.[77] Drawing on the 1970s English language literature about 'the fiscal crisis of the state' (O'Connor, 1973), Rosanvallon (1981) places the French debate on the future of social policy in a broad international context. This is possibly why he uses the expression *État-providence*, which he explicitly relates to the English language phrase 'welfare state'.[78]

As Rosanvallon (1981) himself notes, however, *État-providence* is an old French term coined by opponents of state intervention during the 19th century, decades before the concept of 'welfare state' diffused across the world, starting in the 1940s. For French sociologist Robert Castel (2003), the polemical and antistatist origin of the phrase *État-providence* is one good reason for banning it altogether from the contemporary French social policy language (Castel, 2003: 258).

The first known pejorative occurrence of the word 'providence' in relation to state action appeared in 1849, in an issue of labour newspaper *l'Atelier*. In that issue, labour advocate Anthime Corbon stated that, 'more than one exploited [worker] awaits Providence, in the form of government, to arrive and extract him from the filth with no effort on his own part' (Corbon, quoted in Castel, 2003: 258; see also Cuvillier, 1954: 222). Less than 20 years later, other critics of state intervention such as reformer Émile Laurent (1865: 267) condemned the alleged French tendency to back what he called the *État-providence*, which he tied to Gracchus Babeuf's revolutionary despotism' (that is to say, socialistic authoritarianism).

---

[76] Quote translated from French by Daniel Béland. According to Barbier (2008), another author who helped re-popularize the term *État-providence* in France is researcher Alain Cottereau (1989).

[77] In fact, this book was even featured in Cédric Klapisch's 2002 hit movie *L'Auberge espagnole*, where it symbolises the archetypical French textbook.

[78] The connection between the term *État-providence* and the international, English language literature transcends his book, as the French translation of Gøsta-Esping Andersen's *The Three Worlds of Welfare Capitalism* (1990) bears the title *Les trois mondes de l'État-providence*, which is not an exact translation of the original, English language title (Esping-Andersen, 1999).

As suggested earlier, French scholars like Barbier and Théret (2004) agree with Castel (2003) that the polemic and antistatist past of the term *État-providence* is a good reason for rejecting it, at least as an analytical concept.[79] If Castel employs the term '*État social*', Barbier and Théret (2004) prefer the less controversial concept of '*protection sociale*' (social protection), which is used in France as a synonym for 'social policy' (Barbier, 2008: 26).

The other main reason why the phrase *État-providence* is contested in France is that it refers only to the state component of a social policy system in which employers and labour unions have long played a key role. This is why actors who defend this aspect of French 'social security' reject the term *État-providence* altogether. For instance, left-wing economist Bernard Friot (1998) argues that, in France, the term *État-providence* is meaningless because it reflects a statist vision of social policy that is dominant in Britain but not in his country.[80] As Friot puts it (1998: 37), 'if the expression État-providence could mean something in a Beveridge-style country, it thus makes no sense in a country like ours'.[81] In his book, this author criticises the growing role of direct state financing as an alternative to social insurance contributions.

Even if Castel (2003) does not emphasise this role of 'social partners' in his bold case for rejecting the phrase *État-providence*, one of his arguments against it is that the word '*providence*' may create the impression that social policy is only about passive recipients who are dependent upon state benevolence. More importantly, for Castel (2003: 258), this understanding 'does not take into account its *intermediary* position between the various groups of opposing interests. Yet it is precisely this intermediary position of the state that explains its specific actions'.

First published in 1995, alongside Rosanvallon's second essay on the topic (1995), Castel's work is probably the most influential French social policy book of the 1990s. Considering this, Castel's strong opposition to the phrase *État-providence* cannot be overlooked. But as the above remarks suggest, this is not only about Castel, as the term *État-providence* is more controversial in France than the phrase 'welfare state' is in Britain, for example. This is why *État-providence* is everything but a consensual 'keyword' in contemporary French academic, political,

---

[79]   Barbier (2008: 21) even suggests that, when properly understood in its historical context, the English language equivalent of *État-providence* is 'nanny state' rather than 'welfare state'.

[80]   This basic view is shared by Barbier (2008: 22).

[81]   Quote translated from French by Daniel Béland.

and social discourse. In fact, this term never became a feature of French everyday language and mainstream political discourse (Barbier, 2008: 21). This situation has not prevented some prominent French scholars, sometimes with reluctance (Merrien, 2003), from employing the concept of *État-providence* in their work (for example Ewald, 1986; Bourdelais et al, 1996; Majnoni d'Intignano, 1997; de Luca, 2002).

Solidarity

At a deeper social and political level, in France, political discourse on social programmes is grounded in the Republican tradition, which is inimical to the liberal, individualistic and pro-market language ever present within the Anglo-American world. Instead, since the last quarter of the 19th century, this tradition has stressed the role of solidarity in French society. Although the concept of solidarity is not unique to France, within its Republican political culture, it has taken specific French meanings over the years (Béland and Hansen, 2000).

In France, solidarity became a powerful political concept in the last decades of the 19th century, an era during which politicians and public intellectuals of the recently established Third Republic (1870–1940) attempted to address what was known as the 'social question'. This issue concerned the status of workers in the new industrial era and the struggle between liberalism and socialism as alternative visions of economic and social regulation (Donzelot, 1994 [1984]). Because the advent of the Republic as a political regime did not solve the 'social question', politicians and public intellectuals debated potential ways to fight the socioeconomic insecurity stemming from urbanisation and industrialisation.

Employed decades before by philosopher Pierre Leroux and reframed by well-known figures of the Third Republic like sociologist Émile Durkheim and politician Léon Bourgeois, the concept of solidarity became a 'keyword' in France (Humphreys, 1999) and the central element of solidarism, which Jack Hayward (1961) described as 'the official social philosophy of the French Third Republic'.[82] For Bourgeois, the most central figure of solidarism, then recent trends in biology suggested that, in contrast to what advocates of market liberalism and social Darwinism argued, cooperation rather than competition is the vital principle of both nature and social order (Bourgeois, 1998 [1896]: 23–24). Because all beings are organically tied together in a world of cooperation, interdependence is the dominant

---

[82]   In France, solidarity first emerged as a juridical concept: Hayward, 1959.

positive force in human life, a reality that should be recognised by all. In fact, the interdependence at the centre of human life creates powerful social obligations, which arise from the acknowledgement that each individual has a debt towards the rest of society (Bourgeois, 1998 [1896]: 39). Legitimising social law and social rights (Horne, 2002: 119), the alleged existence of this debt and the more general concept of solidarity justified the development of mutualism and, later on, once the limits of voluntarism became clear, the creation of social insurance schemes. Overall, from the late 19th century on, in the context of the French Republican political culture, the idea of solidarity formed part of the ideological construction of modern social policy in France (Béland, 2009).

Embedded in the Republican tradition and language, solidarity remains a central term in French politics and social policy discourse. This is why references to solidarity abound in contemporary French social science and policy debates (Chevallier, 1992; Rosanvallon, 1995; Paugam, 2007). Yet, in that country, solidarity is a contested concept actors use to frame specific policy proposals. For instance, extensive references to intergenerational solidarity have been made to assess, criticise, or justify various pension reform proposals, both on the left and the right (for example Hénin and Weitzenblum, 2004: 17).

A discussion about the ongoing debate on the future of social insurance illustrates the enduring role of solidarity as a contested 'keyword' in France. As part of this debate, there is a political tension between the 'occupational solidarity' (*solidarité professionnelle*) associated with the fragmented French social insurance system, and the idea of 'national solidarity' associated with citizenship and the role of the state (Béland and Hansen, 2000). This tension is crucial in Pierre Rosanvallon's 1995 book on the future of social policy, in which he stresses the need to expand 'national solidarity' (and the tax based financing associated with it) at the expense of 'occupational solidarity', which is synonymous with social insurance fragmentation. In this book and beyond, the call for 'national solidarity' legitimises Beveridgean statism and a push for universal social citizenship against the occupational logic of Bismarckian social insurance, which has largely dominated French social policy since the late 19th century (Rosanvallon, 1995). This discussion about citizenship and national solidarity points to the issue of social exclusion, which has been central in France since the late 1980s. Now used all around the world, social exclusion is a concept that was coined in France, in the context of a Republican tradition in which solidarity and citizenship inclusion are closely related, at least in political and social policy discourse (Béland and Hansen, 2000).

Social exclusion

The term 'exclusion' (known in English as 'social exclusion' but typically referred to as 'the exclusion' in France) emerged in the mid-1960s, when social commentator Jean Klanfer (1965) used the term to refer to people who are unable to enjoy the rewards of economic prosperity due to irresponsible behaviour.[83] A decade later, René Lenoir (1974) saw 'the excluded' as people who are separated from mainstream society due to factors such as disability, mental illness, and poverty. Even if the meaning of 'exclusion' has changed since the mid-1970s, Lenoir's book is considered as the founding document of the modern social exclusion discourse in France (Frétigné, 1999: 63).

In the 1980s and 1990s, the rise of long-term unemployment and concerns about racism and discrimination helped transform the meaning of social exclusion, a concept typically defined as the lack of social integration related to limited economic opportunities. From this angle, social exclusion is widely perceived as a threat to France's Republican model of integration based on the ideas of citizenship and social solidarity. The discourse about poorer, ethnically diverse French suburbs (*banlieues*) implicitly tied long-term unemployment with geographical isolation. 'The very word *la banlieue*, which creates an image of crime and indigence, graffiti and burned-down cars cut-off from Paris and other French cities highlights the extent to which the extreme deprivation of segments of French society is marginal to the majority's daily existence and life chances' (Béland and Hansen, 2000: 54). In the 1990s, the concept of social exclusion became widely used in French policy and political discourse in part because it reflected and summarised deep anxieties about the future of France's institutions and society, in a context of global economic and social anxieties.

As used in France, 'exclusion' is distinct from 'poverty' and other concepts used to define contemporary social problems in at least two major ways. First, this term has a biographical meaning, as it refers to the personal experience of social and economic isolation typically associated with issues like unemployment and discrimination (Goguel d'Allondans, 2003: 43). Second, social exclusion is grounded in a horizontal, spatial metaphor rather than a vertical understanding of inequality focusing mainly on income disparities (Béland, 2007).

---

[83] The following discussion draws on Béland, 2007. On the history of the concept of social exclusion in France see Silver, 1994; Paugam, 1996; Goguel d'Allondans, 2003.

Beyond these two issues, at the broadest level, the concept of social exclusion can lead to an overly static vision of economic and social order, in which pathways of marginalisation are poorly understood. This is why sociologists such as Robert Castel (2003 [1995]) have rejected it.

Despite these insightful scholarly criticisms, the concept of social exclusion helped legitimise major social policy reforms in France. A clear example of this social exclusion discourse is at the core of Rosanvallon's influential 1995 essay on social policy, which combines the focus on national solidarity mentioned earlier with a call to recognise that the fight against social exclusion necessitates a rethinking of French social programmes. This is true because, for Rosanvallon (1995), the traditional French social insurance system is unable to effectively tackle social exclusion, a task that requires the enactment of new, tax funded programmes aimed at promoting activation and social inclusion, in the name of national solidarity. Even if Rosanvallon's essay is highly controversial, it points to the fact that, in France, the language of solidarity and the language of social exclusion are closely related, at least in the policy discourse.

The popularity of these two concepts stems at least in part from their ideological ambiguity, as they have been used extensively, on the left as well as on the right, to legitimise contrasted policy alternatives. Semantic ambiguity is a potential political asset (Palier, 2005), as it can help bring together coalitions across partisan and ideological divides. This is true because various constituencies can understand concepts such as solidarity and social exclusion in different ways, which may push them to support social policy proposals legitimised in reference to these ideologically and politically ambiguous keywords.

In part because of its ambiguity and related coalition-building quality, the concept of social exclusion has become increasingly influential outside France (Béland, 2007). Such a diffusion process started in the 1980s, when European Commission President Jacques Delors stressed the need for a strong 'social dimension' to the European project. Following this logic, the fight against social exclusion became a European issue. During the 1990s, 'the third EU "poverty programme" was gradually transformed into a fight against social exclusion' (Silver and Miller, 2003: 5). The 2000 Lisbon Council reinforced this EU pledge to combat social exclusion (Begg and Berghman, 2002; van Berkel and Hornemann Møller, 2002). Simultaneously, at the national level, social exclusion became a popular concept in a number of European countries, including the UK, where Tony Blair embraced it, and gave it new meanings, as part of his Third Way government in the late 1990s (Levitas, 2005). Overall, social exclusion is a France-created concept that has had a rich transnational life (Béland, 2007). Although Jean-Claude Barbier (this volume) is right to stress the hegemony of English within European policy circles, the example of social exclusion suggests that non-English terms can have a transnational, European life. Further research should assess whether the story recounted here about social exclusion is part of a larger trend or simply an exception related to the fact that 'exclusion' is spelt the same way, and coveys the same basic meaning, in English and in French.

Conclusion

From the analysis given here, three main lessons can be drawn about the politics of social policy language and concepts, in France and even beyond. First, this case points to the contentious nature of some of the most central social policy concepts in France. As suggested earlier, in that country, *État-providence* is particularly contentious because the intellectuals and politicians who coined the term in the mid-19th century opposed state intervention, and because the term *État-providence* tends to convey the image of an ever powerful and benevolent state that generously offers social benefits to passive and unorganised citizens. Because labour unions are central actors in French 'social security', the idea of *État-providence* is anathema to those who seek to preserve their role. Yet, as 'social security' excludes social assistance and unemployment insurance programmes in France, there is no widely accepted phrase available in that country to subsume all of the state's core social policy activities (Béland, 2011). In France, as in other countries, the semantic struggles over social policy language and concepts point to the political debate over the very boundaries of state intervention (Alber, 1988).

Second, social policy language is embedded in particular, historically constructed political cultures that affect the meaning of key policy concepts. In the case of France, the concept of solidarity, which has been ever present in French social policy since the late 19th century, is closely related to the political and intellectual history of the Third Republic, under which this concept emerged as a response to the 'social question'. But the meaning of solidarity, just like that of social exclusion, has evolved over time in a changing economic, social, and political context. In this changing context, concepts like solidarity and social exclusion become framing devices that help actors make sense of the policy challenges they face while providing symbolic and ideological ammunition used in fights over specific policy proposals. Overall, in France as elsewhere, social policy language remains highly political as well as changing and yet historically rooted.

Finally, regarding the concept of social exclusion, it is fascinating to note that a concept that resonates so strongly within the French universalistic (Republican) tradition can travel so well and far, to a point where it has become a crucial part of the European and, to a certain extent, the global social policy vocabulary. The fact that social policy concepts emerge in specific national contexts does not mean that they cannot have a transnational life, as they can spread to countries with a different political culture and distinct policy institutions. Such diffusion generally involves a 'translation' or adaptation of foreign concepts so that they can properly 'fit in' to their country of adoption (Campbell, 2004). This is why the first Blair government was able to borrow and adapt the concept of social exclusion, which took a distinct political meaning in Britain (Levitas, 2005).

References

Alber, J. (1988) 'Continuities and changes in the idea of the welfare state', *Politics & Society*, 16(4): 451-468.

Baldwin, P. (1990) *The Politics of Social Solidarity: Class Bases of the European Welfare State 1875-1975*, Cambridge: Cambridge University Press.

Barbier, J.-C. (2008) *La longue marche de l'Europe sociale*, Paris: Presses Universitaires de France.

Barbier, J.-C. and Théret, B. (2004) *Le nouveau système français de protection sociale*. Paris: La Découverte.

Bec, C. (1998) *L'assistance en démocratie*. Paris: Belin.

Begg, I. G. and Berghman, J. (2002) 'Introduction: EU Social (exclusion) policy revisited?' *Journal of European Social Policy*, 12(3): 179-194.

Béland, D. (2007) 'The Social exclusion discourse: ideas and policy change', *Policy & Politics*, 35(1): 123-139.

Béland, D. (2009) 'Back to Bourgeois? French social policy and the idea of solidarity', *International Journal of Sociology and Social Policy*, 29(9/10): 445-456.

Béland, D. (2011) 'The politics of social policy language', *Social Policy & Administration*, 45(1): 1-18.

Béland, D. and Hansen, R. (2000) 'Reforming the French welfare state: solidarity, social exclusion and the three crises of citizenship', *West European Politics*, 23(1): 47-64.

Béland, D. and Marier, P. (2006) 'Protest avoidance: labor mobilization and social policy reform in France', *Mobilization*, 11(3): 297-311.

Bourdelais, P. et al. (1996) *État-providence: arguments pour une réforme*. Paris: Le Débat/ Gallimard.

Bourgeois, L. (1998) [1896] *Solidarité*. Villeneuve d'Ascq: Presses Universitaires du Septentrion.

Campbell, John L. (2004) *Institutional Change and Globalization*. Princeton: Princeton University Press.

Castel, R. (2003) [1995] *From Manual Workers to Wage Laborers: Transformation of the Social Question*. New Brunswick: Transaction Publishers.

Chevallier, J. (1992), 'Le réémergence du thème de la solidarité' in CURAPP [Centre Universitaire de Recherches Administratives et Politiques de Picardie] (eds) *La solidarité: un sentiment républicain?* Paris: Presses Universitaires de France.

Cottereau, A. (1989), 'Providence ou prévoyance? Les prises en charge de la santé des ouvriers, au cours des XIXe siècle britannique et français,' *Prévenir*, XIX: 21-51.

Cuvillier, A. (1954) *Un journal d'ouvriers: l'Atelier, 1840-1850*. Paris: Éditions ouvrières.

de Luca, V. (2002) *Aux origines de l'État-providence: Les Inspecteurs de l'Assistance publique et l'aide sociale à l'enfance, 1820-1930*. Paris: Presses Universitaires de France.

Donzelot, J. (1994) [1984] *L'invention du social: essai sur le déclin des passions politiques*, Paris: Éditions du Seuil.

Dorion, G. and Guionnet, A. (1995) *La sécurité sociale*. Paris: Presses Universitaires de France.

Esping-Andersen, G. (1990) *The Three Worlds of Welfare Capitalism*. Cambridge: Polity.

Esping-Andersen, G. (1999) [1990] *Les trois mondes de l'État-providence: essai sur le capitalisme moderne*. Paris: Presses Universitaires de France.

Ewald, F. (1986) *L'État-providence*. Paris: Grasset.

Fraser, N. and Gordon, L. (1994) '"Dependency" demystified: inscriptions of power in a keyword of the welfare state', *Social Politics*, 1(1): 4-31.

Frétigné, C. (1999) *Sociologie de l'exclusion*. Paris: L'Harmattan.

Friot, B. (1998) *Puissances du salariat: emploi et protection sociale à la française*. Paris: La Dispute.

Galant, H. C. (1955) *Histoire politique de la sécurité sociale française, 1945-1952*. Paris: Colin.

Goguel d'Allondans, A. (2003) *L'exclusion sociale: les métamorphoses d'un concept (1960-2000)*, Paris: L'Harmattan.

Guillemard, A.-M. (2000) [1986] *Aging and the Welfare-State Crisis*. Newark, DE: University of Delaware Press.

Hatzfeld, H. (1971) *Du paupérisme à la sécurité sociale, 1850-1940. Essai sur les origines de la Sécurité sociale en France*. Paris: Armand Colin.

Hayward, J. (1959) 'Solidarity: the social history of an idea in nineteenth-century France'. *International Review of Social History*, 4: 261-284.

Hayward, J. (1961) 'The official social philosophy of the French Third Republic: Léon Bourgeois and solidarism', *International Review of Social History*, 6: 19-48.

Hénin, J.-Y. and Weitzenblum, T. (2004) 'Éléments d'évaluation de la réforme des retraites,' *Revue française d'économie*, 18(3): 9-73.

Horne, J.R. (2002) *A Social Laboratory for Modern France: The Musée Social and the Rise of the Welfare State*. Durham: Duke University Press.

Humphreys, J.M. (1999) 'Durkheimian sociology and 20th-century politics: the case of Celestin Bouglé', *History of the Human Sciences*, 12 (3): 117-138.

Klanfer, J. (1965) *L'Exclusion sociale: étude de la marginalité dans les sociétés occidentales*, Paris: Bureau de recherches sociales.

Laurent, É. (1865) *Le paupérisme et les associations de prévoyance* (second edition). Paris: Librairie de Guillaumin.

Lenoir, R. (1974) *Les exclus: un Français sur dix*, Paris: Éditions du Seuil.

Levitas, R. (2005) [1999] *Inclusive Society? Social Exclusion and New Labour* (second edition), London: Palgrave.

Majnoni d'Intignano, B. (1997) *La Protection sociale* (revised edition). Paris: Le livre de proche.

Merrien, F.-X. (2003) *L'État-providence* (third edition). Paris: Presses Universitaires de France.

O'Connor, J. (1973) *The Fiscal Crisis of the State*, New York: St. Martin's Press.

Palier, B. (2002) *Gouverner la sécurité sociale*. Paris: Presses Universitaires de France.

Palier, B. (2005) 'Ambiguous agreements, cumulative change: French social policy in the 1990s' in Wolfgang Streeck and Kathleen Thelen (eds) *Beyond Continuity. Institutional Change in Advanced Political Economies*. New York: Oxford University Press: 127-144.

Palier B. and Bonoli, G. (1995) 'Entre Bismarck et Beveridge: 'crises' de la sécurité sociale et politique(s)', *Revue française de science politique*, 45(4): 668-699.

Paugam, S. (ed.) (1996) *L'exclusion: L'état des savoirs*, Paris: La Découverte.

Paugam, S. (ed.) (2007) *Repenser la solidarité: L'apport des sciences sociales*. Paris: Presses Universitaires de France.

Portonnier, J.-C. (1998) *Glossaire bilingue de la protection sociale. Social Protection: A Bilingual Glossary. Volume 1: Les termes français / The French terms*. Paris: MIRE.

Révauger, J.-P. and Spicker, P. (1998) *Social Protection: A Bilingual Glossary. Glossaire bilingue de la protection sociale. Volume 2: English Terms / Les termes anglais.* Paris: MIRE.

Rosanvallon, P. (1981) *La Crise de l'État-providence.* Paris: Éditions du Seuil.

Rosanvallon, P. (1995) *La nouvelle question sociale: repenser l'État-providence.* Paris: Éditions du Seuil.

Silver, H. (1994) 'Social exclusion and social solidarity: three paradigms', *International Labour Review,* 133(5-6): 531-578.

Silver, H. and Miller, S.M. (2003) 'Social exclusion: the European approach to social disadvantage,' *Indicators,* 2(2): 1-17.

van Berkel, R. and Hornemann Møller, I. (2002) *Active social policies in the EU: Inclusion through participation?* Bristol: Policy Press.

Williams, R. (1976) *Keywords: A Vocabulary of Culture and Society.* London: Fontana.

EIGHT

The language of social politics in Finland

Pauli Kettunen

Among the five representatives of the Nordic model, Denmark, Finland, Iceland, Norway and Sweden, each an exception in its own way, Finland may easily qualify as the most exceptional one. Finland was a latecomer in industrialisation and urbanisation, and it was also the Nordic latecomer in the field of social policies and industrial relations. Connections and conflicts with the Czarist and Soviet Empires are a particular dimension of Finland's history, and the class based Civil War of 1918 and the two wars against the Soviet Union (1939–40 and 1941–44) as a part of the Second World War had many political, not least social political, implications. In a study of concepts and language, the Finnish exceptionality may appear especially striking, as the Finno-Ugric language of the majority of the population of Finland is totally different from the Scandinavian languages.

It would be possible to analyse Finland as one of the new nation-states that were built after the collapse of the Eastern and Central European multi-ethnic empires. Finland was declared independent after the October Revolution, in December 1917. In January 1918, the Civil War began between the socialist Reds and the bourgeois Whites, preconditioned by the international crisis and domestic class based conflicts. It ended in the victory of the Whites in May 1918. Despite the counter-revolutionary outcome of the Civil War, however, Finland was by the Constitution of 1919 established as a parliamentary republic. Again, this solution had its prerequisites in international transformations. The alliance of the White winners with the German Empire lost its basis as the German Empire not only lost the World War but also dissolved through revolution. Importantly, however, parliamentary democracy was sustained in Finland in the 1920s and 1930s as the form of political system, even though it was threatened by right-wing groups, especially in the early 1930s. The sustaining of democratic forms made Finland exceptional among the new nation-states created through the collapse of the empires.

Any explanation of this exceptionality must recognise that the Nordic political traditions had played a crucial role in the Finnish nation building. Sweden lost its Eastern provinces to Russia in the Russian–Swedish War of 1808–09, which was related to the Napoleonic wars. Finland had been an integral part of the Swedish realm and now became the Grand Duchy of the Russian Emperor; however, the old Swedish law and the Lutheran religion remained prevalent. The Finnish nation builders could, by means of real historical references, make use of and contribute to the development of Nordic nationalist myths. Most importantly, these concerned the idealised heritage of the free Nordic peasant who had been capable of local self-government and integrated into the state as the peasantry had formed one of the four estates in the Swedish realm. In the late 19th century, the Finnish polity was shaped on the basis of this constitutional continuity. At the same time the Nordic countries, or *Norden*, came to play an important role in Finland as a framework for international comparison, communication and cooperation in various fields of social knowledge, and 'Nordic' became an ingredient of Finnish national identity.

On the other hand, the making of the Finnish nation and the internally autonomous nation-state in the 19th century happened through the construction of a cultural identity distinct from Sweden's. This also included the shift of language from Swedish to Finnish, the language of the majority of the people, among many families of the political, economic and cultural elite. A central yet contested part of the nation building was the refining of the Finnish language, capable of dealing with politics and sciences and of connecting ordinary and educated people. The coexistence of Finnish and Swedish languages was associated with political controversies about the right way of representing the nation, but it also implied policies of translation that made the structures of meaning of the two languages converge, even though the refiners of the Finnish language eagerly made use of vernacular raw materials when developing the Finnish vocabulary. Currently, the Swedish speaking population comprises only 5% of the whole population. However, in constitutional terms, Swedish is not a minority language but Finnish and Swedish have an equal status as the two official languages of the bilingual nation.

This chapter discusses the conceptualisation of the 'social' in Finland, in what from our present perspective appears as the history of the welfare state. The focus is on the concept of society that, with its specific national and shared Nordic meanings and usages, has played an important role in the defining of the social political agenda and agency. Aimed at tracing the multilayered historicity of concepts, the story begins with how the social political language in Finland was 'temporalised' (Koselleck, 1979, 2003), that is, how the notions of historical change and historical agency were included in concepts, notably the concept of society. The chapter then examines the intertwining of the concepts of society and state, the conceptual relationships between society and economy, the emergence of the concept of the welfare state, and, finally, the political changes associated with the distinction between the welfare state and welfare society.

Society as a temporalised concept

In the 19th century, the intertwined ideas of historical progress and transnational interdependence became crucial ingredients for the notion of modernising the nation-state society. A particular conjunction of temporal and spatial dimensions appears important in how the modernising nation-state society was adopted as the framework for defining social problems and solutions in Europe's Northern periphery. From the latter half of the 19th century onwards, international comparisons became integral in the way the educated elite anticipated social problems and defined sociopolitical tasks. In Finland, which was small and, even by Nordic standards, late to industrialise, such comparisons came to play a particularly prominent role.

A good example is a series of articles, which placed 'the labour question' on the Finnish political agenda in 1874. It was written by Yrjö Koskinen (his original Swedish name was Georg Zacharias Forsman), one of the foremost leaders of the Finnish nationalist movement. Koskinen (1874) argued that efforts should be made to forestall threats to social stability by examining Finnish conditions 'from a European perspective', by trying to learn, in other words, from what was happening in countries that were more highly developed than Finland. Koskinen's articles also demonstrated that both the threat, that is, socialism, and the economic system, which provided a breeding ground for socialism through its inherent conflicts between capital and labour, were perceived as international phenomena. For this pattern of thought, the outside world provided a framework of external preconditions and constraints, hopes and threats, impulses and alarming ideas, models and unpleasant examples, as well as points of reference and limits as to what was possible.

Many ideas and impulses were transferred to Finland via Sweden, but it was only from the 1930s and, especially, after World War II, that Sweden was regarded as itself representing the forefront of modernisation. Nevertheless, contacts with Sweden, of which Finland had been a part before 1809, and the positioning of Finland in *Norden* came to play an important role for the 'comparative imagination' (Sluga, 2004) that was constitutive of the nation as an 'imagined community' (Anderson, 1983). Promoted by intra-Nordic communication in different fields of social knowledge since the late 19th century, 'Nordic' came to represent an active future oriented peripheral perspective towards the varying centres of modernity (Kettunen, 2006; Petersen, 2006).

In general, the Nordic countries developed into small, relatively open economies that were – each country in its specific way – highly dependent on exports and exposed to the cycles and crises of the world economy. This international dependence provided the preconditions for the articulation of strong notions of national economy and national society (Senghaas, 1985: 71–94). In the conceptualisation of social problems and solutions, the concept of society (*samhälle* in Swedish, *samfund* in Danish, *samfunn* in Norwegian, *samfélag* in Icelandic, *yhteiskunta* in Finnish) was assigned a crucial role.

Society was simultaneously an agent and a target of knowledge and politics. In this way, the concept of society became 'a tool for steering the historical movement' (Koselleck, 1979: 344). By means of international comparisons, it was able to *anticipate* its own future; it carried within itself the code of its own future. This capability of society was associated with the capability for *self-criticism*. The concept of society referred to normative criteria and capacities, and these criteria and capacities were then applied to the empirical society in which need, poverty, class divisions, discontent and a lack of discipline were recognised.

With respect to the economy, society was a normative representation of the interests of the whole in a dual sense. 'Society' referred, on the one hand, to the interests of the *national economy* above private economic interests and, on the other, to the *social principle* that put limits to economic action for preserving or reconstructing social cohesion. These dualisms can be found as characteristics of the modern concept of society. However, in the Nordic countries 'society' seems to have been provided with a stronger charge of agency and with a larger amount of normative power than was the case in many other European countries. This extra normative power was included in 'society' as this term was and is often used as a synonym for the *state* or *public power*.

The state called society

'State' and 'society' tend to be confused in Nordic political languages. The use of 'society' as a term for the state or for the totality of the state and the municipalities began much earlier than the era of the welfare state, the large public sector, and corporatism that are sometimes mentioned as the basis for the tendency to 'unify or even identify "state", "society" and "people"' (Knudsen and Rothstein, 1994: 218). Furthermore, this conceptual phenomenon does not only appear in 'social democratic' Sweden, as the Swedish critics of the 'patronising' welfare state have claimed (Trägårdh, 1995), but also in Finland, where social democracy has been, since the Civil War of 1918, much weaker. In all Nordic political languages, 'society' often refers to the state – something current dictionaries confirm – though differences of degree may be found in how frequently this synonymity is present.

Nordic political languages seem to have conserved elements from the political philosophy before the 19th century when civil society did not mean a sphere separate from the state but was a way of conceptualising the state (Riedel, 1975; Bobbio, 1989; Heilbron, 1995). The Nordic use of 'society' for the state implied that the state or public power was supposed to be capable of involving associative, integrative and inclusive principles of 'society' and 'the social'.

According to a plausible hypothesis (Aronsson, 1995, 1997), the development of the Swedish term *samhälle* (society) to refer to the state derives from the tradition of local self-government among the freeholding farmers. In the mid–1700s, when Finland was an integral part of Sweden, the advocators of the Enlightenment adopted this concept and thereby linked Enlightenment ideas and ideals to the local associational practices. The term then referentially expanded to include larger political units, namely, what was becoming called the nation.

Many different 'societies' appeared in political debates, also in one and the same argumentation. For example, in Yrjö Koskinen's Finnish account of the 'labour question' in 1874, the Finnish word for society, *yhteiskunta,* had several meanings:

> *Yhteiskunta, i.e.* the state [*valtio*], is the foundation for all historical progress. The mission of *yhteiskunta* is to watch over all the areas of common life [*yhteiselämä*], including the economic, to see that selfish interests and undertakings do not gain such free rein as would completely doom the lot of the weaker in that battle or as would lead *yhteiskunta* itself into ruin. (Koskinen, 1874: 4)

Besides explicitly identifying *yhteiskunta* with the state, Koskinen saw another level: *yhteiselämä* ('common life' or 'life in common'). The Swedish correlate, *sammanlefnad,* had been used as an equivalent of *societas* in the 18th century translations of Locke and Pufendorf (Saastamoinen, 2003: 43–46). Koskinen's 'common life' carried the meaning of Hegel's *bürgerliche Gesellschaft* (Kettunen, 2003: 183-184). However, this distinction had little analytical force in Koskinen's thought. It is apparent that *yhteiskunta* has multiple meanings in his writing on the labour issue. *Yhteiskunta* (that is, the state) should regulate *yhteiskunta* (societal practices, including economy) in order to bring resolution to the *yhteiskunnallinen* (social) question and, hence, to ensure the existence of *yhteiskunta* (that is, social order) and historical progress.

Koskinen's *yhteiskunta* was defined in a political context in which the Finnish national movement (*Fennomania*) had made 'the will of the people' a fundamental basis of their political argument and of the legitimation of power (Liikanen, 1995). At the same time, they viewed 'the people' and 'its will' as a problem needing oversight and definition. This *yhteiskunta* called for a moral relationship between the state and the people. Implicitly there were two normative kinds of *yhteiskunta*: one referred to the state as carrying out the best interests – and therefore the will – of the people; the other referred to the population living within the order maintained by the state. As a normative concept, *yhteiskunta* offered a means of determining what actions represented the people's real and correct will, and what actions constituted simple rebellion arising from the labour question.

The language of Nordic labour movements implied a strong normative power and agency of society at the same time as 'society', on the other hand, referred to a framework of class conflicts and solidarities, and to a target of criticism, knowledge and politics. In Socialist Party manifestos at the end of the 19th century and the beginning of the 20th century, in Finland as in other Nordic countries, capitalist class society was harshly criticised, the fulfilment of the interest of society was demanded, and transferring the means of production into the ownership of society – that is, socialism – was found necessary. This would happen after the working class achieved the power in society. In this political argumentation, society as an actor and society as a target of critics and politics, as well as the normative and descriptive society, were interlinked by a view on world history and the agency of the working class in the service of history (SDP, 1903; Kettunen, 2000: 176, 2003: 188–9).

The state or public authorities are certainly not in all situations called society, for example, not in law texts. The criteria for situations in which the term 'society' could, and still can, be applied to the state and municipalities stem from the notion of society as the moral order of the relationships between individuals or groups. 'Society' is applied to public authorities in situations where the relationships between public authorities and individuals or public authorities and private actors, often those in the sphere called 'economy', are looked at from this kind of moral point of view.

Arguably, this usage can be found in all Nordic countries, but a particularly strong variant appears in Finland. In the Finnish society-as-state usage, the conception of the state in terms of its societal, associational principles seems to have become subordinated to a mode of thought, in which society carries out the normative force of the state. The influential role of the Hegelian tradition in Finnish nation building, represented especially by the 'national philosopher' of Finland, Johan Vilhelm Snellman, contributed to such a view of the state (Kettunen, 2000, 2003). Later, a notion of politics as the nonpolitical fulfilment of externally determined necessities was reinforced by experiences that were easy to interpret as issues of national existence. This notion was featured in the long-term ideological legacies of the experiences of World War II, especially the strong sense of national unity stemming from the Winter War of 1939–40. During the Cold War, the national political agenda, and the national political agency, were shaped by the necessity to cope with the tight constraints of international politics.

According to the social democratic ideology developed in the Nordic countries, the state could and should be changed into an instrument of political will and planning. However, this mode of thought never achieved the kind of hegemonic position in Finland as it did, in particular, in Sweden. One can say that in Finland the planning reason has been seen as an inherent property of the state itself, and politics is supposed to put into action the agency of the state.

The ideal of national consensus did not imply an absence of conflicts. Finland has a more conflict laden past than the other Nordic countries. The Civil War of 1918, with its class based preconditions, had long-term effects through social memory and political institutions. In the post-World War II era, the relatively strong support of the communists was one of the political phenomena that made Finland exceptional in the Nordic context. In industrial relations, obvious 'low-trust' elements appeared until the 1980s, indicated by comparative strike statistics. The parliamentary system was unstable and short-lived governments were typical until the early 1980s. The Finland of 'too much conflict' and the Finland of 'too much consensus' seem to intertwine. Conflicts were deepened as they easily turned into struggles over the right way of defining and representing the general national interest and the right to talk in the name of 'society'.

Society and economy

The normative standards of society were not only an issue of moral rules but also of the rules of the most rational functioning and the rationalisation of society. They were also rules of how the productive capacities of individuals could be released, as well as rules concerning the contents of those capacities, such as self-disciplined citizenship. In the ideational framework of modernising the nation-state society, the perspectives of economic rationalisation and social integration intersected. In the late 19th century, the concept of society came to refer to the national level of economic activities (*samfundsøkonomi, samhällsekonomi, yhteiskuntatalous*) at the same as it, on the other hand, referred to the social principle putting limits on economic activities in order to preserve or restore social order and cohesion (*socialpolitik, sosialpolitik, yhteiskuntapolitiikka/sosiaalipolitiikka*).

In the 1930s these two aspects became more distinct in Finnish political debate, and it appears that this was inspired by ideological developments in other Nordic countries. The distinction was related to the conceptual construction of 'economy', and it included the idea that governing from society's point of view was not equal to governing from the social point of view.

As an attribute for economic life, the adjective directly derived from the word for 'society' – in Finnish *yhteiskunnallinen*, in Swedish *samhällelig*, in Norwegian and Danish *samfundsmessig* – was increasingly associated with the principles of a 'planned economy' that under the economic depression of the 1930s became, internationally, a popular objective, with various political colours. 'Society' would actively steer and rationalise the economy, and such a steering was 'societal' (Slagstad, 1998: 192). Following the Scandinavian example, Eero A. Wuori's draft of the Finnish Social Democratic economic policy programme spoke of how 'the anarchical system of capitalistic production' could be transformed 'into a plan-based, socialistic system of production under the power and leadership of society ' (SDP, 1933: 119). In the 1940s, during and after World War II, the adjective 'societal' was in many texts still more explicitly associated with regulation and governance in the name of real economic rationality and rationalisation (for example Railo, 1942).

'Social' (*social, sosial, sosiaalinen*), in turn, had a quite different meaning in the context of economic rationalisation. It was associated with the delimiting of, or compensating for, those outcomes of the capitalist economic rationalisation that endangered the welfare of those involved (notably the workers) and threatened the cohesion of society. As these concepts became associated with the distinction between public and private, they also became gendered so that 'societal' came to include a masculine charge and 'social', in turn, a feminine charge. The strong linkages between the concepts of state and society contributed to the masculine connotations of 'societal' that carried over into public power and the domain of public life. As for 'social', its meaning was limited to what existed between society and the family, or between the public and private domains, and was thereby marked as feminine. In the 1940s, *sosiaalinen* and *social* were also adopted in the field of industrial welfare. In large industrial companies, these activities greatly expanded in Finland soon after World War II, carried out predominantly by female 'social workers', often under the direction of male 'social directors' (Kettunen, 2003: 196).

Social policy and societal policy

In the first decades of the 20th century, the state's regulative activities concerning 'the social question' were often called in Finnish *yhteiskuntapolitiikka*, a translation of the German *Sozialpolitik* and Swedish *socialpolitik* (for example Ehrnrooth, 1913). In this compound, *yhteiskunta* referred to the specific target of policy, mainly class relations and the position of the working class. However, *yhteiskunta* brought other connotations to the word: *yhteiskunta* (that is, the state) was the agent that determined and executed these policies, and these policies promoted and strengthened *yhteiskunta* (that is, the prevailing social order within the nation-state).

From the 1930s to the 1960s, the conceptual linkage of social policies and the state was elaborated, not yet by the concept of welfare state, but through the distinction between 'societal' (*yhteiskunnallinen*) and 'social' (*sosiaalinen*). An early explicit distinction between *yhteiskunnallinen* and *sosiaalinen* appears in Eino Kuusi's *Sosialipolitiikka* (Social Policy), a 1000-page textbook published in 1931. Instead of the previously popular *yhteiskuntapolitiikka*, Kuusi chose to refer only to *sosialipolitiikka* from the title on. He argued his decision on the grounds that the words produced different effects on the imagination. In his judgement, the word *sosialinen*:

> is connected to the feeling of commonality, or mutual aid, which is present in *socius* (which is *toveri* ['companion, comrade']). Since *yhteiskunnallinen* also lacks this warmth, *yhteiskuntapolitiikka* does not quite match the concept. Since we lack any other Finnish alternative, I consider '*sosialinen*'

> and '*sosialipolitiikka*' to be the best choices, as they are
> also quite well suited to Finnish. The only caveats is to be
> careful against confusing these words and their meanings
> with what is meant by '*sosialistinen*' ['socialist' as adjective]
> and '*sosialismi*', which mean something altogether different.
> (Kuusi, 1931: 13–14)

However, Eino Kuusi did not by any means abandon *yhteiskunta*. The
motives of social policy in his presentation were full of interests, needs,
demands and obligations of *yhteiskunta*. In his argumentation, *sosialinen*
was associated not only with warmth and interactions between people,
but also with class conflicts that were a threat to social cohesion and to
society itself. Kuusi can be interpreted as wishing to reserve the use of
yhteiskunta and *yhteiskunnallinen* for referring to an essentialist national
cohesion, which had been endangered by the revolution attempted
in Finland in 1918.

In the 1950s, a distinction between *yhteiskuntapolitiikka* (societal
policy) and *sosiaalipolitiikka* (social policy) was developed in a way
reflecting the post-war political changes, especially the increased role of
organised interests and a new ethos of planning. Social policy language,
as it appears in textbooks, developed counter to the mainstream of the
post-war social sciences, which were highly influenced by American
sociology. The distinction of *yhteiskunnallinen* and *sosiaalinen* paralleled
the German *gesellschaftlich* and *sozial*, but it was difficult to find support
from the English language for this kind of distinction.

In his university textbook *Sosiaalipolitiikka* (Social Policy), published in
1955, Armas Nieminen defined a hierarchy between *yhteiskuntapolitiikka*
and *sosiaalipolitiikka*. *Yhteiskuntapolitiikka* was the general concept of
'efforts and measures to organise society so that the conditions of
society are regarded as efficiently suited and right for the purposes'.
Sosiaalipolitiikka was a subconcept of 'measures intended to ensure a level
considered fair in the standard of living, social security and amenities
for society's various groups, families and individuals' (Nieminen, 1955:
43, 95). *Sosiaalipolitiikka* was thus no longer based on a concept of
'class' and class conflicts. Nieminen portrayed the actors and interests
behind *sosiaalipolitiikka* in stating that this kind of policy was 'on the
one hand, a practical expression of the common responsibility felt by
society for its various groups and citizens; on the other hand, it involves
different groups' own activities aimed at promoting and realising their
own self-interests'. He related this tension to another contradiction
that drives social policy: planning based on the knowledge of experts
and involving compromises between differing goals and interests. The

inference is that, for Nieminen, *yhteiskunta* was a social actor functioning as a centre of social solidarity, and with the ability to set up projects and goals based on a scientific knowledge of itself.

In 1961, Pekka Kuusi, Eino Kuusi's nephew, published an influential book, *60-luvun sosiaalipolitiikka* (Social Policy for the Sixties). In this 'plan for Finland', as the ambition was expressed in the subtitle of the English version (Kuusi, 1964), Kuusi further developed the hierarchical order between *yhteiskuntapolitiikka* and *sosiaalipolitiikka*. His perspective differed from Nieminen's in programmatically treating *sosiaalipolitiikka* as a component of *yhteiskuntapolitiikka*, and in calling for the actors of the former to be clear about the general goals of the latter. Pekka Kuusi did not find any essential contradiction between the universal interests of society and the particular interests of various groups, as Nieminen had. Instead, inspired by Gunnar Myrdal's theory of circular cumulative causation (Myrdal, 1957), Kuusi expressed his strong confidence in virtuous circles within modern society: 'Democracy, social equalization and economic growth seem to be fortunately interrelated in modern society. Social policy seems to spring from free and growth-oriented human nature'. (Kuusi, 1961: 8, 1964: 34) Within this fortunately interconnected society, social policy played an important role. In the 'growth-oriented society', 'social' was no longer a counter-principle to 'economic', and the society, 'our society', was simultaneously the subject, object and framework of the growth oriented action.

Nevertheless, also in Pekka Kuusi's argumentation, there was a strong emphasis on national necessities derived from the place of Finland in the world. Finland was situated between two highly dynamic and growth oriented societies: Sweden and the Soviet Union. The mission Kuusi outlined was indeed a matter of life and death: if Finland was to survive between these two societies, he claimed, 'we ourselves are doomed to grow' (Kuusi, 1964: 59).

Kuusi was not advocating any 'third way' between the economic and political systems of Sweden and the Soviet Union. His argument was, rather, an example of the Finnish tendency to avoid any explicit association of social policy with the Cold War confrontation. In reality, this confrontation *was* a significant factor behind social policy considerations. The relatively strong support for communism was a major concern for all those who believed in social policies as a means to reinforce national social cohesion. However, social reforms were typically discussed as functional needs, pragmatic steps along the road of general progress within the limits of the available economic resources, or as issues related to the adjustment of conflicting interests in the name of the common national interest. Kuusi's rhetoric was certainly different: in his programme, Finnish social policies were located in the context of nothing less than world history. However, this meant that they were located in the sphere above – or below – the political and intersystemic confrontations between the East and the West, in which the basic process was the evolution and growth of industrial society, with Sweden and the Soviet Union exemplifying such a society. This version of a convergence ideology had obvious advantages for the national(istic) legitimisation of social policies during the Cold War.

Welfare state

Pekka Kuusi's book of 1961 is often regarded as the plan for the Finnish welfare state, but he did not use the concept of welfare state. Instead, the concept did appear in the critique of the book. The philosopher Urpo Harva, a leading figure in Finnish adult education, argued that the welfare state (*hyvinvointivaltio*) advocated by Kuusi weakens the individual's possibilities to develop his or her human personality (Harva, 1964). Indeed, 'welfare state', as a concept for the role of the state, was until the 1970s most frequently used by right-wing and left-wing critics.

The concept of welfare was much earlier, in the 19th century, associated with social policies, yet with the activities of industrial employers rather than public policies. The Swedish vocabulary for the paternalist policies of industrial companies – in Finland as well as Sweden – made use of the word *välfärd*, welfare. The Swedish terms commonly used for these employer practices were *välfärdsinrättningar* or *välfärdsanstalter* (welfare institutions). In the late 19th and early 20th centuries a popular Finnish translation was *työväenmenestyslaitokset* (institutions for workers' success). Since the 1940s, the adjective 'social' was used as the attribute of these practices.

In the context of governmental activities in 19th century Finland, the word *välfärd* most often referred to the good state of affairs the government in general was supposed to promote. However, associated with cameralistic economic policy ideas, this word was as early as in the mid-19th century also used as an attribute of the state. The term *välfärdspoliti* (welfare polity) appeared in the juridical handbook by Johan Ph. Palmén in 1859. In the Finnish version of Palmén's book, Elias Lönnrot, best known for compiling the national epic *Kalevala*, translated the term as *onnivallinto* (the state of happiness) (Palmén, 1863: 259).

However, these translations of *välfärd* did not transfer into the Finnish term for welfare state as it slowly emerged in public debates in the 1950s. *Hyvinvointivaltio* was a neologism that did not include the old cameralistic or paternalistic layers inherent in the first parts of the compounds *Wohlfartsstaat, welfare state* and *välfärdsstat*. As *hyvinvointi* means both welfare and wellbeing, it is easy to use *hyvinvointivaltio* as a concept for describing socioeconomic circumstances within the borders of a nation-state and not just the role and functions of the state. Actually, this was the way the term, still in the 1960s, appeared in social policy research that was oriented to construct a narrative 'from poverty to welfare state' (Siipi, 1967).

No doubt, the term was also used for characterising the changing functions of the state. One of the first to introduce *hyvinvointivaltio* was the young Social Liberal lawyer Kauko Sipponen, who was impressed by Fabian ideas and British post-war development. In a book, published in 1954 (Repo, 1954), in which a group of educated Finns with different backgrounds discussed contemporary political and cultural phenomena, he defined the welfare state in the context of Cold War confrontation. He had noticed a new way of understanding the role of the state in some Western countries, notably Britain and the Nordic countries, which combined the goal of full employment and the principle of individual freedom. This understanding of the state had resulted in what Sipponen wished to call *hyvinvointivaltio* (welfare state) or *yhteishyvävaltio* (common good state) (Repo, 1954: 242–3; Kettunen, 2008: 154–155, 242). The latter conceptual innovation did not gain any success, but *hyvinvointivaltio* was already shared by some contemporary political authors.

The first political party programme using *hyvinvointivaltio* was the Social Democratic programme for economic policy in 1954, according to which 'the system of social security' was 'a basic feature of the welfare state' (SDP, 1954). Five years later, in its programme for municipal policy, the conservative National Coalition Party opposed the current 'efforts of the state to be a "welfare state"'. The left-wing social policy was subordinating the individual to 'a subservient inmate of a "welfare state" led by a small group of politicians' (Kokoomus, 1959). The same party had in 1957 adopted the German Christian Democratic slogan of 'social market economy' in its general party programme (Kokoomus, 1957). Thus, one can conclude that the National Coalition Party found the welfare state and social market economy to be incompatible ideas.

In the late 1960s and 1970s, *hyvinvointivaltio* was criticised from the left as a new stage of the bourgeois state, serving the material and ideological reproduction of capitalist society. The welfare state was doomed to be incapable of keeping the promise of comprehensive welfare implicated by the term. In Finland as elsewhere, the concept of the welfare state became more common in connection with the international discussion on 'the crisis of the welfare state' in the 1970s and 1980s. By many indicators, these were the decades of the great expansion of the Finnish welfare state.

The era of the expanding welfare state ended in the early 1990s. The conclusions from the intertwined experiences of the emergence of neoliberalism, the globalisation of capitalism, the end of the Cold War, the new phase of European integration and the deep economic crisis in Finland included that much of the previous left-wing critique turned into a defence of the welfare state, and the use of the concept increased. At the same time, however, the concept of a welfare society was utilised in the critique of the welfare state.

Welfare state and welfare society

'Welfare society' was no new term, but it was used in a new way as a tool of the critique of what was seen as an overlarge public sector and a bureaucratic and patronising welfare state. The Organisation for Economic Cooperation and Development (OECD) had been active and influential in modifying and diffusing this concept since the late 1970s (Leimgruber, 2013: 296–300). The conceptual distinction between state and society was linked with the international emergence of 'civil society' in the 1980s as a concept for the sphere of private and voluntary actors and activities. In Sweden, the right-wing critics of the welfare state argued that the conceptual confusion of state and society was a sign of Social Democratic totalitarianism that should be opposed by revitalising civil society (Boréus, 1994).

The international debate in general and, once again, the Swedish impulses in particular played a role in Finland. The distinction between state and society was pointed out, for instance, in the 1996 party programme of the Centre Party, the previous Agrarian Party, which was a main actor in Finnish politics. For the Party, 'state and society are two different things' (Keskusta, 1996). Also in Finland, the concept of civil society, *kansalaisyhteiskunta*, was used in the critique of the welfare state, although not to the same extent as in Sweden. The concept of welfare society, *hyvinvointiyhteiskunta,* appeared in use by those demanding less state and more market. In the 1994 party programme of a short-lived neoliberal party, the Young Finns, the first slogan was 'The Activating Welfare Society' (Nuorsuomalaiset, 1994).

However, in Finland as well as in other Nordic countries, any attempt to create a political alternative by replacing 'state' with 'society' faces the heavy constraints of old conceptual conventions. 'Welfare society' can actually be used to support the legitimacy of the welfare state, because within the Nordic tradition, 'society' represents the general and public against the particular and private and is a positive term for the state. For example, the 1999 party programme of the Finnish Social Democratic Party talked about *hyvinvointiyhteiskunta* (welfare society) instead of *hyvinvointivaltio* (welfare state) (SDP, 1999). 'Welfare society' is an ambiguous term, and in the consensual politics of Finland controversies concerning the welfare state can actually be concealed by talking about welfare society. Attempts to operate with the distinction between welfare state and welfare society sometimes appear, yet these terms are often interchangeable.

In any case, the arguments for a radical deregulation that emerged in the 1980s have been pushed to the margin in Finland and in other Nordic countries. Almost all political parties and interest groups talk warmly and sympathetically about the welfare state. The pro or contra disagreement on the welfare state, still so apparent in the 1980s, has practically disappeared in the Nordic countries and everyone seems to be in favour of the welfare state. Reflecting different political traditions and power structures, the struggle over who owns the history of the Nordic welfare state is most intense in Sweden, where the Social Democrats, using all means, defend their ownership against the bourgeois attempts to claim a role, and less intense in Finland, where the Social Democrats and other heirs of the labour movement tend to see their rivals' views on the welfare state, as a result of a shared national project, as a welcome support for the present welfare state. The historical accounts of the welfare state are weapons in current struggles, albeit less in Finland than in Sweden, where a popular right-wing argument is that their politics for more individual choice represent the true historical essence of The Nordic Way.

In the current political discourse in Finland, rescuing the welfare state is one of the most widely shared objectives. Those concerned about economic competitiveness or advocating austerity politics motivate these concerns by the necessity to create or rescue resources for the welfare state. The welfare state is used as an argument for restrictive immigration policies as well as for the promotion of labour immigration. Those defending the welfare state against the pressures of globalised capitalism argue that the welfare state by its security networks and risk sharing systems actually generates competitive advantages. Rescuing the welfare state seems to be a goal that sanctifies the means and a means that sanctifies the goal.

Current discursive changes are intertwined with long continuities in the conceptualisation of the social in Finland. The concept of society seems to stubbornly perpetuate any accounts claiming that the modern notion of society is too strong and too limited to sustain in a postmodern and globalised world – too strong while referring to 'an integrated holistic entity' (Featherstone, 1995: 134) and too limited due to its ties with the nation-state and national borders. Even in the time of EU citizenship and globalised finance markets, 'society' in Finland and elsewhere rarely extends over the borders of nation-state. 'European society' still means a national society in Europe as it did in the writings of the leader of the Finnish national movement Yrjö Koskinen in 1874. *Yhteiskunta* and *samhälle* are also constantly used as terms for the state and public sector as they were in late 19th century Finland.

The imperatives of competitiveness in globalised capitalism seem to support the image of society as a national entity and contribute to the ideas of the welfare state serving the needs of national competitiveness by means of 'social investments' and 'social capital' (Kettunen, 2011). As former issues on the political agenda of national society have been transformed into external necessities of the global market, the national 'imagined community' (Anderson, 1983) may be strengthened and modified as a prepolitical figure of the competitive national 'we'.

References

Anderson, B. (1983) *Imagined Communities. Reflections on the Origin and Spread of Nationalism.* London and New York: Verso.

Aronsson, P. (1995) 'The possibilities of conceptual history 'from above' and 'from below': Reflections on samhälle 'society' in Sweden, 1700 to 1990', *Historia a Debate, tomo II, Retorno del Sujeto, Actas del Congreso Internacional 'A historia a debate' celebrade el 7-11 de julio de 1993 en Santigao de Compostela,* ed Carlos Barros (1995), 237-260.

Aronsson, P. (1997) 'Local politics – the invisible political culture', in Ø. Sørensen and B. Stråth (eds), *The Cultural Construction of Norden,* Oslo: Scandinavian University Press, 172-205.

Bobbio, N. (1989) *Democracy and Dictatorship. The Nature and Limits of State Power.* Translated by Peter Kennealy. Cambridge: Polity Press.

Boréus, K. (1994) *Högervåg. Nyliberalismen och kampen om språket i svensk debatt 1969-1989.* Stockholm: Tidens förlag.

Ehrnrooth, L. (1913) *Nykyaikainen yhteiskuntapolitiikka.* Suomen työväensuojelus- ja sosialivakuutusyhdistyksen julkaisuja II. Porvoo.

Featherstone, M. (1995) *Undoing Culture. Globalization, Postmodernism and Identity.* London: Sage Publications.

Harva, U. (1964) *Ihminen hyvinvointivaltiossa.* Helsinki: Kirjayhtymä.

Heilbron, J. (1995) *The Rise of Social Theory.* Cambridge: Polity Press.

Keskusta (1996) Keskustan periaatteet. Periaateohjelma. Hyväksytty Keskustan puoluekokouksessa Kouvolassa 1996. *POHTIVA – Poliittisten ohjelmien tietovarasto* (www.fsd.uta.fi/pohtiva/).

Kettunen, P. (2000) '*Yhteiskunta* – "Society" in Finnish', *Finnish Yearbook of Political Thought 2000*, vol 4, Jyväskylä: SoPhi, 159-197.

Kettunen, P. (2003) 'Yhteiskunta', in M. Hyvärinen, J. Kurunmäki, K. Palonen, T. Pulkkinen and H. Stenius (eds) *Käsitteet liikkeessä. Suomen poliittisen kulttuurin käsitehistoria*. Tampere: Vastapaino, 167-212.

Kettunen, P. (2006) 'Power of international comparison – a perspective on the making and challenging of the Nordic welfare state', in N.F. Christiansen et al (eds) *The Nordic Model of Welfare – a Historical Reappraisal*. Copenhagen: Museum Tusculanum Press.

Kettunen, P. (2008) *Globalisaatio ja kansallinen me. Kansallisen katseen historiallinen kritiikki*. Vastapaino: Tampere.

Kettunen, P. (2011) 'The transnational construction of national challenges: the ambiguous Nordic model of welfare and competitiveness', in P. Kettunen and K. Petersen (eds) *Beyond Welfare State Models – Transnational Historical Perspectives on Social Policy*, Cheltenham, UK/Northampton, MA, USA: Edward Elgar, 16-40.

Knudsen, T. and Rothstein, B. (1994) 'State building in Scandinavia', *Comparative Politics* 1/1994, 203-220.

Kokoomus (1957) Kansallisen Kokoomuksen yleisohjelma. Vahvistettu puoluekokouksessa Helsingissä 28-29.4.1957. *POHTIVA – Poliittisten ohjelmien tietovarasto* (www.fsd.uta.fi/pohtiva/).

Kokoomus (1959) Kansallisen Kokoomuksen kunnallisohjelma. Vahvistettu Kansallisen Kokoomuksen valtuuston syyskokouksessa 26 9.1959. *POHTIVA – Poliittisten ohjelmien tietovarasto* (www.fsd.uta.fi/pohtiva/).

Koselleck, R. (1979) *Vergangene Zukunft. Zur Semantik geschichtlicher Zeiten*. Frankfurt am Main: Suhrkamp.

Koselleck, R. (2003) *Zeitschichten. Studien zur Historik. Mit einem Beitrag von Hans-Georg Gadamer*. Frankfurt am Main: Suhrkamp.

Koskinen, Y. (1874) 'Työväen-seikka I-III', *Kirjallinen Kuukauslehti, 1, 4, 8*.

Kuusi, E. (1931) *Sosialipolitiikka I-II*. Porvoo: WSOY.

Kuusi, P. (1961) *60-luvun sosiaalipolitiikka*. Porvoo: WSOY.

Kuusi, P. (1964) *Social Policy for the Sixties: A Plan for Finland*. Helsinki: Finnish Social Political Association.

Leimgruber, M. (2013) 'The embattled standard-bearer of social insurance and its challenger: the ILO, the OECD, and the crisis of the welfare state (1975-1985)', in S. Kott and J. Droux (eds) *Globalizing social rights. The International Labour Organization and Beyond*. Basingstoke and New York: Palgrave Macmillan, 293-309.

Liikanen, I. (1995) *Fennomania ja kansa. Joukkojärjestäytymisen läpimurto ja Suomalaisen puolueen synty.* Historiallisia Tutkimuksia 191. Helsinki: Suomen Historiallinen Seura.

Myrdal, G. (1957) *Economic Theory and Underdeveloped Regions,* London: Duckworth.

Nieminen, A. (1955) *Mitä on sosiaalipolitiikka. Tutkimus sosiaalipolitiikan käsitteen ja järjestelmän kehityksestä.* Helsinki: WSOY.

Nuorsuomalaiset (1994) Nuorsuomalainen Puolue r.p. Yleisohjelma hyväksytty Helsingissä 6. joulukuuta 1994. *POHTIVA – Poliittisten ohjelmien tietovarasto* (www.fsd.uta.fi/pohtiva/).

Palmén, J.P. (1863) *La'in-opillinen käsikirja. Yhteiseksi sivistykseksi.* Suomentanut Elias Lönnrot. Helsinki: Suomalaisen Kirjallisuuden Seura.

Petersen, K. (2006) 'Constructing Nordic welfare? Nordic social political cooperation 1919-1955', in N.F. Christiansen et al (eds) *The Nordic Model of Welfare – a Historical Reappraisal.* Copenhagen: Museum Tusculanum Press.

Railo, P. (1942) *Tie yhteiskunnalliseen suunnitelmatalouteen.* Tampere: Työväen Sivistysliitto.

Repo, E.S. ed. (1954) *Toiset pidot tornissa.* Jyväskylä: Gummerus.

Riedel, M. (1975) 'Gesellschaft, bürgerliche', in *Geschichtliche Grundbegriffe. Historisches Lexikon zur politisch-sozialen Sprache in Deutschland.* Herausgegeben von O. Brunner e.a., Band 2. E-G. Stuttgart: Ernst Klett Verlag.

Saastamoinen, K. (2003) 'Johdatus poliittisiin käsitteisiin uuden ajan alun Ruotsissa', in M. Hyvärinen et al (eds) *Käsitteet liikkeessä. Suomen poliittisen kulttuurin käsitehistoria.* Tampere: Vastapaino, 19-61.

SDP (1903) Sosialidemokraattisen Puolueen ohjelma. Hyväksytty Forssan puoluekokouksessa 17-20.8.1903. *POHTIVA – Poliittisten ohjelmien tietovarasto* (www.fsd.uta.fi/pohtiva/).

SDP (1933) Suomen Sosialidemokraattisen Puolueen talouspoliittiset suuntaviivat, in *Pöytäkirja Suomen Sosialidemokraattisen Puolueen XVI puoluekokouksesta Tampereella 25-18.5.1933.* Helsinki 1934.

SDP (1954) Suomen Sosialidemokraattisen Puolueen talouspoliittinen ohjelma perusteluineen. *POHTIVA – Poliittisten ohjelmien tietovarasto* (www.fsd.uta.fi/pohtiva/).

SDP (1999) Sosialidemokratian periaatteet. Hyväksytty XXXVIII puoluekokouksessa Turussa 29.5.1999. *POHTIVA – Poliittisten ohjelmien tietovarasto* (www.fsd.uta.fi/pohtiva/).

Senghaas, D. (1985) *The European Experience. A Historical Critique of Development Theory,* Leamington Spa: Berg.

Siipi, J. (1967) *Ryysyrannasta hyvinvointivaltioon. Sosiaalinen kehitys itsenäisessä Suomessa.* Helsinki: Tammi.

Slagstad, R. (1998) *De nasjonale strateger.* Oslo: Pax Forlag A/S.

Sluga, G. (2004) 'The nation and the comparative imagination', in D. Cohen and M. O'Connor (eds) *Comparison and History. Europe in Cross-national Perspective.* New York and London: Routledge, 103-114.

Trägårdh, L. (ed.) (1995) *Civilt samhälle kontra offentlig sektor.* Stockholm: SNS Förlag.

NINE

Germany: constructing the 'win-win' society

Stephan Lessenich

Concepts have a life, and like most lives, they are not linear.
(Petersen and Petersen 2013: 48)

Ending class conflict (as we know it): a brief history of conceptual regimes

Concepts have a nonlinear life: What holds for social policy language in general and for the politico-academic concept of the welfare state in particular should be true for the history of 'welfare semantics' (Lessenich, 2003a) in Germany. With Germany having passed through extremely different political regimes throughout the 20th century – imperial authoritarianism, contested democracy, fascist *Volksgemeinschaft*, liberal/communist double stateness, 'post-national' reunification – it is hardly a surprise that German social policy language likewise changed substantially from Bismarck's to Merkel's times. The German welfare language community has moved away from addressing the 'tough' problem(s) of the industrial working class (*Arbeiterfrage*) in the late 19th century and instead headed for the 'soft' issue of activating human capital for the (alleged) knowledge society at the beginning of the 21st. However, with some analytical distance, it may well be said that across this whole period – its eventful history of political transformations notwithstanding – the German welfare discourse revolved around a remarkably stable centreline: the (re)conciliation of economy and society by means of the *Sozialstaat*.

Concepts in the field of social policy are 'essentially contested concepts' (see Collier et al, 2006) – probably even more so than those structuring social reality in other policy domains. The politics of social policy are largely about the continuous political business of 'drawing and redrawing … the contested boundaries of state action' (Béland, 2011: 2; see also Blyth, 1997), that is, of public intervention into private matters. In a way, and to an extent that seems to be quite exceptional when compared to other national trajectories of social policy language, social policy's conceptual history in Germany is a history of theorising and operationalising state–society relations. From its beginnings in the 1840s up to the current state of affairs, German welfare semantics reflect the struggle between statist and civil conceptions of social order. Claims for a 'strong state' as an authoritative instance of public provision (*Daseinsvorsorge*; Günther, 2004) compete with positions arguing for the state's subsidiary role and the prerogative of private entities – the family and/or associations – in the production of welfare (Sachße, 2003; Kaufmann, 2012a) But what at first glance appears to be an irreconcilable clash of philosophies, on a closer look turns out be a matter of dialectical coalescence. What makes German history of sociopolitical thinking and speaking peculiar is the dominance of harmonising concepts in the potentially antagonistic relationship between state and society. From the early days of reasoning in terms of 'social policies' until the present, there has been a conspicuous push towards conceiving the social world as the peaceful coexistence between the 'visible hand' of state intervention[84] and the 'invisible hand' of market processes and social life.

Looking back on a century of welfare state development, then, the evolution of German social policy language may be read as a history of searching and arguing for win–win solutions to the structural conflicts and diverging interests built into modern market society. What is generally at stake in the language game – be it in social policy or any other field of political intervention – is the legitimate definition of what is 'real' and how things 'are':

> Knowledge of the social world and, more precisely, the categories that make it possible, are the stakes, par excellence, of political struggle, the inextricably theoretical and practical struggle for the power to conserve or transform the social word [sic][85] by conserving or transforming the categories through which it is perceived. (Bourdieu, 1985: 729)

For decades, in the German context, the essential categories determining how the social world has been perceived – and thus how it has been understood – have been harmonious concepts that rely on what might

---

[84] Speaking of hands, it has become common to talk of the 'public hand' (*öffentliche Hand*) in German discourse when referring to all sorts of state institutions.

[85] It should properly read 'social *world*' here.

be called, adapting Putnam's (1993) classical terminology, their 'bridging semantic capital'. It is typically in the field of social policy – and its politics – where these categories have been built and rebuilt throughout history. In reconstructing the sequence of different 'conceptual regimes' (Petersen and Petersen, 2013: 48) since the beginnings of modern social policy, we present a (very brief) story of continuity in change: the story of a political struggle to (at least discursively) end social struggle.

The prewar regime: setting the tone – social policy as political mediation

German social policy language began to develop well before the introduction of the workers' insurance systems commonly associated with Bismarck (Kaufmann, 2012b: 58). The term 'welfare state' had already been coined in the socioeconomic academic literature of the 1840s (Petersen and Petersen, 2013: 38–41), and the idea of and discourse about social policy (spelt *Social-Politik* at that time) can be traced back to that same decade. The idea of a police state (*Polizeystaat*), that claims to warrant public and individual security, being much older again than modern social policy language (Kaufmann, 2012c: 336–7)[86], the concept of social policy denotes an ideational innovation insofar as it admits (and takes into account) the autonomy, or, perhaps more accurately, the logical and functional distinctiveness of the social. Social policy, in contrast to an absolutist *gute Polizey* ('good police') proceeding and processing by its own political logics, conceives of itself as a reaction to the social question (*Soziale Frage*). It responds (and means to be responsive) to a novel situation: the social dynamics of an 'economic society' organised around self regulating markets – or, seen from another perspective, the social problems of a civil society being disorganised by market rule.

In their origins, the idea and semantics of social policy – that is, of policing the social – are 'firmly anchored in theories about society itself'

---

[86]   With regard not only to the German case, but to Continental European development at large, Kaufmann (2012c) devises a sequential model of discourses on state roles where the police state is being replaced by the constitutional state in the 19th century, which for its part is superseded by the welfare state in the 20th.

(Kaufmann, 2012b: 59).[87] Most prominently, they follow what may be considered a theory of societal differentiation *avant la lettre*: Hegel's philosophy of right, first published in the early 1820s (Hegel, 1952 [1821]). In line with Hegel's distinction between state and civil society, at the core of the notion of social policy was the sense of a pressing need for a political mediation of social conflict, for 'a kind of interaction between the order-creating power of the state on the one hand and, on the other, the dynamic of concurrent ideas, technical innovations and capitalistic competition that drove civil society' (Kaufmann, 2012b: 59).

The influential work of state theorist and possibly the earliest German sociologist Lorenz von Stein, in the 1840s and 1850s, provides the central intellectual reference for the guiding idea that state interventionism via social policy may be a means of conciliating social dynamics and social order. What von Stein had in mind and advocated was a kind of conservative reformism in the face of a society that had been liberated from feudal ties. Regulating and tempering the drive of social forces was (in the word's double meaning) the *order* of the day: (re)capturing, both intellectually and politically, the autonomous dynamics of the social sphere (Tenbruck, 1981). Based on the theoretical concept of state and society as distinct entities interpenetrating each other, von Stein envisioned a social reform (*Sozialreform*) initiated and implemented by a public administration that he portrayed as 'a neutral third party' (Kaufmann, 2012b: 66) not involved in the structural conflicts characterising industrial society.

In this sense, the intellectual and ideational essence of von Stein's approach to the *Sozialstaat* – which proved to be a lasting legacy for German-style thinking and arguing about social policy – may be said to be a political theory of class compromise through public policy: the 'working state' (*arbeitender Staat*) was meant to solve the worker's question (*Arbeiterfrage*) to the satisfaction of everybody – not only of the workers themselves, but also of the business class. Like all the real-world welfare regimes that would follow in German history – with the exception of the dismal fascist welfare–warfare state – von Stein's imagined '"social state" had the task of both protecting the conditions

---

[87] Kaufmann attributes Germany's early development in social policy thinking to its being a laggard (compared to England or France) in terms of the social problems connected to industrialisation; German social thinkers 'thus had a detached perspective on the new conditions, which aided the development of an autonomous social science' (Kaufmann, 2012b: 60). Unfortunately, academic literature on social policy not only loosened, but almost completely lost its anchoring in social theory in the course of the 20th century.

for private property and hence the development of an independent entrepreneurial capacity, and improving the working and living conditions of labour' (Kaufmann, 2012b: 67). While admitting the fact that labour and capital are antagonistic parties, they nevertheless were claimed to be mutually dependent on each other,[88] and public administration was assigned the task (and imputed the capacity) of 'promoting insight by both the propertied and the un-propertied classes into the complementary character of their interests' (Kaufmann, 2012c: 340).

Thus, from the mid-19th century onwards, it was social policy that seemed to make possible a constructive solution to the economic antagonism shattering and, at least at that time, effectively tearing apart society. Von Stein's institutional design for a political solution to the social question set the tone for things to come, paving the way for a sort of intellectual and discursive path dependence (Mahoney, 2000) in German social policy development. Though it is true that with Bismarck's social insurance legislation (1883–9) and throughout his entire regime, imperial politics favoured the *policing* (read: authoritarian) over the *social* (civil) dimension of social policy, it could not escape the harmonising drift of social reform. The imperial dispatch announcing the establishment of the social insurance system explicitly acknowledged the fact that the worker's question could not be solved only by way of harassing the workers' movement and banning social democratic activity (*Umtriebe*). The authoritarian regime had to admit that, in order to conserve the old social order, it needed carrots as much as sticks. Social insurance proved to be the ideal carrot. And its autocratic roots notwithstanding, the idea and semantics of the (since then called 'Bismarckian') *Sozialstaat*, being an asset for all parties to the industrial game, outlived Bismarck and imperial Germany.

The harmonising intention of state intervention is reflected not only in von Stein's concept of social policy as a means of pacifying class conflict, but also in the more general but not less 'important new basic idea' (Kaufmann, 2012c: 340) of social policy being a matter of combining individual and collective interest(s) – an idea that in the German context also dates back to the 1840s but has never since ceased to be operative. In this sense, social policy denotes a politics of social mediation not only between labour and capital, but also between individual and society, between the individual and the common good. In its most classical formulation, the second axis of the social equation to

---

[88] A concept that is deeply rooted in Catholic social teaching as well and that came to be influential throughout the history of the German *Sozialstaat*.

be established and preserved by the *Sozialstaat* means that 'the members in their totality have the obligation to care for the single individual, just as the single individual has the obligation to care for the totality' (Karl Nauwerck, 1844, cited in Petersen and Petersen, 2013: 40). While the class compromise dimension of German welfare semantics was prolonged into the interwar period and then came to dominate most of post-war social policy history, this wider 'social compromise' dimension[89] was insistently relaunched, as will be seen in more detail later, at the turn of the 20th century.

The interwar regime: losing ground – the welfare state as a political battlefield

The post-imperial Weimar Republic – which constitutionally still signed with the name *Deutsches Reich* – was founded on mainly war driven (or rather defeat driven) class compromise. The wartime nonaggression pact (*Burgfrieden*) between imperial elites and Social Democrats, the Stinnes-Legien Agreement of 1918, signed by the organisational heads of capital and labour (and predetermining central parts of the 1919 Constitution), and the work council law (*Betriebsrätegesetz*) of 1920, establishing mechanisms of effective codetermination at the shop floor: all of these legal (or paralegal) institutions made Weimar seem, at very first glance, to be a pacified and peaceful cross-class polity. In social policy terms, the most important *acquis* of Weimar constitutional law certainly is to be found in the institutionalisation of a whole set of basic social rights assigned to 'the entire working class' (article 162).

But what looked like being the legal gateway to workers' full recognition as qualified citizens, in social reality turned out to be a door that remained locked and blocked. The institutional compromise underlying the Weimar basic rights catalogue stuck to the formula:

---

[89] For an early and conclusive sociological account of this dimension, see Georg Simmel's classic essay on 'the poor' (Simmel, 1965 [1908]; see also Lessenich 2003b). Simmel demonstrates an unmistakable sense for the (social) fact that social policy as 'public help' is a double-edged sword, as it not only serves the individual, but always has an additional – and often primary – social function, protecting the community against the poor individual. In this sense, social policy has an inbuilt tension between two social logics: ethical considerations regarding private rights and individual welfare, and considerations of public policy and the common wealth.

social rights, yes – but not enforceable by law.[90] As a matter of fact, 'the welfare state programme of the Weimar Reich Constitution ... lacked any corresponding resonance in jurisprudence' (Kaufmann, 2012c: 340–1): the basic social rights it stipulated would have needed statutory authorisation and/or judicial support, but in both respects there was administrative reluctance (if not resistance) to implement constitutional law, reducing its catalogue of social rights *de facto* to a political declaration of intent.[91] As such, it eventually remained oddly silent insofar as it did not translate into a hegemonic public discourse on rights for the greater part of Weimar history.

But even so, and rightly, Weimar stands out in German social policy history for the emphasis on the (relative) autonomy of the social vis-à-vis the political, and may well be said to have been the (if only momentary) breakthrough of the welfare state and of welfare state semantics in the German discourse (Kaufmann, 2012c: 340; Abelshauser, 1987). With the Catholic *Zentrum* party occupying the national Ministry of Labour for most of the 1920s, the regime's social administration not only reanimated the idea of mutual dependence between labour and capital, but took a broader initiative for 'corporatist subsidiarity' in the social sector, giving room and political power to civil associations in the organisation of social services. And the introduction of unemployment insurance in 1927 constituted a real institutional innovation, not least because of its supposed susceptibility to moral hazard and its consequential contestedness in the public debate.

Unfortunately, though, the unemployment insurance funds were almost immediately ruined by the Great Depression and the mass unemployment it caused. But had it not been for Black Friday in 1929, the reactionary and nationalist groups and parties in Weimar Germany most probably would have found other ways and vehicles for their antidemocratic and antiwelfarist propaganda. In the desperate struggle over the Republic's fate after 1929, 'both critics and defenders made use of the term "Wohlfahrtsstaat"' (Petersen and Petersen, 2013: 42). It is noteworthy that the term was not only employed pejoratively to attack existing welfare institutions (as is frequently argued in the

---

[90]   This conforms to the 'yes, but ...' logic, which may be said to be built into all the basic institutions of the German social model (Lessenich, 2003c: 200).

[91]   In a certain sense, we find a similar constellation of contingent constitutional rights to work and social security, in this case not being thought of as subjective rights of the individual citizen but as a public obligation assumed by the socialist state, after World War II, in the German Democratic Republic.

literature), but also in a positive, apologetic sense of defending them as a matter of social rights (Petersen and Petersen, 2013: 42–3). For a short instance of history, it was the prewar, state-friendly economist Adolph Wagner's[92] 'economic understanding of the welfare state as associated with social reforms' (Petersen and Petersen, 2013: 41) – a welfare state 'close to present-day definitions' (Petersen and Petersen, 2013: 42) and going beyond von Stein's idea of a 'monarchy of social reform' (Kaufmann, 2012b: 66) – that seemed to have a chance of becoming dominant in German social policy language. But history chose another path, and what was to follow Weimar's 'proto-welfare state' was the racist, exclusionary, war-oriented 'people's welfare' (*Volkswohlfahrt*) of fascist Germany.[93]

The post-war regime: flying high – social partnership as a political philosophy

After World War II, the Western German *Sozialstaat* was to a certain extent constituted (and instituted) *ex negativo*: on one hand, it was sufficiently clear (and effectively ensured by the Western Allies) that it had to represent an explicit break with National Socialism; on the other hand, the socialist welfare state emerging in the eastern part of the country served as another – and possibly even more important – institutional countermodel (Hockerts, 1998).[94] In this constellation, post-war institution building resorted to Bismarck rather than to Weimar, giving special weight to the classical contribution based insurance systems (as opposed to tax financed programmes of public welfare); it was reminiscent of von Stein's (rather than Wagner's) idea of social policy as an agent of class compromise:[95] what was paramount to post-fascist (and anti-communist) policy makers in

---

[92] Wagner is commonly said to have invented the term *Wohlfahrtsstaat* in the 1870s, but see Petersen and Petersen (2013: 39) for competing evidence.

[93] Certainly, the burgeoning welfare state was not the least motive for the violent hatred that not only the Nazis, but the right-wing movement as a whole expressed and acted out against the Weimar Republic.

[94] The institutionalisation and popularity of the social market economy in Western Germany – with the prefix 'social' being the relevant innovation to the liberal discourse – was not least (and maybe mostly) a function of the German Democratic Republic's clamorous self-description as the homeland not only of socialism, but of social security.

[95] 'Von Stein's ... use of the concept "Sozialstaat" foreshadows the dismissal of the term "Wohlfahrtsstaat" after 1945' (Petersen and Petersen, 2013: 40).

the early *Bundesrepublik* was pacifying the battlefield the welfare state had been shown to be in Weimar times. And pacifying that battlefield meant levelling the playing field between capital and labour while incorporating them both into the common enterprise of reconstructing Germany and reviving the dynamics of the German economy.

Beginning with the work of von Stein, '"social policy" (in its German usage) … originated as a concept in social science that has gradually made a practical career in politics' (Kaufmann, 2012b: 59). However, only after 1945 has the concept been effectively anchored in German welfare semantics, and even then, public discourse is dominated rather by the terms *Sozialstaat* and, conspicuously, *Soziale Marktwirtschaft* (Petersen and Petersen, 2013: 40). The broad and common usage of the latter term ('social market economy') in politics and the media since the 1950s symbolises not only the vertiginous rise of economic prosperity in the context of the German economic miracle (*Wirtschaftswunder*), but also the traditional idea of a peaceful cohabitation of economic development and social stability, secured by a *Sozialstaat* that manages to integrate economic and social interests (Lessenich, 2003c: 117–31). Closely connected to this concept emerged, or rather re-emerged (Lessenich, 2003c: 131–43) from the historical memory of World War I, the term *Sozialpartnerschaft* (social partnership), which denoted the fact that capital and labour were no longer deadly enemies, but could (and should) engage in an antagonistic cooperation, advantageous and profitable not only for both of them, but for society at large. Even more ostensibly, talking of social peace (*sozialer Frieden*) became commonplace among the German public in the 1960s and 1970s: employers, unions, and government alike were expected to be open to the idea of cooperation and to processes of interest intermediation – and not least for restraining their individualistic 'pursuit of happiness' if and when necessary for the common good.

Taken together, the semantics of social market economy, social partnership and social peace all paved the way for an informal grand *Sozialstaat* coalition of both big social capitalist (van Kersbergen, 1995) parties – Christian and Social Democrats – and built the ideological setting for the 'politics of the middle way' (Schmidt, 1989) for which Western Germany became famous in the 1970s and 1980s. In this context, it is important to note that German middle way politics, whether right leaning or left leaning, were basically politics for the middle classes that had grown bigger and had profited immensely from the sociostructural 'elevator effect' (*Fahrstuhl-Effekt*; Beck, 1986: 122) owed to stable economic growth and an expanding welfare state. It was the middle classes that were being addressed by emblematic concepts of the German post-war social policy discourse, such as the technical term 'equivalence principle' (*Äquivalenzprinzip*), or the openly political formula of 'achievement justice'[96] (*Leistungsgerechtigkeit*), both of which referred to the idea that social policy should be directed not so much towards redistribution, but rather towards warranting income security and protecting achieved status positions (*Statussicherung*).

As long as the golden age of post-war growth and the Fordist welfare state persisted, the official narrative of the *Sozialstaat* as a huge positive-sum game serving the interests of labour and capital, economy and society, men and women, old and young alike, seemed to be credible to the German citizenry (and even to some of the many millions of migrant workers who had been attracted since the 1950s by the economic boom). But then came Gorbachev, Kohl, and German unification, which, instead of triggering a second economic miracle, initiated a process of substantial (and still ongoing) transformation of social policies in Germany.

The post-unification regime: playing by the rules – social policies for the active society

After the fall of the Berlin Wall and having enjoyed a brief honeymoon, reunified Germany, with its enlarged welfare state embodying 80 million people, started playing by the rules of globalisation, Europeanisation, and neoliberalism, just like any other European Union (EU) member. As envisaged by the EU at large, German social policy development after 1990 (and particularly reforms implemented since the turn of the century) has revolved around the idea of activation. The welfare regime of the Western German provision state (*Versorgungsstaat*) that compensated people for their loss of employment (that is, of their income earning capacity) increasingly came under pressure, going through a kind of retrospective or retroactive public delegitimation. Since the end of the 1990s, it became common sense in debates on social policy that the 'industrial' German welfare state was outdated, having set the wrong incentives by keeping people passive and on welfare (or transfer) dependency (Esping-Andersen, 1996). The new postindustrial philosophy that was being promoted by Christian and

---

[96]   It comes as no surprise that the German *Sozialstaat* has served as inspiration for the ideal-typical conception of Titmuss's 'Industrial Achievement-Performance Model of Social Policy' (Titmuss, 1974: 31), first, and later, Esping-Andersen's 'corporatist' respectively 'conservative' welfare regime (see Esping-Andersen, 1990).

Social Democrats alike (plus by Liberals and Greens) consisted of and insisted on activating people, meaning, first and foremost, bringing them back to work.

The 2003 labour market reforms, which became popular under the shorthand of *Hartz IV*, may be seen as a prototypical (and for that matter highly contested) example of German-style workfare policies. At the core of the activation discourse framing these and other reforms (in pension, health, or family policies) is the epistemic message that in a highly competitive environment, every individual (just like society as a whole) is supposed to play by the rules, which is to say, the rules of the market. Keeping in touch with the market and taking care of one's employability (*Beschäftigungsfähigkeit*) becomes the order of the day. Basically, it may be said that social policy has made a 'subjective turn' (Lessenich, 2008, 2011), effectively shifting the balance of responsibility for welfare production from the state to the individual.

In the emerging 'active society' (Walters, 1997) of the 21st century, the idea of social policy harkens back to its ideological roots, remodifying the meaning and weight of rights and responsibilities as institutionalised by the 20th century's welfare state. Today, individual rights and corresponding public responsibilities lose prominence, with public rights and corresponding individual responsibilities coming to the fore instead. In this process, the idea of 'social rights' is given a radically new meaning, referring not to what the individual may legitimately expect from the larger community, but to the legitimate claim of society for the individual engaging in 'pro-social' behaviour. People are urged to take care not only of themselves as a productive force, but also of social and economic productivity at large. From the activation perspective, society[97] has a legitimate expectation of its individual members to act in the public interest, enhancing and advancing the welfare of the larger collective; individual behaviour is meant to systematically take into account present or prospective public needs.[98] Consequently, what dominates most recent German social policy language is talk about the need to mobilise potential; harnessing untapped resources, including

---

[97] Depending on the discursive context, the interests and needs of 'society' may refer to the larger community, the general public, the national economy, the tax or contribution payer or simply the state itself.

[98] It may be said that in the German case, this tendency towards the responsibilisation of citizens for the common good, and the remoralisation of social policy that goes with it, is a strange amalgam of (as in other countries) neoliberal privatisation pressures, on the one hand, and (as a distinctive German feature) the collectivistic legacy of state socialism mobilising people in the public interest, on the other.

the human capital of women, children, and older people; advancing social inclusion (unequivocally meaning market participation); intensify prevention (the proactive care of one's own health, finance, education, mobility, employability); and safeguarding the sustainability (*Nachhaltigkeit*) of social policies (most prominently: for the sake of generational justice) by individuals *and* society alike.[99]

In summary, what is currently happening in the realm of social policy language is a new but typically German mode of trying to release the tension between state and society, the public and the private, the common good and individual welfare; the process involves projecting 'the social' and its political constitution into, on the one hand, the individual and individual's behaviour, and, on the other, the future and sustainable development. The emerging knowledge order of the activating welfare state centres on the idea that, if every individual acts responsibly today, there will be collective wellbeing tomorrow.

Cutting the long 20th century short: in search of the 'win-win' society

It is certainly problematic when contemporary understanding of social policy language and its central terms 'is automatically projected backwards in time' (Petersen and Petersen, 2013: 38). Trying to avoid this fallacy, what we wanted to suggest in this chapter is that, if analysed retrospectively, the early social policy thinking in Germany had a 'forward projection' in that it set the tone for the concepts and discourses to come. In historical and comparative research, welfare semantics should always be conceptualised as both a dependent *and* independent variable (Lessenich, 2003a): they mirror the development of modern societies just as much as they are drivers of that very development. Since its beginnings, German social policy was concerned with constituting and reproducing a synergetic relationship between state and society and, inextricably linked to this, between individual and collective benefits (Kaufmann, 2012a: 205–8). It was always understood as being – or having to be – 'a combination of socio-ethical with socio-utilitarian principles' (Petersen and Petersen, 2013: 41), a merger of individualistic (or rights oriented) and collectivistic (or duties oriented) principles.

---

[99] It is striking that most of the popular German welfare semantics of the last decade – *Potenziale, Ressourcen, Inklusion, Prävention, Nachhaltigkeit, Generationengerechtigkeit* – was adapted from the European (EU) discourse on social policy (Bruno et al, 2006).

In short, studied through the lens of social policy language, the historical development of the German *Sozialstaat* may be understood as a protracted search for 'win-win strategies' for devising and designing political and social order. In German social policy thinking, society was always seen as being in need of the state (Vogel, 2007). Today, the state in its guise as *aktivierender Sozialstaat* is seeking for ways and means to govern in the name of society, 'socializing' citizens to be and behave as a *homo societalis* (Lessenich, 2011: 324–6). Throughout their history, welfare (state) semantics have been closely tied to politics and power: the concepts and categories constituting social policy language are, in Bourdieu's terms, the stakes (*enjeux*) in the political struggle for symbolic rule. With welfare semantics inevitably changing with time, in Germany as elsewhere, at least one thing is certain: that this tight coupling of language and politics, power and knowledge, will not be changing at all.

References

Abelshauser, W. (ed.) (1987) *Die Weimarer Republik als Wohlfahrtsstaat. Zum Verhältnis von Wirtschafts- und Sozialpolitik in der Industriegesellschaft.* Wiesbaden: Steiner.

Beck, U. (1986). *Risikogesellschaft. Auf dem Weg in eine andere Moderne.* Frankfurt am Main: Suhrkamp.

Béland, D. (2011) 'The politics of social policy language', *Social Policy & Administration*, 45(1): 1–18.

Blyth, M. (1997) 'Moving the political middle: redefining the boundaries of state action', *Political Quarterly*, 68(3): 231-240.

Bourdieu, P. (1985) 'The social space and the genesis of groups' *Theory and Society*, 14(6): 723-744.

Bruno, I., Jacquot, S. and Mandin, L. (2006) 'Europeanization through its instrumentation: benchmarking, mainstreaming and the open method of coordination ... toolbox or Pandora's box?' *Journal of European Public Policy*, 13(4): 519-536.

Collier, D., Hidalgo, F. D. and Maciuceanu, A. O. (2006) 'Essentially contested concepts: debates and applications', *Journal of Political Ideologies*, 11(3): 211-246.

Esping-Andersen, G. (1990) *The Three Worlds of Welfare Capitalism.* Cambridge: Polity Press.

Esping-Andersen, G. (1996) 'Welfare states without work: the impasse of labour shedding and familialism in Continental European social policy', in G. Esping-Andersen (ed.), *Welfare States in Transition. National Adaptations in Global Economies.* London: Sage: 66-87.

Günther, F. (2004) *Denken vom Staate her. Die bundesdeutsche Staatsrechtslehre zwischen Dezision und Integration 1949-1970.* München: Oldenbourg.

Hegel, G. W. F. (1952 [1821]) *Outlines of the Philosophy of Right.* Translated by T. M. Knox. Oxford: Clarendon Press.

Hockerts, H. G. (ed.) (1998) *Drei Wege deutscher Sozialstaatlichkeit. NS-Diktatur, Bundesrepublik und DDR im Vergleich.* München: Oldenbourg.

Kaufmann, F.-X. (2003) *Sozialpolitisches Denken. Die deutsche Tradition.* Frankfurt am Main: Suhrkamp.

Kaufmann, F.-X. (2012a) 'The state and the production of welfare', in F.-X. Kaufmann, *European Foundations of the Welfare State.* New York and Oxford: Berghahn Books: 197-224.

Kaufmann, F.-X. (2012b) 'German origins of a theory of social reform. Hegel, Stein and the idea of "social policy"', in F.-X. Kaufmann, *European Foundations of the Welfare State.* New York and Oxford: Berghahn Books: 58-74.

Kaufmann, F.-X. (2012c) 'What comes after the classic welfare state?' In F.-X. Kaufmann, *European Foundations of the Welfare State.* New York and Oxford: Berghahn Books: 331-353.

Lessenich, S. (2003a) 'Wohlfahrtsstaatliche Semantiken − Politik im Wohlfahrtsstaat', in S. Lessenich (ed), *Wohlfahrtsstaatliche Grundbegriffe. Historische und aktuelle Diskurse.* Frankfurt and New York: Campus: 419-426.

Lessenich, S. (2003b) 'Der Arme in der Aktivgesellschaft − zum sozialen Sinn des "Förderns und Forderns"', *WSI-Mitteilungen,* 56(4): 214-220.

Lessenich, S. (2003c) *Dynamischer Immobilismus. Kontinuität und Wandel im deutschen Sozialmodell.* Frankfurt and New York: Campus.

Lessenich, S. (2008) *Die Neuerfindung des Sozialen. Der Sozialstaat im flexiblen Kapitalismus.* Bielefeld: Transcript.

Lessenich, S. (2011) 'Constructing the socialized self. Mobilization and control in the "active society"', in U. Bröckling, S. Krasmann and T. Lemke (eds), *Governmentality. Current Issues and Future Challenges.* New York and London: Routledge: 304-319.

Mahoney, J. (2000) 'Path dependence in historical sociology', *Theory and Society,* 29(4): 507-548.

Petersen, K. and Petersen, J. H. (2013) 'Confusion and divergence: Origins and meanings of the term "welfare state" in Germany and Britain, 1840-1940' *Journal of European Social Policy,* 23(1): 37-51.

Putnam, R. (1993) *Making Democracy Work: Civic Traditions in Modern Italy.* With R. Leonardi and R. Y. Nanetti. Princeton: Princeton University Press.

Sachße, C. (2003) 'Subsidiarität: Leitmaxime deutscher Wohlfahrts-staatlichkeit', in S. Lessenich (ed.), *Wohlfahrtsstaatliche Grundbegriffe. Historische und aktuelle Diskurse.* Frankfurt and New York: Campus: 191-212.

Schmidt, M. G. (1989) 'Learning from catastrophes. West Germany's public policy', in F. G. Castles (ed), *The Comparative History of Public Policy.* Cambridge: Polity Press: 56-99.

Simmel, G. (1965 [1908]) 'The poor'. Translated by Claire Jacobson. *Social Problems,* 13(2): 118-140.

Tenbruck, F. (1981) 'Emile Durkheim oder die Geburt der Gesellschaft aus dem Geist der Soziologie', *Zeitschrift für Soziologie,* 10(4): 333-350.

Titmuss, R.M. (1974) 'What is social policy?' In R.M. Titmuss, *Social Policy. An Introduction.* Ed. by B. Abel-Smith and K. Titmuss. New York: Pantheon Books: 23-32.

van Kersbergen, K. (1995) *Social Capitalism. A Study of Christian democracy and the Welfare State.* London and New York: Routledge.

Vogel, B. (2007) *Die Staatsbedürftigkeit der Gesellschaft.* Hamburg: Hamburger Edition.

Walters, W. (1997) 'The "active society": new designs for social policy', *Policy and Politics,* 25(3): 221-234.

TEN

Conceptual development of welfare and social policy in Japan

Toshimitsu Shinkawa and Yuki Tsuji

Translating 'welfare'

What strikes researchers who begin investigating the conceptual history of welfare and social policy in Japan is the sheer variety of translations of the term 'welfare'. Depending on the context, people use two different translations: *kōsei* and *fukushi*, and sometimes combine the two as *fukuri kōsei*. The Ministry of Health and Welfare in Japan, established in 1938 and merged in 2001 with the Ministry of Labour into the Ministry of Health, Labour and Welfare, was called the '*Kōsei Shō*.' In contrast, people use the term *fukushi*, instead of *kōsei*, when they say 'he/she is dependent on welfare,' suggesting that the person receives benefits from the system of means-tested social protection. Firm-specific welfare provisions, such as housing, health services, and family allowances, are called *fukuri kōsei*. *Fukushi kokka* is used as a translation of 'welfare state', a term most frequently used by scholars and welfare advocates, but not politicians and the mass media.

As is the case with Western languages, Japanese has another term closely related to the word welfare, that is, 'social security'. Translated as *shakai hosyō*, this term is associated with social insurance schemes in areas such as health care and pensions. By contrast, social welfare refers to means-tested social protection. Welfare is often used in this limited sense of the term. Confusingly, however, the word 'welfare' in 'welfare state' means welfare in the broad sense of the term, including social security, social welfare, and social services. In its recommendation to the government in 1950, the Advisory Council on Social Security classified various social security programmes into four categories: social insurance; public (governmental) assistance; public health and medical care; and social welfare (Advisory Council of Social Security, 1950). It proposed in 1950 that the core of Japan's social security structure should take the form of social insurance schemes financed through payroll contributions. Social policy is also a broad concept, covering welfare, education, labour management, and even peace and order in society. In other words, in Japan, social policy largely means a set of policies regarding all aspects of social life. More often than not, however, social policy specifically means welfare and social security policies. Consequently, in Japan, mapping social policy language and concepts is no easy task. The diversity of the translations of welfare and social policy suggests that, in different time periods, translators used the terms to imply different values and connotations. At the initial stage of modernisation in imperial Japan, where the overriding imperative was to catch up with the West, welfare and social policy were employed to make labour market relations more family-like, improve economic productivity, and demonstrate to the West that modern Japan had become civilised.

As shown in the following sections, Japanese political actors selectively introduced social policy concepts and programmes from Western European countries and the United States, while often modifying them by making a ' Japanese-style' interpretation of them. They sometimes legitimised such a modification by denouncing certain aspects of 'the West'. Whether praised or not, 'the West' in such discourses was represented as an abstract and homogeneous entity, without national specificities. In the initial Japanese modernisation period, 'the West' typically referred to Britain, France and Germany. After World War II, the US Occupation defined Japan's nation rebuilding. As for social policy, the US influence was explicit in the liberal reform of public assistance programmes, but barely witnessed in social security, where prewar social insurance schemes remained intact.

After World War II, the use of welfare and social policy as instruments aimed at promoting economic growth remained dominant and constitutionally guaranteed. According to the post-war Japanese Constitution, the Japanese people have a right to maintain minimum standards of wholesome and cultured living. The Constitution thus seems to grant Japanese people social citizenship rights. In 1967, however, the Supreme Court severely delimited such potential of citizenship rights by ruling that Article 25 defines the obligations of the state, but does not stipulate individuals' (social) rights. Since this ruling, the meaning of social policy in Japan has swung back and forth between welfare as a gift from above and welfare as a citizenship right.

This chapter begins with a brief quantitative overview of the development of social policy language and concepts in Japan. This overview is followed by a more detailed historical discussion of specific time periods, from the ever crucial Meiji Period (1868–1912), which initiated a Japanese-style form of modernisation, to the current period, marked by the considerable restructuring of the social policy arrangements created after World War II.

The frequency of usage

Figure 10.1 shows the frequency with which the word 'welfare' and its related expressions are used by speakers in both Houses of the Diet (the Japanese Parliament).[100] According to Figure 10.1, while *fukushi* had been most frequently used until the end of the last century, *shakai hosyō* has been the most popular at the beginning of the 21st century. The reason behind this shift is that fiscal tightness in social security, caused by increases in pension and health insurance expenditures, has become a serious political issue. Also noteworthy is that the welfare state has never been a popular word in the Diet.

The twin peaks seen in Figure 10.1 are explained as follows. The first peak, soon after World War II, was caused by democratisation under the occupation. The US Occupation, especially the Public Health and Welfare Section in the GHQ/SCAP,[101] led by New Dealers, urged the Japanese government to create a fair framework of welfare provision based on the new Constitution. It resulted in the 1950 revision of the Public Assistance Act, which granted citizens a right to public assistance as well as the right to appeal against a rejection ruling, although the Act preserved many selectivity aspects of the prewar system (Garon, 1997: 218–19). The second peak, in the first half of the 1970s, was due to a legitimacy crisis in the Conservative political regime. The production-first policy conducted by the Liberal Democratic Party (LDP) government led to Japan's economic prosperity which, on the other hand, tended to overlook the quality of urban life, the environment, and social protection. Growing negative assessments of the production-first policy contributed to the rise of anti-LDP civil movements and progressive local governments. To address these dilemmas, the government took major steps towards creating an institutional welfare

---

[100] Japanese words were entered individually into the search system for the Diet minutes and the number of meetings within which the word was stated were counted. A word mentioned several times in the same meeting on the same day counts as one mention. The search system for the Diet minutes is available at http://kokkai.ndl.go.jp/.

[101] The General Headquarters (GHQ) was headed by the General of the Army, Douglas MacArthur, who was appointed Supreme Commander for the Allied Powers (SCAP). GHQ contained several Special Staff Sections, one of which was the Public Health and Welfare Section (PHW), in charge of establishing social security systems.

Figure 10.1: Frequency in the usage of welfare-related terms in the Diet, 1947–2009

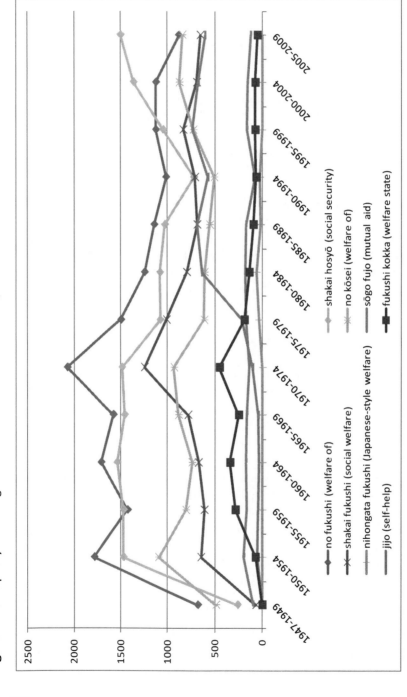

Source: Diet transcripts

state by introducing child allowances and free medical care for older people and improving benefit standards in pension and health insurance to a considerable extent. The increased number of references to the welfare state at that time indicates that the period was an exception in Japanese welfare history. However, the stagflation that emerged following the 1973 oil crisis thwarted the development of universalistic welfare programmes in the short run. Neoliberal attacks on the welfare state emerged in political discourse. When the LDP government clearly steered away from the European-style welfare state (meaning big government, though it had never come into existence in Japan) towards a 'Japanese-style welfare society' (meaning small government), the word *jijo* (self-reliance) was increasingly used.

Now that a quantitative overview of the evolution of social policy language and discourse in Japan has been given, it is time to offer a more detailed historical narrative of the development of social policy concepts over time, from the Meiji Period to the present.

Shifting from mercy to national mobilisation (1870s–1945)

Japan started its modernisation with the aim of 'enriching the country' (through industrialisation) and strengthening military powers (*fukoku kyohei*). To this end, Confucian-like values, such as diligence, frugality, and piety, were emphasised, to discipline the people (the Emperor's subjects). Accordingly, welfare was granted little significance in the governmental agenda. Welfare was nothing more than a gift from above, dispensed by the government at its discretion. Various welfare related concepts were introduced from Britain, Germany, and France, but their ideas were adjusted to the Japanese contexts. Ideas of poor relief (*kyuuhin*) and charity (*jizen*) were introduced from Britain, and social solidarity (*shakai rentai*) from France, but they were interpreted exclusively in terms of the public interest with no reference to individual rights. As the idea of the 'familial state' *(kazoku kokka)* entered the political discourse, the German idea of social policy was more frequently employed to justify its paternalism, statism, and the organic concept of society.

The Meiji government established the Mercy and Relief Regulation (*Jukkyū kisoku*) in 1874. The purpose of the regulation was to alleviate serious poverty soon after it successfully oppressed rebellions by the old class of *samurai*. For the first time in Japanese history, under strict eligibility conditions, the Mercy and Relief Regulation introduced a modest cash allowance awarded exclusively to foundlings and orphans under 13 years old, to people living alone and unable to work due to disabilities, illness, and old age, and to individuals in extreme poverty living with family members, who were under 15 years old or over 70, or who were incapable of working. As there existed no Ministry of Welfare or government social policy office, the Mercy and Relief system was administered by the Home Ministry. At that time, the welfare related translations described earlier, such as *fukushi*, *kōsei,* and *shakai hoshō*, had not yet appeared in the policy discourse. The Mercy and Relief Regulation was based on the principle of strict selectivism and subsidiarity, explicitly stating that poor relief was a gift from the state (Ishida, 1983: 182). The principle of subsidiarity works as follows. The person who cannot help themself should rely upon private welfare, first provided by their family and then by the neighbourhood. The state was supposed to be the last resort, to be appealed to only when no private welfare providers were available (Kinzley, 1991: 7–9). The people were unable to claim public welfare as a social citizenship right.

Nonetheless, groups of scholars and bureaucrats were greatly inspired by social policy development in the 'West' and sought the possibility of establishing a comprehensive public assistance system in Japan. Rising concerns among intellectuals and opinion leaders, about 'social problems' (*shakai mondai*) such as poverty, sanitation, and labour disputes, promoted the institution of the Japan Social Policy Association in 1897, which was modelled on the equivalent German association, the *Verein für Socialpolitik*, established in 1872 (Garon, 1989: 25; Kinzley, 1991: 22–4). Meanwhile, a group of bureaucrats in the Home Ministry committed themselves to liberal-minded reform. Influenced by social policy development in Germany, Gotō Shimpei, the chief of the Home Ministry's Bureau of Hygiene, and his followers, proposed ideas of poor relief and worker's sickness insurance in the 1890s, but never succeeded in obtaining broad support within and beyond the government (Garon, 1997: 39–40). Instead of introducing 'Western-type' social policy, a unique, Japanese way of resolving social problems was recommended.

At the beginning of the 20th century, the new leaders of the Home Ministry, led by Inoue Tomoichi, praised Japanese-style welfare policy and criticised the 'poor laws' witnessed in Britain, Germany and other Western countries. Inoue had visited Western Europe to study welfare programmes, and realised that Western-style poor relief was unable to provide a silver bullet for Japanese social policy (Garon, 1997: 41).[102] He considered the British model so liberal that it could cause

---

[102] He served as chief of the Bureau of Local Affairs in the Home Ministry (1897–1912) and the Governor of the Tokyo Prefecture (1915–19).

welfare abuse, by giving welfare as a right of citizenship (Ishida, 1989: 253–6). Inoue insisted that the Japanese Relief Regulation system be administered under the 'principle of strictly limited assistance', instead of the 'principle of obligatory assistance by the state'. He worried about the possibility that generous public assistance without limitations would ruin the affection, morality, sympathy, and fraternity necessary for maintaining family ties and neighbourhood level mutual aid. The Japanese state, they believed, was, and had to be constructed upon, familial relationship (Ishida, 1989: 248–9).

In the late 1910s, the concept of social work (*shakai jigyo*) appeared in governmental social policy discourse. The Division of Poor Relief in the Home Ministry was reorganised into the Division of Social Affairs in 1919, and its authority and function were reinforced by its upgrade into a fully fledged Department of Social Affairs in 1920. Such changes reflected the concerns of the government with social peace at the time, following the 1918 Rice Riots[103] (Ishida, 1983: 192). The concept of social solidarity *(shakai rentai)*, imported from France, seems to have had some influence on the promotion of social works in Japan. Social solidarity, however, was understood as an indication that society was an organism and that individuals were its parts. Neither social justice nor the obligation of the state was taken into account (Tago, 1922; Ishida, 1983: 268–74).

As industrialisation took hold, the government, aware of increased tensions between labour and capital, passed the Poor Relief Act in 1929. The Poor Relief Act slightly increased the amounts of cash allowance and recognised the obligation of the state to provide the poor with relief partially financed out of the national treasury. It substantially expanded governmental expenditure and coverage (Shinkawa, 2007: 65). Simultaneously, however, the Poor Relief Act denied citizens' right to claim public welfare and excluded those who lost their jobs due to structural changes in the economy.

In 1938, after the outbreak of the Second Sino-Japanese War, the government adopted the term *kōsei* for the first time by establishing the Ministry of Health and Welfare (*Kōsei Shō*). The new Ministry took over the jurisdiction of the Department of Social Affairs in the Home Ministry. The term *kōsei* originates from a classic Chinese history book, and its literal translation is 'thickening people's lives,' meaning

---

[103] Being angry at the skyrocketing price of rice and hoarding by rice merchants in the wake of the Siberian Intervention, millions of people participated in smashing and setting fire to wholesale merchants' stores all over Japan (Garon, 1989: 40–1).

'enriching people's lives' (Kōsei Shō, 1999). During wartime, a new social programme called *Senji Kōsei Jigyō* (wartime welfare project) aimed at increasing and mobilising all national resources for the purpose of winning the all-out war *(sōryokusen)*. In this vein, the state intervened in every aspect of people's private lives in order to enhance the nation's production by cultivating human resources. There were also some references to Nazi Germany's totalitarian use of social work since the 1930s. The Nazi's totalitarian social work was employed to criticise Western individualism and embrace the nation as a community. On the other hand, Japan's welfare model was conceived of as different from Germany's in the respect that Japan maintained her traditional familialism and did not have to rely on Nazi-style dictatorship (Ishida, 1989: 284–5). In the process of total mobilisation, the government employed the paternalistic concept of 'familial state' (*kazoku kokka*) so as to ensure national cohesion. To explain the concept, it was said that the Emperor was the father of the people, and the people, his 'babies' ('*sekishi*').

Establishing the welfare state (1945–1960s)

The end of World War II and the democratisation of Japan led by the Occupation Forces drastically changed both the language and conceptual map of social policy. The US Occupation of Japan was pursued through an indirect rule system, in which the Japanese government retained certain administrative and legal powers while the GHQ/SCAP gave many orders to democratise Japan's social, economic and political systems. The ambivalence of this occupation regime was reflected in social policy. Public assistance schemes were reformed under the strong leadership of the GHQ/SCAP as urgent measures to fight adversity and poverty brought about by the war. On the other hand, the Japanese government (the Ministry of Health and Welfare) took the initiative in establishing and expanding social insurance schemes, such as health insurance, pensions, employment insurance, and workers' compensation (Takahashi and Ozaki, 2000: 46-51).

As mentioned earlier, Japan's new Constitution affirmed social citizenship. The GHQ/SCAP drew up a draft of the new Constitution in February 1946 and handed it down to the Japanese government. The slightly revised version of the draft was passed in the Diet in 1946, and the new Constitution came into effect in 1947. Article 25 stipulates that all people have the right to minimum standards of wholesome and cultured living. Paragraph 2 of Article 25 explicitly states the obligation of the state to promote social welfare (*shakai fukushi*), social security (*shakai hosyō*) and public health (*kōsyū eisei*). To substantiate this principle, the Advisory Council on Social Security issued the 1950 recommendation on major social security issues, which reflected the influence of the 1942 Beveridge Report.

In February 1946, GHQ/SCAP issued the Japanese government with a memorandum, SCAPIN 775, promoting the principle of public assistance, according to which the government should now be responsible for providing 'adequate food, clothing shelter and medical care equally to all indigent persons without discrimination or preferential treatment'. In response, the Japanese government established the Public Assistance Act (literally Life Protection Law) in 1946 and revised it in 1950. In spite of GHQ's explicit call for universalism, the government slipped several modifications into the Act, as it would only offer benefits when applicants were unable to receive necessary support from their families. The Act emphasised the importance of fostering 'independence' and 'self-reliance' among recipients (Garon, 1997: 218–19).

The term *fukushi* is adopted in a number of titles of laws, in conjunction with the category of beneficiaries. The government legislated a series of welfare laws, including the Child Welfare Act (1947), the Physically Disabled Persons Welfare Act (1949), the Social Welfare Act (1951), the Act for the Welfare of the Mentally Retarded Persons (1960), the Act for the Welfare of the Aged (1963), and the Act on Welfare of Mothers with Dependents and Widows (1964). To expand welfare programmes in a comprehensive fashion, some welfare experts proposed the concept of the welfare state (*fukushi kokka*). During the 1950 Diet session, a number of Diet members referred to the welfare state and practices of well established social security systems in advanced industrial countries, ranging from the US to Sweden. The 'welfare state' was apparently a positive term for expressing an ideal towards which Japan should be headed.

The term *fukushi*, however, as shown in the titles of the aforementioned laws, tends to be linked to means- or incomes-tested benefits provided for people in special need. In 1957, Shigeru Asashi, who had received welfare benefits, sued the government on the grounds that low-level welfare benefits were unable to satisfy the right to the minimum standards of wholesome and cultural living guaranteed by Article 25 of the Constitution. Asahi won in the trial court but lost in the Court of Appeal. The Supreme Court did not make a concrete judgement on the case, as Asahi passed away before its final decision, but released its view in 1967 that Article 25 itself defines the obligation of the state but does not directly accord individuals concrete rights. The Court went on to state that while the Public Assistance Act granted people the right to receive welfare benefits, it was left to the discretion of the Minister of Health and Welfare to set 'the minimum standards of wholesome and cultured living'.

In Japan, as in other countries, the concept of social security (*shakai hosyō*) is employed to refer to social insurance schemes covering workers and their families. The 1950 recommendation by the Advisory Council on Social Security insisted that in order to prevent welfare policies from impairing people's idea of individual responsibility, core social security functions must be performed by social insurance schemes in which benefits are derived from contributions. In maintaining the social insurance programmes established in the prewar and wartime periods, the post-war Japanese social security system never really introduced social policy universality based on citizenship. Post-war social security development followed the same social insurance path. For instance, the Employees' Pension Insurance Act (1954), the Workers' Accident Compensation Insurance Act (1947), the National Health Insurance Act (which in 1958 replaced the 1938 National Health Insurance Act), and the Employment Insurance Act (1974) are all social insurance based. The principle of mutual aid (*sōgo fujo*) is often invoked to explain the idea of a social insurance system and to justify the establishment of cooperative associations for employees and for small business owners.

Moving towards a Japanese-style welfare society (1970s–80s)

Social spending in Japan showed a steep increase in the early 1970s. The change can be attributed to the rise of civil movements and the so-called 'progressive' leftist local governments that criticised environmental disruption and overpopulation in urban areas as negative effects of rapid economic growth and production-first policy in the post-war Japan. Their criticisms challenged the legitimacy of the conservative governance in post-war Japan. To cope with the crisis, the ruling alliance (that is, the LDP, the state bureaucracy and business leaders) agreed on the expansion of public welfare (Calder, 1988: 371–5; Shinkawa, 2005: 69–93). By that time, there was a broadly shared perception in the ruling alliance that Japan's endeavour to catch up with the Western countries in economic terms had been completed, and that the next goal would be catching up in terms of welfare and quality of life. Hence, in 1973, Prime Minster Tanaka Kakuei declared the First Year of Welfare (*Fukushi Gan'nen*) and initiated a free medical care programme for older people as well as improved benefit levels for pension and health insurance schemes.

The period of welfare expansion did not last long. The 1973 oil crisis ended the era of rapid economic growth for Japan and brought about serious fiscal deficits. The term 'welfare state' suddenly took on a negative connotation. The ruling alliance, which had expanded welfare benefits for a short time before the oil crisis, devised the concept of a 'Japanese-style welfare society' (JSWS, *Nihongata Fukushi Shakai*) to justify a 'reconsideration of welfare' (*fukushi minaoshi*) by denouncing the Western-style welfare state. Portraying Western-style welfare states (ranging from the UK to Scandinavia) as a major cause of what became known as the 'advanced countries'/British/European disease', which had spread self-indulgence and dependence upon the state among the citizenry while reducing economic productivity, they advocated collectivism as the only true Japanese social policy tradition. In their arguments, advocates of the JSWS claimed that Western-style individualism had led to egocentrism and public dependence, in sharp contrast to Japan's tradition of self-reliance and mutual aid (Shinkawa and Pempel, 1996: 309–22; Shinkawa, 2005: 101).

In the New Economic and Social Plan approved by the Cabinet in 1979, JSWS was officially acknowledged as the approach selected to foster future social and economic development.[104] Self-reliance and mutual aid, especially within the family, neighbourhoods and the workplace, were defined as the essential elements of a true JSWS. The role of the state was to be limited to the 'efficient' provision of 'appropriate' public welfare to those in real need. The increased usage of the term *jijo* (self-reliance) in the political discourse of the 1980s reflected the fact that JSWS ideas prevailed within the country's policy making arena. It should be noted that according to the concept of JSWS, the term 'welfare society' (*fukushi shakai*) is viewed as opposed to the welfare state (*fukushi kokka*). From this perspective, the role of society should be extended to limit the scope of state provided welfare (Ishida, 1989: 298). According to the JSWS perspective, society is assumed to be composed of traditional communities, in which families and face-to-face relations play major roles in the provision of welfare. In the 1978 White Paper on Welfare, for instance, the high rate of three-generation households was praised as a 'hidden asset of the Japanese welfare system' (Kōsei Shō, 1978).

---

[104] The term 'JSWS' was first employed by the government in 1977, by the Economic Planning Agency (Hyodo, 1990).

With the backdrop of soaring budget deficits accelerated by the creation of public works projects aimed at increasing effective demand and ensuring employment in the late 1970s, the LDP government launched an 'administrative reform' in the 1980s, the slogan of which was 'fiscal reconstruction without tax increases.' In 1981, the Interim Commission was established to initiate the administrative reform proposed, 'a welfare society with economic viability', which was but a renewed version of JSWS. The leading political figure on the scene was Nakasone Yasuhiro, who served as Director General of Administrative Management Agency from 1980 to 1982. He was appointed Prime Minister in 1982 due to his prominent leadership in the administrative reform. He substantially followed the policy ideas and political styles of Margaret Thatcher and Ronald Reagan. That is, Nakasone presented himself as a neoliberal leader in Japan. He, however, did not commit himself to welfare retrenchment, by stressing the importance of streamlining administration and cautiously avoiding reference to welfare cutbacks.

To promote economic growth by restraining social security expenditure, the government abolished the free medical care programme for older people and revised the public pension schemes so as to reduce benefits while increasing contribution rates. As a result of such changes, the ratio of total social security expenditure to GDP (Gross Domestic Product) remained at about 11% throughout the 1980s (Kokuritsu Shakai Hoshō Jinkō Mondai Kenkūsho, 2012). This is what the government had planned in adopting the concept of JSWS starting in the late 1970s.

Farewell to the Japanese-style welfare society (1990s)

Since the 1980s, social policy discourse in Japan has prominently featured demographic terms and concepts. As early as 1980, the subtitle of the White Paper on Welfare was 'In Pursuit of Soft Landing on an Aging Society' (Kōsei Shō, 1980). The concepts of 'an ageing society' and 'a longevity society' appeared five times in the White Paper's subtitles during the 1980s. Attempts by welfare bureaucrats to persuade the general public of an oncoming demographic crisis finally proved successful when, in 1990, it was revealed that the 1989 total fertility rate (births per woman) had decreased to 1.57, the lowest ever recorded until then. Stressing such anxieties about fertility, the subtitle of the 1993 White Paper on Welfare was 'For Children, Opening up the Future: Considering Social Support for Childrearing'.

Heightened concerns with population ageing and low fertility led to several important changes in Japanese social policies, especially in the field of social care (Peng, 2002, 2004). Faced with rapid population ageing and the accompanying increase in social expenditure, the government started to boost the number of care workers and facilities starting in the late 1980s. In 1997, the government passed the Long-term Care Insurance Act, thereby providing public support for care of older people *(kaigo shien)*. The new long-term care insurance decreased the range of discretion by the administration and extended entitlements to practically all senior citizens (Tsuji, 2011). At the same time, the government launched the so-called Angel Plan, followed by a New Angel Plan to support childrearing *(ikuji shien)* by expanding the quantity and variety of previously scarce childcare services.

Social support (*shakai-teki shien*) suddenly became popular in the 1990s. It then became urgent to develop social services for childrearing, care of older people, families, and working women. The necessity was also perceived to expand support for homeless and disabled people, unemployed people (especially members of the younger generation), and crime victims. The concept of social support reflected the idea of welfare mix in an age of fiscal austerity. The Director General of the Economic Planning Agency stated in the Lower House in January 1996 that "in order for people to live with a sense of security in the midst of falling fertility and population ageing, the government was going to construct a new social support system by nicely balancing self-help *(jijo)*, mutual help *(kyōjo)*, and public help *(kōjo)*".

To a certain extent, socialisation of not only care of older people but also childcare was necessary to promote women's labour participation. More women needed to be mobilised into the labour market to make up for labour shortage, keep the economy viable and, in turn, make social security and welfare programmes sustainable in the context of the new ageing society. The government asserted the necessity of building 'a Sustainable Social Security System' (*Jizoku Kanō na Shakai Hosyō Seido*). The concept of gender equality has sometimes been employed in the recent social policy discourse as an instrument to expand the labour force and secure tax bases through women's increased labour participation. Lately, profeminist state officials and business leaders have used the term 'work–life balance', promoted by international organisations such as the OECD (Organisation of Economic Co-operation and Development) and ILO (International Labour Organization), reflecting the drive to change assumptions about the role of women in the economy and society in a new demographic environment.

The encouragement of women's labour participation as well as the rejection of the male breadwinner model clearly indicates the end of the government's commitment to the idea of JSWS. The government officially acknowledged the weakened function of family welfare and the need to provide public care services. Firm-specific welfare arrangements, especially corporate pensions, were also in decline. Faced with difficulties in fund management due to the prolonged recession in the 1990s, a large number of companies disbanded their pension funds or shifted benefit-defined schemes into contribution-defined schemes modelled on the American 401(k), in which employers pay fixed amounts of contributions into individual retirement accounts and let employees manage their account. The change reflected a turnaround in labour–management relations. Japanese firms no longer guaranteed lifelong employment and desired more flexibility in employment. Thus, the two major pillars of JSWS, that is, family welfare and firm-specific welfare, had been severely weakened by the end of 20th century. Familialism is still deeply rooted in Japanese society, but social policy is no longer able to count on it.

Woman-friendly concepts and language exist in the context of neoliberal ideas of small government and employment flexibility. Structural reform (*Kōzō Kaikaku*) is a key concept for understanding Japanese neoliberalism. Neoliberals insist on drastic restructuring of the Japanese political, economic and social systems by portraying them as outdated. In 1996, the Hashimoto government set the tone for structural reform, and five years later, the Koizumi government (April 2001–September 2006) largely completed the reform process. Structural reform was promoted as inevitable and indispensable for recovery from the prolonged recession that followed the burst of the Japanese economic bubble in the early 1990s. Under the umbrella concept of structural reform, the Hashimoto government restructured state ministries and agencies, carried out a deregulation of the labour market and introduced the market mechanism in social policy programmes. Under the slogan 'let the market do it', the Koizumi government conducted further labour market deregulation, privatised postal-related services, and continued welfare retrenchment. The Koizumi structural reform was the final blow to the 'Japanese-style welfare society'. Lifelong employment, corporate and family welfare, preferential treatment of the male breadwinner model in taxation and social policy are no longer taken for granted. They are denounced as major factors causing 'rigidity' in Japanese society.

Such policies as to socialise care and promote women's labour participation are comprehensible in the context of structural reform, where their role is to overcome rigidity and enhance labour market flexibility. Together with the younger generation, women constitute a major part of the marginal, lower income and precarious workforce. In the neoliberal discourse of structural reform, social security and welfare are no longer protected as a means by which to reduce inequality and attain social justice. Instead, they are discussed more exclusively in terms of fiscal balance, sustainability, and efficiency. Terms such as 'work–life balance' and 'gender equality' are used in the same vein. Labour market deregulation and reduced social protection have brought about greater wage differentials while increasing the number of poor working people, leading to the power shift in the general election of September 2009, which witnessed the historic defeat of the ruling LDP.

The post-2009 Democratic Party of Japan (DPJ) government apparently took an anti-neoliberal stance by employing such ideas as 'life-first' and 'decent work'. They introduced tuition-free education in public high schools and universal child allowances, as well as stricter regulations protecting the temporary and part-time workforces. These measures, however, did little to fundamentally alter the neoliberal trend that has been exacerbated since the late 1990s. With few policy achievements, the DPJ lost power in the election of December 2012, and the new LDP government, led by Prime Minister Abe, advocated '*Abenomics*', which is a renewed version of the production-first policy, paying little attention to welfare and social protection, in the name of economic recovery.

Conclusion

Welfare and social policy were concepts imported from the European countries to Japan in its initial period of modernisation. Mixed with traditional Confucian values, welfare was initially marginalised as exclusively residual and complementary to self-reliance and mutual aid. Welfare was provided under strict conditions to protect the public interest (peace and order), not to protect individuals. The term 'social policy' became prevalent, as the state was convinced that minimum welfare provision would contribute to the improved quality of human resources and their effective mobilisation. Following the end of World War II, the new Constitution drafted by the US Occupation administration explicitly guaranteed social citizenship, but the Supreme Court of Japan later interpreted the concept in such a restrictive fashion so as to grant the obligation of the state but deny individuals' rights to entitlements.

Accordingly, the term 'welfare state', which is otherwise so closely associated with citizens' rights, has never been used in the Diet except for a short period in the early 1970s. Social citizenship rights have never been predominant in Japan. The word 'welfare' is being marginalised, and 'social security' means nothing more than 'social insurance'. Building a welfare state based on universalism has never been seriously discussed in Japan. Even during the short period of a social policy surge in the early 1970s, political actors focused on raising the benefits granted by established social insurance schemes and never on extending their efforts to create a universal welfare state. Although free medical care for older people existed as a universal policy for those aged 70 and over due to its generous income test, it remained in place only for the period between 1973 and 1982.

The proposal of JSWS indicated the rejection of an idea of an 'institutional welfare state' based on universalism. By creating a JSWS, Japan was expected to avoid the European disease (that is, the welfare state). According to the idea of JSWS, social policy in Japan is subordinated to a 'production-first' policy. Public welfare expansion should be restrained and rearranged in such a way as to maintain the viable economy. The concept of JSWS reaffirmed the importance of maintaining a small government and private welfare functions. Corporate pension and retirement payments were expected to complement modest public pension benefits, while the family (especially wives, mothers and grandmothers) was expected to provide childcare and care of older people.

As population ageing accelerated and fertility sharply declined, however, the JSWS reached its limit. To address the decreasing number of the working-age population, the promotion of women's labour participation became a critical issue in the 1990s. Social services were extended with slogans such as '*kaigo shien*' (support for care of older people) and '*ikuji shien*' (support for childrearing). The government further promoted a fairer burden of family care between men and women by advocating a work–life balance and gender equality. Such women-friendly terms, however, do not necessarily reflect policy inclinations towards a social democratic or an institutional welfare state. They are comprehensible as components of neoliberal 'structural reform', considering the fact that female labour is mobilised mainly as a contingent workforce with low wages and no social protection to enhance flexibility in the labour market.

The DPJ government that ruled Japan after the 2009 election temporarily deviated from the trajectory of welfare development set by the LDP government in its inclination towards universal welfare.

Its policies of free education in public schools and universal child allowance, however, had no major effects, based as they were on credit-claiming politics. There was no grand design for the future. They proposed the idea of combining social security and tax reform (*shakaihosho to zei no ittaikaikaku*), which, however, ended up with an increase in the consumption tax with few social security improvements. The DPJ government also reviewed regulations on the contingent workforce, but the revision remained too minor to improve their working conditions. The concept and ideas of the structural reform still define political discourse; hence, fiscal balance, sustainability, flexibility, and efficiency dominate social policy discourse. Japan's attempts to avoid European welfare states have led it to a system of flexibility, with a thin layer of social protection. Throughout various stages of welfare development, the concept of social citizenship has remained marginal to Japan's social policy discourse.

References

Advisory Council of Social Security (ACSS) (1950) 'A recommendation on social security', in Shakai Hosho Kenkyujo (ed.), *Sengo no Shakai Hosho: Data (Social Security in Postwar Japan: Data)*. Tokyo: Shiseido. Pp. 187–205.

Beveridge, W. (1942) *Social insurance and Allied Services: Report* (the 'Beveridge Report'), New York, NY: Macmillan.

Calder, K. E. (1988) *Crisis and Compensation*. Princeton, NJ: Princeton University Press.

Garon, S. (1989) *The State and Labor in Modern Japan*. Berkeley, CA: University of California Press.

Garon, S. (1997) *Molding Japanese Minds: The State in Everyday Life*. Princeton, NJ: Princeton University Press.

Hyodo, T. (1990) 'Tenkanki niokeru Shaaki Seisaku Shiso (Social Policy Ideas in Transition)', in Shakai Seisaku Sosho Henshu Iinkai (ed.), *Sengo Shakai Seisaku no Kiseki (The Trajectory of Postwar Social Policy)*. Tokyo: Keibunsha, pp. 135–157.

Ishida, T. (1983) *Kindai Nihon no Seiji Bunka to Gengo Shōchō (Political Culture and Linguistic Symbol in Modern Japan)*. Tokyo: Tōkyō Daigaku Syuppankai.

Ishida, T. (1989) *Nihon no Seiji to Kotoba: 'Jiyū" to 'Fukushi' (Japanese Politics and Language: Liberty and Welfare)*. Tokyo: Tōkyō Daigaku Syuppankai.

Kinzley, W. D. (1991) *Industrial Harmony in Modern Japan: The Invention of a Tradition*. London: Routledge.

Kokuritsu Shakai Hoshō Jinkō Mondai Kenkūsho (National Institute of Population and Social Security Research) (2012) *Heisei 22 nendo Shakai Hoshō Hiyō Tōkei (Financial Statistics of Social Security in Japan 2010)* (www.e-stat.go.jp/SG1/estat/List.do?lid=000001103185, accessed March 18, 2013.)

Kōsei Shō (various years) *Kōsei Hakusho (White Paper on Welfare)*. Tokyo: Ōkura Shō Insatsukyoku.

Peng, I. (2002) 'Social care in crisis: gender, demography, and welfare state restructuring in Japan.' *Social Politics*, 9: 411-43.

Peng, I. (2004) 'Postindustrial pressures, political regime shifts, and social policy reform in Japan and South Korea.' *Journal of East Asian Studies*, 4: 389-425.

Shinkawa, T. (2005) *Nihongata Fukushi Rejīmu no Hatten to Hen'yō (Development and Transformation of the Japanese-style Welfare Regime)*. Kyoto: Mineruba Syobō.

Shinkawa, T. (2007) 'Democratization and social policy development in Japan', in Yusuf Bangura (ed.), *Democracy and Social Policy (UNRISD social policy in a development context series)*. Basingstoke: Palgrave Macmillan, pp.62-89.

Shinkawa, T. and T. J. Pempel. (1996) 'Occupational welfare and the Japanese experience', in Michael Shaleve (ed.) *The Privatization of Social Policy?*, Houndmills, Basingstoke: Macmillan Press, pp. 280-326.

Tago, I. (1922) *Shakai Jigyō (Social Work)*: Tokyo: Teikoku Chihō Gyōsei Gakkai.

Takahashi, T. and T. Ozaki (2000) 'Nihon Shakai Hoshō Hō no Keisei Katei 5 (Formation Processes of Japan's Social Security Laws, No.5.)' *Sōka Hōgaku, 29(3): 45-116.*

Tsuji, Y. (2011) 'Re-imagined intimate relations: elder and child care in Japan since the 1990s', in Rianne Mahon and Fiona Robinson (eds), *Feminist Ethics and Social Policy: Towards a New Global Political Economy of Care*. Vancouver, BC: University of British Columbia Press, pp.111-125.

ELEVEN

Transition to the 'universal welfare state': the changing meaning of 'welfare state' in Korea

Huck-ju Kwon

When the current author's book, *The Welfare State in Korea: the Politics of Legitimation*, was published in the late 1990s (Kwon, 1999), many fellow Korean academics and students asked the same question:'Do you think Korea is a welfare state?'The response was,'Korea is not a welfare state, but the book examines the welfare state in Korea'.[105] People were a little confused at this answer. This was because the concept of the welfare state had at least two different meanings. First, in the Korean language, the welfare state (*Pokjikukga*) is a nation-state that provides a comprehensive range of social protection to its citizens, a kind of ideal state of affairs. At the time of the book's publication, the Asian economic crisis that began in 1997–8 had taken its toll. Not only were many Korean citizens hard hit by the economic downturn, but those who escaped it also felt vulnerable due to the lack of social protection. Most Korean people did not consider Korea to be a welfare state in the sense described here. Rather, they felt that Korea fell far short of the mark, and that it should strive further to become a welfare state, a sort of 'good society', which is still the language very much used every day by the Korean media and the general public.

Second, the welfare state is understood as a set of public institutions and policies that aim to provide social protection to citizens. The state (*Kukga*) in the Korean language is a collection of public institutions and policies, and thus the welfare state is a set of public institutions

---

[105]　Throughout this chapter, Korea refers to the Republic of Korea (South Korea) not to the Democratic People's Republic of Korea (North Korea).

and policies that aim to provide social protection for citizens.[106] This second understanding of the welfare state is more analytical than the first one. The author's book (Kwon, 1999) in fact adopts this second definition of the welfare state, as it enables an examination of those public institutions and policies for social protection, even though they may not be able to provide comprehensive social protection to citizens.

Fifteen years after the Asian economic crisis, Korean society was engaged in a debate on the 'universal' welfare state. During the presidential election that took place in December 2012, two leading candidates from the major political parties made it clear that they would pursue policies to establish some sort of 'universal' welfare state once they were elected. The eventual winner, President Park Geunhye, promised that her government would make people happy with the welfare state, which could meet all the different demands of citizens from all walks of life. In order to achieve that goal, she would establish a welfare state that could address the various welfare needs of citizens at the different points of the life course.[107] The opposition party, the Democratic Party, made more specific promises about the 'universal' welfare state. It placed a great deal of emphasis on 'free' social programmes such as free healthcare and childcare.[108] It also made it clear that its social policy programmes would reduce income inequality. Following the debates on the 'universal' welfare state during the presidential election, it seems clear that, in Korea, there is something that can be called the welfare state. Nevertheless, it is a 'selective' welfare state as opposed to a 'universal' welfare state and, the presidential candidates believed, Korea should move towards a 'universal' welfare state. But what does it mean by a 'universal' welfare state, exactly?

These two examples show that, as in other countries analysed in this book, the term 'welfare state' has multiple meanings in Korea. Over the last 50 years, during which it made a rapid transition from a poor, war-torn society to an affluent industrialised country, Korea has evolved from having a minimal structure of welfare programmes to a comprehensive set of institutions and policies for social protection. This chapter argues that, in Korea, the concept of welfare state has referred to

---

[106] In fact, the welfare state was not explicitly defined in the book, *The Welfare State in Korea* (Kwon, 1999). This was done in the edited book, *Transforming the Developmental Welfare State in East Asia* (Kwon, 2005).

[107] This became one of four overall policy orientations of the government. www.president.go.kr/assignment02.php

[108] Democratic Party's Presidential Manifesto (http://minjoo.kr/wp-content/uploads/2012/12/)

at least two understandings: first, an ideal state of affairs that the country should reach, as it strives to become a modern and advanced society; and, second, a set of public institutions aiming for social protection, a simple and analytical notion of institutions. Over the last 50 years, the concept of the welfare state has changed its meaning according to political strategies to establish the welfare state at different conjunctures. In this chapter, It is argued that the understandings of the welfare state moved closer towards the second meaning, while the aspiration for the welfare state as an ideal state of affairs, where a certain level of wellbeing is guaranteed by the state, remains strong, if not stronger than before. It is suggested that the welfare state is one of the essential components of Korea's modernisation project which goes beyond the left and right divide of the Korean politics. This chapter focuses on understandings of the welfare state articulated by policy makers and academics, examining their political strategies to lead Korean society to the welfare state.

Two meanings of 'welfare state' in the context of economic development

In the last five decades, when Korea managed to achieve a remarkable social and economic transformation, economic development was the top priority for virtually all incumbent governments. For this reason, the understanding of the welfare state has been shaped by its relationship to economic development. In this section, two significant historical conjunctures that shaped the meanings of the welfare state in relation to the political strategies for economic development are examined: the first took place in the early 1960s, soon after the military coup in 1961, and the second in the late 1990s, after the 1997 Asian economic crisis.

Government efforts for economic development began in the mid-1950s, when the Korean War ended in a stalemate, but it was the military government established by the 1961 coup d'état that launched a substantial economic development initiative and implemented it in earnest. Its undisputed leader, Park Chung Hee (in office 1961–79), was Chairman of the Supreme Council of National Reconstruction as it launched the First Five Year Economic Development Plan to revitalise the country. In a 1963 speech, Park gave his idea of development a clear purpose, project, and priority:

> I want to emphasise and reemphasise that the key factor of the May 16 Military Revolution was in effect an industrial revolution in Korea. Since the primary objective

> of the revolution was to achieve a national renaissance, the
> revolution envisaged political, social and cultural reforms as
> well. My chief concern, however, was economic revolution
> (Park, 1963: 173).

This speech clearly set out the policy priority of the government, which could be summarised as an 'economy first' policy (Park, 1963: 186). Nevertheless, economic development was not the only policy goal on which the military government focused, as it also recognised the need to address social welfare. Park believed that the Korean government should 'provide all the people in this country with decent lives as human beings' (Park, 1962: 224). Although he made it clear that this would be possible only after the achievement of the overall growth of the economy, he did not simply wait.

In 1962, in fact, Park asked his Cabinet to prepare a policy proposal for social policy programmes (Seo, 1962), and he then announced his intention to introduce social policy programmes in his New Year speech (Seo, 1962). The task to prepare the policy proposal was handed to the Committee for Social Security (CSS) (Ministry of Labour, 1981). The CSS was an informal study group that included bureaucrats from the Ministry of Health and Social Affairs, doctors, and academics who were concerned with the idea of introducing social security programmes in Korea. Although the Ministry of Health and Social Affairs had long planned to give this informal group official status, the move to accommodate the CSS as an official bureau of research was quickly completed, as the military government needed to set up a substantial plan for social welfare.

After only six months of study, the CSS formulated policy proposals regarding unemployment insurance, health insurance, and industrial accident insurance. The CSS reported the proposals to the Supreme Council of National Reconstruction, the Cabinet of the government, for approval. Their recommendation for industrial accident insurance passed through the deliberation process without much difficulty, since the military government was about to embark on an ambitious economic development plan (Son, 1981). The military clearly saw the need for industrial accident insurance, but the proposals for unemployment insurance and health insurance were rejected by the Supreme Council, because they thought that they would impose an excessive financial burden on people. More importantly, the Supreme Council saw these proposals for health and unemployment insurance programmes as rather idealistic (Choe, 1991).

The policy makers assumed that Korean society was not ready to adopt such programmes, which, they thought, only developed societies could afford. Here it is necessary to pay special attention to the understanding of social welfare among CSS members, who were true pioneers in that field. Some of the academics who participated in the CSS had studied social policy in Europe and Japan (Son, 1981; Woo, 2008).[109] For them, it was a genuine 'mission' to introduce social insurance programmes in Korea. The bureaucrats on the CSS who participated from the Ministry of Health and Social Affairs also recognised the need for social insurance. This was why they first started an informal study group seeking to understand the mechanisms of social insurance and explored the possibility of introducing them in Korea. Nevertheless, they did not use the language of the 'welfare state'. At the time, even for them, perhaps the idea of establishing a welfare state seemed too idealistic.

As Park Chung Hee won the presidential election in 1963, which was carried out in a free and competitive manner, the Korean government now had a democratic system. His government vigorously pursued economic development as its top priority. Throughout the 1970s, the Park government managed to achieve economic development, and further social insurance programmes subsequently introduced, such as health insurance and public pensions, were structured in such a way that they could foster economic development policy (Kwon, 1999). For instance, public health insurance, introduced in 1977, only covered workers in large-scale industrial workplaces with more than 500 employees, while poor people and other vulnerable groups were excluded from coverage. Industrial workers received the coverage because they were considered to be of strategic importance for economic development. Such policy logic, driven by economic consideration, gave a distinctive characteristic to the welfare regime in Korea, which the current author refers to as a 'developmental' welfare state (Kwon, 2005).

However, in Korea, other policy paradigms have emerged alongside the traditionally dominant 'economy first' approach. Let us fast-forward to the late 1990s. In December 1997, in the wake of the Asian economic crisis, long-time opposition leader Kim Dae-jung was elected to the presidency. The Kim government launched the 'productive' welfare initiative, which initially came to the fore as a response to the economic crisis, but later became a government policy

---

[109] Some of the CSS members studied in France and Japan, and others had a progressive political orientation before they joined the CSS (Woo, 2008).

priority. The weaknesses of the developmental welfare state in Korea (based on a narrowly growth focused system only providing social protection to those strategically important for economic development, combined with a heavy reliance on family or informal networks for social support) were painfully exposed during the economic crisis of 1997–8 (Goodman et al, 1998; Kwon, 2001). Faced with a severe economic crisis, the newly formed Kim government convened a tripartite committee, in which the government, business, and labour were able to reach a social consensus for reform. The government quickly implemented social policy reforms to enhance social protection for vulnerable citizens. This swift response was also related to economic structural adjustment and the government's related plan to implement labour market reform. To facilitate this process, the Kim government saw the need for social protection programmes for unemployed and poor people. The Employment Insurance Programme, consisting of unemployment benefits and training schemes, was extended and strengthened in terms of coverage and benefits. The government also strengthened the benefits of the public assistance programme for poor people. Together with the Employment Insurance Programme, it placed a strong emphasis on training and workfare in order to help unemployed people and low income families to re-enter the labour market. The government intended to use these welfare initiatives to bring the Korean economy through structural transformation leading to a more high-tech orientation. With this approach, the concept of social policy, which was once understood in terms of a trade-off in relation to economic policy, became an essential part of economic policy (Kwon, 2005).

The Kim government continued making social protection its main policy priority. In his 2000 Independence Day address, President Kim promised that his government would launch a 'productive' welfare initiative (Presidential Office, 2000). The President made it clear that his government would serve the welfare needs of the people while meeting the demands for economic development. It was a significant break from the past policy paradigm, which saw social policy as a mere instrument for economic consideration. The Kim government initiative put social welfare as a key policy priority on a par with economic development, although the concept of 'productive' welfare was still in use. Following this initiative, the government integrated the fragmented National Health Insurance into the new National Health Insurance Corporation, a single national agency for health insurance administration and finance. This restructuring of National Health Insurance would enhance the redistributive effects of public health insurance by pooling together all income groups into a single risk pool. More importantly, in 2000, the Kim government introduced the Minimum Living Standard Guarantee, which was based on the idea of social rights and replaced the stringent means-tested public assistance programme. The changes in policy worked to extend social protection to poor and vulnerable people.

Figure 11.1 shows public spending on social protection in Korea over the decade after the Asian economic crisis. Since the Kim years (1998–2003), public spending on social protection has increased steadily but its relative proportion within the government budget has remained stable. In contrast, spending through social insurance has increased sharply as the National Pension Programme, the Employment Insurance Programme, and National Health Insurance have matured. The Long-term Care Insurance, which was also introduced in 2008, contributed to the increase in social spending. In short, there is a rather wide range of social insurance programmes and income support programmes in place in Korean society.

Because of the steady extension of existing programmes and introduction of new programmes to the system, there was a significant change in the language of the welfare state. Here it is necessary to follow how social policy scholars used the concept of welfare state, as they are the first group of people to reflect such changes in the discourse. As mentioned earlier, in the late 1990s, the current author used the concept of welfare state to refer to the set of public institutions and policies for social protection (Kwon, 1999), but the term 'welfare state' to denote such public institutions and policies for social protection was not used very often. Once the Kim government extended existing social policies and introduced new programmes in the late 1990s and early 2000s, scholars began to use the term the 'welfare state' as an analytical term rather than as an ideal state of affairs.

For instance, in a paper published in the book entitled *Debates on the Nature of the Welfare State in Korea* (Kim, 2002), Seong (2002) used the term the welfare state to refer to social welfare institutions and policies. The title of the paper, which was written in Korean, can be translated as 'Democratic consolidation and the development of the welfare state: comparison between the Kim Young Sam and the Kim Dae-jung governments'. It compared social policy under two presidents in the late 1990s. Seong's paper maintained that there was a strong growth in the welfare state in Korea under the Kim Dae-jung government (Seong, 2002). Later , Jeong (2009) edited a new volume with the same title as Kim's 2002 book (*Debates on the Nature of the Welfare State in Korea II*). In the 2009 volume, there were a number of chapters using the

Figure 11.1: Public spending on social protection in Korea

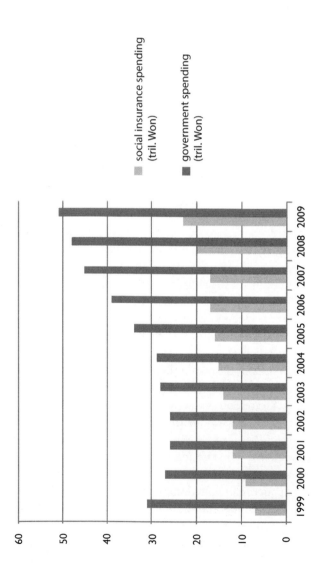

Source: http://kosis.kr/ups/ups_01List01.jsp?grp_no=&pubcode=KP&type=F (social indicators in Korea) Values given in trillions of Won (Korean currency)

concept of the welfare state as an analytical concept, although some of the chapters used the welfare state as the ideal state of affairs, in which a certain level of wellbeing is guaranteed by the state. In other words, the 2009 book featured both definitions of the welfare state.

This section has shown that the welfare state as an ideal had long existed in Korea and that some social policy measures were introduced when Korea began to embark on economic development under the rationale of 'economy first'. In contrast, today, the growing currency of the welfare state as an analytical term is a reflection of the development of the welfare state in Korea. More specifically, there is a comprehensive set of social policies and programmes in Korea that can be called a 'welfare state'. This reality is related not only to the expansion of social programmes but also to their changing nature. Until recently, the welfare state gradually moved from a selective to a more inclusive developmental state, although it was not inclusive enough to cover the whole population (Kwon, 2005).[110]

From development to the 'universal' welfare state

In this section, the way in which the concept of a 'universal' welfare state has emerged as the embodiment of a 'good society', and its impact on social policy, are explored. From the 1960s until the 1980s, although it was seen as a remote possibility at the time, the welfare state as an ideal state of affairs had been an aspiration for Korean society. From the 1980s until now, on two occasions, explicit political commitments have been made to realise such an aspiration. The first commitment came about in the early 1980s, when the Chun Doo-whan government (in office 1980–7) launched a welfare state project. The catchphrase used by the government at that time was, 'Let's Construct a Welfare State' (*Pokchi Kukka Kŏnsŏl Hacha*). The second was in the lead-up to the 2012 presidential campaign, when the 'universal' welfare state became one of the main policy issues for political parties. The concept of the welfare state as an aspiration for a society where a high level of wellbeing is guaranteed has been further articulated by the new concept of the 'universal' welfare state (*'Popyeonjŏk' Pokchi Kukka*). Why did the Chun government put the welfare project first for their political programme and what impact did it have? What is the rationale for introducing a new notion of the universal welfare state? What are the implications for social policy?

---

[110] Some argue that the Korean welfare state became more liberal under the Kim government.

The first political project for the welfare state began with the Chun government. In 1979, President Park was assassinated by his security chief, and subsequent political events took place in a highly uncertain situation. No one was sure whether such a catastrophic event would lead to democratisation or further deterioration into authoritarian politics. In the end, another military general, General Chun, who was in charge of investigation of the assassination, took over power through a palace coup d'état. Chun forcefully quelled political competition from other civilian politicians and made himself President through a rubber stamp election. What was very interesting was that he issued a manifesto on social welfare to seek support from the Korean people. He adopted the political catchphrase, 'Let's Construct a Welfare State' (*Pokchi Kukka Konsôl Hacha*) (Kwon, 1999). His determined effort to emphasise social welfare was a deliberate move to distance himself from the previous government; President Park and his government had prioritised economic growth over social welfare, although some social programmes had been introduced during his incumbency. In terms of economic policy, it is important to note that the Chun government's main priority was stabilisation rather than growth, another contrast to the previous government's policy (Haggard and Moon, 1990).

With the welfare state project, the Chun government tried to convey the political message to the public that this government was serious about achieving one of the ideals of the Korean society: the welfare state, a term epitomising a good society. In terms of practical programmes for implementation to realise such a policy commitment, the Chun government decided to strengthen the public assistance programme. The programme was introduced in 1965 and was a means–tested policy providing meagre benefits to very poor people. As Table 11.1 shows, the number of recipients of that public assistant programme declined throughout the 1960s and 1970s. Rapid economic development in this period raised the level of income among low income households, and reduced the number of poor people in Korea. Considering that only very poor people, who did not have enough to survive on their own, were eligible for assistance, the reduction in the number of recipients was hardly surprising. In 1980, the Chun government raised the income ceiling of the means test for public assistance and, as a consequence, the number of recipients increased sharply (Ko, 1990). Apart from strengthening the public assistance programme, the Chun government did not continue efforts to bolster social programmes. His government, however, pursued a stabilisation policy, carrying out structural reform of major industries and keeping government spending in check (Haggard and Moon, 1990).

Table 11.1: Number of recipients of the Public Assistance Programme, 1965–90

	Housing, income and medical supports	Income and medical supports	Medical supports	% of the total population
1965	288	72	3,563	13.66
1970	306	63	2,116	7.71
1975	375	52	904	3.77
1980	339	47	1,500	4.95
1985	282	63	1,928	5.52
1990	340	81	1,835	5.26

Source: Korea Statistical Yearbook (1966, 1986, 1990)

According to Haggard and Moon (1990), within the Chun government, the welfare initiative was promoted by people with a military background, and the stabilisation policy was backed by the bureaucrats from the Board of Economic Planning and Ministry of Finance. There was inevitable tension between the welfare initiative and economic stabilisation policy. Once Chun consolidated his power, he was inclined to rely more on bureaucrats than on military personnel for his economic and social policy. The welfare manifesto became marginalised while economic stabilisation remained at the fore of the government's overall policy direction. In the end, the 'welfare state' in the broad sense of the term remained an elusive ideal for the Korean public.

In the previous section, the shift in the meaning of the welfare state following the productive welfare initiative by the Kim government was discussed. If the concept of the welfare state now refers to social welfare institutions and policies, how could one still describe the welfare state as an ideal, as in the broader definition of the concept discussed earlier? In recent years, the concept of the 'universal welfare state' appeared in the public debate to refer to such an ideal welfare state.

The concept of the 'universal welfare state' appeared for the first time in Korean politics during the local election for the Educational Authorities in 2010. Kim Sang-gon, one of the candidates for the Educational Authority in the Kyunggi Province surrounding the Seoul metropolitan area promised that he would provide all children in primary schools with free school lunches. At the time of the election, only children of poor households were exempt from paying for school lunches, while other pupils needed to pay a monthly fee for lunches. Candidate Kim promised that all children would have free lunches, regardless of the level of family income. This electoral pledge brought about a wide range of responses from politicians and the public in general. Kim Sang-gon explained his idea in the following statement:[111] "… in the advanced capitalist society it is natural that basic welfare should be provided universally to the public. As Korea is now preparing to enter the group of advanced societies, basic welfare should be guaranteed for everyone no matter who gets political power". While there were strong criticisms of the statement in the political establishment, the public initially received it very well. The general public's embrace of his message was an unexpected response, since people in the establishment, politics, the government and the media still felt it was premature for Korea to establish a welfare state comparable to those in Western European countries (Koh, 2012). To take advantage of the situation, other candidates in the election jumped on the bandwagon and embraced the idea of universal social policy. For instance, Kwak Nohyun, candidate for the Educational Authority for Seoul metropolitan area, argued that welfare is not only for the poor:[112] "… in the school, universal welfare should be guaranteed. There should be no children stigmatized. Children of rich households should be eligible. … Universal welfare should be for everyone". Although it was not certain whether their promise of free school lunches for everyone influenced election results, these two candidates, who supported universal welfare, won their seats in the end.

With their eyes on the upcoming general election in April 2012, the main opposition party, the Democratic Party, went on to say that their government would make health care free, removing patient copayments for National Health Insurance. The Democratic Party also promised that they would halve university fees. The Democratic Party placed strong emphasis on the concept of 'free' welfare provision.[113] During the general election, such efforts were not, however, received very well by the public. It was seen as a fiscally unsustainable commitment grounded in populism. The Democratic Party was accused of recklessness by the mainstream media. Faced with such a strong backlash, the Democratic Party shifted its policy emphasis from 'free' to 'universal' welfare, but it was not clear what 'universal' welfare would mean, if not free.

---

[111] Interview with Kim Sangon, *Hangyore Daily*, April 2010.
[112] Interview with Kwak Nohyun, *Poli News*, May 2010.
[113] 21 March 2012, *the Maeil Economy*.

One of the underlying reasons the Democratic Party was so desperate about welfare policy was that the leading political figure of the governing party at the time, Park Geunhye, gave social welfare high policy priority. It was a different policy stance from that of her party, which had maintained a neoliberal position. She wanted to project herself as a national leader representing the whole population rather than a particular political tendency. She maintained that every citizen would need social support from the state, not only poor people. She further argued that welfare benefits should be tailored to each citizen's needs, varying according to their position in the life cycle. It was a bold move, since the incumbent government under President Lee Myungbak (in office 2008–13) did not consider welfare a high priority.

During the presidential election in 2012, both major parties, the governing Saenuri Party and the opposition Democratic Party, promised that they would pursue a 'universal' welfare state once they were elected. However, the two political parties were not given a clear definition of the 'universal' welfare state. First, this concept may mean that the state would provide citizens with welfare provisions for free. In other words, social services are provided free at the point of delivery. Although the Democratic Party withdrew their commitment for free health care, both major parties supported free childcare for families with children under five. Such a reform would increase fiscal expenditures, which in turn would require tax increases, but the governing party was not very clear about such potential increases, while the opposition party was willing to increase tax.

Second, to establish a 'universal' welfare state in Korea, it would be necessary to include those who are currently excluded from social insurance coverage. As shown in Table 11.2, social insurance programmes cover less than half of the population in the relevant categories. For instance, only 42.5% of working-age people are covered by public pension programmes such as the National Pension Programmes and Government Employees Pension Programmes. Furthermore, only 41.2% of workers are covered by the Employment Insurance Programme. This high level of noncoverage means that a large segment of the population facing income losses is not entitled to any state protection. Regarding the Minimum Living Standard Guarantee, only 46.4% of poor people receive income support, as the others are not entitled because they have family members who are responsible for supporting them. In a nutshell, the 'welfare state' in Korea is still far from 'universal', as it does not cover all the relevant risk categories for the entire population. Despite all the talk about universality, it is not

Table 11.2: Coverage of social insurance programmes in 2012

Social Programmes	Categories	People covered by the programmes	People not covered by the programmes
Public pensions	Working-age people	42.5% (Contributors to the national pensions or government employees pensions)	57.5 % (Non-contributors, and economically inactive people)
Employment insurance	Employed people	41.2% (Regular employees and some short-term contract workers)	58.8% (Part-time workers, family business employees and self-employed people)
Minimum Living Standard Guarantee	On low income (below the poverty line)	46.4% (People without family members responsible for support)	53.6% (On low income, people with family members responsible for support)

Source: Kang (2011), National Assembly Budget Office (2009) and Park (2008)

clear how the incumbent Park government would bring those outside the 'welfare state' into the main fold of social insurance.

Third, in order to claim that Korea has established a 'universal' welfare state, in which citizens are guaranteed a decent level of wellbeing, a sort of ideal state of affairs that used to be implicit in 'welfare state', there would have to be a sharp increase in the amounts of public provision. For instance, old age pensions, which are provided to people over age 70, are only one fifth of the average wage of working people and should be raised to a higher level in order to be considered genuinely universal. Another example is health care. Although National Health Insurance covers the entire population, the medical treatments that are covered within National Health Insurance are still limited. The extension to those previously uncovered treatments will also cost a great deal.

Although the concept of the 'universal welfare state' has yet to be clarified in Korea's political discourse, it has set the direction of social policy for the foreseeable future, as both major political parties have promoted the idea. They agree that the universal welfare state can be an effective response to 'new social risks' in Korea (Myles, 2002; Kwon et al, 2010; Pang, 2011). Among these new social risks, the dramatic demographic transition to the ageing society poses the most serious threat. While in most Organisation for Economic Cooperation and Development (OECD) countries, the transition from an ageing to an aged society (the proportion of the elderly population from 7% to 14%) took about 100 years, it should only take 19 years in Korea (from 2000 to 2019). With such demographic transition, it seems clear that every citizen will need social protection at some point in their life, in the form of either social services or social insurance. Political parties seem to agree that a 'universal' welfare state could be economically useful, as it could maintain Korean society's productive potential. In the end, the Korean concept of the welfare state remains closely tied to economic imperatives.

Conclusion

This chapter has examined the changing meaning of the term 'welfare state' in Korea, contrasting its two different meanings: an embodiment of a 'good society' and an analytical term referring to specific institutions and policies. Originally, in the 1960s, the welfare state referred to an ideal state of affairs, when a small number of social programmes were introduced in the country as part of economic reform. Although a range of social insurance programmes had subsequently been implemented in Korea, the welfare state as an ideal remained an elusive goal in Korean society. It was only after new social programmes were introduced and existing ones were extended in the late 1990s that the welfare state as an analytical term became used by academics and policy makers to refer to a concrete set of social policies and institutions. Today, as a new social ideal, the 'universal' welfare state appears to set the goal for an ever changing Korean society. Such fluctuating meaning of the welfare state is a reflection of Korea's transition from a poor to an affluent society, and the related development of social policy this brought about in particular. Analytically speaking, this change constitutes a shift from a developmental welfare to a universal welfare state.

Despite this transformation, this chapter has revealed that there has been a remarkable continuity in Korean society in the prevalence of the enduring belief that citizens should be guaranteed a decent standard of living. It is true that, in Korea, the recent emergence of the welfare agenda is due to increasing political competition in democratic politics. It is also true that demographic shifts and subsequent increases in 'social risks' have been among the main reasons for the support of the middle class towards a 'universal' welfare state. Nevertheless, democratic competition and the social shift towards post-industrialisation are only part of the story. Such strong continuity can only be fully explained by Korea's modernisation project, which is about economic development, democracy and the welfare state. The idea of President Park Chung Hee that the 'economy [should come] first and welfare [should come] later', (Park, 1963) the notions of Kim Dae-jung's 'productive welfare', and now the 'universal welfare state' all converge in principle with the belief that Korea should strive for the 'welfare state' as a good society. It is a fair observation that such consensus has existed not only among policy makers but also among Korean people, throughout Korea's economic transition.

What is important in the present context is that the 'universal' welfare state is no longer an ideal state of affairs for the future. It is now knocking at the door. Korean society is now faced with the immediate task of deciding what the 'universal' welfare state should be like. Who should be eligible for benefits? Who should pay for the 'universal' welfare state? How should the system be implemented? These are some of the questions waiting to be answered.

References

Choe C. (1991) *History of Korean Social Policy Research,* Seoul: Korea Institute of Social Security (in Korean).

Goodman R, White G and Kwon HJ. (1998) *The East Asian Welfare Model: Welfare Orientalism and the State,* London: Routledge.

Haggard S and Moon CI. (1990) Institutions and economic policy: theory and a Korean case study. *World Politics* 42: 210-237.

Jeong M. (2009) Debates on the nature of the welfare state in Korea II. Seoul: Human-being and Welfare (In Korean).

Kang, S (2011) 'Estimation of the blind spot of the national pension programme and the impact on old age poverty in relation to the maturity of the programme', *Fiscal Studies*, vol. 4, no. 2, (in Korean)

Kim Y-M. (2002) Debates on the nature of the welfare state in Korea. Seoul: Human-being and Welfare (In Korean).

Ko I-d. (1990) Reform of the public assistance programme and policies for the poor. In: KDI (ed.) *National Expenditure and Policy Goals.* Seoul: KDI (in Korean).

Koh W. (2012) Analysis of political discourse on welfare agenda in Korea. *Economy and Society* 95.

Kwon HJ. (1999) *The Welfare State in Korea: The Politics of Legitimation,* London: Macmillan.

Kwon HJ. (2001) Globalization, unemployment and policy responses in Korea: respositioning the state? *Global Social Policy* 1: 213-234.

Kwon HJ. (2005) Transforming the developmental welfare state in East Asia. London: UNRISD/Palgrave.

Kwon, HJ, Dong, G and Moon, H-g. (2010) Economic crises and the welfare state in Korea: reforms and future challenges. *Korea Journal of Policy Studies* 24.

Ministry of Labour. (1981) *Fifteen Year History of Industrial Accident Insurance,* Seoul: Ministry of Labour, Korea (in Korean).

Myles J. (2002) A new social contract for the elderly?, In: Esping-Andersen G. (ed.) *Why we need a New Welfare State.* Oxford: Oxford University Press, 130-172.

National Assembly Budget Office (2009) *Issues in the Revised Budget in 2009,* Seoul: National Assembly Budget Office (in Korean).

National Statistical Office (1966), *Korea Statistical Yearbook,* NSO.

National Statistical Office (1986), *Korea Statistical Yearbook,* NSO.

National Statistical Office (1990), *Korea Statistical Yearbook,* NSO.

Pang H. (2011) Forced choice: retirement from the job for life and reemployment. *Korean Sociology* 45.

Park C.H. (1962) *Our Nation's Path: Ideology of Social Reconstruction,* Seoul: Hollym.

Park CH. (1963) *The Country, Revolution and I,* Seoul: Hollym.

Park, N (2008) 'Evaluating ten years outcome of the Minimum Living Standard Guarantee', *The Forum of Health and Welfare,* No. 167 (in Korean).

Presidential Office. (2000) *DJ Welfarism: A New Paradigm for Productive Welfare in Korea,* Seoul: Presidential Office.

Seo Ba. (1962) The pledges of the 5.16 military revolution and the idea of the welfare state. *Supreme Council Review* 9 (in Korean).

Seong K. (2002) Democratic consolidation and the development of the welfare state: Comparison between Kim Young Sam and Kim Dae-ju government. In: Kim Y-M (ed.) *Debates on the Nature of the Welfare State in Korea.* Seoul: Human-being and Welfare (in Korean).

Son J. (1981) A study of the policy process of social policy making in Korea. *Department of Political Science.* Seoul: Seoul National University.

Woo M. (2008) Industrial accident insurance. In: Yang J (ed.) *Social Policy Making Process in Korea.* Seoul: Nanam (in Korean).

TWELVE

The Dutch 'caring state'

Kees van Kersbergen and Jaap Woldendorp[114]

The Dutch term used to describe the welfare state is '*verzorgingsstaat*'. '*Verzorgen*' means 'to take care of', but also 'to care', and implies 'to nurture', 'to tend to' and 'to nurse'. The word '*verzorging*', for instance, also appears in the term '*verzorgingshuis*' (nursing home). The distinct connotation of the Dutch term is paternalistic and reminiscent of charity in its emphasis on obligation rather than rights: it is the state's obligation to help weak people in society. This connotation is heavily loaded by the heritage of religious political actors, especially the Catholic People's Party (*Katholieke Volkspartij* – KVP)[115], one of the main original protagonists of a passive, benefit oriented conception of the welfare state (Van Kersbergen and Becker, 1988).

The seemingly literal translation of the term 'welfare state' as '*welvaartsstaat*' was popular in the first years after the Second World War. The term quickly fell into disuse, however, partly because it was an incorrect translation of the English term ('*welvaart*' means prosperity), and partly because the Social Democrats, who adopted and preferred the term, lost the ideological language struggle with the Roman Catholics. The Social Democrats, too, started to use the term '*verzorgingsstaat*', in addition to the more restrictive terms 'social security' and 'social provisions', which were the most common words used, at least until the 1980s. The term '*verzorgingsstaat*' has prevailed in the political debate, especially since the mid-1980s. Most recently, however, the notion of '*verzorgingsstaat*' seems to have lost its hegemony in political discourse, while no other expression has replaced it yet.

---

[114] We would like to thank Lars Thorup Larsen, Barbara Vis, and the editors of this volume for their very helpful comments and suggestions.

[115] Christian Democracy in the Netherlands is the outcome of a merger in the 1970s between the Katholieke Volkspartij (KVP) and the two large Protestant parties, the Anti-Revolutionary Party (*Anti-Revolutionaire Partij* – ARP) and the Christian Historical Union (*Christelijk-Historische Unie* – CHU). The ARP organised the '*Gereformeerden*', a 19th century breakaway group from the original Protestant '*Hervormden*' of the CHU (in English '*gereformeerd*' and '*hervormd*' both translate as reformed).

These shifts in descriptive terms can be taken as an ideational characterisation of the political struggle over social and economic policy in the Netherlands in the post-war construction, expansion and reform of the 'welfare state'. This history starts in 1944, when the Committee Van Rhijn on *Sociale Zekerheid* (Social Security) produced a policy paper for the Dutch government in exile in London, based on the famous Beveridge Report (1942). It contained policy recommendations for insurance against sickness, accidents at work, disability, unemployment, and old age, but also for welfare (social assistance: '*bijstand*', '*steun*'),[116] a minimum wage, and protection against unfair dismissal, and marks the start of the acceptance of discussions, definitions and issues relating to the Anglo-Saxon term 'welfare state' in the Netherlands.

This chapter comprises five main sections. Section one discusses the period 1945 to 1958, which covers the construction phase of the Dutch welfare state and in which the notions of welfare state and social politics compete in the struggle over words. Section two covers the period 1958 to 1967, in which the notion of the '*verzorgingsstaat*' emerged, but did not yet become the dominant expression. Section three focuses on the period 1968 to 1976, in which the Dutch welfare state reached its zenith as a total 'caring' state. Section four discusses the period 1977 to the mid-1990s, when the Dutch welfare state ran into trouble and the term '*verzorgingsstaat*' started to lose its positive meaning. Section five discusses the period since 1995, in which the language of activation became dominant.

Welfare state or social policy: 1945–58

The main proponents of welfare state development after World War II were the Social Democrats and the Roman Catholics, with the support of the affiliated trade unions of both camps. The term '*welvaartsstaat*' was first used in an academic context in 1952, but was quickly embraced by the Social Democrats in the same year (Donner, 1957: 559). They preferred this term, while the Catholics referred to '*sociale politiek*' (social politics/policy). The two Protestant political parties and the Liberal Conservatives, in contrast, fostered anti-interventionist if not state-sceptic conceptions (Van Kersbergen, 2009). The main Protestant party (ARP), for instance, uses the term '*sociale politiek*' for the first time in its electoral manifesto for 1956, only to inculcate that social

---

[116] *Bijstand* is the term used in political and judicial language, *steun* is the colloquial expression. *Bijstand* translates as support, aid, assistance, benefit, help or relief, whereas *steun* is support.

policy must first and foremost 'provoke and reinforce a sense of self-responsibility in individual persons and the various circles of life in society' (ARP, 1956: 6).

For the Social Democrats, although they initially disagreed on the specific meaning of the concept (Donner, 1957: 559), the term '*welvaarststaat*' came to denote the ultimate aim of social and economic policies, to create prosperity, and was conceived in contrast to the passive adjustment policies during the Great Depression, which had reinforced impoverishment (see for example Banning, 1954; Oosterhuis, 1956). In the period just after the war, however, the main focus of the Social Democrats was on '*wederopbouw*' (reconstruction), '*bestaanszekerheid*' (existential security) and a '*rechtsorde van de arbeid*' (a [just] rule of law covering labour relations), constituting a '*sociale verzorgingsstaat*' (social caring state) (see for example PvdA, 1951: 82). In electoral manifestos, the term '*welvaartsstaat*' is only used once, by the Social Democrats in 1956 (PvdA, 1956).

The Catholics, in contrast, were inspired by Vatican oriented '*sociale politiek*' (social politics/policy). '*Sociale politiek*' aimed to mitigate the negative income effects of sickness, old age and unemployment due to personal factors or economic ups and downs, but not to regulate those economic ups and downs as the Social Democrats wanted (see for example Roebroek and Hertogh, 1998: 271–8).

The main conflict between the Social Democrats and the Catholics concerned the role of the state and social partners in the organisation and implementation of social security, which reflected fundamental differences in basic notions of state and society (and their interrelationship). The Social Democrats had statist ideals and opted exclusively for tax-financing of social security based on majority parliamentary decisions. The Catholics, in contrast, had corporatist beliefs and wished for (legally based) social insurance schemes run by employers and employees and only a subsidiary role for the state in case of inadequacy of protection (Hertogh, 1998: 149–61).

The Social Democrats also opted for an interventionist approach to control the economic cycle. Hence, the first Social Democratic Minister of Economic Affairs, Hein Vos, created the '*Centraal Plan Bureau*' (Central Planning Bureau, that is, the Netherlands Bureau for Economic Policy Analysis). This institute was originally designed to actually devise plans for the economic reconstruction of the Dutch economy. However, it was quickly reorganised by subsequent Catholic Ministers of Economic Affairs to forecast economic developments and analyse the effects of economic policies (see for example Roebroek and Hertogh, 1998: 271–5).

The Social Democrats and the Catholics concluded a compromise that came to define the Dutch welfare state. They agreed on company or industry-wide compulsory social insurance for unemployment, sickness, and company pensions, financed by the contributions of employees and employers and run by bipartite organisations and pension funds. For social risks like old age and widows and orphans a compulsory, state-governed, pay-as-you-go, so-called people's insurance would be the model. Both Social Democratic statist and Roman Catholic corporatist beliefs came to underlie the social security system to cover different types of social risks.

This compromise marked the end of the political and ideational struggle over social policy and '*maatschappelijke ordening*' (there is no literal translation in English but the Dutch term refers to the organisational principle of society) between Social Democrats and Catholics that had taken place since the end of World War I. The Social Democratic idea of social policy and socialisation of production organised by the (democratic) state had stood in opposition to the Catholic idea of the organic society and free enterprise, based on the principle of subsidiarity, in which the state only stepped in if and when hierarchically lower communities proved unable to cater for the social wellbeing of their members. The Protestant principle of sovereignty in one's own circle interpreted state and society as two separate spheres of life, which in practice meant that their views on social (and economic) policy were more or less identical with the anti-interventionist conceptions of the liberals of various persuasions (Hertogh 1998: 165–205; Roebroek and Hertogh 1998: 247–65).

One key impact on social policy language, which can be read as an effect of Catholic dominance over social democracy, was that the emphasis on the notion of state, such as in welfare state, disappeared from government policy language and also gradually from Social Democratic discourse. In 1953, for instance, the Social Democratic Minister of Social Affairs and Public Health, J.G. Suurhoff, declared in Parliament: 'People in a free society should principally be responsible for their own means of existence .... Social security from the cradle to the grave, as it is called, is a slogan that you will never hear yours truly utter' (as cited in Ruppert, 1965: 29).

A crucial area of agreement in the social policy image of all political actors was the concept of the male '*kostwinner*' (breadwinner) and his dependent family as the focal point and principle of all social policies (see for example Bussemaker, 1993: 98–9; Hertogh, 1998: 311–20). The breadwinner principle also strongly affected female labour force participation: it had inspired laws that prohibited women entering the labour market and had obliged the state (until 1957) to fire its female employees when they got married (Blok, 1978).

With regard to economic policy, the implementation of Social Democratic (Keynesian) interventionist ideas was blocked by the non-Social Democratic parliamentary majority led by the Catholics (see for example Roebroek and Hertogh, 1998: 267–80). The model of economic recovery and social security that evolved from the Catholic–Social Democratic coalitions that ruled until 1958 included a low wage policy for export-led job creation, minimum protection against sickness, unemployment and old age, and the creation of a bi- and tri-partite corporatist system covering various aspects of social policy. In exchange for wage moderation (national, government directed wage policy), workers obtained jobs and limited social rights to secure their existence ('*bestaanszekerheid*').

Paternalism, passivity and generosity for the male breadwinner: 1958–67

In the 1960s, the term '*welvaartsstaat*' had already fallen into disuse and the term '*verzorgingsstaat*' surfaced. The latter expression was first coined in 1957 by sociologist Verwey-Jonker and later elaborated by sociologist Thoenes (Thoenes, 1962: 124; WRR, 2006: 32). In the latter's view, the '*verzorgingsstaat*' was a system of government care for the collective wellbeing of its subjects ('*onderdanen*'). Collective wellbeing as an object for government intervention covered all economic, social and cultural needs of citizens. Both paternalism (the obligation of the government to look after the economic, social and cultural wellbeing of its subjects) and generosity (government policies should cover the complete economic, social and cultural wellbeing of citizens) stand out in this definition. Various pro-welfare state actors could recognise their own central beliefs in the term, including '*bestaanszekerheid*' (existential security), '*sociaal recht*' (social rights), and '*rechtvaardigheid*' (justice). Interestingly enough, Thoenes based his definition quite literally on M. Penelope Hall's (1952) characterisation of the 'welfare state'.

However, the consensus on the welfare state was not limited to the Social Democrats and Catholics. In this period the Dutch welfare state was extended and completed by coalition governments of the Catholic People's Party, the two Protestant parties, and the Conservative Liberals. With the gradual demise of the national, government directed wage policy and the ensuing wage explosions, all benefits were significantly increased. The male breadwinner, in spite of increasing criticism, remained the focus and principle of all social policies (see for example Visser and Hemerijck, 1997: 33–5; Hertogh, 1998: 353).

The general self-image among political actors was that they were perfecting the system of social security. The term *'verzorgingsstaat'* obtained a definite positive connotation, although the electoral manifestos of the main parties in the 1960s primarily referred to social insurance and social provisions in their pleas for improving social security. Moreover, the system's increasing generosity (see van Kersbergen and Becker, 1988) became a source of political pride for both Social Democrats and Christian Democrats, including the two Protestant parties. The Conservative Liberals also participated fully in the completion of the 'caring' state (see for example Hertogh, 1998: 351; Roebroek and Hertogh, 1998: 345–9).

The total 'caring' state: the legal minimum wage and the net linking of wages and benefits: 1968–76

During this relatively short period, the Dutch *'verzorgingsstaat'* reached its zenith. In 1969, the statutory minimum wage was introduced under the aegis of a Catholic Minister of Social Affairs. Political debates were phrased in terms of what would still be a socially acceptable minimum. The term the 'social minima' emerged to refer to the bottom group of low income earners and welfare beneficiaries. In 1974, the Social Democratic minority government of Den Uyl (1974–7) introduced the linking of wages, benefits and pensions in the public sector to the statutory net minimum wage and to the average rise in collectively agreed wages in the market sector (Visser and Hemerijck, 1997: 132–134), which produced the persistent growth in public spending that later became the hallmark of the so-called Dutch Disease. This was particularly the case because the net linking became statutory in 1979, under a Christian Democratic–Conservative Liberal coalition (Van Kersbergen, 2009: 138).

The social policy discussions in this period were dominated by a social democratic discourse and were worded in terms of solidarity, equality, and redistribution. The term 'levelling of incomes' especially became a catchphrase, referred to positively by the left and negatively by the right. The Christian Democratic parties sought a halfway point and talked rather about 'a more just distribution of income', to be achieved not by redistribution, but by 'boosting the incomes and wealth acquisition by the lower income groups of workers' (ARP, KVP, CHU, 1971: 9). The Social Democrats believed the net linking of wages and benefits to be a crucial instrument to increase equality.

The declaration of the Social Democratic-led government stated that its policy aimed at the abolishment of inequality and disadvantage via the reduction of the existing inequality in income, property, power and knowledge (see Roebroek and Hertogh, 1998: 376). The Social Democratic government was a minority coalition, but the left wing of the three Christian Democratic parties in particular also supported the equality project. The Conservative Liberals also supported the total caring state (see for example Roebroek and Hertogh, 1998: 345–9).

In this period, the first systematic criticism of the male breadwinner oriented character of the social security system was formulated by feminists, who pointed out the inequality in the social security system. Feminist ideas resonated well with the Social Democratic emphasis on social equality and it was the Social Democratic government that started an emancipation policy (Bussemaker, 1993: 120–4; Roebroek and Hertogh, 1998: 376). The Christian Democratic parties were slower to adopt this criticism, kept using the term breadwinner, and formulated a somewhat ambiguous position on the matter in their common political programme for the elections of 1977. On the one hand, they argued that the level of a social benefit should take into account whether the beneficiary is a breadwinner or not. But on the other hand, they also stated that a married couple must be able to choose who is regarded as the breadwinner (CDA, 1977).

For the Christian Democrats, occupied with the fusion process between the two Protestant parties and the Catholic party, the central terms in the social policy debate were 'responsibility' and the 'responsible society'. This language was part of an effort to merge the Protestant idea of sovereignty in one's own circle and the Catholic concept of subsidiarity. The terms 'responsibility' and the 'responsible society' pointed to the belief that the state and the relevant societal institutions (for example trade unions, building societies, schools, and the family) should share responsibility for social wellbeing. Based on these ideas and reflecting the prevailing mood, Christian Democratic women also argued that there were no arguments to reproduce existing inequalities between men and women. However, they argued that such inequalities had to be dealt with in harmony, within the family. Social policy was to be designed with an eye on protecting the family as the fundamental unit of society (Bussemaker, 1993: 126–7).

The Conservative Liberals slowly changed their central conception from freedom within the community to freedom of individuals from the community and equal opportunities for women. However, they were initially relatively reluctant to dispose of the breadwinner principle, because it might force a woman onto the labour market and hence would limit freedom of choice. This changed, when the Conservative Liberals accepted the principle of economic independence as their key concept (Hellendoorn, 2012: 211–13).

Austerity and retrenchment: moderating and reforming the 'caring' state: 1977–95

As the preceding paragraph explains, all political actors took pride in the construction of the total caring state for the male breadwinner. However, in the late 1970s and the 1980s the system experienced severe problems following the oil crises of the 1970s. The explosive influx of claimants to the various social security schemes – unemployment and disability – and social assistance, in combination with the net linking of wages and benefits mentioned earlier, was exhausting the insurances' and state financial capacity, despite generous gas revenues, and introduced a new discourse of austerity and retrenchment, which led to a fundamental criticism, rethinking and then remodelling of the passive welfare state (see for example Visser and Hemerijck, 1997: Ch 6; Roebroek and Hertogh, 1998: 380–2).

The term '*verzorgingsstaat*' appeared for the first time in the Christian Democratic and Conservative Liberal electoral manifestos of 1981. The Christian Democrats noticed that despite the '*verzorgingsstaat*' some individuals and specific groups were still lonely or isolated (CDA, 1981). The Conservative Liberals argued that they had cooperated to establish the '*verzorgingsstaat*', but that increasing unemployment, in combination with the recruitment of migrant workers, indicated that the expansion of the redistributive '*verzorgingsstaat*' had reached its limits (VVD, 1981).

By 1986, both Christian Democrats and Conservative Liberals had adopted a much more negative discourse to discuss the '*verzorgingsstaat*'. Christian Democrats, while claiming credit for its positive aspects, argued that the '*verzorgingsstaat*' had become too big by shifting all social problems to the state, instead of addressing them within the '*verzorgingsmaatschappij*' (caring society) (CDA, 1986). Conservative Liberals also argued that the '*verzorgingsstaat*' had become too all-encompassing and was suffocating society (VVD, 1986). Social Democrats, by contrast, explicitly stated that the party wanted to hold on to the basic principles of the '*verzorgingsstaat*': the state accepts co-responsibility for employment and social security and essential public services (PvdA, 1986).

Moderation ('*matiging*') and the retreating state ('*terugtredende overheid*') gradually became the new buzz words and expressed the belief that the further (financial) expansion of the welfare state had to be curbed.

A euphemism for retrenchment, moderating the caring state became the key aim of successive governments: lowering benefits by reducing the replacement rate, restricting criteria for eligibility and duration, not executing the statutory linking, and not indexing the minimum wage. Studies by the Organisation for Economic Co-operation and Development (OECD), especially the yearly *Economic Outlook*, but also the country reports, had started to influence policy ideas in the early 1980s because they showed that the Netherlands had the lowest employment/population ratio of all OECD countries (Visser and Hemerijck, 1997: 24; see also Binnema, 2004). To launch the language of moderation and legitimise it, the '*Inactieven/Actieven*' ratio (I/A ratio) was introduced, that is, the ratio between inactive (including pensioners) and active members of the total population over 15 years of age. This number clearly pointed to an increasingly bad employment performance, which stirred up anxiety about the sustainability of the '*verzorgingsstaat*' (Green-Pedersen et al, 2001; Vis and van Kersbergen, 2012).

The language of moderation extended to wages as well. The statutory minimum wage was not consistently indexed and wage rises in general were minimal, and a whole new language was invented to describe the de facto (but not the de jure) delinking of wages and benefits, such as 'linking at a distance' or protecting the '*real* social minima' only. The yardstick was another prominent statistic, the 'Arbeidsinkomen Quote' (AIQ), which showed that total wages as a proportion of Gross National Income had been steadily rising. In addition, in the market sector unions and employers had forged an exchange between wage moderation and early retirement schemes and shorter working weeks ('*arbeidstijdverkorting*') in order to provide jobs for the younger generation (see for example Visser and Hemerijck, 1997: Ch 5).

Moderation turned into a reform agenda, starting in 1987 with the restructuring of the social security system (Rigter et al, 1995: 374–7) and reaching its high point with the reform of the Disability Scheme in 1993 and the complete overhaul of the organisation of the social security system in 1995, which dismantled the bipartite corporatist governance structure (Vis et al, 2008; Vis & van Kersbergen, 2012: 12).

The reform of the Disability Scheme was heavily disputed between the Christian Democrats, who were in favour of reform, and the Social Democrats, who initially were dead set against any moderation or reform of the scheme. Hence, the Lubbers III (1989–94) government of Christian and Social Democrats was in a deadlock that was only resolved after a few years of massaging and cajoling the Social Democrats into accepting reform. First, through public discussions and the invocation of a crisis rhetoric (Kuipers, 2006), the Dutch welfare state was diagnosed as an ailing patient. Prime Minister Lubbers stated: 'Nederland is ziek' (the Netherlands is sick), highlighting the alarming fact that in 1990 the number of disability claimants was rapidly approaching one million, that is, three and half times the scheme's capacity (Vis & van Kersbergen, 2012: 10–11). This invoked a sense of urgency that also started to emerge among Social Democrats and led to an increasingly alarmist political discourse. Second, by blunt power politics: the Christian Democrats threatened to forge a new coalition with the Conservative Liberals to push through the reform. The Social Democrats had to rethink their position and find a way to survive electorally once they decided to support retrenchment and reform. In the end the Social Democrats found a scapegoat and blamed the explosive and continuous growth of claimants on the bipartite corporatist administration of the social security system. Social partners had jointly abused the Disability Scheme to give redundant older employees lifelong high benefits until they reached the official retirement age of 65 (Kuipers, 2006: 152–163; Vis & van Kersbergen, 2012: 12).

The feminist critique of the gender inequality implied by the male breadwinner principle and European pressure in favour of the equal treatment of men and women translated into social security reform. Social Democrats had adopted a more liberal discourse, stressing participation and individual responsibility (Hellendoorn, 2012: 215). Moreover, the emancipation of women came to be seen as a potential contribution to economic growth, as an increasing number of working married women would necessitate more commercial and social services, creating badly needed new jobs. Social Democrats also wanted social security benefits to become completely individualised (Hellendoorn, 2012: 215–16).

Initially, under pressure of rapidly increasing unemployment, Christian Democrats rather reversed to the male breadwinner principle and blamed economic stagnation and unemployment on the increased labour supply of (married) women. This was construed as an egoistic thirst for money and consumerism that was fuelled by a belief in gender equality. Instead of mutual solidarity based on discipline and self-sacrifice, people, that is to say women, were argued to have shifted their own responsibility for the family onto the state. Later in the period working married women became accepted, although a preference for traditional family friendly policies persisted. With regard to social security policies, Christian Democrats agreed to abolish criteria discriminating against women, but remained staunchly in favour of protecting the male breadwinner with a minimum wage (Hellendoorn,

2012: 216–17). The Conservative Liberals, in contrast, unreservedly opted for individualisation and hence wanted to do away with all male breadwinner clauses in social security (Hellendoorn, 2012: 212–14).

Simultaneously with this shift regarding the position of (married) women in the social security legislation, the 1980s witnessed the first development towards what later became known as the essence of the Dutch Miracle: the Dutch job machine. Already in the early 1980s, a significant shift from full-time (male) employment in industry towards a hefty increase in more flexible, part-time employment in the service sectors became visible. Most of these jobs were taken by (married and younger) women who replaced more expensive (and less flexible) male breadwinners (Elfring and Kloosterman, 1989). The basis for this was a deal (first negotiated in 1982) between employers that later introduced a new term: the Polder Model. This term initially described the tripartite system of negotiated deals that focus on job growth in return for wage moderation, but was gradually more generally applied to typify the complex blend of consensus building mechanisms. By the early 2000s the term had acquired a pejorative meaning when it was being used to describe the 'stickiness' of the process of social and political consensus building (see Woldendorp, 2005; Bos et al, 2007). In a similar vein, the 'verzorgingsstaat' became associated with problems and failures instead of with solutions and successes.

From the 'caring' to the 'activating' state: the period since 1995

The moderation of the 'caring' state reached its pinnacle in the mid-1990s with the gradual introduction of a more active and service oriented social policy paradigm, exemplified by the ideologically important (and later exported) neologism 'flexicurity', the launching of the idea that social policy is not a cost but has economic value (it is a 'productive factor') as it promotes political and social trust, and the belief in social investments, for instance in workers' skills and qualifications (employability).

The origin of the new paradigm can be traced back to a recommendation from the Dutch Government Council for Scientific Research that was published in 1990: *A Working Perspective. Labour Market Participation in the 1990s* (WRR, 1990). The report proposed a break with the past and recommended that labour market participation became the overarching goal of policy. It launched most of the terms of the activation paradigm, with a particularly strong focus on flexibility and participation. A comparison between the Swedish and the American models gave birth to the idea (although not yet to the term) of flexicurity. The Swedish job security model forces people to accept a job or training, whereas the American flexible market model compels people to accept low paid and low quality jobs. The Council argued that the Netherlands had neither, but needed both. The leading intellectual of the Council, Hans Adriaansens, introduced the term 'flexicurity' in interviews in the 1990s. The term became the key concept in public debates on the Flexibility and Security Law (Wilthagen et al, 2004), which was prepared by the coalition of Social Democrats and Conservative Liberals that had as its motto 'Job, jobs, jobs'.

The new social policy paradigm, with the core idea of flexible labour contracts with social security rights, was adopted and officially launched at a high level, agenda-setting conference organised by the Social Democratic Minister of Social Affairs and the European Commission in 1997, during the Dutch Presidency of the European Union (EU) and in anticipation of the EU Amsterdam summit of June 1997. The conference brought together ministers, high level policy makers of the EU, representatives of trade unions and employers' organisations, and experts on the welfare state (Ministry of Social Affairs and Employment, 1997) and did much to change the discourse on social policy in the direction of the crucial concepts of flexicurity, social investment and activation.

The new paradigm of the 'activating welfare state' was initially a Social Democratic project, albeit supported by the Conservative Liberals, who were particularly keen on the more stringent policies that were part of activation policies. It took Christian Democracy until the end of the 1990s to make the ideational switch from their passive conceptions of moderation and reform to embrace the new paradigm in social policy thinking. The 1998 electoral manifesto, for instance, has a chapter entitled 'Balance between market and society' and – in addition to a section on traditional solidarity – contains a large section on labour market flexibility and social security (CDA, 1998).

In the Social Democratic model of the activating *'verzorgingsstaat,'* jobs had to be created by the market and the state. State intervention was needed to further job creation in the market, but it was also to create 'additional' jobs in the public sector. Such jobs had to be subsidised because indispensable organisations like schools, social work organisations, and hospitals were incapable of financing them due to tightening budgets. Subsequent Christian Democrat and Conservative Liberal governments did not fundamentally diverge from the agenda of activation, although they did dispense with the most clearly Social

Democratic aspects of it, such as job creation and subsidising jobs in the public sector.

Changing coalitions since 2007 have adopted the new language and the concept of 'activation' has assumed an unchallenged status. Even the financial crisis of 2008, although reinstating some Keynesian ideas, has not altered this. In fact, the crisis response makes use of the activation apparatus already installed and in the spirit of the paradigm, policy makers are inventing new instruments to prevent mass unemployment and by ensuring that redundant workers would in some way retain their relation with the labour market, making use of neologisms, such as 'part-time unemployment'.

However, the Dutch debate on the welfare state since the financial crisis has become more permeated with crisis speech. The Conservative Liberals and Christian Democrats, governing until 2012, believed that a quick return to a balanced budget was indispensable for economic recovery and opted for drastic retrenchment. The Social Democrats also prioritised a balanced budget, but sought an optimal balance between retrenchment, tax increases, and continuation of demand stimulating and social investment policies.

During the electoral campaign in 2012 the Social Democrats were involved in a fierce electoral battle with their competitors on the left (the Socialists) who headed the polls. The Socialists had embraced a conservative–protective position with regard to the welfare state, that is, they were unwilling to fully adopt the dominant activation and flexicurity agenda. In fact, the Socialists' electoral manifesto of 2012 contained several proposals to reverse flexicurity and activation measures, such as reducing the number of flexible contracts and the preservation of employment protection (SP, 2012). Surprisingly, however, the Social Democrats managed to win the competition for left voters and became the second party after the Conservative Liberals.

In spite of the increasing emphasis on activation and the Europe-wide embracing of the model of the social investment state (see van Kersbergen and Hemerijck, 2012), the notion of '*verzorgingsstaat*' that became the dominant term in the 1980s has been remarkably resilient as a key concept in daily political discourse, at least until fairly recently. It has been the prime term to describe the Dutch welfare state. However, it seems to be disappearing from contemporary political discourse, as is shown by its use in 2012 election manifestos (see Table 12.1).

Table 12.1: Welfare state political discourse in the Netherlands, 2012: terms used in election manifestos

Political party	'Verzorgingsstaat' Welfare state	'Investeringen' Investments	'Hervorming' Reform	Other
Christian Democrats	0	50	13	
Social Democrats	1 (negative)	71	19	
Socialist Party	0	43	3	Social Security (10 – Defensive)
Conservative Liberal	0	15	0	
Populist Right	0	0	0	Social Security (1 – Defensive)

Sources: CDA, 2012; PvdA, 2012; PVV, 2012; SP, 2012; VVD, 2012

The combination of the Conservative Liberals and Social Democrats in power seems most likely to uphold and reinforce the activation image as it was their coalition governments that introduced it in the first place.

Conclusion

During the period 1945 to 1958, which covers the construction phase of the Dutch welfare state, the Social Democrats were led by the notion of the *'welvaartsstaat'* (welfare state), while the Catholics relied on a conception of *'sociale politiek'* (social policy) that directly drew on Vatican social thinking. All political actors in their more concrete political proposals around social policy, however, tended to speak of social security, social insurance and social provisions.

The notion of the *'verzorgingsstaat'* emerged in the period 1958 to 1967, although it did not yet become the dominant expression to characterise the Dutch welfare state. The systematic expansion of the Dutch welfare state, implemented by the Christian Democrats, in their period in coalition with the Conservative Liberals, was governed by the belief that increasing prosperity allowed the extension of social insurance and social provisions so as to establish more social security.

The Dutch welfare state reached its zenith in the period 1968 to 1976 as a total 'caring' state. The Social Democrats aimed to increase social equality by linking economic growth, wages and benefits. Their (perhaps somewhat naïve) idea was that Dutch society had enough solidarity to allow for political intervention aimed at a massive redistribution of resources. Although the Christian Democrats had a similar notion of solidarity, it was only the left wing of the religious parties that supported the Social Democratic project of redistribution. The concept of 'levelling of incomes' permeated the social policy debate.

In the period 1977 to the mid-1990s the Dutch welfare state ran into trouble. In this period the term '*verzorgingsstaat*' was used much more frequently in political discourse than before, but at the same time the term's positive connotations started to give way. The '*verzorgingsstaat*' became increasingly associated with predicament, failure and ultimately crisis, often expressed in a medical parlance, portraying society and the 'welfare state' as patients with ill-health.

During the period since 1995 the Dutch welfare state discourse started to revolve around the concepts of 'activation', 'flexibility and security', and social investment. The language of activation helped to forge a coalition between the Social Democrats and the Conservative Liberals, at the exclusion of the Christian Democrats, who until the late 1990s clung to their essentially subsidiary notion of a generous yet passive welfare state. The political discourse was enriched with a host of new terms, including social investment, flexicurity, and employability, as a predominantly Social Democratic attempt to launch the alternative idea of an activating welfare state to replace the passive '*verzorgingsstaat*'. The financial crisis may have caused the return of a language of retrenchment and financial and fiscal prudence, but has – so far – not led to a disintegration of the activation discourse.

We conclude by highlighting three key developments. First, the connotation of the term '*verzorgingsstaat*' changed from paternalistic, to seemingly neutral and essentially positive with reference to its accomplishments and success, to almost entirely negative, unless it is accompanied with adjectives such as 'activating'. Second, the political and discursive significance of the term '*verzorgingsstaat*' is in decline, and it is perhaps even at the verge of extinction. Third, there seems no alternative word or phrase available that is acceptable to the various competing political actors and that can express the goal and perhaps reality of the current Dutch welfare state, although the term 'activation' has acquired a firm position in Dutch social policy language.

References

ARP (1956) Electoral manifesto (http://pubnpp.eldoc.ub.rug.nl/ FILES/root/verkiezingsprogramma/TK/arp1956/arp56.pdf, p. 6; 26-09-2012)

ARP, KVP, CHU (1971) *Gemeenschappelijk Urgentie Program 1971–1975*, http://pubnpp.eldoc.ub.rug.nl/FILES/root/verkiezingsprogramma/ TK/arpchukvp1971/arp-chu-kvp71.pdf, p.

Banning, W. (1954) *Ons socialisme, de Partij van de Arbeid in Nederland. Een verweer en appel naar aanleiding van het Mandement 1954 en de daarop gevolgde discussies.* Amsterdam: PvdA.

Beveridge, W. (1942) *Social Insurance and Allied Services* (the 'Beveridge Report'), Cmnd 6404, London: HMSO.

Binnema, H. (2004) 'The Netherlands: How OECD ideas are slowly creeping in' in K.A. Armingeon, M. Beyer (eds) *The OECD and European Welfare States.* Cheltenham: Edward Elgar: 113–125.

Blok, E. (1978) *Loonarbeid van vrouwen in Nederland, 1945–1955.* Nijmegen: SUN

Bos, D., M. Ebben, and H. Te Velde (eds) (2007) *Harmonie in Nederland. Het poldermodel van 1500 tot nu.* Amstedam: Bert Bakker.

Bussemaker, J. (1993) *Betwiste zelfstandigheid. Individualisering, sekse en verzorgingsstaat.* Amsterdam: SUA

CDA (1977) *Niet bij brood alleen. Programma CDA Tweede-Kamerverkiezingen 1977*, http://pubnpp.eldoc.ub.rug.nl/FILES/root/verkiezings programma/TK/cda1977/cda77.pdf

CDA (1981) Election Manifesto (http://dnpp.eldoc.ub.rug.nl/FILES/ root/programmas/Verkiezingsprogramma/1981/cda.pdf, p. 72; 01-08-2012)

CDA (1986) Election Manifesto (http://dnpp.eldoc.ub.rug.nl/FILES/ root/programmas/Verkiezingsprogramma/1986/cda86.pdf, p. 2; 01-08-2012)

CDA (1998) Election Manifesto (http://dnpp.eldoc.ub.rug.nl/FILES/ root/programmas/Verkiezingsprogramma/1998/cda98.pdf, pp. 62–64; 01-08-2012)

CDA (2012) Election Manifesto (http://verkiezingen.cda.nl; 01-08-2012)

Donner, A.M. (1957) *Over de term 'welvaartsstaat'.* Mededelingen der KNAW (Nieuwe Reeks 20, nr. 15). Amsterdam 1957.

Elfring, T., R.C. Kloosterman (1989) De Nederlandse 'job machine'. *Economisch-Statistische Berichten*, 74(3718): 736–740

Green-Pedersen, C., K. van Kersbergen, A. Hemerijck (2001) Neo-liberalism, the 'third way' or what? Recent social democratic welfare policies in Denmark and the Netherlands. *Journal of European Public Policy*, 8(2): 307–325

Hall, M. Penelope (1952) *The Social Services of Modern England*. London: Routlegde & K. Paul.

Hellendoorn, M. (2012) *Kostwinners en verliezers. De consequenties van individualisering van inkomensvorming voor de economische positie van vrouwen (1950–1990). Een sociologische analyse*. Amsterdam (PhD-thesis VU University)

Hertogh, M. (1998) *'Geene wet, maar de Heer!' De confessionele ordening van het Nederlandse socialezekerheidsstelsel (1870–1975)*. Den Haag: VUGA

Kuipers, S. (2006) *The Crisis Imperative. Crisis Rhetoric and Welfare State Reform in Belgium and the Netherlands in the Early 1990s*. Amsterdam: Amsterdam University Press

Ministry of Social Affairs and Employment (1997) *Social Policy and Economic Performance. Employment, Activating Welfare State and Economic Competitiveness*. The Hague: Ministry of Social Affairs and Employment

Oosterhuis, H. (1956) Een rechtsorde van de arbeid. *Socialisme en Democratie*, 2: 44–48

PvdA (1951) *De Weg naar Vrijheid. Een socialistisch perspectief* 1951. Amsterdam: De Arbeiderspers

PvdA (1956) Election Manifesto (http://dnpp.eldoc.ub.rug.nl/FILES/root/programmas/Verkiezingsprogramma/1956/pvda56.pdf; 01-08-2012)

PvdA (1986) Election Manifesto (http://dnpp.eldoc.ub.rug.nl/FILES/root/programmas/Verkiezingsprogramma/1986/pvda86.pdf, p. 3; 01-08-2012).

PvdA (2012) Election Manifesto (www.pvda.nl; 01-08-2012)

PVV (2012) Election Manifesto (www.pvv.nl; 01-08-2012)

Rigter, D.P., E.A.M. van den Bosch, R.J. van der Veen, A.C. Hemerijck (1995) *Tussen sociale wil en werkelijkheid. Een geschiedenis van het beleid van het ministerie van Sociale Zaken*. Den Haag: VUGA

Roebroek, J.M., M. Hertogh (1998) *'De beschavende invloed des tijds'. Twee eeuwen sociale politiek, verzorgingsstaat en sociale zekerheid in Nederland*. Den Haag: VUGA

Ruppert, M. (1965) *De welvaartsstaat. Een inleidende beschouwing*. Kampen: Kok.

SP (2012) Election Manifesto (www.sp.nl/2012/verkiezingen/SP-verkiezingsprogramma-nieuw-vertrouwen-print.pdf)

Thoenes, P. (1962) *De elite in de verzorgingsstaat*. Leiden: Stenfert Kroese (1st edition)

Van Kersbergen, K. (2009) 'Religion and the welfare state in the Netherlands'. In K. van Kersbergen, P. Manow (eds) *Religion, Class Coalitions, and Welfare States*. Cambridge: Cambridge University Press: 119–145

Van Kersbergen, K., U. Becker (1988) 'The Netherlands: a passive social democratic welfare state in a Christian Democratic ruled society' *Journal of Social Policy*, 17(4): 477–499.

Van Kersbergen, K., A. Hemerijck (2012) 'Two decades of change in Europe: the emergence of the social investment state' *Journal of Social Policy*, 41(3): 475–492

Vis, B., K. van Kersbergen (2012) 'Towards an open functional approach to welfare state change: pressures, ideas, and blame avoidance'. *Public Administration* (doi: 10.1111/j.1467-9299.2012.02071.x)

Vis, B., K. van Kersbergen, U. Becker (2008) 'The politics of welfare state reform in the Netherlands: explaining a never-ending puzzle.' *Acta Politica*, 43 (2): 333–356

Visser, J., A. Hemerijck (1997) *'A Dutch Miracle'. Job Growth, Welfare Reform and Corporatism in the Netherlands*. Amsterdam: Amsterdam University Press

VVD (1981) Election Manifesto (http://dnpp.eldoc.ub.rug.nl/FILES/root/programmas/Verkiezingsprogramma/1981/vvd.pdf, p. 1; 01-08-2012)

VVD (1986) Election Manifesto (http://dnpp.eldoc.ub.rug.nl/FILES/root/programmas/Verkiezingsprogramma/1986/vvd86.pdf, p. 3; 01-08-2012)

VVD (2012) Election Manifesto (www.vvd.nl)

Wilthagen, T., F. Tros and H. van Lieshout (2004) 'Towards "flexicurity"? Balancing flexibility and security in EU member states. *European Journal of Social Security*, 6(2): 113–136.

Woldendorp, J. (2005) *The Polder Model: From Disease to Miracle? Dutch Neo-corporatism 1965-2000*. Amsterdam: Thela Thesis

WRR (1990) *Een werkend perspectief. Arbeidsparticipatie in de jaren '90*. Den Haag: WRR (Rapport 38).

WRR (2006) *De verzorgingsstaat herwogen. Over verzorgen, verzekeren, verheffen en verbinden*. Den Haag: WRR/Amsterdam: Amsterdam University Press.

THIRTEEN

Panacea, problem or perish: social policy language in New Zealand

Neil Lunt

New Zealand has long been at the forefront of continuous reforms of its economic and social welfare system. Since colonisation by the British in the 19th century, the settler state was a powerful driver of economic development and, later in the century, state intervention emerged across labour markets, health and social assistance, including the establishment of old age pensions in 1898. As Phillips (2011) writes, 'The Liberal reforms of the 1890s attracted international interest and signified the nation's distinctive egalitarian ethos'. Such innovations led to New Zealand being called a 'social laboratory', a reputation that continues to have contemporary resonance.

The view of state intervention was reinforced during the economic depression with the first Labour government (1935–49) introducing the 1938 Social Security Act and free public health care and education. The needs of wartime contributed towards centralisation, and the aftermath saw government intervention maintained through economic management around which there was growing consensus. As a mirror to British Butskellism, the role of the New Zealand state was similarly reoriented into that of manager rather than architect. In politics, the choice appeared that of selecting the party most equipped to manage and there was an accompanying narrowing of ideological debate (Lunt, 2006a). Social policy intervention was premised on income and employment security and social services were seen as facilitating economic growth and development (O'Brien and Wilkes, 1993; Castles and Shirley, 1996). Many commentators viewed the post-war period as the apogee of progress and New Zealand was scripted as the 'half-gallon, quarter-acre, pavlova paradise' (Mitchell, 1972).[117] As Henderson (2005:

---

[117] A 'half gallon' was the standard size for New Zealand pubs selling beer; 'quarter acre' referred to the size of suburban land plots on which homes were built; a 'pavlova' is a New Zealand dessert, similar to a meringue.

118) notes the account of the 1950s and 1960s 'Typified a country where people could own their own land and home; enjoy wholesome, locally produced food and drink; and where pride in the pioneering spirit was strong."Paradise" meant the land of plenty, and was a source of immense national pride'.

The country presented itself as a model of social democracy, racial harmony, natural beauty and economic abundance with the redistributive nature of the welfare state and ideas of 'one-nation New Zealand' underpinning prevalent ideas of identity and citizenship.

While social rights were arguably the basis for a consensus and 'imagined community' (Anderson, 1983), in reality 'the Maori problem' and 'problem families' were centre stage of the policy and politics during the post-war period. Throughout the 1950s, New Zealand social fabric was being further stretched by ongoing urbanisation that now encompassed the indigenous Maori population (around one in seven of New Zealanders are Maori) migrating from tribal homelands to cities in search of work. The rhetoric of 'social problems' was linked to individualised welfare interventions, and a deficit-driven approach of correction and resolution. Such a paradigm was evident for a range of population groups including older people and young people (Lunt, 2003).

The pavlova paradise was also assailed by growing economic pressures from the end of the 1960s. Assumptions of full employment came increasingly under pressure. Britain joining the European Economic Community in 1973 saw shifting trade allegiances: whereas previously it was a major recipient of New Zealand meat and dairy produce it was now expected to conform to the 'common agricultural policy' and trade relationships of the European Community. Combined with oil price increases and economic slowdown, New Zealand policy makers faced mounting challenges. From growth of 2.1% per annum from 1955–72, the loss of markets, combined with weaker global competitiveness and rigid conditions within labour and product markets, saw growth fall to 0.5% 1972–92 (Carroll, 2012). In the 1950s, the per capita Gross Domestic Product (GDP) of New Zealand was 6th highest in the world – by 1992 it had fallen to 19th in the Organisation for Economic Co-operation and Development (OECD) (Easton 1997 cited in Carroll, 2012).

After 1984, perceptions of a bloated public sector, red tape, and distorted markets were presented as structural problems under a neoliberal analysis, and the solutions were then argued to lie in fostering the free flow of people, products and capital. Demand management of the economy, import and capital controls, and public sector ownership and delivery gave way to supply-side solutions focused on incentives, a freer labour market, and individual and family responsibilities. There was a disassembling and reassembling of the welfare machine through legislation, organisational restructures, and new policy missions. The impacts of these changes on living standards, the machinery of government, and labour markets have been well documented. The unemployment rate peaked at 10.6% in 1991 and 1992 and the 1991 Employment Contracts Act introduced a model of individualised wage bargaining. Within the public sector there was a focus on government outputs, major corporatisation of functions, and a raft of privatisations, including Telecom New Zealand and New Zealand Steel (see for example Boston et al, 1996; Kelsey, 1997; Duncan, 2007; Lunt et al, 2008).

The aim of this chapter is to complement the 'real' restructuring of welfare delivery mechanisms with a language focus, tracing how the concepts 'welfare state' and 'welfare' have fared within New Zealand. In shaping social relationships, language operates to naturalise and to neutralise dissent (Edelman, 1964, 1971, 1988). Uncovering such discursive strategies reveals the hidden paths of reform and provides opportunities for resistance (Fairclough, 2000: 167) and gives insight into the rhetorical nature of social welfare politics itself (Finlayson, 2004). Discourse is a core mechanism through which welfare is restructured and populations are 'governed' (Fairclough, 2000), because when continuously performing policy work language performs ideological work (Marston, 2000). There are a range of concerns, including the use of binary devices within policy messages and stories, and political tactics and techniques involving narrative, myth, metaphors, frames, and vocabulary. These linguistic issues are intertwined with core social policy debates around the place of power, and how inequality and privilege are generated and sustained within politics and society. The following discussion provides analysis of the overall trends and developments of discursive articulation of 'welfare' and 'welfare state'. It outlines five distinct periods and explores in greater detail the implications of how language is used in contemporary social policy debates within New Zealand.

New Zealand's welfare state

Welfare state and social welfare as panacea

The 'welfare state' entered into use after the Second World War to describe a range of social security and services provision,[118] and during the 1950s the term became widespread within New Zealand (NZ Labour Party, 1949; Scott, 1955). The concepts of welfare and welfare state became accepted parlance across policy, practice, administration and academia and viewed as broadly welcome goals. A new epoch was projected, one focused not on material want but on addressing 'behavioural problems' focused on child welfare, probation, and integration of Maori people (Green et al, 1954). The ageing population faced evils of poverty, poor housing and loneliness; elsewhere juvenile delinquency was seen as an emerging social ill; illegitimacy was on the rise, and the Maori 'problem' was constructed in the fields of education, employment, income, housing, health and justice (Marsh, 1952; Tasker, 1953; Mazengarb Report, 1954; Schwimmer, 1960; Sears 1969).

There was a rapid growth of welfare professionals (Child Welfare Officers, Probation Officers, and Maori Welfare Officers) in post by the mid-1950s, and increased emphasis was being placed on their training. This growth helped cement the practice of the intimate welfare encounter, and aspirant welfare professions entered the debate over resources. Close at hand for politicians and public servants were the intellectual resources of social science, social research, social administration, and social work that promised immediate benefits in helping to reverse this incipient social malaise.

But not only was a welfare system being wrought via policy measures and professional practices, there was also the establishment of a conceptual edifice. Within policy and politics the welfare state entailed particular things. *Empirically* it was shorthand for publicly funded services and benefits including old age pensions, benefits for families and those experiencing hardship and loss of employment, health services, and education. *Politically,* it pointed towards a dominant consensus and a narrowing ideological debate around the state's role and the nature of citizenship. *Economically,* it centred government economic intervention, reflecting a rejection of interwar fiscal and monetary

---

[118]   The term 'welfare state' was coined during the war years by Archbishop William Temple as a counter to the Nazi 'warfare' state.

practice. In *social–cultural* terms it invoked a sense of identity, and these evocations underpinned a one-nation project of assimilating Maori and emigrant populations into being fully fledged 'New Zealanders'. The term 'welfare state' was thus effectively depoliticised, synonymous with progress, and accepted by parties of both left and right.

Until the 1970s support for the welfare state and public provision encompassed education, health, housing as well as income maintenance and pensions (Palmer, 1977). The academic and political literature suggests that the symbolism of the welfare state was strong, and its definition included financial support and a wide range of areas of public delivery. The (re)emergence of complex social problems – including poverty and inequality during the 1960s – began to erode such complacency. In the 1970s, as a result of new costs and growing challenges to provision, 'welfare state' and 'welfare' began to assume negative connotations (a point noted in passing by McClure, 1998: 207, 258). Throughout the 1970s, 'social welfare' continued to refer to the provision of monetary benefits and support services for both universal and targeted services, but this was soon to give way to a politicisation and residualisation of terms.

The problem of 'welfare' and 'welfare state'

The post-war settlement ended abruptly with election of the fourth Labour government (1984–90). The subsequent deregulation, liberalisation, corporatisation and privatisation were influenced by Chicago School economics, public choice and agency theory. The period witnessed the desire both to reduce public expenditure levels *and* to translate spending concerns into a new set of economic concepts contained within a market paradigm. Thus *Economic Management* (New Zealand Treasury, 1984), a Treasury Briefing paper, repackaged complex policy problems to present them as having elegant first-principle solutions. The emphasis within documents and discussions during this time was on axiomatic workings, assumptions of rational economic actors, and producing objective and neutral accounts.

As an illustration, 'welfare' became a dispassionate economic measurement, drained of interests or values: 'A poorly functioning economy limits opportunities for welfare gains ...' (New Zealand Treasury, 1984: 119). Welfare state and social justice became incommensurable within an economic paradigm elevating individual and market concepts. The neoliberal strategy influenced by Public Choice Theory began to flood the political terrain with economic concepts and understandings. For example: 'Another failure of many programmes which are targeted at low-income households is that the benefits are largely 'captured' by middle and upper-income households (New Zealand Treasury, 1984: 258), while 'Areas of extra potential for diminished state provision and increased incentives for efficiency over the longer term are education (at all levels), institutional health and welfare care (especially for the elderly) and rental housing' (New Zealand Treasury, 1984: 258). Such a strategy was unable however to fully achieve its aim – of forging a new consensus. From the late 1980s a focus on the 'undeserving poor' (young people, women at home, people retired early, and Maori and Pacific populations) complemented and, ultimately, replaced the more abstract notions of homogenous economic actors within labour markets. Attempts to present an alternative view of policy and discourse included the 1988 Royal Commission on Social Policy (Royal Commission on Social Policy, 1988). But messages were submerged within the analysis of the 6,000 submissions, and the four volumes of the report weighed in at nearly 6 kg. As Barnes and Harris (2011: 79) note, it was 'rushed, mammoth, convoluted, in some places repetitive and in other places contradictory, poorly organized ...'.

The election of the right leaning National Party in 1990 saw a reforming agenda further implemented within the social policy sphere and a third phase of welfare narrative. In putting a human face on what were perceived as problems, the welfare state and social welfare were increasingly equated with spending on income maintenance for particular groups. A growing emphasis across the political spectrum was on how 'welfare payments' undermined self-reliance and threatened to induce 'dependency' (National Party, Manifesto 1987: 26). The early 1990s marks an important watershed: in most documents concerning welfare and social welfare the delivery of health, education, and income support payments are identified as separate service areas allowing a selective universalism to be preserved from a residual rump of 'benefits'.

Social security benefits were cut in 1991, and accompanying this were stricter waiting periods to qualify or requalify for benefit receipt, and the Family Benefit was abolished altogether. Reforms were driven by concern about whether economic growth would benefit all sections of the population, and a worry that children in families and the Maori and Pacific populations would be left behind as the economy picked up (Ministry of Social Policy, 2001). Alongside these reforms was the shift to a language that individualised, blamed and moralised. A campaign was consolidated around themes of a 'dependency culture' and 'underclass', as well as the fiscal costs resulting from increased benefit numbers.

Between 1990 and 1999 national-led administrations undertook a number of discursive strategies (Lunt, 2008):

Building a brand to support the new mission. From 1994, national administrations sought to develop a 'Welfare to Wellbeing' brand under which its broad objectives could be advanced (Player, 1994).

Hyphenating and prefixing. Vogue terms were increasingly those of 'welfare spending', 'welfare cost', 'welfare drift', and 'welfare dependency' (National Party, 1990; New Zealand Treasury, 1996: 100). New populations were aligned as 'welfare-dependent communities', 'welfare-dependent families', and along with 'benefit dependent' such terms were presented as both explanatory and prescriptive (see O'Neill, 1997).

Residualising welfare. As evidenced through policy documents and political debates, welfare became a term of abuse, and along with 'beneficiaries' used exclusively pejoratively. Terms such as 'bludger' and 'welfarism' seeped into New Zealand usage, influenced in large part by American intellectual and media exchanges. As one commentator captures, the debate became refocused in a particular way: 'Though education, health care, public housing and provisions for the disabled are undoubtedly programmes identified within the welfare state, 'welfare reforms' has come to denote a more limited target' (Paz-Fuchs, 2008: 2).

Binaries. These included the new brand launched by the Department of Social Welfare around Welfare *versus* Wellbeing (Player, 1994; Department of Social Welfare, 1994, 1995, 1996). Equally, welfare was contrasted with self-sufficiency, and dependence and independence presented as mutually exclusive.

Presenting groups as 'problem' groups. Familiar deserving/undeserving distinctions were introduced around the spectre of beneficiaries, the feckless, and the workshy, and these had frequent racialised undertones regarding Maori and Pacific peoples (those New Zealanders with connections to islands including Samoa, Tonga, Fiji and the Cook Islands). A new binary pitched the beneficiary *versus* the taxpayer, thereby narrowing coverage of the deserving.

Introducing new terms and developing concepts. The term dependency is not new (see New Zealand Treasury, 1987, 1990, 1993; Department of Social Welfare, 1991), however, from the mid-1990s it was less used descriptively. Through the 1990s, and reflecting developments overseas, dependency was presented as 'long-term reliance on benefits', and served as shorthand for intergenerational cycles of reliance among promiscuous and workshy populations. While dependency can be seen to be relational (we are all dependent in various ways at various points in time), under this emerging understanding it became an individual flaw (see Fraser and Gordon, 1994).

While the previous attempt to dissolve welfare and the welfare state had used economic language this was clearly a more abrasive, head-on attack. Underpinning most reforms was the belief that welfare change should reconfigure institutions and policies (focusing on supports, incentives and sanctions) but also needed to effect a broader cultural project to shift how welfare, responsibility and citizenship were conceptualised. In part, this required 'educating' the public about issues including welfare dependency. From 1997 'social responsibility' and 'strengthening families' emerged as key notions which have their genealogy in debates around dependency.

Displacement and dissolution

The election of a series of broadly centre-left Labour led coalitions (1999–2008) saw reform debates being placed within a social democratic Third Way framework (Lunt et al, 2008). Labour governments perceived their role as steering a middle course between global competition, and ensuring more equitable distribution of opportunities and outcomes. The emphasis was on the information based economy and ensuring the labour market was highly skilled, innovative and responsive (New Zealand Government, 2000; Clark, 2002). Welfare benefit numbers were a concern and particular at risk groups targeted for intervention included long-term unemployed people; sickness and invalid beneficiaries; young jobseekers; sole parents; mature jobseekers; Maori people; Pacific Peoples ; and new migrants. Improved incentives and signals for labour market participation were recurring leitmotifs. Labour opposed workfare measures and instead sought to improve job search and coaching provision and attempted to 'make work pay'. Labour clearly signalled the importance of 'investment' in individuals and communities to increase stocks of social capital rather than 'spending'. Alongside such immediate responses towards building employability were longer-term investments – changes to paternity benefits, the thrust of the knowledge based economy, and the commitment to basic literacy and eliminating innumeracy (Lunt, 2006b). A central rationale was that 'investing' in families and children, through providing resources and strategies, would ensure the successful transition of children and young people into future 'citizen-workers' (also see Lister, 2003).

The period also marked the end of a more acerbic moralisation of public welfare provision that was evident under National Party led administrations during the 1990s. A reading of a range of political speeches and policy documents of Labour administrations (1999–2008) suggests an important shift in the debate towards 'modernisation' and 'social development'.

In attempts to 'modernise' Labour's intention was to align its traditional values with the perceived imperatives of globalisation and challenges of what was frequently termed the 'knowledge economy':'A modern welfare state can't be just a safety net, it has to be a trampoline, bouncing its clients back into full and meaningful participation as quickly and effectively as possible' (NZ Labour Party, 1996: 325). Labour's modernisation project sought to revise the organisation and delivery of benefits, as well as the principles of the system itself (see Clark and Maharey, 2001). Modernising welfare provision and commitment to 'active labour market' intervention were to harness new employment realities of global markets. Policy documents drew a sharp distinction between traditional approaches to 'social welfare' and the vision of 'social development'. Occasional references to the welfare state were now prefixed or hyphenated with 'reform', 'modernisation' and 'new'.

As a notion social development has distinctly local origins with a Ministry of Social Development advocated in the early 1970s (one was actually established in 2001), and 'social development' as accepted terminology (see Kelsey and O'Brien, 1995). It draws upon the traditional appeal of community development within New Zealand, and also hails to the longstanding notions of indigenous advancement. Its combination of social *and* development attempted to displace the economic human with a more interdependent social being. Social development is tailored for New Zealand conditions and potentially has a powerful conceptual grab; carrying meaning that is both normative and prescriptive rather than simply descriptive.

Social development entailed commitment to supporting and caring for vulnerable members of society (social protection), and a notion of social investment. Cross-sectoral social policy activity focused on achieving desirable outcomes, and the reduction of social exclusion (Ministry of Social Policy, 2001; Bromwell and Hyland, 2007). What may be discerned as a 'social-investment state' signals an emphasis on education and training to develop human capital, activation policies and welfare to work, enhancing future opportunities rather than tackling current inequalities, and investment in children (Jenson and Saint-Martin, 2003: 79; Lister, 2003; Dobrowolsky and Jenson, 2005).[119]

---

[119] 'Active social policy' and investment were first mentioned in New Zealand and overseas at the beginning of the 1990s.

A focus on health and education facilitates 'investment' in individuals and communities while simultaneously appealing to public and voter opinion far more than does spending focused around forms of residual 'welfare'. The concepts of investment and social development remain embedded in future opportunities rather than present inequalities.

The version of social development advanced also drew upon 'work-focused welfare' and the economic–social policy fusion of the early 1990s. What was relatively inchoate under national has begun to mature under Labour administrations. Schmidt (2001: 252) identifies how the transformative power of discourse occurs when it is absorbed by an opposition party, and as with Third Way developments elsewhere New Zealand Labour sought to reconfigure policy and presentation accordingly.

Active labour market policy emphasises *rights and responsibilities:* 'mutual obligation', 'conditionality', or the melding of 'rights and responsibilities' are central to debates. Sanctions were increasingly a focus of welfare policy, and while 'social development' ostensibly captures the role of markets, families, state and community, state responsibility appeared to be more about matching individuals with markets than more robust notions of inclusion.

Two readings of 'investment' are possible: that current investment will lead to future savings; and second, that current investment leads to benefits and improvements in the longer term. Much of the term's appeal however lies in its ambiguity: 'Government intervention can be conceived as a "social investment" because there are benefits from policy that is well-designed and implemented' (Ministry of Social Policy, 2001: 6).

The notion of social investment also serves a clear tactical function where a distinction is drawn – irrespective of whether it can be maintained in practice – between good and bad public spending. The emphasis is upon refocusing state spending and selective advancement of universalism around health and education, which are argued to be worthwhile investments of New Zealand public funds. According to this intervention logic, measures aimed at promoting active labour markets and developing supply-side responses will produce beneficial outcomes downstream, notably paid work. In identifying understandings of welfare and wellbeing, the investment rationale and expected dividend centre tightly on paid work. As a result welfare is literally *reworked* out of debate, displaced by the emphasis on solely paid activity. As with attempted discursive redrawing of the 1980s welfare has shifted from being an opportunity (1950s); to being dependency (1990s); to being irrelevant (due to globalised and modern labour markets). The final section moves to the fifth discursive development in the post-2008 national administrations

Return to recession

The National Party won the 2008 election and formed a coalition agreement amid what were seen as 'extraordinarily difficult times for the country and the world' (Key, 2008). Initially distinctions between National's prognosis and that of its Third Way predecessor were difficult to identify: 'Paid work is the route to independence and well-being for most people, and that is the best way to reduce child poverty' (Key, 2008), although the Labour mantra of 'making work pay' has under National become a 'tax structure that rewards hard work' (Key, 2009).

The policy approach of 2008–9 was best encapsulated as 'growth deferred' – a government circumscribed by the wider global economic climate and biding time while avoiding unnecessary state intervention. As the Prime Minister stated: 'The task of Government is not to claim to be that [economic] engine, but instead to do all that we sensibly can to keep that engine humming, tuned and free to go up a gear' (Key, 2009). Post-2009 grave economic challenges remained and rising unemployment prompted support for employers and for those losing work, as well as an emphasis on youth opportunities. A policy position was discernible beyond those who were job ready and unemployed, to focus on sickness and invalid benefit recipients and lone parents (Garlick, 2012). The 2010 Future Focus policy package stressed the centrality of work, corresponding obligations and sanctions. A Welfare Working Group (2011) highlighted the role of early investment and forward liability for benefit payments. There remains frequent talk of welfare dependency but also of the investment agenda. Terminology has altered, for example: 'Discussion of the social development approach has largely disappeared from the policy agenda' (Garlick, 2012: 298), although tussles to balance social protection with preventive and early intervention social investment do remain. Continued emphasis on investment within current policy and discourse now carries a strong actuarial twist. This includes completing an annual valuation of the costs of individuals remaining on benefits for their lifetime: 'Underpinning the investment based approach is a focus on the long-term social and financial costs of welfare dependency' (Bennett, 2012). There has been a renaming of benefits with Sickness Benefit and Invalids Benefit replaced by Jobseeker Support and Supported Living Payment from 2013. Discourse has a strong focus on welfare as part of the 'welfare system' and how the system prevents people reaching their full potential by 'trapping' and not offering appropriate incentives. New terms have emerged (including 'young beneficiaries' and 'beneficiary parents'), however language is used far more circumspectly than in the early 1990s. While the discursive shift is being continued it is less an obvious sideswipe reminiscent of the 1990s, when groups were pilloried in political discourse. The emphasis has become a more indirect one, with groups brought into focus because they do not fit within the dominant paradigmatic emphasis that is the 'relentless work focus'.

Conclusion

The chapter has explored the changing social policy language around state intervention and social responsibility, identifying five periods in the post-war era and documenting the language shifts. During the prosperous post-war period, social welfare and the welfare state were seen (to paraphrase Gallie, 1956) as 'essentially accepted concepts' and considered a constituent of growth and development. Post 1984, a neoliberal market vision and corresponding social citizenship emerged, and a version of the Nozickean economic human helped shape social policy language. During the 1990s abstract formulations of welfare were replaced by more direct critique of welfare populations and associated institutions. Labour-led administrations undertook a substantial rethink during the 1990s, and the investment and social development vocabulary and conceptualisation sought to reframe social policy (Lunt, 2010). There are clearly limits around what a renaming can achieve and dangers of engaging in a politics of euphemisms (Schram, 1995: 24). But as this chapter has outlined, there is ongoing contestation of the language landscape. Attention to such discursive articulations remains an important and parallel activity to studying machinery and 'real' policy work. A recent review of social policy management and organisation concluded: 'Across a range of recent developments, one can trace both signs of the past – abiding issues, unresolved tensions, long-standing controversies – and signs of the future, of new direction for an organisation which continue to evolve'. (Garlick, 2012: 300) Such a view applies equally to the ongoing discursive agenda of welfare, welfare state and social policy reform.

References

Anderson, B. (1983) *Imagined Communities: Reflections on the Origins and Spread of Nationalism*, London, Verso.

Barnes, J. and Harris, P. (2011) 'Still kicking? The Royal Commission on social policy, 20 years on', *Social Policy Journal of New Zealand*, vol 37, pp. 70-82.

Bennett, P. (2012) 'Budget 2012: extra funding for welfare reforms, Social Development', Wellington, National Party.

Boston, J., Martin, J., Pallot, J. and Walsh, P. (eds) (1996) *Public Management: The New Zealand Model*, Auckland: Oxford University Press.

Bromwell, D. and Hyland, M. (2007) *Social Inclusion and Participation: a Guide for Policy and Planning*, Wellington, Social Inclusion and Participation Group, Ministry of Social Development.

Carroll, N. (2012) *Structural Change in the New Zealand Economy 1974-2012*, Draft paper for the Long Term Fiscal External Panel, Wellington: Treasury.

Castles, F.G. and Shirley, I. (1996) 'Labour and social policy, gravediggers or refurbishers of the welfare state', in F.G. Castles, Gerritsen, R. and Vowles, J. (eds), *The Great Experiment: Labour Parties and Public Transformation*, Auckland: AUP.

Clark, H. (2002) *Growing an Innovative New Zealand*, Wellington: New Zealand Government.

Clark, H. and Maharey, S. (2001) *Pathways to Opportunity: From social Welfare to Social Development*, Wellington, New Zealand Government.

Department of Social Welfare (1991) *Towards Welfare That Works*, Wellington, DSW

Department of Social Welfare (1994) *From Welfare to Well-Being 1994/5*, Wellington, DSW.

Department of Social Welfare (1995) *From Welfare to Well-Being 1995/6*, Wellington, DSW.

Department of Social Welfare (1996) *From Welfare to Well-Being 1996/7*, Wellington, DSW.

Dobrowolsky, A. and Jenson, J. (2005) 'Social investment perspectives and practices: a decade of British politics', *Social Policy Review 17: Analysis and Debate in Social Policy* (eds) M. Powell, L. Bauld and K. Clarke, Bristol, Policy Press.

Duncan, G. (2007) *Society and Politics: New Zealand Social Policy*. 2nd edition. Auckland: Pearson Education-SprintPrint Prentice Hall.

Edelman, M. (1964) 'The symbolic uses of politics', Chicago, University of Illinois Press.

Edelman, M. (1971) *Politics as Symbolic Action: Mass Arousal and Quiescence*, Institute for Research on Poverty, Monograph Series, Chicago, Markham Publishing Company.

Edelman, M. (1988) *Constructing the Political Spectacle*, Chicago, University of Chicago Press.

Fairclough, N. (2000) *New Labour, New Language*, London, Routledge.

Finlayson, A. (2004) 'Political science, political ideas and rhetoric', *Economy and Society*, vol 33, No 4, pp. 528-549.

Fraser, L. and Gordon, N. (1994) 'A genealogy of dependency: tracing a keyword of the U.S. welfare state', *Signs*, vol 19, no 2, pp. 309-336.

Gallie, W.B. (1956) 'Essentially contested concepts', *Proceedings of the Aristotelian Society*, vol 56, pp. 167-198.

Garlick, T. (2012) *Social Developments – An Organisational History of the Ministry of Social Development and its Predecessors, 1860–2011*, Wellington, Ministry of Social Development.

Green, W.A. E., Oram, C.A. and Schwimmer, E. G. (1954) *Social Services in New Zealand: A Study Group Report Presented to the Wellington Branch of the Institute of Public Administration, 11 November 1954*. Wellington.

Jenson, J. and Saint-Martin, D. (2003) 'New routes to social cohesion? Citizenship and the social investment state', *Canadian Journal of Sociology*, vol 28, no 1, pp. 77-99.

Henderson, A. (2005) 'Activism in 'paradise': identity management in a public relations campaign against genetic engineering, *Journal of Public Relations Research*, vol 17, no 2, pp. 117–137.

Kelsey, J. (1997) *The New Zealand Experiment: A World Model for structural Adjustment*, Auckland, Auckland University Press/Bridget Williams Books.

Kelsey, J. and O'Brien, M. (1995) *Setting the Record Straight: Social Development in Aoteroa New Zealand*, Wellington, ANGOA.

Key, J. (2008) Speech from the Throne, 9 December, New Zealand Parliament, Wellington.

Key, J. (2009) 'Jobs and growth', Speech to the Waitakere Enterprise Business Club, 4 February.

Lister, R. (2003) 'Investing in the citizen-workers of the future: transformations in citizenship and the state under New Labour', *Social Policy & Administration*, vol 37, 5, pp. 427-443.

Lunt, N. (2003) 'Knowledge for policy: the emergence of evaluation research within New Zealand', in Lunt, N., Davidson, C. and McKegg, K. (eds) *Evaluating Policy and Practice: A New Zealand Reader*, Auckland: Pearson Education.

Lunt, N. (2006a) 'New Zealand', in Fitzpatrick et al (eds) *International Encyclopedia of Social Policy*, London: Routledge.

Lunt, N. (2006b) 'Employability and New Zealand welfare restructuring', *Policy & Politics* vol 34, No 3, pp. 473-494.

Lunt, N. (2008) 'From welfare state to social development: winning the war of words in New Zealand', *Social Policy and Society*, vol 7, No 4, pp. 405-418.

Lunt, N. (2010) 'Welfare reform and the reshaping of New Zealand citizenship', in A. Nevile (ed.) *Human Rights and Social Policy: A Comparative Analysis of Values and Citizenship in OECD Countries*, Edward Elgar.

Lunt, N., O'Brien, M. and Stephens, R. (2008) (eds) *New Welfare New Zealand*, Melbourne: Thomson Press.

Marsh, D. C. (1952) 'Old people in the modern state' *Political Science*, March, 23–28.

Marston, G. (2000) 'Metaphor, morality and myth: a critical discourse analysis of public housing policy in Queensland', *Critical Social Policy*, vol 20, no 3, pp. 349-373.

Mazengarb Report (1954) *Special Committee on Moral Delinquency of Children and Adolescents*. Wellington.

McClure, M. (1998) *A Civilised Community: A History of Social Security in New Zealand 1898-1998*, Auckland, Auckland University Press in association with the Historical Branch, Department of Internal Affairs.

Ministry of Social Policy (2001) *The Social Development Approach*, Wellington, Ministry of Social Policy.

Mitchell, A. (1972) *The Half-Gallon, Quarter-Acre, Pavlova Paradise*, Christchurch: Whitcomb.

National Party (1987) Manifesto, Wellington, National Party.

National Party (1990) *Economic and Social Initiative*, Wellington, National Party.

New Zealand Government (2000) *Opportunity, Capacity, Participation: Government Employment Strategy*, Wellington.

NZ Labour Party (1949) *An Era of Plenty*, Wellington, NZ Labour Party.

NZ Labour Party (1996) *New Heart, New Hope*, Manifesto, Wellington, NZ Labour Party.

New Zealand Treasury (1984) *Economic Management*, Briefing Paper, Wellington: NZ Treasury.

New Zealand Treasury (1987) Treasury Briefing Paper, Wellington, NZ Treasury.

New Zealand Treasury (1990) Treasury Briefing Paper, Wellington, NZ Treasury.

New Zealand Treasury (1993) Treasury Briefing Paper, Wellington, NZ Treasury.

New Zealand Treasury (1996) Treasury Briefing Paper, Wellington, NZ Treasury.

O'Brien, M. and Wilkes, C. (1993) *The Tragedy of the Market*, Palmerston North: Dunmore Press.

O'Neill, R. (1997) 'Strategic framework of government-community partnerships: Opotiki development projects a case study', *Social Policy Journal of New Zealand*, vol 9, pp. 27-43.

Palmer, G. (1977) *The Welfare State Today: Social Welfare Policy in New Zealand in the Seventies*, Auckland, Fourth Estate Books.

Paz-Fuchs, A. (2008) *Welfare to Work: Conditional Rights in Social Policy*, Oxford: Oxford University Press.

Phillips, J. (2011) 'The New Zealanders', *Te Ara - The Encyclopedia of New Zealand*. www.TeAra.govt.nz/en/the-new-zealanders/4/4

Player, M. (1994) 'Welfare to Well-Being', *Social Policy Journal of New Zealand*, vol 3, pp. 77-81.

Royal Commission on Social Policy (1988) *The April Report* (Volumes I-IV), Wellington, Royal Commission on Social Policy.

Schmidt, V. (2001) 'The politics of economic adjustment in France and Britain: when does discourse matter?' *Journal of European Public Policy*, vol 8, no 2, pp. 247-264.

Schram, S. F. (1995) *World of Welfare: The Poverty of Social Science and the Social Science of Poverty*, Minneapolis/London, University of Minnesota Press.

Schwimmer, E. G. (1960) Government and the changing Maori. *New Zealand Journal of Public Administration*, vol 22, pp. 13–37.

Scott, K. J. (ed)(1955) *Welfare in New Zealand*. Wellington, NZ Institute of Public Administration/ Oxford University Press.

Sears, A. (1969) 'Trends in illegitimacy' *New Zealand Social Worker*, vol 5, pp. 15–20.

Tasker, J. F. (1953) 'Older people in New Zealand' *New Zealand Journal of Public Administration*, vol 15, pp. 1–13.

Welfare Working Group (2011) *Reducing Long-Term Benefit Dependency*, Recommendations, Wellington, School of Government at Victoria University of Wellington and the Institute of Policy Studies.

FOURTEEN

Evolving social policy languages in Spain: what did democracy and EU membership change?

Ana M. Guillén and David Luque

This chapter analyses the historical evolution of the social policy languages and concepts in Spain. It focuses on the changing meanings of 'social security' (*seguridad social*) and 'welfare state' (*estado del bienestar*) but it also takes into account how entitlements and recipients were defined and how these notions changed over time.

The interest in the Spanish case for analysing the evolution of social policy language is derived precisely from its peculiar historical development. Modern[120] social policy was initiated in Spain in 1900. The development of social insurance followed the Bismarckian model from then until the end of Franco's authoritarian regime in 1975. However, since the advent of democracy, the Spanish social protection system has become a mixed model à la Esping-Andersen (1990); in other words, it has been based on a combination of social democratic, conservative-corporatist, and liberal principles, where policy areas differ with respect to institutional design. For instance, while the income maintenance system remains broadly rooted in Bismarckian principles, health care, education, and, partially, social care services, have been universalised following the social democratic model. The analysis in this chapter focuses on the ways in which social policy language in Spain's various policy areas reflects the influence of the Bismarckian, social democratic and liberal models of welfare capitalism.

---

[120] By 'modern' we mean a social protection system based on social rights as opposed to discretionary public or private action. In previous centuries, private and public institutions provided social protection. Among private ones one can cite guilds, mutual associations, and the Catholic Church. There were public health care centres mainly in large towns, called *Casas de Socorro* and *Hospitales Generales,* and a scheme for medical assistance in rural areas, termed *Asistencia Pública Domiciliaria.* Also the *Beneficencia* was in charge of poor relief.

The chapter is divided into two main sections. The first section addresses briefly the language used in the origins and early construction of the Spanish social protection system during Franco's dictatorship (1939–75). The second section explores the evolving meanings of 'social security' and 'welfare state' during the democratic period (1975 to the present). Changes in the historical construction of social policy language were brought about not only because of the advent and consolidation of a democratic regime, but also because of the inclusion of Spain in the European Economic Community in 1986.

Social policy languages: origins and historical construction of the Spanish social protection system

As already stated, the Spanish social protection system was initiated in the late 19th century with a debate grounded on 'the social question' (*la cuestión social*). This constituted a fundamental ideological turning point: people in need should no longer be protected only by charitable bodies and institutions, but the state was to play a direct (but still limited) role in the provision of social protection, understood as a social right. The reformist ideological turn was possible, among other things, thanks to a change in the official position of the Catholic Church, namely the upsurge of Social Catholicism as expressed in the 1891 Rerum Novarum encyclical of Pope Leo XIII (Guillén, 1990).

At the turn of the century a Bill on employers' liability for labour accidents was passed. Shortly after, in 1908, the National Insurance Institute (*Instituto Nacional de Previsión*, INP) was established and charged with the development of social insurance schemes. The new schemes followed the principle of 'subsidised freedom' (*libertad subsidiada*), meaning that the INP could delegate its administrative powers to private entities. In this early period, both the legal norms and the INP itself referred to 'popular insurance' (*previsión popular*) rather than to social protection. Compulsory social insurance schemes were created for retirement (1919), maternity (1926), and labour accidents (1932), leaving the coverage of other risks to either voluntary public or private insurance. It was the 1919 Bill introducing retirement pensions that used the term 'social policy' (*política social*) for the first time. Political turmoil and authoritarian periods hindered the legal proposal for introducing a coordinated set of public compulsory insurance schemes (*seguros sociales obligatorios*) until the Second Republic (1931–6), an initiative blocked by the outbreak of the Civil War in 1936.[121]

The Francoist regime, in place by 1939, quickly decided to introduce compulsory insurance schemes in the 1940s for retirement pensions and invalidity, healthcare, and maternity, as a way to compensate both the victors and the losers of the Civil War, and as a means of social appeasement. This constituted, as Velarde (1990) portrayed it, the 'first switch' of the Spanish social protection system. Franco's ideology with regard to social policy was closer to that prevailing in Nazi Germany or Fascist Italy at the time than to the new economic and social policy ideas associated with British thinkers such as Beveridge and Keynes. This means that the first Francoist governments were more inclined to pursue the creation of a social insurance system aimed at protecting only workers and their dependents than a universal system aimed at all citizens. Furthermore, the Francoist ideology favoured the Bismarckian principle of the male breadwinner model, as did the highly influential Catholic Church. In other words, the social order revolved around conservative principles: men should sustain families and women should stay at home, taking care of the children, and of sick, older, and disabled people. Hence, the policy pursued a set of compulsory occupational insurance schemes, while social care services remained poorly developed well into the late 1960s. These schemes were initially aimed at 'economically weak workers' (*productores económicamente débiles*) in the industrial sector, a peculiar choice in terminology, from a comparative perspective. Official, legal, and academic social policy language referred in general to the 'providence state' (*estado providencia*) or the 'social state' (*estado social*) during this period.

According to Rodríguez Cabrero (1989: 80), the historical foundations of the Spanish welfare state can be found in the period from 1963 to 1975. It was in 1963 that the Basic Law on Social Security (*Ley de Bases de la Seguridad Social*, BL) was passed, and from 1967 onward, it was implemented. This constitutes the crucial 'second switch' of the Spanish social protection system (Velarde, 1990). The BL introduced the term 'social security' in Spanish social policy language for the first time. Moreover, from a comparative perspective, it included several interesting elements in its design. Using the terminology of the time, 'risks' (*riesgos*) covered previously by independent social insurance schemes were now renamed 'contingencies' (*contingencias*) in order to underscore the novel uniformity of protection of the system. Another particular term, still

---

[121] On the origins of the Spanish welfare state, see Guillén (1990); de la Calle Velasco (1997).

used, was 'regulatory base' (*base reguladora*), referring to the formula to calculate the amount of the initial pension. Other than these terms, the language used was similar to that in any other European social security system. No terminology stemming from religious or conservative family conceptions was incorporated in the social security legal texts and the new legal terms were broadly used and accepted by all actors. Conversely, the legislation on family protection did reflect the existing conservative ideology by referring to the traditional Christian family as the foundation of society.

By the time of Franco's death in 1975, the term 'social security' had become broadly used in everyday language by politicians, public and private institutions and organisations, and the population in general, as a synonym for social protection. Spanish people continue to use it nowadays in this sense. The advent of democracy and European Union (EU) membership, however, brought about significant changes in the use of social policy language, as the next section shows.

Democratisation and Europeanisation: from 'social security' to 'welfare state'

The onset of the transition to democracy period in 1975 constitutes the landmark for what Spanish academics call 'the process of consolidation of the Spanish welfare state' (Rodríguez Cabrero, 2011) or the 'third switch' of the Spanish social protection system (Velarde, 1990). This process of consolidation is marked by four factors: the establishment of a democratic political regime, essential to be able to term a social protection system a 'welfare state'[122]; the shift of the basic principle informing access to and provision of healthcare and education services towards a social democratic one; the decentralisation of powers to the regions in some policy areas; and the growing Europeanisation of social policies since Spain's integration into the EU in 1986, but also before that time as preparation for entry (Rodríguez Cabrero, 1989; Guillén, 1992; Guillén, 2010). Profound laicisation of Spanish society and a widespread reaction against the prominent role played by the Church under Francoism were conducive to a much weakened position of the Catholic Church in the policy making process.

---

[122] Many experts agree that the social security system was only able to be referred to as a 'welfare state' when democracy became a reality. See, for example, Rodríguez Cabrero (2004); de la Calle Velasco (1998); Comín Comín (1996).

Pursuing the completion of a welfare state

In the second half of the 1970s, the social policy debate was centred on how to attain a well-developed welfare state similar to other more advanced European ones, and to pursue the narrowing of pre-existing protection gaps. All political and economic actors, as well as social ones (the social partners, interest groups, associations) agreed with this course of action, but while the left-wing parties and the unions favoured the swift introduction of expansionary reforms into the social protection system, right-wing parties and the employers' association preferred to see a slower pace of change. In general, both the different political actors and the population admired the Nordic social democratic model of welfare. However, while the left-wing parties and the unions were in favour of turning healthcare and education services into a universal, citizenship-based model, they wanted the income maintenance system (pensions, unemployment) to remain organised along occupational (Bismarckian) lines.

Article 41 of the democratic Constitution of 1978 endows the state with the responsibility of 'maintaining a public regime of social security for all citizens, which is to guarantee assistance and sufficient social protection in the face of need, especially in situations of unemployment. Complementary protection is to be optional.' In accordance with such principles, the first major reform of the social security system took place in 1978 by incorporating the representation of social agents into the management of the system and by improving management through the division of the old INP into four national institutes devoted to protection in the fields of pensions and invalidity, unemployment, healthcare, and social services.

Income maintenance à la Bismarck

The 'contingencies' of retirement, invalidity, and widowhood have remained grounded in occupational and contributory principles.[123] Hence, the language used by all actors and by the population in this domain has remained Bismarckian (the usual language of social protection systems based on social insurance for workers and their dependents; it differs from either universal entitlements based on citizenship or access based on means testing). As stated earlier, such Bismarckian language was already introduced at the beginning of the

---

[123] For analysis of the evolution of the pension system during democracy in Spain, see Chuliá (2011).

20th century in Spain, and it used terms such as 'replacement rates', 'minimum contributory periods', 'salaried years to calculate the initial pension', 'pension formula', and so on. The Spanish system also counts on a minimum and maximum contributory pension. 'Top-ups' for minimum pensions (*complementos a mínimos*) bear great weight in the redistribution mechanisms within the pension system, and constitute a meaningful concept for the population in general. Since the early 1980s, an informal consensus, so far unbroken by either socialist or conservative governments, has allowed for the 'improvement of the lowest pensions' (*mejora de las pensiones mínimas*), so that the average contributory pension reached the level of the minimum wage (attained in 1995), and later the minimum contributory pension reached the same level (attained in the early 2000s).

Another uninterrupted aspect of the informal consensus on pensions consists of what is termed both in the normative and in common political and administrative language[124] as 'convergence of special regimes with the general regime', referring to the equalisation of all workers in terms of conditions for access and entitlements to economic transfers. This implies incorporating the 'beneficiaries' or workers of special regimes into the general regime in order to enjoy better conditions. The last and most recent incorporations have included agrarian salaried workers and home helps. The reform of the pension system has been guided up to the present by the decisions of the so-called 'Toledo Pact', reached in 1995 among all parties with parliamentary representation, unions, employers' associations, and other social interests. Unemployment protection also remains mainly based on occupational (that is, employment) principles, so that typical Bismarckian terminology such as 'minimum contributory periods' and 'replacement rates of previous salary' also apply.[125]

Social democratic health and education services coupled with regional autonomy

The reform of healthcare and education services produced a marked innovative shift in social policy language towards social democratic

---

[124] We indicate that this term is used in legal language but also in common political and administrative language because there are cases in which the latter develop either a shorter or different term.

[125] This terminology is also used in non-occupational schemes such as those of the UK and the US, but the origin is clearly Bismarckian systems, where social protection was, and still is, aimed at workers rather than citizens.

terminology based on universal access grounded in citizenship and equity (equal treatment for equal need, irrespective of wealth). Such reform was backed by a broad coalition including the leftist parties (the Socialist Party was in office for 14 years starting in 1982), the unions, regional governments and civil society associations. The reform entailed a major and novel departure from the pre-existent Bismarckian principle of social insurance for workers and their dependants. Primary healthcare was reformed in 1984, establishing healthcare centres (*centros de salud*) and improving the working conditions of general practitioners, who have always been public-salaried employees and the gatekeepers of the system right from its inception as a compulsory insurance scheme. In this way, the new term 'healthcare centres' (*centros de salud*) replaced the old 'ambulatories' (*ambulatorios*). Also, general practitioners, previously called 'bedside doctors' (*médicos de cabecera*) became 'family doctors' (*médicos de familia*). The teams of health professionals in charge of primary care, including doctors, nurses, social workers, and psychologists have come to be known as 'primary healthcare teams' (*equipos de atención primaria*).

But the major departure from Bismarckian principles on the one hand, and central state management on the other, took place in 1986, with the approval of the General Law on Healthcare (*Ley General de Sanidad*). It grouped all pre-existent healthcare public networks (the broadest by far being Social Security) into a National Health System (SNS). The 1986 reorganisation also prompted the devolution of powers to autonomous regions in this policy domain (powers had already been devolved to Catalonia in 1983). In this way, by 2002, 17 regional healthcare systems were in place.

Furthermore, the popularly called 'decree on universalisation' incorporated all previous poor relief beneficiaries into the SNS in 1989. Since the electoral victory of the national Socialist Party in 1982, the term 'universalisation' (*universalización*) has carried a lot of symbolic and political weight for labour unions, leftist parties and associations, and the population in general, as it also does in the UK, Sweden, and even Canada. As a consequence of this move, population coverage for healthcare became quasi universal. Also, individual health cards were issued for all 'users' (rather than 'patients'), first in the Basque Country and then in the rest of Spain. Despite these moves towards the transformation of a system based on social insurance into a universal national health service, access based on citizenship was never approved legally, so that it remains conditional on being a worker or the dependant of a worker. In other words, we are talking here about a 'de facto', not 'de jure', universalisation. The result in terms of communication is that, in everyday language, people still talk about 'going to the social security doctor' or 'the social security hospital', or they refer to the healthcare system by the acronym of their corresponding regional service, this latter habit constituting an interesting change in common vocabulary. Hence, it tends to be only politicians or social partners who refer in their written and oral declarations to the 'National Health System'. The use of the term 'individual health card' (*tarjeta sanitaria individual*) has become widespread in everyday life, which is because patients must show it when accessing any of the services provided (primary, specialist, and hospital care, and also for prescriptions and diagnostic tests) (Guillén and Cabiedes, 1997). Citizens also have access to an individual European health card on request, valid for two years. No individual cards are used in any other policy domain. Workers have an official document of affiliation to social security, called '*cartilla de la seguridad social*', in paper format.

In the 1990s, legal, academic, and political vocabulary changed again, all in the same direction. As a result of the Maastricht Treaty, the Stability Pact and the age of austerity, member state governments had to aim not only for equity but also for efficiency in social protection policies in order to attain the required fiscal balance. On the one hand, the EU required this for countries to join the European Monetary Union (EMU); on the other hand, both the Spanish government and the public were eager to comply. This brought about a new terminology shared by all actors. Simultaneously, British reforms undertaken by Thatcher and summarised in the White Paper entitled *Working for Patients* (Department of Health, 1989), came to represent the example to be followed in other EU countries, especially those with a national health service. 'Users' became 'clients' and such terms as 'freedom of choice', 'managed competition', 'co-payments', 'sustainability', 'cost control policies', 'rationalisation', and 'new public management' gained presence in Spanish public debates. However, in Spain, and possibly due to the closeness in time of the universalisation reform of 1986, such terms have not taken root among the population. It has been hard for people to accept that austerity measures were needed so soon after the adoption of a social democratic healthcare system. While efficiency goals came to stay, the vocabulary of experts, academics, and politicians has shifted to issues of 'quality of services' and 'preventive' action in the 2000s. This is hardly surprising in the case of Spain: the implementation of the 1986 reform and the devolution of powers to the 17 autonomous regions were both completed in 2002. In this context, it is only normal that language should insist on 'consolidation', 'coordination' among levels of governments and different territories, and 'enhancing quality'.

In terms of size and cost, healthcare and education have been the main social policy domains devolved to the autonomous regions. Regional powers have also been extended to other areas, namely, social services, housing, non-contributory pensions, and active labour market policies. This has triggered the use of terms like 'regional welfare regimes' among academics for comparative purposes (Gallego and Subirats, 2011), given that autonomous regions can, at their discretion, develop complementary social protection policies in addition to compulsory ones. Regional governments and actors tend to use the same terminology, only translated into written regional languages where those languages are co-official, that is, in the three 'special status' or 'historical regions' (the Basque Country, Catalonia, and Galicia). Also significant is that, as a consequence of the introduction of the new universalist social democratic principle into the social protection system, the so-called 'separation of financing sources' (*separación de las fuentes de financiación*) was agreed upon by the Toledo Pact in 1995 and enacted in 1999. This means that social contributions are to be used to finance solely contributory cash transfers, while non-contributory ones and welfare services are to be financed through general revenues. Such reform has now been almost completed.

It is probably only in the realm of primary and secondary education that resistance to change on the part of the Catholic Church has taken place under democracy, regarding two specific issues. The first concerns resistance to a shift in religious teaching from '(Catholic) Religion' to 'Religions' or 'Ethics', a battle that was lost by the Church. The second is related to confessional 'concerted schools' (*colegios concertados*). Concerted schools are publicly financed but privately managed schools, many of them operated by the Church. These schools are always struggling to retain the levels of public funding, something that is usually easier under right-wing than under left-wing regional governments. Beyond the field of education, the enactment in 2010 of a Law about abortion on demand has also caused a lot of public controversy, with the Church and the Popular Party (PP) intensely resisting such a move. The PP, currently in office, has announced a revision of the Law.

Moves to overcome residualism in social assistance

The contributory income maintenance system has been complemented by economic transfers aimed at workers who have either failed to complete minimum contributory periods or exhausted the contributory transfers, or at people who have never accessed the labour market. However, rather than being called 'assistance' (*asistenciales*), these transfers are called 'non-contributory': they include 'non-contributory pensions' (for older or disabled people or families with dependants, introduced in 1990), and 'social salaries' (*salarios sociales*) or 'minimum income transfers' (*rentas mínimas de inserción*), aimed at households headed by people of working age, which were introduced at regional level in the late 1980s and early 1990s. Minimum income transfers include labour activation policies as opposed to social salaries that are mere cash transfers (Laparra, 2004; Arriba and Pérez, 2007).

Apart from contributory unemployment transfers (*prestaciones por desempleo*), unemployment protection has also come to include 'non-contributory subsidies' (*subsidios de desempleo*) for ex-workers having exhausted the contributory transfer period and 'activation unemployment subsidies' (*rentas activas de inserción*). All 'non-contributory' income maintenance transfers can be characterised as assistential because access to them is based on scarcity of resources (means testing; *comprobación de medios*) at the household level rather than at the individual level. It could thus be interpreted that non-contributory transfers are based on a 'liberal' or 'residual' principle.

Actors and social policy languages

Though reference to 'the Spanish welfare state' (*Estado del bienestar español*) has become common among all political, social, and economic actors since the advent of democracy in Spain, the main political parties show differences in their discourses in accordance with their social democratic (*Partido Socialista Obrero Español*, PSOE) and conservative/ neoliberal (*Partido Popular*, PP) ideologies. Predictably, unions and employers' associations also sustain different narratives on what principles should guide welfare state development.

In the field of pensions, the PSOE and the unions defend the public system and understand the private tier as a complementary scheme, never as a substitute for public schemes. Both acknowledge the need for 'rationalisation' and the introduction of cost control measures due to population ageing, expanded life expectancy, and other such factors. The PP and the *Confederación Española de Organizaciones Empresariales* (CEOE), together with the banking sector, support a much more intense development of private schemes but fear the loss of support of the older electorate. During its time in government (1982–96), the PSOE was able to universalise healthcare and education policies, and also to devolve powers to the regions in these domains, thanks to union support and population preferences (León and Guillén, 2011). While unions have always opposed the abandonment of the occupational principle in the area of income maintenance policy, they have been very much in favour of universalising welfare services, especially those considered to be 'basic', such as healthcare and education. The PP and the CEOE do not challenge this position, but advocate the separation of state functions in order to reduce the size of the state and public administration and to enhance 'free choice of provider'. Nonetheless, the establishment of a universal system of care for dependants was backed by all relevant actors in 2006. In electoral programmes, conclusions of party congresses, and public declarations of all major collective actors, little attention is paid to policies (cash transfers or services) aimed at the protection of people of working age, with the outstanding exception of unemployment policies. In other words, the housing and financial needs of young people in search of their first job and wanting to start a family seem to be forgotten.

Last but not least, the EU has influenced the adoption of new social policy terminology (Guillén and Álvarez, 2004). Spanish political and social actors and the population in general have traditionally shown great enthusiasm for the EU, the construction of the single market, and belonging to the Eurozone. Moreover, there has always been a wish to appear to be a deserving member state, this circumstance easing the incorporation of Eurospeak, at least in those social policy areas of action in which the EU is involved. For example, the narrative of 'activation' quickly took root during the 1990s. Also, Spain followed suit in the evolution of terminology produced at the EU level: 'fighting poverty' in the 1980s, 'fighting social exclusion' in the 1990s and 'promoting social inclusion' in the 2000s. Gender equality mainstreaming by the EU has also had a direct impact on the terminology used for equal pay, work–life balance, and care policies. Gender Equality Plans enacted since the early 1980s and, very prominently, the so-called 'Equality Law' (*Ley para la Igualdad Efectiva entre Mujeres y Hombres*) passed in 2007 are proof of the adoption of EU terminology in contemporary Spanish social policy.

A final note is needed on the most recent period of economic and financial crisis. Unsurprisingly, since the outburst of the crisis in the autumn of 2008, new terms have entered the public debate and the political agenda. Up to mid-2010, the political discourse of the Socialist government (in office since 2004) centred on the need to use the welfare state as an 'anti-cyclical stabiliser'. From then on, and due to the ever-growing and sustained debt crisis, the motto has turned to the need to attain 'balanced budgets and reduce public deficits'. Much resented budget cuts (*recortes*) have become the leitmotiv of everyday life for citizens and the subject of many conversations. Cuts are presented by the new Conservative government (in office since December 2011) as 'the only way out of the crisis'. In the realm of pensions, the 'sustainability factor' (*factor de sostenibilidad*) entered the public debate in 2013. As for the language developed in the context of street protests (for example, that of the '*indignados*'), it has never entered social protection debates, probably due to their anti-establishment character, as *indignados* reject bipartisanism and advocate deliberative democracy. Moreover, no specific terminology has been advanced by protest movements regarding social policy. In 2012, labour unions, together with various social associations,[126] celebrated several so-called 'social summits' (*cumbres sociales*). Such a term constitutes the introduction of new terminology in the array of actions of social protest against welfare state retrenchment.

Conclusion

This chapter has shown how the historical context produces significant changes in the evolution of social policy languages. In the case of Spain, not only time but a change of political regime was crucial to approach the social protection system as a 'welfare state' rather than a 'social security' system. Democracy brought about a search for inclusiveness of all the population in social protection by means of universalising welfare services and adding non-contributory schemes to the income maintenance system. Spaniards viewed the social security system inherited from Francoism as incomplete and suffering from protection gaps, while attaining an inclusive social protection system was equated to the construction of a democratic fully fledged welfare state.

Also, as hypothesised in the introduction, the adoption of new principles in different areas of the social protection system under democracy was conducive to the incorporation of new terms that were in accordance with such new principles. From the analysis, it may easily be concluded that, because of the differing trajectories underpinning the social protection pillars, a different terminology and language is used nowadays, which is very much in accordance with the grounding principle of each one, be it Bismarckian (income maintenance), social democratic (healthcare, education) or liberal–residual (social assistance).

Changes in the language used have been fostered from within and without the country, because of integration into the EU and also

---

[126] Among such associations are, for instance, *Sindicato de Técnicos de Hacienda, Jueces para la Democracia, Ecologistas en Acción, Unión de Actores, Asociación de Consumidores, Afectados por los Recortes de la Ley de Dependencia, Plataforma de los Trabajadores de la Función Pública.*

because of the admiration of foreign social democratic protection systems by leftist political elites (at both the national and regional levels) and the labour unions. Internal drivers have consisted mainly of diverse political ideologies and ideas of modernisation and changing population preferences. The widespread belief in regional autonomy causing a modification of governance patterns has also produced new terminology.

At present, and in the context of very deep and everlasting economic crisis, social policy languages are changing again. Discontent with the EU, political parties, and political elites in general is growing rapidly. Regional autonomy is also increasingly contested. In contrast, support for the welfare state remains strong (del Pino, 2007). What modifications this will bring about in social protection narratives, discourses, and terminology remain to be seen.

References

Alarcón Caracuel, M.R. (1999) *La Seguridad Social en España*. Aranzadi: Pamplona.

Arriba González de Durana, A. and Pérez Eransus, B. (2007) 'La última red de protección social en España: prestaciones asistenciales y su activación', *Política y Sociedad*, 44 (2): 115-133.

Chuliá, E. (2011) 'Consolidation and reluctant reform of the pension system', in *The Spanish Welfare State in European Context*, edited by A.M. Guillén and M. León. London: Ashgate, 285-303.

Comín Comín, F. (1996) 'Las formas históricas del Estado de Bienestar: el caso español', in *Dilemas del Estado de Bienestar*, Madrid: Fundación Argentaria.

de la Calle Velasco, M.D. (1997) 'Sobre los orígenes del Estado social en España', *Ayer*, 25: 127-150.

de la Calle Velasco, M.D. (1998) 'El sinuoso camino de la política social en España', *Historia Contemporánea*, 17: 287-308.

del Pino, E. (2007) 'Las actitudes de los españoles hacia la reforma del Estado de Bienestar', *Política y Sociedad*, 44 (2): 185-208.

Department of Health (1989) *Working for Patients*, London: DH.

Esping-Andersen, G. (1990) *The Three Worlds of Welfare Capitalism*. Cambridge/Princeton: Princeton University Press.

Gallego, R. and Subirats, J. (2011) 'Regional welfare regimes and multi-level governance', in *The Spanish Welfare State in European Context*, edited by A.M. Guillén and M. León. London: Ashgate, 97-117.

Guillén, A.M. (1990) 'The emergence of the Spanish welfare state: the role of ideas in the policy process', *International Journal of Political Economy*, 20, 3: 82-96.

Guillén, A.M. (1992) 'Social policy in Spain: From dictatorship to democracy,' in *Social Policy in a Changing Europe*, ed. by Ferge, Zsuzsa y Jon Eivind Kolberg. Boulder, Colorado: Campus/Westview, pp. 119-142.

Guillén, A.M. (2010) 'Defrosting the Spanish welfare state: the weight of conservative components', in *A long Goodbye to Bismarck: The Politics of Welfare Reforms in Continental Europe*, edited by B. Palier. Amsterdam: Amsterdam University Press, 183-206.

Guillén, A.M. and Álvarez, S. (2004) 'The EU's Impact on the Spanish welfare state: the role of cognitive Europeanization', *Journal of European Social Policy*, 14, 3: 285-300.

Guillén, A.M. and Cabiedes, L. (1997) 'Towards a national health service in Spain: the search for equity and efficiency', *Journal of European Social Policy*, 7, (4): 319-336.

Laparra, M. (2004) 'La travesía del desierto de las rentas mínimas en España', *Documentación Social,* 135: 57-76.

León, M. and Guillén, A.M. (2011) 'Conclusions', in *The Spanish Welfare State in European Context*, edited by A.M. Guillén and M. León. London: Ashgate, 305-312.

Prats, J. (2005) 'La crisis de la reforma educativa socialista y la contrarreforma conservadora en España', *Perspectiva*, 23 (2): 255-278.

Rodríguez Cabrero, G. (1989) 'Orígenes y evolución del Estado de Bienestar español en su perspectiva histórica. Una visión general', *Politica y Sociedad*, 2: 79-87.

Rodríguez Cabrero, G. (2004) *El Estado del bienestar en España: debates, desarrollo y retos*. Madrid: Fundamentos.

Rodríguez Cabrero, G. (2011) 'The consolidation of the Spanish welfare state 1975-2010', in *The Spanish Welfare State in Europena Context*, edited by A.M. Guillén y M. León. London: Ashgate, 17-38.

Velarde Fuertes, J. (1990) *El tercer viraje de la Seguridad Social en España*. Madrid: Instituto de Estudios Económicos.

FIFTEEN

Social policy language in the United States

Jennifer Klein, Daniel Béland and Klaus Petersen

Policy discourse in the United States (US) has drawn on languages about labour, citizenship, and family. Beyond the specifications of formal citizenship (birth in the US, naturalisation procedures, freedom and unfreedom, voting rights), there is a language that shapes understandings of citizenship – rights and obligations, membership or inclusion, and individuals' relationship to the state. From the mid-19th century, industrial capitalism sparked mass migration and immigration, intensive urbanisation, wage work, and the lack of work. The rapidly changing nature of American democracy, historian Michael Katz noted, also brought with it new questions about who merited help and what the limits of social obligation would be (Katz, 2001: 341). The terms and concepts used became a constitutive element in US social policy language.

Yet social policy is also a story of contestation and, in this respect, language and discourse matter. 'The substance of American politics,' finds Gary Gerstle, 'changed dramatically over time as different groups gained and then lost control of [an articulated political] language ...' (Gerstle, 1989: 9). The development of US social policy language was not only about ideology and party politics. First, since the late 19th century, there has been a persistent tension between the charity reform conception of the 'deserving' and the 'undeserving' and the labour/industrial reformers' concerns about the social and health hazards of industrialism and protecting the wage earner and wage income.

Bridging family and market, the language of social policy reflected (and indeed intended to shape) the expected gender roles of workers, non-workers/dependants, and citizens. The Progressive Era (1880s–1910s) rhetoric of the family wage for a male breadwinner seeped into all policy language. From the incipient moments of industrial era social policy, welfare advocates sought to separate motherhood from 'breadwinning'. Public relief was supposed to 'honour motherhood' and support it; yet in every era, there has been a resentment that poor people were not seeking and maintaining employment in the paid labour force.

Questions of citizenship related to race and immigration were ever present. How did the language of social policy reconfigure citizenship to include those outside its boundaries (women, African-Americans, immigrants), and by the late 20th century, to exclude others and thereby reconfigure citizenship once again? For a brief moment in the 1960s, especially through the social struggle and political organising of African-Americans and welfare recipients, a new articulation of need, rights, and property came together through three major Supreme Court cases to capture welfare rights for poor women on public assistance. Nonetheless, the terms of social policy have drawn persistent racial and gender boundaries, even as policies themselves changed. The 'deserving' and the 'undeserving' categories are still with us (Steensland, 2008).

Finally, the meaning of key social policy concepts such as 'welfare' and 'social security' has changed over time, sometimes in a radical way. Such semantic changes are political in nature, as they are related to concrete policy developments and political struggles over social programmes and the boundaries of citizenship. Just as Americans have used particular terms and rhetoric to demarcate inclusion and exclusion, the words Americans have used to make sense of US social policy allegedly allow them to draw a clear line between public and private, state and market. But they mostly have led to a great deal of confusion (and denial) among Americans as to what is 'public' and what is 'private'. These are drawn by and through the divisions of American federalism. The federal structure of American governance should be understood in two dimensions: the division of sovereignty among local, state, and national (or federal) government; and the separation of powers among legislative, administrative, and judicial branches of governance. It would be ahistorical to claim simply that American political culture has always been 'anti-statist'. Rather, we have to investigate how different levels and branches of government have competed with each other to gain power and authority, or restrain the realm of action of law and citizens.

Foundations: the Progressive Era

With the industrialisation, geographical expansion, and urbanisation of the US in the 19th century, development oriented politicians and social reformers alike turned to what was known as 'the general welfare clause' of the US Constitution to support 'positive government'. Found in Article I, Section 8, it grants the US Congress the power to 'lay and collect taxes, duties, imposts, and excises, to pay the debts and provide for the common defence and general welfare of the United States'. During the 19th century, party politicians, civil and sanitary engineers, and urban planners used this invocation of the 'general welfare' to expand government involvement in internal improvements, such as highways, canals, paved streets, and transportation; public water and sewerage; public schools and parks; and building inspection. Yet as the US experienced the emergence of a mass property-less working class, class stratification, and mass unemployment from the 1880s onward, trade unionists and reformers began to argue for a link between protecting particular individuals – young women, pregnant women, and orphans, for example – and protecting the general welfare of the nation. What they saw as the police power of the state should ensure the 'public welfare'. In either case, 'welfare' had positive registers, signifying wellbeing, good health, prosperity and contentment (Gordon, 1994: 1–2; Katz, 2001: 2).

At the end of the 19th century, with the first emergence of militant industrial unrest, national trade unions, and successful industrial regulation, federal courts transformed the legal meanings of property and liberty to push the administrative state out of this role. Courts took free labour ideology, which stressed a man's liberty, right to earn, and independence, and generated a new legal meaning that melded liberty and property under the right to contract. 'The privilege to contract is both a liberty and a property right', declared the Illinois Supreme Court in 1895. Courts then redefined labour as property. State industrial protection laws (either regulatory or social welfare) were rendered unconstitutional because they interfered with this 'freedom of contract' (Forbath, 1991: 85–91; Woloch, 1996: 12–13). Constricting the meaning of the police power of the state, men's right to contract would take precedence over community protection (Boris, 1994: 47). 'Freedom of contract' displaced the general welfare clause – and became a general impediment to welfare state development in the US until the 1930s. Moreover, since women would still receive some forms of state protection, the term welfare began transmuting into something feminised, disdained, and ultimately, debasing.

Both social reformers and male trade unionists used the rhetoric of 'family wage' to prop up the claims and dignity of working-class men. Male and female social policy advocates and industrial reformers assumed a male breadwinner should support a non-working wife and children. The reality, however, diverged in two key ways: few working-class families earned a 'family wage' and many women were single mothers. Yet the rhetorical emphasis on the family wage insisted that women should remain in the home, no matter how poor they were and how much they indeed lacked male support. Not perceived as breadwinners who could make claims to earn benefits, these mothers received little support to combine paid employment and family care (Gordon, 1994; Nadasen, Mittelstadt and Chappell, 2009).

When it came to protecting women from the hazards of the industrial economy, reformers – male and female – sought to 'save the home'. They not only represented the interests of women and children as identical; they analogised the hierarchical relations of parent and child to men and women, and state and women. Since the 1880s, courts had relied on freedom of contract doctrines to block labour regulations for male workers; the citizen-worker (male) had to have unhindered freedom of contract to arrange the terms of his labour, and bosses (also male) had the same, as a property right. How, then, could society use the state to protect the working conditions of women? Here reformers deployed rhetorical constructions about women's reproductive role and motherhood, a language that was not only gendered but racialised as well (they used the term 'mothers of the race'). Protective labour laws, such as maximum hours or proscriptions against night work, relied on arguments that women were physically weak; their reproductive system needed protection; and 'women, like children, ... constituted a special class that needed protection as men did not'. If children were wards of an adult, women should be seen as wards of the state. The landmark Supreme Court case, Muller v Oregon (1908), upheld this argument, setting up a decades-long ambivalence about sexual difference, labour standards, and the role of the state (Woloch, 1996: 5–18; Goodwin, 1997). It positioned women as dependent, in contrast to men as independent, in terms of socio-legal status.

Widows' pensions, one of the most significant social policies of the Progressive Era (Skocpol, 1992), did the same, even while offering direct cash support to women. Widows' pensions were small cash payments from the government to support single mothers' ability to care for children and prevent children from being sent out to work or to orphanages. The pension filled in for the absent male breadwinner. It was middle class women's groups who advocated and fought for it: the General Federation of Women's Clubs and National Congress of Mothers. Without being eligible to vote, their activism, resting on this maternalist ideology, won passage of mothers' pensions at the state level, starting in Illinois in 1911. Six years later, 35 states had enacted a programme, and all but two states had passed a law by the time of the New Deal (Nadasen, Mettelstadt and Chappell, 2009: 14).

The rhetoric surrounding mothers' pensions would have a long lasting impact. First, it asserted that women's claim to support was as mothers, not as workers – a reflection of the influence of the charity realm. Second, aid did not go to just any mother. The term 'widow's pension' revealed more accurately the values and expectations of those who created and implemented the programmes and thereby attempted to draw boundaries between the 'worthy' and the 'unworthy' poor. Seeking to mould poor, and especially immigrant, women into 'proper Americans', administrators granted aid only to widows. Potential recipients had to show piety, moral character, and willingness to learn English. Women whose husbands divorced or deserted them or who never married did not receive widows' aid; they were the 'undeserving poor'. And although a maternalist ethos undergirded the programme, its framers did not want men to shirk their roles as family providers. Advocates, administrators, and legislators did not want women to be too comfortable supporting themselves, so the amount was always meagre and insufficient. Black women were assumed to have always worked and therefore were fit for ongoing wage work. Counties could choose to opt in and half of them did not because they had 'suitable home' (behavioural) requirements that arbitrarily excluded black people (Nadasen, 2005: 10). It most certainly was not an entitlement. Mothers' pensions would subsequently influence what would later become known as 'welfare' – with a much more pejorative meaning than in the 19th century or early 20th century (Gordon, 1994: 38–50; Nadasen, Mittelstadt and Chappell, 2009).

The Great Depression and New Deal

The Great Depression began in the United States in 1929, before spreading to Europe and East Asia over the following two years. It broadened into a decade-long period of mass unemployment and insecurity. The majority of Americans, of course, did not own stock, but the 1929 stock market crash rippled widely and deeply. Four million workers were out of work by December 1929. Many millions worked only part time or intermittently. Average real wages fell by 16% in two years. Single mothers and children fell into even deeper poverty and rapidly exhausted poor relief and mothers' aid. State legislatures ceased to allocate funds to widows' pension programmes (Gordon, 1994: 185–6).

The Great Depression had a devastating social impact on American society in part because of the limited social protection available at both the federal and the state level. Starting in 1933, Democratic President Franklin Delano Roosevelt (FDR) launched the New Deal, an ambitious reform programme that focused on economic recovery and public works, which aimed at fighting unemployment. The first phase of the New Deal, from 1933 to 1935, mainly focused on emergency relief and public works; although still within the poor relief tradition, it did, however, shift the provision of aid from the local or state level to the federal government. Starting in 1934–5, New Dealers in Congress and FDR pressed forward with a legislative agenda of permanent, long-term 'security', especially as pressure mounted from the grassroots in the form of marches by unemployed people, industrial strikes, and a mass old age movement, the Townsend Movement, demanding pensions. In August 1935, FDR signed the Social Security Act, the most crucial social policy legislation ever enacted in the US. Importantly, this complex legislation was grounded in the explicit dichotomy between contribution-based social insurance and means-tested social assistance.[127] In the field of social insurance, the Social Security Act created a federal old age insurance programme (based on payroll tax) and a federal tax that created incentives for states to enact their own unemployment compensation programmes. In the field of social assistance, the Act created grants-in-aid to the states for programmes supporting poor older people, blind people, and the dependent children of poor single mothers. It did not include sickness insurance or a disability pension; the latter would not be enacted until 1956. The Social Security Act helped popularise the concept of 'social security', which referred not only to all the components of the 1935 Social Security Act but also to social programmes in general. In 1942, the International Labour Office (ILO) published Oscar Stein's book, *Approaches to Social Security* (International Labour Organization, 1942), which contributed to the diffusion of the concept of 'social security' beyond US borders (Witte, 1951: 8).[128]

The advent of such 'social security' generated an ideology of security in the US (Klein, 2003). The politics of the New Deal put security at the centre of American political and economic life. The enactment of federal mortgage assistance, bank deposit insurance, minimum wages, Social Security, and laws bolstering labour's right to organise created social and economic entitlements that legitimised the modern state. Though initially excluding many women, Latinos, and African-

---

[127] On this issue and its ideological consequences, see Fraser and Gordon, 1992. This paragraph draws on Béland, 2011.

[128] A year earlier, President Roosevelt and British Prime Minister Winston Churchill had already favoured this transnational diffusion of the expression 'social security' by embedding it in the Atlantic Charter (Altmeyer, 1966: 5).

Americans, the entitlement to economic security was capable of being expanded upon, and indeed would be, as various groups of Americans mobilised to demand inclusion and full citizenship rights. New Dealers identified economic security as a grand national project, 'a great cooperative enterprise' among 'the citizens, the economic system, and the government' (Social Security Board, 1937). Hence, the meaning of security necessarily entailed an element of public power. The New Deal legitimised the right to security for wage workers, but over the next few decades, various players clashed over who would define security. Prior to the New Deal, the craft union-based American Federation of Labor, primarily composed of skilled, white men, dominated the labour movement and had a hostile view of the state. With the emergence of a new industrial union movement in the mid-1930s, federated nationally as the Congress of Industrial Organizations (CIO), unions organised the mass of ethnic manufacturing workers, including women, and became key supporters of the New Deal welfare state. The politics of security as it played out beyond the New Deal years would involve a political struggle among business and labour; commercial insurers and non-profit, community-, or labour-controlled means of social provision; the state; and private capital (Klein, 2003).

Security, Social Security, and America's post-World War II welfare state

During World War II, the social meaning and legitimacy of 'security' intensified. Fighting against the fascists, American workers knew that hard work and sacrifice on the home front and abroad was a fight, as the CIO put it, to 'Insure Your Future ... For Peace–Jobs–Security'. Urging American workers and their families to 'vote for Collective Bargaining and Full Employment, Lasting Peace and Security', the CIO saw the rights of the National Labor Relations Act, Social Security, and the international struggle for democracy as inseparable: The broad problems of world security and the personal problems of individual security seem to merge (Klein 2003).

When the war ended and the economy reconverted to civilian production, this vision of security was widely shared. The Life Insurance Association of America praised the political commitment to security and linked domestic and international security as twin imperatives. Praising the new efforts at 'collective security' after the war, it stated with assurance, 'just as has been proven that completely self-reliant individuals cannot exist in a modern world, the same rule applies to people collectively, and that utter self-reliance cannot protect the nations of the earth from scheming aggressors'. Freedom and security were compatible concepts, not competing ones (Klein, 2012).

While they were willing to accede to workers' demands for security, American business leaders sought to reprivatise the meaning of security. Ideologically, this meant resuscitating a more individualised understanding of risk and security. Business leaders fought back to tip the balance of power in their favour, a project that was as much ideological as economic. To counter the growing pressure of the new labour movement and welfare state, corporations turned to 'welfare capitalism' – a wide range of social welfare benefits, from insurance and pensions to paid holidays, athletic and leisure programmes to mortgage assistance and even college scholarships, offered by the firm. The proliferation of so-called private benefits, however, was buttressed by public policies, particularly state support for collective bargaining and tax subsidies for health insurance. Government had a presence and yet its role became increasingly obscured, as the boundaries between public and private blurred (Klein, 2012).

During and immediately following the war, in the public sector, the broad understanding of 'social security' associated with the 1935 Social Security Act remained dominant (Béland, 2011). Yet, after the early 1950s, a narrower definition of 'social security' triumphed, and the concept now refers only to the federal old age insurance created in 1935 (Altmeyer, 1966: 5–6; Weir, Orloff and Skocpol, 1988: 7). This is the case in large part because, following its post-war expansion, the programme became the largest and most popular component of the Social Security Act. This meaning contrasts with the broad use of the term 'security' discussed earlier, which transcended public social programmes to apply to private, employer-sponsored benefits (Klein, 2003). The administrators of social insurance, who worked within the Social Security Administration, expected the public assistance titles of the original Social Security Act (or, what was called 'welfare') to fade away, as more men qualified for social insurance as breadwinners and could thereby support a dependent wife. The pension would continue the old notion of the family wage. Thus there was a perpetual ideological elevation of old age insurance – as something earned by workers – over 'welfare', grudgingly given to poor people who did not earn anything (Fraser and Gordon, 1992). Consequently, this ideological emphasis occluded the presence of other forms of public assistance within the original Act.

In the American political and policy discourse, the European-born concept of 'welfare state' did not replace 'social security' in the popular political lexicon or in reference to social programmes as a whole, as is the case in other countries like the UK. Instead, in US political discourse, the concept of 'welfare state' has long proved highly contentious, and it is frequently associated with negative connotations. In the late 1940s, the term 'welfare state' became an ideological weapon in the hands of conservatives who raised the spectre of a new totalitarianism in the context of the Cold War. In an analysis published by the Legislative Reference Service of the Library of Congress in 1950, Asher Achinstein devoted a full chapter to 'The welfare state, socialism, and communism', introducing the discussion as follows: 'The more extreme opponents of the "welfare state" describe it as "socialism" and the more moderate refer to it as the halfway house to Socialism' (Achinstein, 1950: 61). Former Republican President Herbert Hoover, speaking in the late 1940s, called the welfare state a 'disguise for the totalitarian state' before declaring that his country was already 'on the last mile to collectivism'. He warned Americans to beware of 'these European infections' (Hoover, 1952 [1949]). Even current office holders followed his lead. Republican Governor Thomas E. Dewey attacked what he called the 'ever-growing, nobody-can-feed-you-but-us philosophy of the welfare state' (Dewey, quoted in Katz, 2008: 5, 84).

With the coalescence of a New Conservatism, influenced by welfare state critic and free market champion Friedrich von Hayek's *Road to Serfdom* (1944) (distributed also through *Reader's Digest*), organisations such as the Foundation for Economic Education and American Enterprise Association began circulating 'educational' materials to call into question New Deal programmes (Phillips-Fein, 2009). In 1949, an editorial in the *Hartford Courant* (22 November) noticed that 'The phrase, Welfare State, certainly can be tortured for political purposes, and President Truman even warned his political allies against using the concept "welfare state", as it was becoming a 'scare word' (*Los Angeles Times* 19 February 1950). This was the result of an intense campaign from opponents of tax increases and 'statism'. Hence, the term 'welfare state' was attacked when the *Los Angeles Times*, a conservative newspaper, asked its readers to come up with negative synonyms for it, and among many proposals, the list of readers' suggestions included: 'Santa Claus State', 'everything for nothing state', and 'hand-out state'. Business interest groups, academics, church leaders, and politicians used the term 'welfare state' in their attack on social reforms. 'Reactionary hunted around for a new phrase', George Meany, the secretary-treasurer of the American Federation of Labor (AFL) stated in a speech in the US Congress in April 1950 (quoted in Procter, 1950: 115).

Even though the critics dominated the public debate, several voices defended not only social reforms and President Truman's Fair Deal, but also the concept of 'welfare state' against what was considered unfair accusations. Historian Henry Steele Commager, placing the US within an internationally comparative context, defended the welfare state by drawing a clear line between it and socialism:

> Whatever this may be, it is not socialism. The essence of socialism is the public ownership and management of the means of production, capital, land and property, by the state. Soviet Russia is, in a large measure, a socialist country; Britain and Scandinavia are as yet far from true socialism. By contrast, the United States retains, even after two generations of public regulation, even after 16 years of the New Deal, an economy of private enterprise. By contrast the American program remains a conservative one, and – it is proper to add – a democratic one (Commager, 1949).

At the same time, because many women had moved into precisely the government positions that handled social welfare, economic planning, and labour policy, Conservatives used the anti-communist Red Scare to launch a gendered attack on the welfare state in the late 1940s and early 1950s. They stoked fears of a 'femmocracy' turning the US government towards socialistic purposes. 'Conservatives who charged that the civil service was riddled with Communists devoted much attention to high ranking women', writes Landon Storrs (2013: 86, 88, 89–106), accusing them of creating a 'womb-to-tomb' state. Although the concept of 'welfare state' has gradually entered the US academic discourse in its broader, European meaning, today it is rarely used by politicians, except perhaps when they want to put a negative spin on existing social programmes.

As far as social policy language is concerned, beyond broad concepts such as security, Social Security, and welfare state, in the 1950s and early 1960s, we also find increasing emphasis on 'ending dependency' and on 'rehabilitation'. Post-war welfare and medical authorities shared a concern about 'dependency', defined in social, psychological, physical, and gendered terms (on the history of the concept of dependency in the US, see Fraser and Gordon, 1994). Professionals in each realm, for example, agreed that large numbers of public welfare recipients suffered from chronic illness or physical impairments. With the right intervention – or care – these individuals should and could be moved off public assistance, the categorical aid programmes for poor older, and disabled people, and children. They deployed notions of rehabilitation towards the goal of ending dependency. The rhetoric of rehabilitation fused medical, social, and economic registers.

The language of rehabilitation too had roots in the New Deal. In his first inaugural address, President Franklin Roosevelt announced: 'Our greatest primary task is to put people to work' (Roosevelt, 1938: 13). In its emergency relief phase, New Dealers saw themselves as emphasising work relief over the 'dole'. Work meant independence, not dependency, a condition associated with people considered unemployable, such as those who were helpless or derelict, young or old, and the wife and mother.

After World War II, welfare agencies and officials within the federal Social Security Administration deployed notions of rehabilitation towards the goal of ending dependency, believing that it could help patients or clients achieve some final state of independence (Boris and Klein, 2012). The 1956 amendments to Social Security promised a means to accomplish that task. They authorised demonstration projects, with the goal of helping to 'restore public assistance recipients more quickly to their maximum economic and personal independence'. Advancing the social rehabilitation agenda, the 1956 Amendments proposed to refashion Aid for Dependent Children (ADC) around public services to reduce dependency and encourage self-support, while still protecting a mother's right to claim assistance. In reality, such a shift remained aspirational because Congress did not provide sufficient funds to match state spending on such services (Bureau of Public Assistance, 'Review of Public Assistance Achievements in 1956'; Mittelstadt, 2005: 12–13; 37–42; 65–7).

That situation would begin to change in the 1960s. In his 1962 State of the Union address, President John Kennedy called for a shift in public welfare to emphasise 'services instead of support, rehabilitation instead of relief and training for useful work instead of prolonged dependency'. The 1962 Social Security Amendments did put the money behind this agenda with the explicit aim of 'ending dependency'. Rehabilitation also justified work and training programmes for parents receiving the newly renamed Aid to Families with Dependent Children (AFDC), including fathers and other relatives, although liberals remained divided on the implication. At this stage, AFDC would combine income support with work requirements, reclassifying poor mothers as 'employables'. This designation as 'employable' would take on heightened importance in coming years, when Congress enacted more punitive workfare measures. This contestation came to a head in Newburgh, New York, in the early 1960s. Angry welfare oponents unleashed a public attack against women on welfare, explicitly labelling them 'able-bodied but unemployed', and therefore of 'questionable morals', and as more African-Americans came on the rolls, with the old terms, dating to the days of slavery, 'shiftless and lazy'. On the other hand, welfare proponents believed rehabilitation could respond to all these charges (Mittelstadt, 2005: 100–1, 118–19, 122; Boris and Klein 2012: 74–5).

Rehabilitation propped up dominant social assumptions about family and employment. Through welfare support services, such as home care, counselling, and therapeutic services, men could become breadwinners again and women could perform household tasks and care for family members. Welfare reform in the name of rehabilitation would teach the deficient work ethic, female 'respectability', and the domestic ideal (Boris and Klein 2012: 60–1). Not rights in themselves, these supports positioned men and women back within the paradigm of contract and earned benefits and the family wage.

The Great Society and the War on Poverty

In the mid-1960s, following a landslide Democratic presidential and congressional victory triggered in part by the November 1963 assassination of President Kennedy, President Lyndon Johnson launched two ambitious and related reform programmes known as the Great Society and the War on Poverty. The concept of the Great Society referred to a general programme aimed at fighting inequality and improving the lives of Americans. The War on Poverty was a more specific yet highly ambitious campaign that sought to eliminate poverty from the land altogether. In contrast to the 1930s, this new round of liberal reform explicitly intended to include – and enfranchise – African-Americans, Latinos, poor people, older people, immigrants, and farm workers. The War on Poverty led to the implementation of social and community programmes aimed at creating employment and educational opportunity for poor people. From a political standpoint, both the Great Society and the War on Poverty represented responses to the civil rights movement and the 'rediscovery of poverty' associated with the work of authors such as John Kenneth Galbraith (1958) and Michael Harrington (1962), who lamented the widespread poverty in the midst of unprecedented economic prosperity. During the 1950s, the words 'poverty' and 'the poor' had disappeared from mainstream American public discourse; economists hardly looked at poverty. Growth was the watchword of the era. Now, policy makers and intellectuals worked to define both a theory and a response to poverty (O'Connor, 2001: 139–46) – and for Lyndon Johnson, eager to prove his legitimacy and escape Kennedy's shadow, it had to be grand.

Johnson and the Democratic Congress passed over 80 pieces of legislation as part of this agenda, covering everything from civil rights to immigration, clean air regulations, higher education grants and loans, parks and national wilderness areas, housing, elementary and secondary schooling, legal services for poor people, and a National Endowment for the Arts and the Humanities. The 1965 Immigration and Nationality Act finally ended the 1924 racially discriminatory national origins quotas and allowed family reunification. The Great Society also built on the foundation of the New Deal and Social Security Act, expanding the reach of AFDC and bringing the most significant addition to social insurance, Medicare (universal, public social insurance for hospital care for older people) and its companion, Medicaid (means-tested public health insurance for poor people). The latter two were monumental achievements that liberal and labour activists had worked for since the end of World War II. Yet the split between Medicare, a national benefit for retired pensioners, and Medicaid, a state-by-state, variable programme for poor people, continued the structural and rhetorical legacies of the distinction between 'social security' for the deserving and 'welfare' for the less deserving. The Law explicitly referred to potential Medicaid enrollees as 'recipients', while calling those in Medicare 'beneficiaries' (Quadagno, 2005: 74–5; Engel, 2006: 48–9).

The 1960s and 1970s witnessed the triumph of a more inclusive concept of citizenship that articulated a broad concept of rights. As previously embedded discriminatory policies and occupational exemptions were gradually dismantled, African-Americans won greater inclusion in the social welfare system. Further, rights-based movements and social struggles among people with disabilities, senior citizens, public sector workers, Native Americans, women, and Latinos generated myriad new economic and social rights. Some social rights became recognised as 'entitlements', a term that would become increasingly contested in subsequent decades. Mothers on public assistance mobilised as part of the National Welfare Rights Organization (NWRO), not only pressing for expansion of public assistance and racial equality but challenging the stigmatising distinction that had separated welfare from other forms of social support. As Alversa Beals, a Nevada mother on welfare who became active in the movement, put it, it was the first time she 'had heard the words "welfare" and "rights" put together' (Orleck, 2005: 98). At the end of the decade, the welfare rights movement won three cases altering the meaning of welfare, rights, liberty, and property. *King v Smith* struck down welfare rules that revoked benefits if a 'substitute father' was found in the house, even if he provided no child support; *Shapiro v Thompson* ended residency requirements; and

Goldberg v Kelley ruled welfare benefits were 'not a gratuity' but an entitlement, and recipients therefore had a constitutional right to a fair hearing (Orleck, 2005:132–3). For a brief moment, poor women had been able to use rights language to shift some of the terms of American social policy.

A renewed conservative discourse on 'welfare dependency' linked to ideas of a pathological culture of poverty and family structure, however, would undermine these gains in the 1980s and the early to mid-1990s. Neither liberals nor conservatives had shaken free of the assumptions of an obsolete family wage ideal. The language of family wage still masked a 'deeply sex- and race-segregated labor market'. (Chappell, 2010: 134) Even at the high point of the War on Poverty, liberals expected antipoverty policy to restore a male breadwinner family structure. When poor families did not conform to that model, the Liberal Coalition opened the door to the perception that the 'AFDC program produced undesirable family and work behaviours among the poor' and to political attacks on AFDC that soon undermined its political viability (Chappell, 2010: 11, 17).

Never referred to as 'welfare', the benefits that the white middle class and working class relied on – Social Security, home mortgage subsidies and tax deductions, higher education grants, unemployment compensation, health insurance – became, in a sense, invisible assistance to Americans. The more visible forms of support – public housing and public assistance – were increasingly perceived negatively and began generating hostile opposition in the late 1960s and early 1970s. This anger, combined with bitter confrontations over school busing for racial integration and rising property taxes, turned the hopeful War on Poverty into the 'war on welfare'.

The War on Welfare and beyond

Although it had a positive meaning during and after the Progressive Era, by the 1960s, the concept of 'welfare' (Katz, 2008: 2) had taken on an increasingly negative and racial meaning, as it became synonymous with social assistance offered 'mainly to unmarried mothers, mostly young women of colour, under Aid for Families with Dependent Children [AFDC]' (Katz, 2008: 1). Embedded in profound gender and racial prejudice, 'welfare' became closely associated with dependency and the 'undeserving poor' (Fraser and Gordon, 1994; Katz and Thomas, 1998; Steensland, 2008; Béland, 2011).

With a fully articulated anger against welfare in the 1980s, leading Democrats as well as Republicans spoke of work, independence, deservingness, and markets. This time, poor men *and* women should be pushed into the low wage, paid labour market. The welfare state, or 'nanny state' (a term which echoed the earlier 'womb-to-tomb' phrase), should no longer interfere with the labour market. The rhetorical legacy of 'dependency' dominated, displacing a realistic focus on poverty and adequacy. (On the links between these two phrases, see Storrs, 2013).

By 1992, when Democratic candidate Bill Clinton ran for president and promised to 'end welfare as we know it', 'everyone knew that he meant AFDC – the most disliked public program in America' (Katz, 2008: 1). But it also would entail the compulsion to work, whether one had young children at home, no child care, or only poverty wage jobs to choose from. For many citizens and politicians, 'welfare' had become the exact opposite of the ever popular 'Social Security' (OASDI), a situation that reinforced the traditional dichotomy between social assistance ('welfare') and social insurance ('Social Security') in the US (Fraser and Gordon, 1994). Even though it was actually a miniscule expenditure in the national budget, conservatives could easily tap into decades of ideological denigration to justify the 1996 abolition of AFDC and the end of a right to public assistance. The 1996 legislation replaced it with a 'workfare' scheme based on strict time limits known as *Temporary* Assistance for Needy Families (TANF). Through workfare and lifetime caps, the notion of 'personal responsibility' through work displaced welfare as an 'entitlement' (even though most women on AFDC had always worked).

Nor did President Clinton truly defend the notion of security when pushing for his national health programme in 1993 and 1994. Americans were imagined as consumers of health services rather than citizens contributing to a system of shared savings. The Clinton Democrats used a market language that militated against social solidarity. They refused to frame health security as a public good, and economic security as a social project. While conservative Republicans took over Congress soon after (and health reform went down in flames), the Clinton Democrats in a sense helped ideologically lay the groundwork for Social Security privatisation to percolate onto the agenda next (Klein, 2003: 272–3). The next president, a conservative Republican, eagerly took it on, insisting Americans had to turn to markets and the private realm to establish that persistently elusive political ideal of 'independence'.

In the wake of the 11 September 2001 attacks, with the exception of the enduring popular support for the Social Security programme (Béland, 2005), security in the broad sense of the term seemed to have lost its social or economic meaning. The only security in political discourse now is security from terrorists. 'Homeland Security' became infused with one single meaning: security against armed attack. The policy prescription was the Patriot Act: expanded surveillance of American citizens. President George W. Bush's proposed 'ownership society' was the perfect analogue to homeland security. The high security alerts signal an atomising security imperative: stay home, lock your family inside, and seal yourself off. The 'ownership society' is a similar concept. It harkens back to a mythic, pre-industrial yeoman farmer – the only worthy citizen because of his solitary virtue and property ownership. Re-establishing antique notions of 'worthy' and 'unworthy' citizens that Social Security mostly did away with, 'ownership society' throws risk back onto the fortunes of the individual. The ideological posturing of the 'ownership society' is a fundamental assault on the idea of 'social security' in the broad sense of the term (Klein, 2007).

Although financial markets have generated enormous wealth in the past two decades, Americans in the 21st century face stagnant wages, persistent underemployment, unaffordable health insurance that the 2010 Patient Protection and Affordable Care Act struggles to improve, shrivelling or collapsing private pensions, and home foreclosures with the start of the 2008 financial crisis. The pressures of long-term care have gone unrelieved, never having been included discursively or programmatically under the federal social insurance system. Since the 1980s, employers have been allowed to subvert the National Labor Relations Act, the ability of workers to join unions, and the collective bargaining that had made possible the allegedly 'private' side of Social Security. That had required the public support of the state, which workers lost under successive conservative regimes. And yet, as people scramble for stability, financial and corporate scandals have continued to grow in scale. In 2011, the brief but intense emergence of the Occupy Wall Street movement suddenly insisted that Americans retrieve and revivify the other meanings of security. Security flourished as a political value in America when it germinated in the soil of shared social responsibility. This is why, in the US as in other countries, the historical analysis of social policy concepts and language is necessary to recover lost meanings and explore their potential political power.

References

Achinstein, A. (1950) *The Welfare State*, Public Affairs Bulletin No 83, Washington: Library of Congress Legislative Reference Service.

Altmeyer, A. J. (1966) *The Formative Years of Social Security*. Madison: University of Wisconsin Press.

Béland, D. (2005) *Social Security: History and Politics from the New Deal to the Privatization Debate*. Lawrence: University Press of Kansas.

Béland, D. (2011) 'The politics of social policy language,' *Social Policy & Administration*, 45(1): 1-18.

Bureau of Public Assistance, 'Review of public assistance achievements in 1956,' 2, RG47, Records of Social Security Administration, BPA, Family Services Master Subject Files, Box 17, file 600.05 1954, National Archives and Records Administration. College Park, MD.

Boris, E. (1994) *Home To Work: Motherhood and the Politics of Industrial Homework*. New York: Cambridge University Press.

Boris, E. and J. Klein (2012) *Caring for America: Home Health Workers in the Shadow of the Welfare State*. New York: Oxford University Press.

Chappell, M. (2010) *The War on Welfare: Family, Poverty, and Politics in Modern America*. Philadelphia: University of Pennsylvania Press.

Commager, H. S. (1949) 'Appraisal of the welfare state', *New York Times Magazine*, 15 May.

Engel, J. (2006) *Poor People's Medicine: Medicaid and American charity care since 1965*. Durham: Duke University Press.

Forbath, W. (1991) *Law and the Shaping of the American Labor Movement*. Cambridge, MA: Harvard University Press.

Fraser, N. and Gordon, L. (1992) 'Contract versus charity: why is there no social citizenship in the United States?' *Socialist Review*, 22 (July-September): 45-68.

Fraser, N. and Gordon, L. (1994) "Dependency" demystified: inscriptions of power in a keyword of the welfare state', *Social Politics*, 1(1): 4-31.

Galbraith, J.K. (1958) *The Affluent Society*. Boston, MA: Houghton Mifflin.

Gerstle, G. (1989) *Working-Class Americanism: The Politics of Labor in a Textile City, 1914-1960*. Princeton: Princeton University Press.

Goodwin, J. (1997) *Gender and the Politics of Welfare Reform: Mothers' Pensions in Chicago, 1917-1929*. Chicago: University of Chicago Press.

Gordon, L. (1994) *Pitied but not Entitled: Single Mothers and the History of Welfare*. Cambridge: Harvard University Press.

Harrington, M. (1962) *The Other America: Poverty in the United States*. New York: Macmillan.

Hayek, F.A. (1944) *The Road to Serfdom*. London: Routledge.

Hoffman, B. (2001) *The Wages of Sickness: The Politics of Health Insurance in Progressive Era America*. Chapel Hill: The University of North Carolina Press.

Hoover, H. (1952) 'The last miles to collectivism', In S. Glueck (ed.), *The Welfare State and the National Welfare. A symposium of Some of the Threatening Tendencies of Our Times*, Cambridge Mass: Addison–Wesley Press: 180–181.

International Labour Organization (1942) *Approaches to Social Security: An International Survey*. Montreal: International Labour Office.

Katz, M. B. (2001) *The Price of Citizenship: Redefining the American Welfare State*. New York: Metropolitan Books.

Katz, M. B. (2008) *The Price of Citizenship: Redefining the American Welfare State* (Updated Edition). Philadelphia: University of Pennsylvania Press.

Katz, M. B. and Thomas, L.R. (1998) 'The invention of "welfare" in America', *Journal of Policy History*, 10 (December): 399–418.

Kessler-Harris, A. (2001) *In Pursuit of Equity: Women, Men, and the Quest for Economic Citizenship in 20th Century America*. New York: Oxford University Press.

Klein, J. (2003) *For All These Rights: Business, Labor, and the Shaping of America's Public-Private Welfare State*. Princeton: Princeton University Press.

Klein, J. (2007) 'Welfare and security in the aftermath of World War II: How Europe influenced America's divided welfare state' in Maurizio Vaudagna, (ed.), *The Place of Europe in American History: Twentieth Century Perspectives*. Torino: Otto Editore, 215–242.

Klein, J. (2012) 'The politics of security', in *Liberty and Justice For All? Rethinking Politics in Cold War America*. Kathleen Donohue, ed. Amherst: University of Massachusetts Press.

Lieberman, R. (1998) *Shifting the Color Line: Race and the American Welfare State*. Cambridge: Harvard University Press.

Mink, G. (1990) The lady and the tramp: gender, race, and the origins of the American Welfare State', in *Women, The State, and Welfare*. Linda Gordon, ed. Madison: University of Wisconsin Press.

Mittelstadt, J. (2005) *From Welfare to Workfare: The Unintended Consequences of Liberal Reform, 1945-1965*. Chapel Hill, NC: University of North Carolina.

Nadasen, P. (2005) *Welfare Warriors: The Welfare Rights Movement in the United States*. New York: Routledge.

Nadasen, P., J. Mittelstadt, and M. Chappell (2009) *Welfare in the United States: A History With Documents, 1935-1996*. New York: Routledge.

Nelson, B. J. (1990) 'The Origins of the Two-Channel Welfare State: Workmen's Compensation and Mothers' Aid', in *Women, The State, and Welfare*. Linda Gordon, ed. Madison: University of Wisconsin Press.

O'Connor, Alice. (2001). *Poverty Knowledge: Social Science, Social Policy, and the Poor in Twentieth-Century U.S. History*. Princeton: Princeton University Press.

Orleck, A. (2005) *Storming Caesars Palace: How Black Mothers Fought Their Own War On Poverty*. Boston: Beacon Press.

Phillips-Fein, K. (2009) *Invisible Hands: The Making of the Conservative Movement From the New Deal to Reagan*. New York: W.W. Norton & Co.

Procter, L. C. (1950) *The Welfare State:* A Debate Casebook. Austin, TX: Travis Pub. Co.

Quadagno, J. (2005) *One Nation Uninsured: Why the U.S. Has No National Health Insurance*. New York, NY: Oxford University Press.

Roosevelt, F.D. (1938) *Public Papers and Addresses of Franklin D. Roosevelt*, vol 2 New York: Random House.

Skocpol, T. (1992) *Protecting Soldiers and Mothers: The Political Origins of Social Policy in the United States*. Cambridge, MA: Belknap Press.

Social Security Board (1937) Foreword in *Annual Report of the Social Security Board: Letter From the Social Security Board Transmitting First Annual Report*, Washington D.C.: Government Printing Office.

Steensland, B. (2008) *The Failed Welfare Revolution: America's Struggle over Guaranteed Income Policy*. Princeton: Princeton University Press.

Storrs, Landon R.Y. (2013). *The Second Red Scare and the Unmaking of the New Deal Left*. Princeton: Princeton University Press.

Weir, M., Orloff, A.S. and Skocpol, T. (1988) 'Introduction: understanding American social policy'. In Margaret Weir, Ann Shola Orloff, and Theda Skocpol, *The Politics of Social Policy in the United States*. Princeton: Princeton University Press, pp. 3-27.

Witt, J. F. (2004) *The Accidental Republic: Crippled Workingmen, Destitute Widows, and the Remaking of American Law*. Cambridge: Harvard University Press.

Witte, E. E. (1951) *Five Lectures on Social Security*. Rio Piedras, Puerto Rico: 'Labor Relations Institute (University of Puerto Rico).

Woloch, N. (1996) *Muller v. Oregon: A Brief History With Documents*. Boston: Bedford Books.

Conclusion: comparative perspectives on social policy language

Klaus Petersen and Daniel Béland

This edited volume has offered comparative, historical, and political perspectives on the development of social policy concepts and language in a number of advanced industrial countries. For decades, social policy scholars and practitioners have used concepts such as 'welfare state' and 'social security' without paying much attention to where these concepts come from and how their meanings have changed over time. The previous chapters in our volume have addressed this question by exploring the social policy language of relevant international organisations: Organisation for Economic Co-operation and Development (OECD); European Union (EU); International Monetary Fund (IMF) and World Bank; and of countries spread across four continents (Asia, Australasia, Europe, and North America). These chapters have explored the characteristics of social policy concepts and language. In this brief concluding chapter, we discuss the main findings of our volume and outline an agenda for research on the history and politics of social policy concepts and language.

Main findings

As the chapters of this volume demonstrate, social policy language has evolved in close connection with the building of national social policy institutions. This language has been shown to have significant variation across time and space. Similar concepts have acquired different meanings and connotations, and some countries have preferred some concepts to others.

The most notable example of conceptual stability is Germany, where 'welfare discourse revolved around a remarkably stable centreline: the (re)conciliation of economy and society by means of the *Sozialstaat*' (see the chapter on Germany in this volume). Even though German society was subjected to profound social upheavals (two world wars and the 1933 Nazi takeover of power), the concept of the *Sozialstaat* continued to serve as a common frame of reference in German social policy debates.

As other chapters of this volume illustrate, 'welfare state' is probably the most influential of the key social policy concepts to be found (and translated) in most national contexts. In Britain, New Zealand, Sweden, and Denmark, for example, 'welfare state' became an almost hegemonic term in the post-war era. The chapter on Britain clearly shows that enthusiasm for this new term was hardly universal, and the critics included not only ideological opponents of social reforms but also prominent social policy figures such as William Beveridge and T.H. Marshall. In this way, analysing social policy language can provide a window to more critical analyses of the often simplistic or romantic narrative of the Golden Age of the welfare state (on this issue see Wincott, 2013). In Finland, while 'welfare state' also became an important concept, it competed with the concept of 'society'. In the Nordic countries 'society' could refer to the public sphere (and the state). However, as in New Zealand, 'society' could reappear as part of an antistatist concept of 'welfare society' (see also the chapters on Finland, Denmark and Sweden, and Japan).

An explicitly comparative perspective highlights the importance of not overemphasising the 'welfare state' as some kind of expression of political consensus for social policy reform. In several countries where 'welfare state' entered the social policy discourse, it failed to gain a strong foothold or was looked upon with scepticism. A prominent example here is the United States, a country where the concept of 'welfare' has been associated with negative images of alleged social parasitism (often gendered or racialised). In the Netherlands, we also find that '*verzorgingsstaat*' (the caring state) was preferred to the more literally translated '*welvaartsstaat*'. Like their sister parties in North West Europe after 1945, the Dutch Social Democrats had used 'welfare state' as a depiction of the New Jerusalem. However, in the 1950s, as part of a broad political compromise between Social Democrats and Catholics, the more statist idea of 'welfare state' lost political momentum.

A second influential concept in the post-war period was that of 'social security'. Following Roosevelt's New Deal in the 1930s, this term became a key concept of American social policy language, and during World War II became part of Allied war propaganda (used, for instance, in the 1941 Atlantic Charter). A genuine study of the transnational diffusion of 'social security' is still lacking, but it is noteworthy that the first Beveridge Report (1942) actually presented itself as offering a 'Plan for Social Security' (at the same time Beveridge obviously preferred the term 'social insurance'). In France, *sécurité sociale* became widely known after World War II and was used extensively in French social policy language. Parallel to the descriptive use of *sécurité sociale,* the chapter on France also points to the use of the older concept of *État-providence,* which was clearly more polemical and pejorative, having emerged from the French anti-statist tradition.

Not all countries have had a dominant social policy concept prevailing over a prolonged period of time. We have seen several examples of significant changes due to political regime shifts, the sudden emergence of a distinct social policy language, or strong external influences. In Hungary and Poland, for instance, the development of social policy language was heavily structured by regime changes at both the beginning and the end of the Cold War. In both countries, an originally German-inspired social policy tradition was reconceptualised after 1945 within a Marxist communist worldview. This did not leave much room for the emergence of a distinct social policy vocabulary in its own right, nor for any interchange with social policy concepts in the West. After the end of the Cold War, however, Western European terminologies had a strong impact on both Hungarian and Polish social policy discourses.

Japan and Spain also witnessed dramatic regime changes that affected social policy language. We saw how Japan had a long tradition of importing and translating Western concepts such as 'social security' (*shakai hosyō*) and, later, 'welfare state' (*fukushi kokka*), or 'welfare society' (*fukushi shakai*). In fact, the Japanese case points to translation as a methodological challenge for the comparative study of social policy language. On one hand, translations facilitate diffusion processes from one language and one country to another. On the other hand, such translations are rarely literal, especially when it comes to political concepts. In most cases, translations also include some elements of adaptation in order to adjust imported concepts to the new context.

In the chapter on Spain, we also find examples of translations of imported concepts such as 'welfare state' (*estado del bienestar*), and 'social security' (*seguridad social*), with the latter becoming widely used in everyday discourse. The transition to democracy following Franco's death in 1975 coincided with Spain's entry into the Common Market in 1986, and the influx of European social policy ideas led to a revival of the concept of the 'welfare state' in Spain. Meanwhile, at the other end of the planet, in Korea, we find examples of importation and translation of West European social policy concepts such as 'welfare state' (*Pokchi Kukka*). However, the chapter on Korea shows that 'welfare state' is a temporal concept that includes promises, ideals, and hopes for the future (see also the chapter on Finland for a discussion of this role of temporality).

In terms of social policy language, the transnational organisations analysed in this volume – the OECD, the EU and the two Bretton Woods institutions (IMF and the World Bank) – differ from the countries studied. The social policy language of these transnational organisations was not based on a set of national social policy institutions, nor was it the result of any sort of formalised political process. All these organisations were established in order to coordinate and influence national states while using specific concepts and languages as tools to do so. The chapter on the OECD shows how this organisation has become an important arena not only for formulating a new social policy language that reframed the role of the state in social policy but also for promoting this language internationally through reports and policy advice. The OECD's language has emphasised the importance of employment as well as the need for 'active social policy' and a shift from 'welfare state' to 'welfare society'. This reconceptualisation of the state–society–individual nexus gained a foothold in several of the countries analysed in this volume.

The IMF and the World Bank, despite varying approaches, have long focused on 'development' and 'modernisation' as key concepts. Due to their truly global mandate, they have turned their attention beyond the OECD countries in order to formulate strategies for economic growth, social stability and poverty reduction in the developing world, based on concepts such as 'social safety net'. For the OECD, the IMF and the World Bank, it is clear that some countries have played a more decisive role than others with respect to the formulation of development strategies and the social policy language embedded in them. As for the EU, it has a more formalised decision making process and is forced to balance the interests of its member countries. Consequently, it becomes more problematic to talk about a stand-alone EU social policy language. However, the chapter on the EU clearly shows that distinct social policy ideas and concepts have been diffused through various European arenas across member states. Although concepts of such as 'flexicurity' and 'social investment' have emerged in specific national contexts, the career of these concepts illustrates the role of the EU in transnational policy language and diffusion.

Some general patterns emerge from the discussion of individual countries. We find three aspects of importance for future research on social policy language:

First and second order concepts

If we look beyond the key concepts or 'first order concepts' discussed earlier (such as welfare state, social security, or welfare society), we find a social policy language that is more narrowly attached to specific groups (such as experts, bureaucrats, welfare critics, philanthropic actors or the Church) or to specific policy subfields (such as old age pensions, family policy or social services). The history of social policy is a history of professionalisation and institutionalisation, and new groups of professionals or new social programmes have actively contributed to the development of social policy concepts and language. Such 'second order concepts' may take on a life of their own while in other conjunctures they may serve to either support or challenge key social policy concepts. One example that runs through several of the chapters (especially that on the OECD) is the language of the New Left, where a more critical perspective utilised concepts such as 'social exclusion', 'inequality', or a stronger focus on 'wellbeing' (vis-à-vis formal rights). Another later language stream is that of neoliberalism, popularising discussions of 'privatisation', 'freedom of choice', 'consumers', or 'competition' within the mainstream social policy vocabulary. This global trend is discussed further in the chapters on New Zealand and the OECD. Most recently, we find the language attached to social investment strategies promoted by the EU and diffusing to many countries within and outside Europe (Parlier et al, 2011).

Timing and historical waves

If we turn to the issue of timing, the studies in this volume show cross-national patterns or even stages in the historical development of social policy language. Around 1900, the idea of modern social policy became established in several European countries, and with the emergence of new disciplines and institutions, a modern social policy discourse crystallised in the form of new concepts of social protection. The chapters analysing early periods of social policy language show that modern social policy language did not emerge independently from existing traditions. In Denmark, Sweden and the United States, the older distinction between 'deserving' and 'undeserving' poor people persisted, and the more interpersonal (and religiously-grounded) language of the philanthropic tradition became integrated into modern social policy language. Similarly, in France, the concept of 'solidarity' embedded in the Republican tradition has continued to play a role until the present day. This continuity with traditional concepts and distinctions has helped legitimise new social programmes.

The second 'stage' – starting in the 1930s in some countries and after 1945 in others – is characterised by the growing emphasis on the role of the state in social policy provision and language. In this context of social policy expansion, the concept of the 'welfare state' was mobilised by both social reformers and critics of statist tendencies. It is important, however, to underline that within these two 'stages', we find major variations from country to country. In Germany, Denmark, Britain, the Netherlands, France, and to some degree also Finland, New Zealand, and the United States, key social policy concepts developed early and often led to the emergence of well-established and nationally distinct social policy languages. These languages changed over time, but the existence of early, well-developed concepts meant that the social policy language in these countries was characterised by the presence of historical legacies and changes through incremental forms of drift and layering (Hacker, 2004; Mahoney and Thelen, 2010; Carstensen, 2011) rather than dramatic 'paradigmatic shifts' (Hall, 1993). The most significant example of continuity is in Germany, where the concept of '*Sozialstaat*' (and the social policy language related to it) survived three political regime changes. In other countries, such as Hungary, Poland, Spain, South Korea, and Japan, which established their modern social policy language in recent decades, we find that political regime changes had a much more dramatic effect on such language.

Starting in the 1970s and 1980s, developments in social policy concepts and language in different countries began to converge. The international debate about the apparent 'crisis of the welfare state' meant that existing social programmes faced extensive criticisms, while neoliberalism provided uniform answers to the 'crisis'. This reality affected social policy language in all the countries studied in this volume. During this period, ideas about competitiveness, free choice, work incentives, and privatisation entered social policy language. This convergence in social policy language is related to the influence of new social policy ideas and concepts advocated by international organisations. The OECD, IMF and World Bank became leading advocates of social policy reform, typically demanding activation, a slimmer and leaner public sector and a stronger emphasis on growth in the private sector, among other things. The EU also joined the chorus, favouring the addition of concepts such as 'social investment' and 'flexicurity' to the international social policy vocabulary. The country chapters demonstrate that these new ideas and concepts were picked up in national policy debates. Overall, in part because of the influence of these transnational actors, the general tendency was a shift towards a market oriented social policy language that challenged the more statist language of the post-war era. These recent streams of social linguistic innovation from the 1960s onwards share the historical situation that they had to react to, or engage with, the welfare state as a phenomenon already in place. Following Paul Pierson's (2001) category of 'the new politics of the welfare state', we also find the new languages of social policy developed in a markedly different context than the language used in previous periods. However, as the studies here point out, the development of a new social policy language can include both new concepts and the re-emergence (and reframing) of older concepts.

National and transnational patterns of social policy

This transnational dimension of social policy language is far from new. Comparing countries, we find both overlapping patterns and a strong degree of interdependence, which is consistent with other studies of transnational history and diffusion (Rodgers, 1998; Conrad, 2011; Obinger et al, 2013). This research attempts to identify centres and peripheries in the international development of social policy language. In the late 19th century, for instance, Germany became the epicentre of social policy in Europe and beyond. So-called Bismarckian social insurance attracted international attention, and German social policy thinking was discussed throughout the world. These German policy and intellectual developments affected social policy language not only in neighbouring countries such as Hungary or Denmark, but even as far away as Japan.

The dominance of German scholarship in this field changed during the 20th century. The German tradition remained an important element of the social policy language in several countries, but other centres of social policy thinking also emerged. French ideas had some influence in Japan. British debates during the interwar and World War II years were picked up in Scandinavia and spread throughout the Commonwealth, including New Zealand. The study on Finland in this volume clearly shows how the other Nordic countries became a yardstick for social policy debates in Finland, and the intense Nordic social policy cooperation led to social policy ideas and concepts travelling easily within the region (Petersen, 2006). Internationally, the 'Nordic model' also attracted attention (Musial, 1998; Marklund and Petersen, 2013). On one hand, it had iconic status as the most progressive social policy model, combining economic growth, equality, and social protection.

On the other hand, it was also cited as a dystopia with excessive state intervention in the everyday life of citizens.

Finally, the important role played by the United States in the post-war era should not be overlooked. During the 1930s and 1940s, the concept of 'social security', as articulated by Roosevelt's New Deal, diffused throughout the world. During the Cold War era, the United States served as a model of modernisation for the entire Western World (de Grazia, 2005; Ellwood, 2012). Even though European welfare regimes took a different pattern of development than the American welfare state (Esping-Andersen, 1990), it is possible to trace American influence on European social policy debates at the time. American scholars had a great influence on European social sciences (Thue, 2006; Rausch, 2007), and in Europe, the experts (and politicians) trained in the social sciences became the 'ideological innovators' (Skinner, 1989) of social policy language.

Comparing the country studies with the three chapters dealing with international organisations indicates that such organisations are typically more dynamic than national systems and are able to change their social policy concepts and language according to the changing political goals of the organisation. This conclusion reflects the fact that by nature these organisations are 'open systems' capable of profound ideational change (Béland and Orenstein, 2013), and that they can serve as 'epistemic communities' (Haas, 1992). The three chapters on the EU, the OECD and the IMF and World Bank all demonstrate how a change in an organisation's agenda through a top-down process leads to a significant change in concepts and language. Countries do not work in the same way. Except for changes caused by dramatic political revolutions, national social policy language develops much more slowly, often through modest, gradual changes to existing concepts and languages (on incremental ideational processes, see Carstensen, 2011).

Political struggles over state power

Finding patterns and tracing national variations in the development of social policy concepts and language should not allow us to forget that at both the national and transnational levels, such language and concepts are central to ongoing political struggles over the boundaries of state action. These struggles take different forms and concern issues such as the public/private mix, the respective role of the state versus the individual or the family, and the universalistic versus residual nature of social programmes, among other things. In other words, these struggles are largely about who has the main responsibility for providing and producing social welfare. Overall, the studies in this volume suggest that analysing social policy concepts and language is a window to understanding political struggles over the role of the state.

Perspectives and agenda for future research

In this volume, we argue that the study of social policy language should be part and parcel of welfare state analysis. There are several reasons. First, we need to have a better and more precise understanding of the concepts we use as analytical tools. Most of the social policy concepts we use as researchers are also key concepts in the political debate, which is why we need to be rigorous in the way we handle them. This intellectual rigour must feature a new historical and comparative awareness that enables us to understand the development of our social policy concepts and language, both over time and across time and space. This is why it is essential to map out the different meanings and understandings of popular social policy concepts.

Second, another reason why social policy language should be part of welfare state analysis is that such language is an integral part of the political processes that make and remake social programmes. The analysis of such language is necessary for the analysis of the politics of social policy, from a comparative and historical standpoint. Social policy language, as an essential element of political and expert discourse, participates in the construction and reconstruction of social policy systems. Such language and the concepts embedded in it are the target of political forces seeking to change or preserve specific social programmes.

Third, by systematically looking at the language of social policy and the policy debates over its core concepts, we can gain a new perspective on the politics of social policy, both in specific countries and at the transnational level. We think this is one way of addressing the problem of methodological nationalism within comparative social policy research (Kettunen and Petersen, 2011; Obinger et al, 2013). Systematic comparative studies of social policy concepts and language open the way towards an enhanced understanding of how 'national welfare states' are linked together (or not) through ideational and policy diffusion.

What are the next steps for analysis of social policy concepts and language? The most important step will be to integrate the analysis of social policy language into social policy analysis generally. Social policy scholars and practitioners, regardless of their theoretical or political orientation, have much to gain from bringing social policy conceptual history and language into their analyses. We are forced to become more self-reflective about the concepts we use, while gaining a better understanding of the politics of ideas surrounding social programmes.

At a more specific level, the case studies featured in this volume point towards a number of promising research themes. First, there is a need for more and better knowledge about the link between the national and international and transnational social policy debates. Several case studies in this volume demonstrated the importance of international organisations and of diffusion processes in the development of social policy ideas and concepts. However, more work is needed to fully grasp the mechanisms and processes involved when these concepts traverse national boundaries. Future work could include a discussion about the politics of creolisation[129] and translation (see the chapter on the EU in this volume), or more detailed studies of the 'career' of specific social policy concepts over time and space. Within the EU, ideas and concepts diffuse through international English and these 'ideas' and 'concepts' (or policy recipes) circulate and influence the discourses of those participating in specific policy forums as a currency which can be useful for them – and in some cases, we find translation, adaptation or transformation making its way into their national languages. However, it is clear that the translation of policy concepts is not an innocent process and that it might entail misunderstandings, political manipulation, and even cultural hegemony (for instance: what is the consequence of the dominance of English for the development of social policy language?).

Another overarching question in this respect centres on the structures which affect the diffusion of social policy language. The chapters in this volume have pointed to the importance of transnational institutions and cooperation, regions and regional cooperation (such as Nordic cooperation or the EU), formal interdependencies such as the British Commonwealth, or the Cold War. However, much more work on diffusion processes is needed.

Second, beyond the issue of transnational and ideational diffusion, the analysis of social policy concepts and language should be used as a legitimate and fruitful analytical lens through which scholars can re-examine social policy ideas and institutions, as well as institutional change. The use of a specific social policy language is typically attached to concrete institutional configurations, and the contestation or reframing of key concepts (or the introduction of new concepts) is

---

[129]   In the Americanisation literature, 'creolization' (Kroes, 1996: 168–9) refers to the processes of 'domestication' or 'hybridization' that take place when an object, symbol or phenomenon moves from its place of origin to another social context.

intimately related to the politics of institutional change. Conversely, the chapters in this volume demonstrate that a well-established social policy language is associated with a certain form of institutional continuity. From this perspective, the analysis of social policy concepts and language could help social policy scholars to better understand social policy stability and change and the interplay between welfare state institutions and social policy language.

Third, we call for studies that transcend the group of advanced industrial countries and international organisations analysed in this volume. The chapter on the social policy language of the IMF and the World Bank shows how these two organisations paid direct attention to developing countries in Africa, South America and Asia. Recent studies of developmental aid (Maul, 2009) and of the history of modernisation theory (Gilman, 2003) demonstrate that social policy was a key feature of developmental aid programmes. The Swedish social theorist Gunnar Myrdal concluded 40 years ago that 'the Welfare State is hesitantly and very slowly widened to be conceived as a Welfare World' (Myrdal, 1972: 11). However, this expansion of the welfare state can also be analysed as part of a Cold War strategy of offering a viable alternative to Communist promises of social progress (Petersen, 2013).

Fourth, the studies from our volume raise the question of why some concepts have a long and international career while others have a much more limited and local impact. Based on the studies in this volume, one could speculate that language and concepts very clearly connected to concrete political actors (or political ideologies: Freeden, 2003) tend to live and die with them. The socialist social policy language of Poland and Hungary are illustrative cases, but we also find other, less dramatic examples in other countries. Conversely, lasting concepts like '*Sozialstaat*', 'social security', or 'welfare state' are much more open to divergent interpretations and mobilisation by actors from different political and ideological camps, which may explain why they have a longer life expectancy and more potential for transnational diffusion. The analysis of why some ideas and concepts have more 'valence' (that is, potency) than others is the new frontier of ideational analysis (Cox and Béland, 2013). The analysis of social policy language can make a direct contribution to this intellectual project. A related question is the relationship between the 'old' social policy language about poverty and 'the poor' and the 'modern' social policy language of the 20th century. As discussed earlier, the chapters of this volume show examples of both continuity and change. We suggest approaching this question more systematically by looking for historical layers in the national social policy languages that are activated or reactivated over time. It is possible for actors to evoke language from earlier periods, as when present day Social Democrats depict workfare policies as being in the tradition of the old slogan of the labour movement of 'right and duties' (originally aimed at the privileged classes). One can also study how old distinctions between 'deserving' and 'undeserving' welfare recipients have been maintained in more moderate form in modern social policy languages.

Fifth, researchers also need to turn their attention to the relationship between social policy language and comparative welfare state research. In particular, we should study how social policy language creates and transcends well-established welfare regime typologies and how similarities and differences in social policy language correspond with the dominant typologies in comparative welfare state research. A fruitful point of departure here is the dominant typology of the three worlds of welfare capitalism developed by Gøsta Esping-Andersen (1990). The individual chapters in this volume do not explicitly address this question, but as suggested earlier, the two chapters on the Nordic countries give evidence of a distinct Nordic social policy language. The other countries, however, do not exhibit a direct link between social policy language and a welfare regime typology. The chapters on the English speaking countries (the UK, New Zealand and the United States) do not clearly spell out a liberal social policy language across the three cases. In the other European countries – often grouped in the so-called 'continental model' – it is difficult to identify any clear patterns. Nevertheless, much more work is needed before we jump to any firm conclusions on the topic. Additionally, future research could emphasise the relationship between social policy language and concepts, on one hand, and enduring forms of ethnic, gender, and sexual inequalities directly related to the development of social programmes, on the other. These concepts can reflect, reinforce or challenge such forms of 'durable inequality' (Tilly, 1999). Following the work of Nancy Fraser and Linda Gordon (1994) and others, for instance, it is clear that the gender inequality–social policy language nexus has played an important role in the United States (and to some extent also in the Netherlands, Sweden and Denmark). However, more comparative perspectives on this nexus would certainly enrich the general social policy literature.

Finally, we encourage researchers to combine qualitative and quantitative analysis of social policy concepts and language. The statistical data in the Introduction and in the chapter on Japan show the illustrative value of counting words, but much more can certainly be done in this respect. More and more online resources (full-text databases) and large-scale digital initiatives such as Google Books have become available to researchers, making it possible to trace the use of concepts over time (for a discussion on this see Michel et al, 2010, as well as the more critical approach of Gooding, 2012). Moreover, more research is needed to further map ideational diffusion, explore the origins and careers of individual social policy concepts, provide more quantitative evidence about the comparative development of such concepts, and even study the impact of key documents and reports on changes in social policy language, over time.

To sum up, there remains considerable work to be done in this emerging field of research. We therefore hope that welfare studies scholars, encouraged by the issues raised in this volume, will pursue research in social policy concepts and language as an essential element of contemporary policy research.

References

Béland, D. and M.A. Orenstein (2013) 'International organizations as policy actors: an ideational approach,' *Global Social Policy*, 13(2): 125-143.

Beveridge, W. (1942) *Social Insurance and Allied Services* (the 'Beveridge Report'), Cmnd 6404, London: HMSO.

Carstensen, M.B. (2011) 'Ideas are not as stable as political scientists want them to be: a theory of incremental ideational change,' *Political Studies*, 59(3): 596-615.

Conrad, C. (2011) 'Social policy history after the transnational turn', in P. Kettunen and K. Petersen (eds), *Beyond Welfare State Models. Transnational Historical Perspectives on Social Policy*. Cheltenham: Edward Elgar.

Cox, R.H. and D. Béland (2013) 'Valence, policy ideas and the rise of sustainability,' *Governance*, 26(2): 307-328.

Ellwood, D. (2012) *The Shock of America: Europe and the Challenge of the Century*. Oxford: Oxford University Press.

Esping-Andersen, G. (1990). *The Three Worlds of Welfare Capitalism*. Cambridge: Polity Press 1990.

Fraser, N. and Gordon, L. (1994) '"Dependency" demystified: inscriptions of power in a keyword of the welfare state', *Social Politics*, 1(1): 4-31.

Freeden, M. (2003) *Ideology: A Very Short Introduction*. Oxford: Oxford University Press.

de Grazia, V. (2005) *Irresistible Empire. America's Advance through Twentieth-Century Europe*. Cambridge MA/London: The Belknap Press.

Gilman, N. (2003). *Mandarins of the Future: Modernization Theory in Cold War America*. Baltimore/London: John Hopkins University Press.

Gooding, P. (2012) 'Mass ditization and the garbage dump: the conflicting needs of quantitative and qualitative methods', *Literary and Linguistic Computing*, 28: 425-431.

Haas, P. (1992) 'Introduction: epistemic communities and international policy coordination', *International Organization*, 46: 1-35.

Hacker, J.S. (2004) 'Privatizing risk without privatizing the welfare state: the hidden politics of welfare state retrenchment in the United States,' *American Political Science Review*, 98: 243-260.

Hall, P.A. (1993) 'Policy paradigms, social learning and the state: the case of economic policymaking in Britain.' *Comparative Politics* 25(3): 275-296.

Kettunen, P and K. Petersen (eds) (2011), *Beyond Welfare State Models: Transnational Historical Perspectives on Social Policy*. Cheltenham: Edward Elgar.

Kroes, R. (1996). *If You Have Seen One You've Seen the Mall: Europeans and American Mass Culture*, University of Illinois Press.

Mahoney, J. and K. Thelen (eds) (2010), *Explaining Institutional Change: Ambiguity, Agency and Power*. Cambridge: Cambridge University Press.

Marklund, C. and K. Petersen (2013) 'Return to sender. American images of the Nordic welfare state and Nordic welfare state branding', *European Journal of Scandinavian Studies*, 43: 245-257.

Maul, D. (2009) 'Help them move the ILO way: the International Labor Organization and the modernization discourse in the era of decolonization and the Cold War', *Diplomatic History*, 33, 387-404.

Michel, J.-P., Shen, Y.K., Aiden, A.P., Veres, A., Gray, M.K., The Google Books Team, Pickett, J-P., Holberg, D., Clancy, D., Norvig, P., Orwant, J., Pinker, S., Nowak, M.A., and Aiden. E.L. (2010) 'Quantitative analysis of culture using millions of digitized books', *Science*, 331: 176-182.

Musial, K. (1998) *Roots of the Scandinavian Model: Images of Progress in the Era of Modernization*. Baden Baden: Nomos Verlag.

Myrdal, G. (1972) 'The place of values in social policy', *Journal of Social Policy*, 1: 1-14.

Obinger, H. et al (2013) 'Policy diffusion and policy transfer in comparative welfare state research, *Social Policy & Administration*, 47 (1): 111-129.

Parlier, B, Morel, N, and Palme, J. (eds) (2011) *Towards a Social Investment Welfare State? Ideas, Policies and Challenges.* Bristol: Policy Press.

Petersen, K. (2006) 'Constructing Nordic welfare? Nordic social policy cooperation 1919-1955' in Christiansen, N.F., Petersen, K., Edling, N. and Haave, P. (eds) *The Nordic Model of Welfare: A Historical Re-Appraisal* (pp. 67-98). Copenhagen: Museum Tusculanum.

Petersen, K. (2013) 'The early Cold War and the Western welfare states', *Journal of International and Comparative Social Policy.*

Petersen, K., Stewart, J., and Sørensen, M. K. (eds) (2012), *American Foundations and the European Welfare States.* Odense: University of Southern Denmark Press.

Pierson, P. (eds) (2001) *The New Politics of the Welfare State*, Oxford/New York: Oxford University Press.

Rausch, H. (2007) US-amerikanische Scientific Philanthropy in Frankreich, Deutschland und Großbritannien zwischen den Weltkriegen. *Geschichte und Gesellschaft* 22, 73–98.

Rodgers, D.T. (1998) *Atlantic Crossings: Social Politics in a Progressive Age.* Cambridge, MA: Belknap Press.

Skinner, Q. (1989) 'Language and political change' in T. Ball, J. Farr and R.L. Hansen (eds) *Political Innovation and Conceptual Change*, Cambridge: Cambridge University Press: 6-23.

Thue, F. W. (2006) *In the Quest of a Democratic Social Order: The Americanization of Norwegian Social Scholarship 1918-1970.* Oslo: University of Oslo.

Tilly, C. (1999) *Durable Inequality.* Berkeley: University of California Press.

Wincott, D. (2013) 'The (golden) age of the welfare state: interrogating a conventional wisdom', *Public Administration*, 91, 4: 806-822.

Index

(Page locators in *italics* indicate exclusive reference to notes.)